WELSH FAMILY HISTORY

**WALES: THE OLD AND NEW COUNTIES**
**(SHOWING LOCATION OF MAIN ARCHIVE REPOSITORIES)**

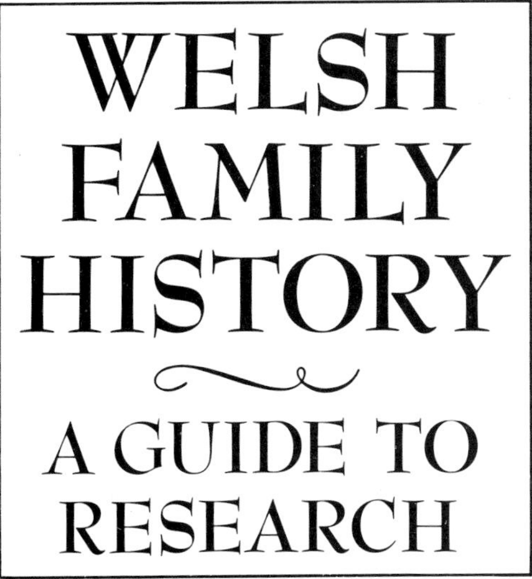

# WELSH FAMILY HISTORY

## A GUIDE TO RESEARCH

Edited by John Rowlands and Others

ASSOCIATION OF
FAMILY HISTORY SOCIETIES
OF WALES

ISBN 0 9520727 0 X

First Impression—March 1993
Second Impression—December 1993

Published by the Association of Family History Societies of Wales in conjunction with the Federation of Family History Societies.

Distributed by the Federation of Family History Societies, The Benson Room, Birmingham & Midland Institute, Margaret Street, Birmingham B3 3BS.

Cover design by Elgan Davies of the Welsh Books Council.

*Typeset and Printed in Wales by*
*J. D. Lewis & Sons, Gomer Press, Llandysul, Dyfed.*

# Contents


| | | | |
|---|---|---|---|
| List of Figures | | | vii |
| Notes on contributing authors | | | ix |
| Editorial preface | | | x |
| Chapter | | | |
| 1 | Introduction | *Hafina Clwyd* | 1 |
| 2 | Archive Repositories in Wales | *Geoffrey Veysey* | 3 |
| 3 | Family History Societies of Wales | *Stewart Blackwell* | 8 |
| 4 | Parish Registers and Bishop's Transcripts | *John Watts-Williams* | 13 |
| 5 | Civil Registration and the Census | *Sheila Rowlands* | 29 |
| 6 | Nonconformity | *Muriel Bowen Evans* | 36 |
| 7 | The Surnames of Wales | *Sheila Rowlands* | 57 |
| 8 | Place Names | *Bedwyr Lewis Jones* | 73 |
| 9 | Some Basic Welsh for Family Historians | *M. Auronwy James* | 81 |
| 10 | The IGI for Wales | *Chris Pitt Lewis* | 93 |
| 11 | Estate Records | *David W. Howell* | 104 |
| 12 | Maritime Records | *Lewis Lloyd* | 123 |
| 13 | Wills and Other Records of Inheritance | *Gareth Haulfryn Williams* | 140 |
| 14 | Education Records | *David A. Pretty* | 152 |
| 15 | Parochial Records | *John Rowlands* | 166 |
| 16 | The Welsh at Law | *Chris Pitt Lewis* | 181 |
| 17 | The Records of the Courts of Great Sessions for Wales | *Murray Ll. Chapman* | 188 |
| 18 | Printed and Manuscript Pedigrees | *Michael P. Siddons* | 209 |
| 19 | Migration: Some Perspectives | *W. T. Rees Pryce* | 227 |
| 20 | Emigration | *David Peate* | 254 |
| 21 | The Freeholders | *Evan L. James* | 269 |
| 22 | Miscellaneous Sources | *D. Emrys Williams and Others* | 280 |
| 23 | Select Bibliography | | 298 |
| Index | | | 310 |

# List of Figures
(including tables and appendixes)


| | | |
|---|---|---|
| | Wales: The Old and New Counties | Frontispiece |
| 3-1: | The Clwyd FHS Centre at Ruthin | 9 |
| 4-1: | The Survival of Parish Registers | 16 |
| 6-1: | Distribution of local christenings, Tre-lech a'r Betws | 50 |
| 7-1: | The change from John to Jones and David to Davies | 63 |
| 7-2: | A comparison of the incidence of surnames | 68 |
| 11-1: | Formation of the Wynnstay Estate c.1500-1740 | 106 |
| 11-2: | Wynnstay, Denbighshire | 116 |
| 15-1: | Poor rate assessments, Llanrhystud, Cardiganshire | 169 |
| 15-2: | Examination as to settlement (Thomas Thomas) | 172 |
| 15-3: | Pedigree chart from examination as to settlement | 174 |
| 15-4: | Pedigree chart from bastardy bond | 177 |
| 17-1: | The Jurisdiction of the Council in the Marches of Wales | 190 |
| 17-2: | Example of a challenge pedigree | 194 |
| 17-3: | Exchange of pleadings | 197 |
| 17-4: | Example of genealogical information derived from Pleadings | 198 |
| 17-5: | Example of genealogical information from an Examination | 201 |
| | Appendix: List of Plea Rolls, Chancery Pleadings and Gaol Files | 208 |
| 19-1: | Key terms in migration studies | 228 |
| 19-2: | Long-distance life-time migration | 230 |
| 19-3: | Counties of absorption and dispersion | 232 |
| 19-4: | Some patterns of migration | 233 |
| 19-5: | Ravenstein's Laws of Migration, 1885 | 234 |
| 19-6: | Life-time migration within north-east Wales, 1851 | 238 |
| 19-7: | Migration patterns to the Ogmore and Garw Valleys, 1881 | 242 |
| 19-8: | Welsh migration to England, 1881 | 245 |
| | Appendix: Some key concepts in migration studies | 252 |
| 21-1: | Landownership—Wales and Cardiganshire, 1873 | 270 |
| 21-2: | Pedigree of Llangrannog families | 274 |
| 21-3: | Fforchgwm, Llanllwchaearn, Cardiganshire | 277 |
| 21-4: | A family of Llanllwchaearn | 278 |
| 22-1: | The Survival of Bidding Letters | 282 |

# Notes on Contributing Authors

**Hafina Clwyd** is an active family historian and serves on the committee of the Clwyd Family History Society. She is an author, journalist and broadcaster and was the Editor of *Y Faner.* She is a member of the Gorsedd. With her husband, Cliff Coppack, she has been part of the Editorial Group responsible for this book.

**Geoffrey Veysey** is the County Archivist of Clwyd, is the Honorary Secretary of the Welsh County Archivists' Group, and represents Record Office interests on the Association of Family History Societies of Wales. He is the author of *Guide to the Parish Records of Clwyd.*

**Stewart Blackwell** is a retired civil servant. He was the founder Chairman of the Clwyd Family History Society and was made its first Life Member. He has run classes on family history research both for the WEA and the Extra-Mural Department of the University of Wales at Bangor.

**John Watts-Williams** is Assistant Keeper in the Department of Manuscripts and Records at the National Library of Wales. He is the co-compiler of the *Cofrestri Plwyf Cymru/Parish Registers of Wales* which is an essential handbook for family historians with Welsh ancestry.

**Sheila Rowlands** has taught family history for more than 12 years and is a Director of the residential courses in family history which are run at the University of Wales at Aberystwyth. She has edited the journals of family history societies in both England and Wales, and is joint editor of *Family History News & Digest,* the official journal of the Federation of Family History Societies. She is a member of the Editorial Group responsible for this book.

**Muriel Bowen Evans** is a local and family historian and teaches history for the Extra-Mural Department of the University of Wales at Swansea. She is the Editor of *The Carmarthenshire Antiquary.*

**Prof. Bedwyr Lewis Jones**, who died in the summer of 1992, was Professor of Welsh at the University of Wales at Bangor. He was an author and broadcaster of great note who had the gift of bringing his knowledge and enthusiasm to ordinary people. Wales is the poorer for his untimely death.

**Dr. Auronwy James** has been an active family historian for many years and was, until recently, the genealogical researcher on the staff of the National Library of Wales. She has an especial interest in the study of Englynion.

**Chris Pitt Lewis** is a solicitor with the Land Registry. He is a past Chairman of the Gwent Family History Society and has contributed to various publications on the Welsh section of the IGI.

**Dr. David Howell** is Senior Lecturer in History at the University of Wales at Swansea. He has published extensively and his two books *Land and People in Nineteenth-Century Wales* and *Patriarchs and Parasites* are essential background reading for family historians.

**Dr. Lewis Lloyd** is a lawyer by training but now teaches Politics at Coleg Harlech. Local, family and maritime history are spare-time interests. He is the author of *Australians from Wales,* and is one of the Editors of *Cymru a'r Môr/Maritime Wales.*

**Gareth Haulfryn Williams** is Principal Archivist and Museums Officer with the Gwynedd County Council. He has done academic research on the Probate Records of Caernarfonshire: 1630-1690 and published widely on both professional and historical matters. He is the resident expert on family history for a series on Radio Cymru.

**David Pretty** is Head of History at Ysgol Gyfun Rhydfelin. He has previously published articles and books on history generally, and in particular on the development of Education in relation to his home county of Anglesey.

**John Rowlands** is a Chartered Civil Engineer. He is the Chairman of the Association of Family History Societies of Wales and has chaired the Editorial Group which has been responsible for this book. He is a Director of the residential courses in family history which are run at the University of Wales at Aberystwyth. He has lectured extensively in this country and abroad on Welsh research, and is joint editor of *Family History News & Digest.*

**Murray Chapman** is also a Chartered Civil Engineer. He is the Chairman of the Powysland Club, the premier county historical society in Wales. He is an authority on the contents of the records of the Courts of Great Sessions which, thanks to his efforts, are now becoming recognised as a major source for family historians with Welsh ancestry.

**Dr. Michael Siddons** is a Fellow of the Society of Antiquaries. He was formerly the head of the medical service for the staff of the Commission of European Communities in Brussels. He is author of *The Development of Welsh Heraldry.* The first volume of this three-volume work was published in 1991 and the two companion volumes (a Welsh armorial, and an ordinary of Welsh arms) are expected to be published in 1993.

**Dr. Rees Pryce** is Senior Lecturer and Staff Tutor in the Social Sciences with the Open University in Wales. He is a member of the Open University Course Development Team on Studies in Family History, and is the author of some 50 books and articles mainly on cultural and historical geography.

**David Peate** is a local and family historian. He is a co-founder and past Chairman of the Powys Family History Society. He has a long-standing interest in emigration (particularly from Montgomeryshire) and is now a professional genealogist specialising in emigrant connections.

**Dr. Evan James** has recently retired as a lecturer in local history with the Extra-Mural Department of the University of Wales at Aberystwyth. He has a personal interest and involvement with family history research and this has been a significant feature of his local history work.

**Emrys Williams** was, prior to his retirement in 1985, Senior Assistant Keeper in the Department of Manuscripts and Records at the National Library of Wales.

# Editorial Preface

The idea of a handbook dealing with those aspects of family history research which are different in Wales from other contexts has been discussed within family history circles in Wales since the early 1980s. By 1986 the establishment of the highly popular 'Family History in Wales' Courses at the University of Wales at Aberystwyth provided a ready-made group of authors capable of covering most aspects which would need to be dealt with in the book. While the University initially intended to publish such a book as an adjunct of its courses, responsibility for this was eventually taken over by the Association of Family History Societies of Wales, partly because the majority of prospective authors were members of one or other of its constituent societies, but mainly because of the extensive publishing, sales and distribution network for family history material which is available to it.

The final decision to go ahead was taken soon after the Fourth British Family History Conference had been successfully hosted by the Association in Aberystwyth in the summer of 1987. The decision was also taken to steer the book to publication through an Editorial Group drawn from within the family history movement in Wales. Inevitably the members of the Group came from a wide area—mainly north Wales—and we were grateful for the hospitality and quiet working conditions provided by the White Lion Hotel at Bala for the majority of our meetings.

Steering this book to publication has not been without its difficulties and delays. However, the Editorial Group would like to record its gratitude to all the authors; their courtesy, cooperation and competence has been in welcome contrast to other influences which have certainly delayed the production of this book and, at one stage, even threatened its very existence.

Some authors have recorded specific acknowledgements to those who have helped them with their chapters or the work on which it has been based. We feel sure that all the authors would wish us to express our gratitude to the staff of the many archive repositories in Wales whose cheerful cooperation has helped further the cause of family history. More specifically we would wish to thank the County Archivist of Dyfed for permission to use the Examination shown in Fig 15-2; also the National Library of Wales for providing the illustration of Wynnstay used in Fig 11-2, as well as allowing us to work from a colour photocopy of the Pedigree Roll in their possession which has been used for the front cover. Permission to use this was given by the owner, the late Lt.Col. Hopton Addams-Williams of Llangybi, Gwent. We would also like to thank Catherine Camfield for assistance with typing and in particular for the immediacy of her response at moments of crisis (of which there were many). Victor and Shirley Williams gave invaluable help with reading the final proofs.

Finally, the Association would like to record its thanks to the Federation of Family History Societies for its valuable support for the publication of this book and its willingness to store and distribute it thereafter.

John Rowlands
Chairman, Editorial Group

Aberystwyth
March 1993

# 1. INTRODUCTION

Hafina Clwyd

Family history has a long tradition in Wales. According to the Laws of Hywel Dda it was incumbent on all families to know their relatives to the ninth remove (**i'r nawfed ach**) and each and every one was responsible for the well-being and welfare of all the others. More than two centuries later (in 1188) Giraldus Cambrensis (**Gerallt Gymro**) went on his crusading journey through Wales and he noticed that the Welsh had many vices and virtues. Among the latter he noted that we were witty and voluble, musical and hospitable. Above all, he said, even the lowest of the low was able to recite from memory his family tree, naming at least six or seven generations. This ability probably gave rise to the proverb 'As long as a Welshman's pedigree'.

It is commonly assumed by those approaching research into their Welsh ancestry for the first time—possibly after considerable experience in other contexts—that tried and tested methods used with success elsewhere can be applied to Welsh research. In some ways this does, indeed, hold true, particularly in the need to work from the known towards the unknown. However, the poor survival rate for many key records and the unique social, cultural, religious and linguistic characteristics which have prevailed in Wales over the centuries require a radically different attitude and approach to many aspects of research. A simple example will illustrate this. The survival in Wales of the patronymic system of naming—in some areas until well on into the nineteenth century—presents many pitfalls for unwary researchers using records of a British state which assumes a society with settled surnames.

It must be stressed from the outset, however, that this book is not a step by step guide for complete beginners. Instead it is aimed at those with some knowledge of research generally who are either experiencing difficulties with their Welsh lines or who are, perhaps, coming to Welsh research for the first time. It has been assumed, therefore, that most readers will have a basic understanding of family history research through reading such standard works as Pelling's *Beginning Your Family History* and the various Gibson Guides and other guides which are published by the Federation of Family History Societies.

The Editorial Group had two main aims in mind when steering this book to publication. First it wanted to give readers an insight into the social, cultural, religious and linguistic background of Wales and the ways in which this can affect family history research. Secondly, it wanted to help dispel the widely held belief that these aspects pose insurmountable barriers to progress in researching Welsh ancestors. In order to achieve those aims the Group has commissioned contributions from a wide range of specialist authors and the book as a whole should be viewed as a collection of essays under a unifying theme. It hopes that readers will feel it has gone some way towards achieving both those aims and will enjoy the variety of styles and change of pace this brings to the book.

Clearly it would be unrealistic to expect that every aspect of research could be covered in a book of this size. Indeed the Editorial Group has constantly been faced with the need to decide what to leave out rather than what to put in. It has also had to limit severely the number of pages given over to each author. As a result, the book does not attempt to deal at any length with those aspects of research such as, for example, Civil Registration and the Census which are the same as those in England; nor too is there more than passing reference to such sources as Trade Directories, Maps, etc.

Perhaps the most striking omission from the chapters included in this book is one on Newspapers. This reflects the powerful influence of the Welsh language—the oldest living language in Europe—and its importance in everyday life. Many Welsh language newspapers have existed over the years and it would not be possible to do them justice as an important source for family historians in an English language book.

Finally, the Group hopes that researchers will read as much as possible about the history of Wales generally and about their area of interest in particular. To be successful with family history research in Wales it is imperative to understand the locality to which the research relates and thereby identify one's ancestors in their specific social, cultural, religious and economic context.

**Anniddig heb drig, heb dras**

Unhappy is the one without land, without lineage.

# 2. Archive Repositories in Wales

Geoffrey Veysey

No less than forty-one repositories in Wales are listed in the second edition of *British Archives: A Guide to Archive Resources in the United Kingdom,* published in 1989. These range from libraries, museums and record offices to a cathedral library and the British Steel Corporation. Any records which contain details of individuals will be of interest to family historians in search of their Welsh ancestry. British Steel's centre at Shotton holds records of its Welsh workforce, and the South Wales coal archive in Swansea University College Library contains information on miners and the mines which were once such overwhelming features of the landscape.

The genealogist, however, will probably first confine his searches to one of the many non-specialist archive repositories in Wales which hold, and can readily make available, evidence of the past life of its inhabitants. Of the repositories listed in the 1989 guide, seventeen have holdings considered sufficiently extensive or valuable to justify the employment of one or more professionally qualified archivists.

In many respects the pattern of archive-keeping in Wales is similar to that in England, although there are variations as a result of historical developments and the role played by the National Library of Wales. Before its foundation at Aberystwyth in 1907, manuscript material was collected by the larger borough libraries founded in the late nineteenth century, especially in the more populous areas of South Wales. From the beginning, the National Library aimed to collect local records, and published a brochure in 1938 drawing attention to the importance of Welsh local records and to the advantages 'of bringing them into one central institution'. As it had been established before most other Welsh repositories, including county record offices, it was able to accumulate many holdings of particular interest to the family historian which in England are likely to be found in a county archive.

As one of the copyright libraries, the National Library of Wales receives a copy of most of the books published in the United Kingdom and specialises in material relating to Wales. Its three departments, of Manuscripts and Records, Printed Books, and Pictures and Maps, together house millions of books, newspapers, manuscripts, deeds, documents, prints and maps concerned with the Principality. The holdings of the department of Manuscripts and Records are of especial importance to genealogists. Among them are the probate records of Wales including wills proved in Welsh dioceses from the earliest surviving records in the second half of the sixteenth century until January 1858, and register copy wills, 1858-1941. The records of all the dioceses of the Church in Wales are also to be found there, together with bishop's transcripts (some dating from the 1660s), marriage allegations and bonds of the eighteenth and nineteenth centuries, and tithe maps and apportionments. It shares custody of parish registers and parish collections with county record offices. Over the years it has built up extensive accumulations of nonconformist records, especially those of the Welsh Calvinistic Methodist Church (Presbyterian Church of Wales) together with estate collections and personal papers from all parts of Wales. Particular mention must be made of its holdings of mediaeval and later pedigrees as genealogical source material. Its collection of legal and administrative records include the records of the court of Great Sessions, 1543-1830, transferred from the Public Record Office and covering the whole of Wales except Monmouthshire (now Gwent). These courts corresponded approximately to the English Assize courts although their jurisdiction was wider.

Apart from the borough libraries and the library of the University College of North Wales at Bangor, which has large deposits of family and estate collections relating to North Wales, the National Library dominated the scene until the setting up of county record offices in Wales. These have had the effect of slowing down any tendency there might have been towards the centralisation of important records. Every Welsh county now houses one or more record offices maintained by its county council (see Frontispiece) where official and local material of relevance to its history is stored and made available. In England county record offices were mostly a development of the 1930s; in Wales progress came a little later. Monmouthshire appointed a consultant archivist in 1938, and the first Glamorgan archivist took up his post in 1939, but the majority of the repositories were established only after the Second World War, in Caernarfonshire (1948), Flintshire (1951), Merioneth (1952) and Carmarthenshire (1959). Local government reorganisation in the 1970s, which merged several old counties into new creations, also led to the setting up of additional record offices. There are now twelve repositories which by and large relate to the pre-1974 counties, Powys being the last county to establish an archive service in 1984. Since 1974

Glamorgan has been divided into three separate administrative counties. The archive service is based in Cardiff (for Mid and South Glamorgan) with an area office at Swansea which became an independent service for West Glamorgan in April 1992.

Central to the county collections are the Quarter Sessions records which cover all aspects of county government until the establishment of county councils in 1889. Caernarfonshire's records date from 1541, Denbighshire's from 1647, Breconshire's from 1670, and most of the other Welsh counties from around the middle of the eighteenth century. Quarter sessions rolls, land tax assessments, enclosure awards, poll books, and electoral registers (from 1832), will be of interest to family historians. Record offices also hold county council and local authority records including rate books and collections relating to the poor law and education. Agreements with the Church in Wales since 1976 have allowed county archive repositories (except Powys) to take in deposits of parish registers, so that virtually all the registers of the ancient parishes in Wales are either in their custody or that of the National Library. Like the Library they all hold growing collections of nonconformist registers, chapel records, family and estate papers, records of businesses and industries, which will contain information of interest to family historians. There are records of the Society of Friends for the whole of Wales dating from the 1660s in the care of the Glamorgan Archive Service. Maritime records are especially strong in Gwynedd, while merchant ship agreements and crew lists for ships registered at Welsh ports, 1863-1913, are held by the maritime counties and at the National Library (for Cardiganshire). The Glamorgan Archive Service has custody of seamen's records up to the early 1970s from the Registry of Shipping and Seamen.

All the record offices and the National Library have leaflets and information available on their holdings or have published guides, handlists and booklets. Most have also compiled short guides, some for sale, to their genealogical sources. A reader's ticket and prior booking of a microfilm or fiche reader may also be required, so that readers would be well advised to contact a repository before paying a first visit. This will, in any case, be necessary because a further reorganization of Welsh local government, including the creation of new unitary authorities to replace the present counties, is planned in the next few years.

Of the other repositories employing archivists, the library of the University College of North Wales at Bangor has considerable collections of estate papers of North Wales families, and mine and quarry records. The library of University College, Swansea, has trade union, political and private records relating to the South Wales coalfield, together with early records of Swansea borough. Its collections also include genealogical material once in the Royal Institution of South Wales. Swansea City Archives, established in 1974, has rate books of the nineteenth and twentieth centuries, electoral registers from 1839, poll books and freeman's records dating from 1760. The Welsh Folk Museum at St Fagans, near Cardiff, opened in 1948, is rich in collections relating to Welsh folklore and photographic, film and sound archives, in addition to diaries and account books of the Welsh farming and craft community.

Undoubtedly there are records of potential interest to family historians in the local collections of many libraries throughout Wales. They may include original manuscript material, books and pamphlets, some of them scarce, as well as copies of local newspapers, printed directories, electoral registers and microfilms of the census returns, 1841-91, which are also to be found in the county record offices.

Repositories in Wales as elsewhere are under pressure from lack of funds but they are all endeavouring to meet the needs of growing numbers of family historians who are calling on them for assistance and information about their Welsh ancestry.

## ADDRESSES

### LIBRARIES AND MUSEUMS

The National Library of Wales, Aberystwyth, Dyfed SY23 3BU. (Tel: 0970 623816)

University College of North Wales Library, Bangor, Gwynedd LL57 2DG (Tel: 0248 351151)

University College of Swansea Library, Singleton Park, Swansea SA2 8PP (Tel: 0792 205678 ext. 4044)

Welsh Folk Museum, St Fagans, Cardiff, CF5 6BX (Tel: 0222 569441)

### RECORD OFFICES

**Clwyd**

Clwyd Record Office, The Old Rectory, Hawarden, Deeside, Clwyd CH5 3NR (Tel: 0244 532364)

Clwyd Record Office, 46 Clwyd Street, Ruthin, Clwyd LL15 1HP (Tel: 0824 703077)

**Dyfed**

Dyfed Archive Service, County Hall, Carmarthen, Dyfed SA31 1JP (Tel: 0267 233333 ext. 4182)

Carmarthenshire Record Office, County Hall, Carmarthen, Dyfed SA31 1JP (Tel: 0267 233333 ext. 4182)

Pembrokeshire Record Office, The Castle, Haverfordwest, Dyfed SA61 2EF (Tel: 0437 763707)

Cardiganshire Record Office, Swyddfa'r Sir, Aberystwyth, Dyfed SY23 2DE (Tel: 0970 617581 ext. 2120)

**Glamorgan**

Glamorgan Archive Service, County Hall, Cathays Park, Cardiff CF1 3NE (Tel: 0222 780282)

West Glamorgan Record Office, County Hall, Oystermouth Road, Swansea SA1 3SN (Tel: 0792 471589)

Swansea City Archives Office, The Guildhall, Swansea SA1 4PE (Tel: 0792 302126)

**Gwent**

Gwent County Record Office, County Hall, Cwmbrân, Gwent NP44 2XH (Tel: 0633 832214)

**Gwynedd**

Gwynedd Archives Service, Victoria Dock, Caernarfon

(letters to be addressed to: County Offices, Shirehall Street, Caernarfon, Gwynedd LL55 1SH)

Caernarfon Record Office, Victoria Dock, Caernarfon, Gwynedd (Tel: 0286 679095)

Dolgellau Record Office, Cae Penarlâg, Dolgellau, Gwynedd LL40 2YB (Tel: 0341 422341 ext. 3301/2)

Llangefni Record Office, Shirehall, Llangefni, Gwynedd LL77 7TW (Tel: 0248 750262 ext. 269)

**Powys**

County Archives Office, County Hall, Llandrindod Wells, Powys LD1 5LD (Tel: 0597 826088)

# 3. The Family History Societies of Wales

Stewart Blackwell

As is well known the Welsh have for centuries had a feeling for family kinship. Indeed, in Chapter 1, reference has been made to the observations about this by Giraldus Cambrensis in 1188 when he described how in Wales a person by the name of Rhys could be known as 'Rhys, son of Gruffydd, son of Rhys, son of Tewdwr, son of Einion, son of Owen, son of Howel, son of Cadell, son of Rhodri Mawr' and so on.

Today, more than 800 years on, that feeling continues—indeed, in recent years with added momentum. It is surprising, therefore, to find that, at the end of the 1970s, there was only one family history society (The Genealogical & Heraldic Society of Wales, located in Cardiff), purporting to cover the whole of Wales. It was unrealistic, however, to hope that a single society could cover all Wales and from it evolved the South Wales Family History Society with more limited horizons.

The pattern changed, however, when the Clwyd FHS was formed in May 1980 covering the interests of those with ancestors in north-east Wales—the historic counties of Denbighshire, Flintshire and a small part of Merionethshire around Corwen. Later the same year, two further societies were formed: the Gwynedd FHS in north-west Wales covering Anglesey, Caernarfonshire and most of Merionethshire, and the Powys FHS in mid-Wales which covered the counties of Breconshire, Montgomeryshire and Radnorshire.

In 1981, the Gwent FHS came into existence and its area coincides almost exactly with the ancient county of Monmouthshire. A year later, the Dyfed FHS was formed and its area of interest covered the pre-1974 counties of Cardiganshire, Carmarthenshire and Pembrokeshire. In 1983 the South Wales FHS was re-formed as the Glamorgan FHS.

We have, therefore, been fortunate in having six very active family history societies in Wales for the last ten years. Each is run by a committee and honorary officers elected at an Annual General Meeting, and family historians generally owe them a great debt for their voluntary work.

The societies have similar, but not identical, constitutions, enjoy charitable status, and have similar aims. They encourage and help people interested in family history in their particular county and also people with ancestors from that county but living elsewhere, including those overseas. Annual subscriptions are modest and members receive help and assistance in many ways. Each society publishes a journal (free to members) two or three times a year. Members are encouraged to submit the names they are researching for inclusion in the columns of these journals or in a separate *Directory of Members' Interests* and this can frequently lead to contact with distant cousins. The entries are updated and distributed from time to time. In addition, the journals generally have reasonable space (normally free) for members to seek information on their queries.

The societies hold regular meetings—often monthly—at various venues throughout their county. Programmes include talks, visits and Members' Evenings when members are told about current research, share their experiences and obtain practical help. Overseas visitors are always most welcome at these meetings. Current research projects include transcription of monumental inscriptions from churches and graveyards (often threatened by clearance and development), transcription and indexing of ancient parish registers, preparation of census indexes, marriage indexes, etc. Some societies have made substantial progress recording monumental inscriptions and others have concentrated on parish register transcriptions.

Some Welsh societies have a panel of members who will try to resolve a particular problem for a fellow-member living some distance from their Record Office, but they normally deal only with a specific item and not with open-ended requests for information. Some may provide lists of experienced people who will undertake research for a fee.

At the beginning of 1988, Clwyd Family History Society opened its own Centre in Ruthin in a former vestry and schoolroom (see Fig 3-1), leased at a peppercorn rent from the Trustees and Deacons of Ruthin Welsh Baptist Chapel. The building, erected in 1870, had become derelict and it was converted and restored at a cost of £1500.

The Centre, which is open to members, contains a wealth of information on local, social and family history, some of which is not available elsewhere in Clwyd or, indeed, North Wales. To name just a few sources: the 1988 International Genealogical Index for Great Britain, Indexes of Welsh Wills proved in all four ancient dioceses (Bangor, St Asaph, St David's and Llandaff), Bartrum's *Welsh*

Fig. 3-1: The Clwyd FHS Centre at Ruthin

*Genealogies AD 300-1400*, and much other information held on microfiche and microfilm, can all be consulted. It is hoped that this Centre might be the fore-runner of similar centres established by the other societies in Wales.

In March 1981, the Welsh family history societies then in existence founded the Association of Family History Societies of Wales as a co-ordinating body to promote and foster the study of family history throughout Wales and to publish material of interest to Welsh genealogists and family historians. Hence, the publication of the book of which this forms one chapter.

The Council of the Association meets in mid-Wales normally in March, July and October. It co-operates fully with the Federation of Family History Societies and makes any necessary representations to official bodies worldwide on matters affecting family history research in Wales.

Quite apart from the family history societies of Wales, mention should be made of the Guild of One-Name Studies, which has over one thousand members who are researching particular surnames in depth. They record every occurrence of that name in a particular area and this obviously includes Wales. As yet no-one has had the temerity to register the common Welsh surnames of Jones, Davies, Thomas, Williams, etc, but names of patronymic origin such as Alban, Meredith and Prothero have been registered. A list of registered surnames can be obtained from the Guild, Box G, Society of Genealogists, 14 Charterhouse Buildings, Goswell Road, London EC1M 7BA.

Throughout the centuries Welsh people have migrated to London to seek fame and fortune or simply to earn their livings. It is therefore, perhaps, not surprising that all the Welsh family history societies have members now living in the London area who have ancestors born in Wales. In recent years, several societies—namely those in Dyfed, Glamorgan, Gwynedd and Powys—have joined together to organise meetings at the Society of Genealogists for these members and any others who care to attend. Full details are available from the Society of Genealogists or from the family history societies concerned.

Education is another area in which members of Welsh family history societies play a leading role. For some years each winter and spring, more experienced researchers in several counties have run well-attended courses of about ten weeks' duration on 'Tracing Your Ancestors'. The courses are usually sponsored by the extra-mural departments of the colleges of the University of Wales or by the Workers' Educational

Association, and beginners have found them particularly helpful. Each summer since 1986, members have taken a major part in residential courses offered by the University of Wales, Aberystwyth, for those interested in tracing their Welsh ancestry. The latter cover both basic research and more specialised aspects of Welsh family history and many of the contributors to this book are also speakers on the courses.

From the previous paragraphs, the advantages of joining a family history society, covering the county where ancestors lived, must be self-evident. The geographical coverage of each society has already been given and the names and addresses of current Honorary Secretaries can be obtained from the appropriate County Record Office or the National Library of Wales (see Chapter 2). In addition, the Federation of Family History Societies (c/o The Benson Room, Birmingham & Midland Institute, Margaret Street, Birmingham B3 3BS) always has an up-to-date list.

# 4. Parish Registers and Bishop's Transcripts

John Watts-Williams

## Introduction

Wales has no history of keeping parish registers separate from England. The union of Wales with England coincided with the Reformation in Europe. The establishment of a national church in England along Protestant lines meant automatic membership for all the king's subjects, Welsh and English alike, and when, in September 1538, Henry VIII issued an order to every parish priest to start keeping a record of all weddings, christenings and burials in their respective parishes, it applied to Wales as well as England.[1]

Many of the king's subjects suspected that the introduction of parish registers meant new taxes. One of the Herberts of Abergavenny was arrested for repeating, over a noggin of Gloucestershire ale, the common gossip he had picked up in London and Abingdon that tribute should be paid for christening, burying and wedding.[2] Henry VIII took a dim view of such rumour-mongering and hastened to explain that the order to keep a register had nothing whatsoever to do with raising taxes but was intended purely 'to avoid disputes touching ages, titles, or lineal descents and whether any one was the King's born subject or not'.[3] Taxes or no taxes, parish registers may well assist us with our lineal descents. Whether they will help us to avoid disputes concerning those descents is, however, another matter. We are likely to find them throwing up quite as many questions as answers.

Part of the fascination of parish registers from 1538 to 1812 is their eccentricity. The manner in which entries were to be made in the parish registers was prescribed by law in the sixteenth century, but it was not until 1813 that every parish in England and Wales was issued with register books which contained printed columns and headings ensuring a common standard in the amount of detail recorded for baptisms and burials. Before 1813 it was the responsibility of each parish to provide its own register, and every clergyman largely pleased himself regarding the format of the entries he made in it, although nearly all parishes had adopted a more or less standard form of entry for marriages following the *Act for the better preventing of Clandestine Marriages* which came into effect in 1754. Before that date weddings were recorded in the same plain, unruled registers as the baptisms and burials.

The task of keeping a register has remained among the routine duties of the Anglican[4] parish clergy from 1538 to the present day. Baptisms and burials are being recorded today in Wales in precisely the format introduced in 1813, and indeed, many small parishes are still struggling to fill the one-hundred-page, eight-entries-per-page, registers they received at that time; but parish registers are no longer as vitally important as they once were. By the 1830s it had been evident for some time that parish registers were failing to meet the needs of the modern industrial state which was then emerging. Some other more effective method of recording vital events had to be found. A General Register Office superintending a network of local register offices was set up, and in 1837 it began to keep a central register of all the births, marriages and deaths in England and Wales, irrespective of religion (see Chapter 5). Since 1837 parish registers have played a less demanding role than that which Henry VIII envisaged, but they continue to perform a useful function as Anglican registers pure and simple. Indeed, family historians may still find valuable information in them for a period when civil registration can be difficult to search for Welsh families.

## Finding parish registers

Parish registers are essential reading, therefore, only before 1837, though they may be useful after that date as a supplement to other sources such as the General Register Office records and the census returns. For the searcher eager to get cracking on parish registers, there are two main questions to be answered at the outset: to which parish did an ancestor belong, and which registers, if any, have survived for that parish? Before 1837 Wales had about one thousand Anglican churches, all keeping their own separate registers of baptisms, marriages and burials. Life will be very much easier if somehow we can reduce to a handful the number of parishes whose registers we need to search. That means doing our homework thoroughly beforehand in order to identify our ancestor's parish of origin. Once the parish has been identified, the guide book, *Cofrestri Plwyf Cymru/Parish Registers of Wales (CPC/PRW)*[5] will give us the basic information we need concerning its registers: which of them have survived, which dates and events they cover, and where they are available for searching.

Nearly all surviving parish registers of baptisms, marriages and burials before 1813 will be found at one of two places: at the county record office in whose territory the parish lies; or at the National Library of Wales in Aberystwyth. A few others remain in their parishes. Many registers covering the period 1813-1837 have also been transferred to these public repositories. The depositing of original registers began at the National Library during the 1950s. By 1975 the registers of some three hundred parishes had been placed there for safekeeping. In 1976 the various record offices, serving most, but not all, of the counties of Wales, also began to collect parish registers and by 1986 there were fewer than twenty parishes which had not deposited at least one of their registers at the appropriate county record office or the National Library. The year 1986 saw the publication of *CPC/PRW* and little material change has occurred since that time in the information it contains concerning the location of registers or the dates covered by surviving pre-1813 registers. For an update on the availability of registers which are noted in *CPC/PRW* as being with the incumbent it is advisable to contact either the National Library of Wales or the appropriate county record office.

## Survival of parish registers

The survival rate of parish registers in Wales is, in general, not as good as that of parish registers in England. Fig 4-1 gives a rough comparison of the survival rate for the thirteen counties of Wales and a sample of four counties of England (Hereford, Gloucester, Oxford, and Shropshire).[6] The statistics, from which the chart has been compiled, are based on the date of the earliest entry recorded in the surviving registers of each parish.[7]

Sixteenth century registers are fairly common survivors in England: well over a hundred parishes in the county of Suffolk alone possess registers going back to 1538-1540, and all four English counties included in the chart have a 40-50% survival rate for their pre-1600 registers. Of the Welsh counties, only Flint comes anywhere near them; and, of all the Welsh parishes, there is only one, Gwaunysgor (Flintshire), which has a register beginning in 1538. Only three other parishes have entries earlier than 1550: Conwy (Caernarfonshire) 1541; Llandegfan (Anglesey) 1547; and Llanddewi Skirrid (Monmouthshire) 1549. Bracketing the other ancient parishes according to the dates of commencement of their registers gives some idea of the overall survival

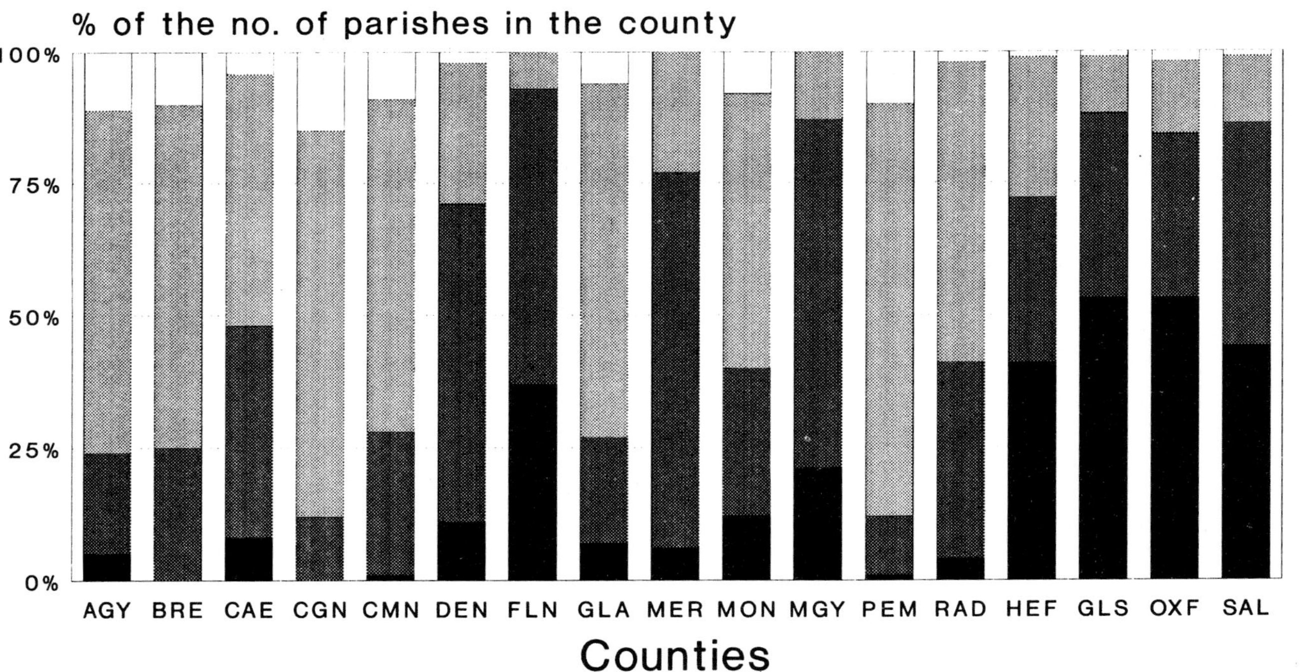


Fig. 4·1: The Survival of Parish Registers

rate: 1551-1600: 65 parishes; 1601-1660: 90; 1661-1700: 200; 1701-1753: 300; 1754-1812: 250; 1813 + : 70 parishes. Only one in six of the old parishes of Wales has a register beginning before 1660; and only slightly more than one in three has a register beginning before 1700. The distribution of parishes with pre-1700 registers is uneven, favouring north more than south, east more than west. In terms of dioceses, the order of precedence is, roughly speaking, St Asaph, Bangor, Llandaf, St David's. The highest proportion of the parishes in the 1754-1812 and post-1813 brackets is in the southern counties of Cardigan, Pembroke, Brecknock, Glamorgan and Carmarthen. The only northern county which has suffered losses of parish registers on a similar scale is Anglesey.

The main reasons for the poorer rate of survival of parish registers in Wales compared to England were, undoubtedly, ineffective organisation, and poverty at the parish priest level. A quiet disregard of royal and episcopal authority prevailed in some areas with impunity. As one writer observed in 1795, 'church registers have been so shamefully neglected in this country [ . . . ] that very few parishes can furnish one twenty years old'.[8] His remarks refer primarily to part of the large and unwieldy diocese of St David's (which covered most of south Wales), where the combination of remote churches, sparse population, poor livings, low standards of priests, and slack supervision by the higher clergy was at its worst, and where, it goes almost without saying, the rate of survival of parish registers is at its most dismal;[9] but they are equally applicable to other parts of Wales, and reflect badly on the Church's efficiency in those areas too. In the diocese of Llandaf in 1781, a vicar explained his inability to produce at the bishop's visitation any register prior to 1770 by pointing out that 'the parish being so very small, and of so few inhabitants, I suppose very little attention was paid to this article by my predecessors'.[10] Some of the poorer parishes could hardly afford the cost of acquiring a register. One curate complained in 1771 that he had no register books because 'the parishioners expect the impropriator to furnish them with those books, which he refuses to do'.[11] In the diocese of Bangor, the vicar choral of the cathedral church itself, which was also the parish church of Bangor (Caernarfonshire), confessed in 1776 that 'there is no parish rate by means whereof the churchwardens may be enabled to provide register books, register rolls, or other things required of them'.[12]

It is also worth remembering that Wales was a predominantly agrarian country with a generally low density of population throughout most of the period of parochial registration 1538-1837. Its largest town at the first census taken in 1801 was Merthyr Tudful (Glamorgan) with under 8,000 inhabitants. The combined effects of indigenous population growth, internal and inward migration, and large-scale industrialisation which changed radically the face of the principality during the nineteenth century were at that time only just beginning to show themselves. By 1831 the population of Merthyr Tudful had shot up to over 22,000, while the population of Wales as a whole almost doubled between 1800 and 1850 until at the time of the 1851 census it stood at 1,163,000. It is difficult to visualise some of our present-day conurbations as scenes of rural bliss, but the fact is that, in 1781, when asked whether there was a separate register of marriages in the parish, the incumbent of Barry (Glamorgan) wrote, 'No, but all our marriages are entered upon the same register as our births and burials'; and the incumbent of Penarth (Glamorgan) replied, 'The same [register] doth for all uses in our little parish'.[13] So both of those south-eastern parishes were, at that date, akin to the joint curacy in the north-western remoteness of Anglesey which, having a more original excuse for not keeping a separate register of marriages, declared that 'there has been no clandestine marriages in this parish, therefore there is no occasion for such a register'.[14]

Of course, there are plenty of instances of registers whose loss owes more to individual acts of negligence or accidental circumstances of varying degrees of credibility. At Cilymaenllwyd (Carmarthenshire) in 1765 it is alleged that the vicar was in a state of panic because his servant girl had put the parish books in the oven.[15] At Cadoxton-juxta-Neath (Glamorgan), there was a tradition, summarised in a stanza, which spoke of 'the demented wife of a former incumbent casting the church registers into the vicarage fire and dancing with glee at the spectacle'.[16] Invading Frenchmen have been blamed for the disappearance of registers at Llanwnda and Letterston (both Pembrokeshire); a cow with an indelicate palate for turning one unidentified Anglesey register into a churnful of milk and other assorted bovine by-products; and a gun-toting parson and his well-born companion for using the registers of an unnamed parish in Carmarthenshire to charge their firearms.[17] Humid storage conditions, common enough in Wales's wet climate, have not helped much in the preservation of parish records, as, for example, at Henllan Amgoed (Carmarthenshire) where it was reported in 1831 that 'the entries of Baptisms etc. were written upon loose scraps of paper and deposited in a damp chest, and are now completely decayed'.[18] Nor has excessive heat. The earliest register of Christchurch (Monmouthshire) containing baptisms, marriages and burials from 1695 to 1736 is a useless solid block of parchment after shrinking and melting in the fire which gutted the parish church as recently as 1949.[19] A change of incumbency was often a hazardous time. One vicar confessed in 1781 that he had delayed obtaining a new register 'in hope that I should have got something from the old curate who have served [the parish] for near fifty years, but I imagine the whole is lost'.[20] Another went so far as to advertise in 1828 for the safe return of the oldest register belonging to his parish which was said to have been taken to the next county by one who had been vicar some forty to sixty years previously;[21] and, in 1831, two parishes reported that they had failed to recover their old registers of marriages from a former parish clerk and the executors of a former incumbent respectively.[22]

## Nature of content

Even if the register we wish to see is still in existence, there is no guarantee that the information we are hoping to find is recorded in it. Poor record-keeping was a common failing. 'The entring down into this register was omitted from ye year 1755 to the year 1758 by the late curate Mr.Hope' is inscribed in one register by an incumbent anxious to absolve himself from any blame; and in another the inscription reads: 'From 1757 to 1771 Mr.Powel the curate neglected to register'.[23] Such lengthy gaps are, of course, self-evident. It is the occasional omissions which are virtually impossible to spot. For instance, one minister excused his failure to register promptly the baptism of the local squire's twins in 1737 'by reason of my being indispos'd in the mean-time'; and, in 1806-7 in another parish, the baptisms of two children of well-to-do families 'was omitted in their proper places owing to timely notice having not being [*sic*] given to the curate—they were not baptized by him'.[24] In those two cases, the omissions were made good; but the big question is how many other similar events remained unrecorded because of the clergy's forgetfulness, indisposition, or inadvertency.

Bad habits often contributed to poor record-keeping. It was common practice for the clergy to make rough notes of events as they occurred and to enter them in the register at a later date, on the following Sunday if the rules were strictly obeyed. In the diocese of Llandaf, as late as 1800, the diocesan registrar remarked that 'many of the parish registers are badly kept, and in one instance, (and I fear there are many more), which came to my knowledge on the death of the curate, no entry whatever was made, but the transcripts written from detached scraps of paper'.[25] Even when the clergyman kept his rough notes in a draft register or a notebook rather than on loose scraps of paper, he might forget to transfer them to the proper register. The former incumbent of one Cardiganshire parish, having received an enquiry concerning an entry which had obviously been omitted from the register when he was in charge, replied, with no hint of remorse, that 'it appears by the old Pocket Register kept by me that Thomas son of Thomas and Margaret Jenkin of Dolychgennog was baptized the 14th day of August in the year 1786. This is a fact you may depend upon its reality and your entering it upon the Register and afterwards to certify its being there can not be attended with any great impropriety. It is marked in my book as if already entered there'.[26]

Nobody knows how far the rate of recording in Wales was affected by clandestine marriages, but there is evidence to suggest that such marriages were common throughout the principality during the seventeenth and early eighteenth centuries. Some clandestine marriages are recorded in parish registers, but, presumably, many more of them went unrecorded. There was no recognised centre for their solemnization, but, at one stage, there was 'a parcel of strolling curates in South Wales, and some there were also in North Wales, who for a crown or at most a guinea, would marry anybody under a hedge';[27] and cases involving the performance of clandestine marriage were frequently brought before the consistory courts.

Yet, in spite of this catalogue of mishap and negligence, it should be noted that there are parishes in Wales which do possess a good set of registers, and that, although the registers of Wales come a poor second to those of England in terms of early survivals, they may, on the whole, compare favourably with those of Scotland and Ireland and some other European countries.[28]

## Nonconformity and parish registers

When we search a parish register and fail to turn up the entry we hoped or expected to find, we tend to assume that the person for whom we are looking was a nonconformist. Whereas our assumption may well be true, it is worth noting some points before rushing off to look for the register books of the various non-Anglican denominations. In the first place, the entry may be missing because of poor record-keeping as explained above. In the second place, parish registers do not necessarily exclude nonconformists: occasionally you will come across references to Roman Catholics, Quakers, Dissenters, Methodists and the like among the baptisms and burials, but, more often than not, there is nothing in the entries to distinguish nonconformists from the rest; and, as far as marriages are concerned, it is important to note that during the period 1754-1837 the only nonconforming communities allowed by law to perform wedding ceremonies according to their own custom were Jews and Quakers. Everybody else had to be wed in a church duly licensed for the solemnization of marriage according to the rites of the Church of England. As Jews and Quakers were not particularly numerous in Wales during that period, it is reasonable to suppose that virtually all the marriages which took place in Wales between 1754 and 1837, involving nonconformists and conformists alike, were recorded in the parish registers of the Church of England.

In the third place, the spread of the old dissent, which put down its roots in Wales in the mid-seventeenth century, was slow and unspectacular before the last quarter of the eighteenth, but phenomenal after 1800. The number of Baptists has been estimated at about 500 in 1689, rising to 1,500 in 1760, and over 9,000 in 1800; the number of Independent churches grew from 87 in 1742 to about 100 in 1775, to 257 in 1815, and to about 500 in 1839; and when, in 1811, the Calvinistic Methodists officially joined the ranks of nonconformity, the Anglican cause was reeling. By 1851 the Anglicans were in the minority in nearly every part of Wales, and eight of every ten Welsh men and women, who attended a place of worship, went to chapel rather than to church.[29]

The effects of nonconformity on the fulness of parish registers are, therefore, probably more marked only from about 1780 onwards. At the time of the 1811 census, for instance, the curate of Llandygwydd (Cardiganshire) remarked that it was difficult for him 'to ascertain the numbers of baptisms and burials taking place in this parish among the numerous dissenters of various denominations. They may nearly average the number [of Anglican baptisms and burials I have counted for the years 1801-1810]. From a comparison of the average of ten years of our register 120 years ago when there were no dissenters with our present, I infer that our population has greatly increased'.[30]

He obviously made no effort to record the births/baptisms or burials of the nonconformists in his parish, and, if we are to believe the statistics gathered as part of the 1831 census survey, there must have been many more clergymen like him. For the published figures show that during the

1820s the annual average number of births not entered in the parish registers of Wales was 3,513, which gives a total of 35,130 unentered births over the whole ten-year period 1821-30. As the number of baptisms which were entered in the parish registers over the same period amounted to only 176,689, it seems that, towards the end of the era of parochial registration 1538-1837, for every five recorded baptisms there is one baptism (probably the very one we are looking for) not recorded. The comparable ratio for England is one unentered baptism for every twenty-six entered. Burials are usually less defective than baptisms: the 1831 census returns suggest an average of 1,101 unentered burials a year for the 1820s. Although irreligion contributed to these discrepancies, there can be little doubt that most of them are the result of the nonconformist boom.[31] The early part of the nineteenth century was precisely the period which saw many Welsh nonconformist churches gaining in confidence and beginning to keep their own separate registers.

## Detailed content

The nature of parish register entries has been discussed in detail by R.W. McDonald in an article which includes examples from all parts of Wales, while England's have been analysed extensively by various authors.[32] Their observations need no rehearsal here. Essentially there is little difference between Wales and England in the form and content of entries, not even in language. Latin (before 1733) and English were the official languages for keeping such records in Wales as well as England. Welsh, the everyday language of the overwhelming majority of the population, was banned from official use and is encountered in parish registers, almost without exception, only in place-names, personal names, and marginal notes.[33]

Bear in mind that the events recorded in the registers are Christian ceremonies performed in accordance with the rules and regulations of the Church of England. The usual date recorded in the register is the date of baptism, not the date of birth; the date of burial, not the date of death. Sometimes you will find registers which record the date of birth as well as the date of baptism, but they are not very common. A detailed study of parish registers in England for demographic purposes concluded that, at the beginning of the three hundred year period of parochial registration, infants were usually baptized when they were two or three days old, and that near its end the average gap between the date of birth and the date of baptism had lengthened to about four weeks. As far as I know, nobody has yet attempted such a detailed analysis of the parish registers of Wales so that, for the time being, one must assume that the Welsh pattern followed the English in this particular. So *Richard son of the Reverend Mr Lucas born 26th March baptized 26th April 1771* was probably of a typical age for infant baptism in the late eighteenth century, while *Eleanor daug*[*hte*]*r of John Thomas of Typoeth (six weeks old) by Rachael uxor* [*baptized 2 March 1804*] was perhaps noteworthy as being a little overdue, leaving *Anne Davies, daughter of Tho*[*mas*] *Davies* [ . . . ] *publickly xtened in this church and married on the same day* [*17 December 1807*] as, most definitely, a late starter.[34]

## Bishop's transcripts

The laws of the Church of England, commonly called its Canons, were first codified during the years 1597-1603. One of these canons made it obligatory for every parish in England and Wales to send annually to the bishop of the diocese a copy of its register for each successive year. The bishop was to be responsible for preserving these copies, popularly known in archival and family history circles as bishop's transcripts or, for short, BTs, in the diocesan registry. In England bishop's transcripts going back to the canon of 1603 and beyond are commonplace. In Wales, except for a few border parishes which belonged to English dioceses, there is none earlier than 1661. As with parish registers, north Wales is better served by BTs than the south. Both the diocese of St Asaph and the diocese of Bangor have some transcripts dating from 1661-62, but mostly they cover the periods 1670-1850 and 1675-1880 respectively. In south Wales the main body of BTs for the diocese of Llandaf does not begin until 1725, while those for the diocese of St David's fall into three distinct categories: parishes in the archdeaconries of Carmarthen and Gower which generally have transcripts beginning in 1671; parishes in the archdeaconry of Brecon which have a smattering of transcripts dating from 1685 and a main series beginning in 1700; and parishes in the archdeaconry of Cardigan and St David's which have some transcripts dating from the last quarter or so of the seventeenth century and then nothing for virtually the whole of the eighteenth century until the main series begins in 1799.

If registers and bishop's transcripts are available for your chosen parish, it is wise to check both. They do not always agree and sometimes supplement one another; and some incumbents seem to have considered the transcripts more important than the register. For example, the parish of Llanfihangel Rhydieithon (Radnorshire) has a register and BTs which between them supply the records of fourteen separate events in the twelve month period January 1734/5 to December 1735: eight baptisms, two weddings, and four burials. Five of the fourteen entries are to be found in both the register and the bishop's transcripts; two more in the register only; and the remaining seven in the BTs only.

## Other transcripts of parish registers, copies and indexes of entries

During the second half of the twentieth century, parish registers have become far more accessible to searchers. The days of tramping from one church to the next in the footsteps of the old breed of antiquarians are over. As a result, enthusiasts have been able to take up the challenge of transcribing and indexing registers at an ever-increasing pace in recent years. For example, dedicated individuals and associations have engaged themselves in the compilation of marriage indexes for several of the historic counties. Family history societies are well to the fore in this work and should be consulted with regard to projects completed, in progress, or being planned. Paradoxically, increased accessibility has led to restricted access to the original registers. To preserve these unique records from the damaging effects of overhandling, some repositories now insist on the use of microfilm copies or facsimiles by searchers. There is also a good deal of exchange of microfilm and facsimile copies between the repositories so that the same records may be consulted at more than one access point; and do not ignore the many copies of and extracts from parish registers in manuscript, typescript or print, which were produced by previous generations of enthusiasts, and which now often reside in the same repositories as the original records themselves. Very occasionally they may redeem a loss as in the case of the aforementioned register damaged by fire at Christchurch (Monmouthshire).

The bishops' transcripts are also now more accessible to the public. They were transferred from the various diocesan registries to the National Library of Wales during the 1940s. Since 1950 the Genealogical Society of Utah, working from microfilm copies, has steadily incorporated a vast amount of data from the BTs in its International Genealogical Index for Wales. Yet, it is still too early to speak of a comprehensive index which covers all of the events recorded in the parish registers and the bishop's transcripts; and, even if it were available now, it would, in view of the comparative lack of variety in

Welsh surnames, be of limited use to those searchers who set out with only a vague notion of their Welsh connections: there is absolutely no substitute for the methodical association of a person's name and dates with a particular locality or parish.

## Search and photocopying services

The repositories welcome written enquiries concerning the availability of sources, and, if it is not possible for you to pay them a personal visit and carry out your own research, their staff will usually do simple searches such as the confirmation of a single entry in the parish registers without charge. For lengthier and more complicated searches, however, you may be referred to independent researchers. The National Library of Wales has, since January 1988, provided a fee-paying research service of its own, details of which may be obtained by contacting the Library directly. The authorities of the Church in Wales are strict in their photocopying policy with regard to original parish registers: they allow the piecemeal photocopying of single entries under the careful supervision of the repositories, but permission to photocopy registers, in whole or in more considerable part, is seldom given. There is, on the other hand, no restriction on the photocopying of bishop's transcripts.

**NOTES TO CHAPTER 4**

[1]Public Record Office, Burnet IV, 341; Wilkins III, 815: Thomas Cromwell's Injunctions to the Clergy, dated 5 September 1538, summarised in *Letters and Papers, Foreign and Domestic of the reign of Henry VIII*, ed. by James Gairdner (London: HMSO, 1893), vol.XIII, pt.II, p.114, no.281. See also pp.xxiii-xxiv of the same work for further background material. Wales lost its independence in 1282, but the legislation designed to eradicate those features which made it different from England was passed in 1536 as 27 Hen VIII, c.26, *An Acte for Lawes & Justice to be ministred in Wales in like fourme as it is in this Realme*, the first of the Acts of Union.

[2]PRO, Sir Walter Denys to Thomas Cromwell, 24 September 1538, including the confession of Lewez Herbert of Aburgavene in Wales, 18 September, in *Letters & Papers*, pp.158-59, no.413.

[3]PRO, Burnet, VI, 223: Henry VIII's Circular to the Justices of the Peace, December 1538, in *Letters & Papers*, pp.485-86, no.1171.

[4]The term 'Anglican' refers to the reformed Church of England, the established religion of the English state. The Welsh church was an integral part of the Established Church of England until 1920, when it was disestablished by act of Parliament, and became a separate Province within the Anglican Communion under its adopted name of 'The Church in Wales'.

[5]C.J.Williams and J.Watts-Williams, eds, *Cofrestri Plwyf Cymru/Parish Registers of Wales* (Aberystwyth: National Library of Wales & Welsh County Archivists' Group in association with the Society of Genealogists, 1986)

[6]The county codes used in this Fig. are as follows: AGY Anglesey; BRE Brecknockshire; CAE Caernarfonshire; CGN Cardiganshire; CMN Carmarthenshire; DEN Denbighshire; FLN Flintshire; GLA Glamorgan; MER Merionethshire; MON Monmouthshire; MGY Montgomeryshire; PEM Pembrokeshire; RAD Radnorshire; HEF Herefordshire; GLS Gloucestershire; OXF Oxfordshire; and SAL Shropshire (Salop). [They are also used in the notes which follow.]

[7]The statistics for Wales are gathered from *Cofrestri Plwyf Cymru/Parish Registers of Wales*; and those for England from D.J.Steel, *National Index of Parish Registers*, V, 3rd edn. (London: Society of Genealogists; Chichester: Phillimore, 1976) and *Original Parish Registers in Record Offices and Libraries* (Matlock: Local Population Studies, 1974, and its four supplements, 1976-82).

[8]Gwinfardd Dyfed in his 'Statistical Account of the parish of Fishguard in Pembrokeshire' in *The Cambrian Register for the year 1795* (London, 1796), p.260.

[9]Erasmus Saunders, *View of the State of Religion in the Diocese of St David's about the beginning of the eighteenth century* (London: John Wyat, 1721; replica reprint, Cardiff: University of Wales Press, 1949); Walter T.Morgan, 'Yr Eglwys Sefydledig yng Nghymru 1700-1735' in *Hanes Methodistiaeth Galfinaidd Cymru*, ed. by Gomer Morgan Roberts (Caernarfon: Llyfrfa'r Methodistiaid Calfinaidd, 1973), I, 43-80, and 'The diocese of St David's in the nineteenth century', *Journal of the Historical Society of the Church in Wales*, vol.21, no.26 (1971), 5-49; vol.22, no.27 (1972), 12-48; vol.23, no.28 (1973), 18-55.

[10]National Library of Wales, Church in Wales Records, LL/QA/9, parish of Llansanffraid (MON), whose population in 1801 totalled 22 persons. The vicar remarked further that 'most of this parish is occupied by one gentleman, and but himself within the parish capable to serve the office of churchwarden . . . I reside within a quarter of a mile of the church but not in the parish. There is no parsonage house and but two other houses within the parish'.

[11]NLW, LL/QA/5, item 1676, parish of Monkswood (MON) (pop. 1801: 110 persons). The curate served two other churches both of which had their own registers. To compensate for no register at Monkswood he claimed, 'I always keep a book of my own and return yearly copies of it to the Registrar's Office'.

[12]NLW, B/QA/5, fol.8r, parish of Bangor (pop. 1801: 1,770). On fol.4r, the junior vicar admitted that there was no register of births and burials, but that he had 'caused an acc't to be kept and a return to be made into the Registrar's Office. There is a proper register book for marriages duly kept'.

[13]NLW, LL/QA/8. In 1763, Barry (pop. 1801: 70) had but four farmers and five cottages, and there were only twelve families in Penarth (pop. 1801: 72) (NLW, LL/QA/1). See *The Diocese of Llandaff in 1763: the Primary Visitation of Bishop Ewer*, ed. by John R.Guy (Cardiff: South Wales Record Society, 1991).

[14]NLW, B/QA/6, fol.423r, parish of Llanallgo and Llaneugrad (pop. 1801: 196 and 207 persons respectively).

[15]NLW Facs. 75, Phillipps of Cilsant family papers, p.7.

[16]D.Rhys Phillips, *The History of the Vale of Neath* (Swansea: D.Rhys Phillips, 1925), p.74.

[17]*Abstract of the Answers and Returns made pursuant to* [*the Population Act, 1831*], *III, Parish Register Abstract* (London, 1834), p.472; R.M.& G.A.Benwell, 'Interpreting the Parish Registers and Bishop's Transcripts for Anglesey and Llŷn' in *Anglesey Antiquarian & Field Club Transactions* (1975), 69-140 (p.77); and 'Parish Registers and their Perils' in *Carmarthenshire Notes and Miscellany for South West Wales*, reprinted from *The Welshman*, ed. by Arthur Mee, II, 25.

[18]*Parish Register Abstract*, p.433.

[19]Now at NLW. Fortunately there is a transcript of the register by Joseph Bradney (1859-1933) in NLW MS. 7586D.

[20]NLW, LL/QA/9, parish of Llanddewi Rhydderch (MON) (pop. 1801: 304).

[21]The vicar of Llanberis (CAE) in *Y Gwyliedydd*, 6 (1828), 24.

[22]*Parish Register Abstract*, p.444, parish of Nantglyn (DEN) and p.455, parish of Caerau (GLA).

[23]NLW, parish register of Llanfihangel Rhydieithon (RAD), 1750-85, fol.5r; and Glamorgan Archive Service, parish register of St.Andrew's Major (GLA), 1744-91, p.6.

[24]NLW, parish registers of Llanbadarn Trefeglwys (CGN), 1724-85, fol.111, and Cardigan (CGN), 1653-1808, p.123 respectively.

[25]*Reports from the Select Committee appointed to inquire into the state of the Public Records of the Kingdom, &c* (House of Lords, 1801), p.314 (Appendix L.15.b).

[26]NLW, parish register of Eglwys Newydd (CGN), 1773-1812, p.37.

[27]Oxford, Christ Church, Wake MSS, Arch.W.Epist. 21, ccxcviii, fol.419, W.Wootton to Abp Wake, 23 February 1720/1, quoted by R.Brown, 'Clandestine Marriages in Wales', *JHSCW*, vol.25, no. 30, 66-71 (p.69), after N.Sykes, *Church and State in England during the Eighteenth Century* (Cambridge: Cambridge University Press, 1934), 221.

[28]In Scotland, registers 'rarely survive for country parishes before 1700 or even later' (E.McLaughlin, *Parish Registers*, 31-32); in Ireland, where registers were not obligatory until 1634 and the standard of record-keeping not high, a thousand pre-1869 Anglican registers were lost in the destruction of the Dublin PRO in 1922 (Marilyn Yurdan, *Irish Family History* (London: Batsford, 1990), 127-28); in France, where parochial registration began in 1539, the curés were often negligent, edicts being made in 1667 and 1673 to improve the quality of parish registers, and in 1737 to require greater care in the registering of deaths (Roland E. Mousnier, *The Institutions of France under the Absolute Monarchy 1598-1789: Society and the State*, transl. by Brian Pearce (Chicago and London: University of Chicago, 1979), 700); 'Swedish registers survive in numbers only from the 1680s' (E.A.Wrigley & R.S.Schofield, *The Population History of England 1541-1871: A Reconstruction* (London: Edward Arnold, 1981), 2).

[29]T.M.Bassett, *The Welsh Baptists* (Swansea: Ilston House, 1977), 92-93; R.Tudur Jones, *Hanes Annibynwyr Cymru* (Abertawe: Undeb yr Annibynwyr Cymraeg, 1966), 190. For tables of places of worship, sittings and attendants see the *Census of Great Britain, 1851. Religious Worship. England and Wales. Report and Tables* (London: HMSO, 1853), pp.ccxiii, ccxxxiii-iv; and, for further analysis, *The Religious Census of 1851: A Calendar of*

*the Returns relating to Wales* (2 vols.), ed. by Ieuan Gwynedd Jones and David Williams (Cardiff: University of Wales, 1976).

[30]NLW, parish register of Llandygwydd (CGN), baptisms and burials 1803-12, p.6. The population of the parish in 1811 was 877. Over the ten years 1801-10, although the burials (97) entered in the register outnumbered the baptisms (78), the population of the parish had actually increased by 79.

[31]*Parish Register Abstract*, 483. For evidence of irreligion see, for example, E.D.Jones, 'Some aspects of the history of the Church in North Cardiganshire in the eighteenth century', *JHSCW*, 3 (1953), 100-110 (pp.109-10); W.T.Morgan, *JHSCW*, 22 (1972), 26-27; Owen Chadwick, *The Victorian Church*, 3rd edn. (London: A.& C. Black, 1971), 4-5; and W.L.Mathieson, *English Church Reform 1815-1840* (London: Longmans, Green, 1923), 17-18.

[32]R.W.McDonald, 'The Parish Registers of Wales' in the *National Library of Wales Journal*, XIX (1975-6), 399-429. For England, see D.J.Steel, E.McLaughlin, and others.

[33]The ban was reinforced by Henry VIII's Acts of Union.

[34]The first and last of these quotations are taken from the parish register of Cardigan (CGN), 1653-1808, pp.98 and 125; the other from the parish register of Lampeter(CGN), 1746-1805, p.43.

# 5. Civil Registration and the Census

Sheila Rowlands

## Civil Registration

The introduction of the civil registration of births, marriages and deaths on 1 July 1837 affected England and Wales together and equally. As a source for family history, this topic is well covered in introductory guides to research[1] and this chapter assumes that readers will be familiar with the general background. Some Welsh researchers need no more guidance than such guides provide, since it is quite possible with many families to move backwards without major problems, generation by generation, to the start of civil registration.

To the newcomer, however, this seemingly straightforward process may have many pitfalls in Welsh research. The sad truth is that many researchers have serious difficulties in relatively recent times, the main cause being the large numbers of entries in the civil registration indexes relating to our small stock of surnames. For this reason, all who seek their recent ancestors in Wales are well advised not to omit the essential stages of writing to and interviewing relations, however distant, and of searching every possible avenue for family memorabilia which will provide details of birth or baptism, marriage, death or burial. School and service records, newspapers, wills and obituaries are a few examples of sources which may help solve problems of identification. Every discovery of this nature makes the journey through civil registration easier and in many cases it makes the difference between success and failure. Such are the problems of finding Welsh individuals with very common names in the civil registration indexes that alternative sources are always to be recommended first!

Records of birth, marriage and death have been recorded in a dual system from the outset in 1837: the events were recorded by local registrars, details were kept locally and copies were sent to the General Register Office in London.[2] Information in the form of a certificate may, therefore, be obtained from either source. The quarterly indexes covering England and Wales at St. Catherine's House are open to searchers and certificates may be ordered there. The consolidated indexes provide names in alphabetical order, together with the registration district and a reference number (unique to these indexes).

In recent years, microfilm and microfiche copies of these indexes have become widely available both in Britain and overseas. Microfiche has many advantages in use and, being less expensive, may even be within the reach of individuals to purchase.[3] The National Library of Wales has coverage from 1837 to 1983 and other record offices and libraries in Wales are, increasingly, acquiring copies, whether for some or all of the period. Microform copies may also be seen in Mormon Family History Centres throughout the world as well as in a growing number of public libraries.

The certificate on which information is issued nowadays may be bilingual in English and Welsh, since such forms were instituted for use in Wales in 1963. The production of nineteenth and early twentieth century information on these modern forms should not mislead the purchaser into thinking that the originals would have been bilingual: they would have been on the standard (English language) forms which are illustrated in most basic family history guides.[4]

The researcher into Welsh family history is all too often presented with too many people of the same name in the same quarter in Welsh registration districts. One of the first steps should be to ensure that the right area is being searched. The nineteenth century Welsh registration counties, which include the registration districts, do not necessarily coincide with the more familiar administrative counties. For example, Newcastle in Emlyn Registration District straddled the administrative counties of Cardigan, Pembroke and Carmarthen; the county of Anglesey lay in the three registration districts of Anglesey, Bangor and Carnarvon. Maps of the districts may be seen at St Catherine's House or referred to in the printed Census Report for 1851 in large libraries. The Institute of Heraldic and Genealogical Studies[5] has produced a general set of maps of registration districts at different dates, and some Welsh family history societies have produced detailed maps of their locality, showing boundaries and anomalous areas. A useful recent guide lists districts and sub-districts.[6] Armed with such finding aids, one may plan research to best effect, taking full account of adjacent registration districts and eliminating improbable ones in the national indexes.

The researcher, even then, might locate several possible entries in the General Register Office indexes. Full details should be noted and then there are two possible approaches to obtaining a certificate.

First, the reference checking system at St Catherine's House may be used to eliminate some of the possibilities. Briefly, this enables one to state a known fact or facts about an event in order (for a fee) to allow the correct certificate to be identified. This is much cheaper than buying a succession of wrong certificates. A leaflet explaining the system in detail is available from the General Register Office. Though it may still prove expensive in a difficult case, many average problems in Welsh research can be solved this way.

When using the microform indexes it is important to take down full details, including the reference number. Without these details, the cost of obtaining a certificate by post is increased considerably. In any case, those who are unable to get to London themselves should consider using the services of a record agent, who can order the certificate in person much less expensively, even taking the agent's fee into account. A word of warning, however, in that a record agent who is unfamiliar with Welsh surnames and place-names may well be as easily confused as anyone else: confidence and local knowledge count for a great deal in finding one's way around the maze of civil registration in Wales, and some precise questions about experience in this specific field would be sensible.

Alternatively, the family historian should consider approaching the local Superintendent Registrar, who will have full records for that specific district only.[7] (It should, however, be borne in mind that a number of registration districts have been rationalised or amalgamated over the years in Wales.) As long as family historians approach registrars politely and with due regard for the priorities of their job (which is to register vital events and not to help us), they will almost always receive courteous assistance. Indeed, a great many Welsh family historians have reason to be thankful for their help, for their expertise is invaluable when searching local indexes. Bear in mind always that the General Register Office index reference numbers have no relevance whatsoever to the local registrar, therefore you should not quote them. Simply give name, year and quarter, and any identifying detail you can provide in the case of birth or death.

In the case of marriages, you may well find that it is easier to use the General Register Office and its indexes, since the lack of a single index to marriages at the local level means that the registrar needs first to know the church, chapel or register office where the event took place. The General Register Office indexes allow you to cross-refer between bride and groom (who will each have an identical registration district and reference number) and to pinpoint a marriage more easily. As an example, a marriage sought for Thomas Jones in Anglesey in the year

1852 produced a glut of possibilities. His bride's name, Mary Roberts (also very common), had been found from a child's birth certificate. Thomas Jones and Mary Roberts had the same registration district and reference number in only three cases. A form for the reference checking system was completed, in this case supplying the groom's occupation as weaver, since this was the only further detail known. A matching certificate was received, and further research proved it to be the correct one. This is a simple example, but one which could be repeated in most Welsh families, and illustrates how an initially daunting search can often prove to be reasonable.

Some difficulties in locating births in Wales will be due to the non-registration of the infants concerned, particularly in the early decades of civil registration. This was prevalent throughout England and Wales before penalties were introduced in 1874. In rural areas, where baptism was sometimes ignorantly thought to be an acceptable alternative, any available church and chapel registers should be searched. In the fast-growing industrial towns, apathy and indolence led to many parents not registering some of their offspring. That this happens can be demonstrated by anyone researching an uncommon Welsh name (and there are some) for a one-name study, for gaps in the indexes can be clearly illustrated; this leads to great frustration and much fruitless searching in the case of common names.

Patience and doggedness are the best allies when searching for Welsh families during the period of civil registration, and too many family historians give up without searching all the obvious trails. It has to be said that the only real solution to this problem would be a similar arrangement, at least for the older documents, to that used in Scottish civil registration, whereby (for a fee) the actual registers are available for inspection. During the preparation of this book the necessary legislation to bring this about for England and Wales has been much deferred, but it would transform Welsh research at one of its most difficult stages, since all good family historians develop an instinct for their own John Jones, Mary Evans or David Thomas, folk who have been rendered almost invisible in the indexes.

## The Census

There are a small number of special features to record relating to the census in Wales. For the most part, the requirements which applied to England also applied to Wales.[8]

From 1841, a Welsh translation of the household schedule was available, though the enumerators' books were to be completed in English. That this was strange to some enumerators can occasionally be deduced, for example in the Westfa area of Llanelli in 1851, where the enumerator filled in relationship, condition, occupation and birthplace in Welsh, but then crossed them out and substituted the English equivalents.[9] It may also explain a great many of the strange 'mongrel' versions of house and farm names which appear throughout Wales, such as Tanhouse for Tanws and The Voel for Y Foel.[10]

From 1871 onwards, if the householder completed a schedule in Welsh, the enumerator would indicate this with a 'W' in the first column. It is difficult to say how accurately this was recorded but, when found, it is of great interest to descendants. Its presence is a reliable sign that Welsh was used, but its absence does not prove the contrary.

From 1891, a question on the ability to speak Welsh has been included, and householders' schedules for Wales and Monmouthshire indicated whether individuals spoke either English or Welsh exclusively, or if they spoke both. The bald figures have long been available but, again, individual cases interest the modern family historian. They illustrate, at least, how census information depends on the interpretation of the questions.[11] From 1901, such returns were not to be made for infants under the age of three. For other age groups there must have been considerable confusion as to how much proficiency in either language was required to qualify as a speaker.

The returns must be viewed on microfilm or microfiche, and may be seen in an increasing number of places including, outside Wales, the Public Record Office, Chancery Lane, London, and Mormon Family History Centres worldwide. The National Library of Wales has microfilm copies for the whole of Wales for 1841-1881, with 1891 on microfiche. Copies for the old counties and other subdivisions of Wales may be seen at many county record offices and county libraries in Wales. Border areas are sometimes to be found in the record offices of the adjoining English counties. A Gibson Guide lists locations of such copies.[12] The release of the 1891 census returns on microfiche, with the possibility of the purchase of such a limited (and relatively inexpensive) area as a sub-district by individuals,[13] now makes it feasible for family historians with problems in Wales around the end of the nineteenth century to have easy access, presenting a new opportunity to make progress at a time when civil registration is particularly difficult.

Searching the census can often be very easy in Wales, where many parishes had small populations. The need to look at all available census years should be stressed, for this is undoubtedly the way to build up a detailed picture of ancestors in their family and local setting, so essential for progress in Welsh research. The larger towns are inevitably much more difficult but many street indexes now exist at the Public Record Office, with copies at the National Library of Wales and some record offices. The latter, in any case, often have their own local finding-aids.

Modern transcripts of the census exist for some areas of Wales. The most popular year for such projects has until recently been 1851, since it was the first to indicate a reasonably accurate birthplace and helps to locate the origins of people born before civil registration. Details of work completed or in progress by Welsh family history societies and by individuals are shown in a survey of 1851 Census Indexes[14] and in a further Gibson Guide.[15] Most Welsh transcribers see the value of fairly full transcripts, since surname indexes alone are not of great value in the land of the Joneses!

The 1881 census is being transcribed for the whole of England and Wales under the auspices of the British Genealogical Record Users Committee, with the Church of Latter Day Saints taking a prominent role. The production of the complete index on microfiche (some Welsh counties have been among the first to be published) will add considerably to the possibilities of finding missing Welsh ancestors in relatively modern times. It is a pity that transcribers were not asked to copy the indication that forms were completed in Welsh, referred to above.

For background reading about the census generally there is a useful Public Record Office publication;[16] for Wales one can hardly do better than to read the excellent HMSO publication by Edward Higgs.[17] Few general works devote space, as this one does, to specifically Welsh aspects of the subject: detailed references are given for examples of Welsh household schedules and enumerators' books and the problems of interpreting the answers relating to language are described.

**NOTES TO CHAPTER 5**

[1]For example: Andrew Todd, *Basic Sources for Family History—1: Back to the Early 1800s.* (Ramsbottom: Allen & Todd, 1987), and George Pelling, *Beginning Your Family History* (Birmingham: FFHS, 1990). Pauline Saul & F.C.Markwell, *The Family Historian's Enquire Within* (Birmingham: FFHS, 1991) indicates potential problems in civil registration and provides useful addresses. A list of current FFHS publications is available from FFHS, Benson Room, Birmingham & Midland Institute, Margaret Street, Birmingham.

[2]The General Register Office, St Catherine's House, Kingsway, London WC8 6JP.

[3]Enquiries should be addressed to The General Register Office, Smedley Hydro, Trafalgar Road, Birkdale, Southport, Merseyside PR8 2HH, marking the envelope 'Microfiche Sales'. This address should also be used for all postal applications for certificates.

[4]Pelling (1990)

[5]Institute of Heraldic & Genealogical Studies, Northgate, Canterbury. Also helpful in this context, as long as the reader bears in mind that anomalous county boundaries are not described, is M.E.Bryant Rosier, *Index to Census Registration Districts* (1992).

[6]Ray Wiggins, *St Catherine's House Districts* (Author, nd)

[7]Local registrars are listed in the telephone directory; a useful publication is *District Register Offices in England & Wales*, 8th ed. (East Yorkshire FHS, 1991).

[8]Only the 1841-1891 censuses are considered here, but some earlier nominal lists exist for Wales; see Jeremy Gibson and Mervyn Medlycott, *Local Census Listings 1522-1930: Holdings in the British Isles* (FFHS, 1992)

[9]PRO: HO 107/2468, folio 451.

[10]I am grateful to Hafina Clwyd for this suggestion.

[11]In the Rhondda in 1891, Daniel Einon and his son-in-law, David Davies, near neighbours and of very similar background and age (there was only thirteen years between them) gave their language as Welsh only and English only, respectively. Both were literate men, known to be fluent in both languages and needing English for their work, but speaking Welsh at home. (RG 12/4423, folios 8 and 10). K.Schurer, 'The 1891 census and local population studies', *Local Population Studies* 47 (Autumn 1991) has interesting comments on and background to this topic.

[12]Jeremy Gibson, *Census Returns 1841-1881 on Microfilm: A Directory to Local Holdings in Great Britain* (FFHS, 1988).

[13]Details are available from Reprographic Ordering, The Public Record Office, Ruskin Avenue, Kew TW9 4DU.

[14]*1851 Census Index Survey: England, Wales and Channel Islands*. (FFHS, 1992).

[15]Jeremy Gibson, *Marriage, Census and other Indexes for Family Historians*. (FFHS, 1992).

[16]Susan Lumas, *Making Use of the Census*, Public Record Office Readers' Guide No.1. (London: PRO Publications, 1992). The same author's *An Introduction to the Census Returns of England and Wales* (FFHS, 1992) will become available while this book is in the press.

[17]Edward Higgs, *Making Sense of the Census: the Manuscript Returns for England and Wales, 1801-1901*. Public Record Office Handbooks No.23. (London: HMSO, 1989).

# 6. Nonconformity

Muriel Bowen Evans

## Introduction

The visual evidence of Nonconformity in Wales is all around us: chapels of a variety of styles and several denominations; chapels which have had an inextricable place in our social and community life. The poet T.Rowland Hughes was moved to comment:

> Nid ydynt hardd, fy ffrind, i chwi,
> ein hen addoldai mawr, di-ri,
> ond hwy a'n gwnaeth,
> o'r blychau hyn y daeth
> ennaint ein doe a'n hechdoe ni,
> os llwm eu llun, os trwsgl eu trem,
> Caersalem, Seion, Soar, a Bethlehem.[1]

Clearly the historian eschews one-influence explanations for the patterns of the past, and a variety of factors interacted to form modern Wales. Nonetheless the roles of Nonconformity were so dynamic that if those searching for their Welsh ancestors wish to understand their social milieu they must take account of Nonconformity. Moreover, by the second half of the nineteenth century, the proportion of chapel adherents amongst those who attended places of worship was so high that almost all researchers into family history in Wales must expect to have had some Nonconformist connections.[2]

In short, let it be said at the outset that if you are Welsh you are quite likely to have had some chapel-going ancestors. And when you find them you will be in touch with a whole range of experiences and yearnings which were mainstream in our history.

## Some Preliminary Explanations

What's in a name? Well, let us start with some clarification of the use of the words **church** and **chapel** in the context of Nonconformity. Although we talk of the meeting place as a chapel, the body of members form a church.

A Nonconformist is 'a member of a religious body which is separated from the Church of England'—or in our case the Church in Wales.[3]

The early Nonconformists of England and Wales were also described as Dissenters. Today Nonconformists are often referred to as members of the free churches, the word 'free' having an organisational rather than a financial connotation.

One of the difficulties experienced by researchers arises from the fact that at no stage have the Nonconformists been one homogeneous body. There have been and are a variety of denominations. In the sixteenth and seventeenth centuries terms such as Congregationalist, Independent, Presbyterian, Baptist and Quaker emerged. The first three arose from views of church government, the Congregationalists or Independents maintaining the authority of the local church while the Presbyterians favoured a hierarchical system. Baptists also maintained the authority of the local church but their name arose from a belief in the baptism of believers, while Quaker was a term of mockery from a man of the law.[4] Later, the Unitarians and Methodists appeared along with some other smaller groups.

Most of these denominations have or had a place in the religious history of Wales.[5] This is not the occasion to discuss their theological nuances, but their story is part of the history of our country. The unifying structures of the present-day denominations in Wales vary according to the underlying philosophy of the persuasion, some being far more prescriptive than others. Likewise the degree of congregational control allowed to individual churches varies from denomination to denomination.

## The Origins and Early History of Nonconformity

To begin at the beginning, the first objections to conformity, in England, appeared almost contemporaneously with the establishment of the Church of England. A group who came to be called Separatists favoured withdrawal from the state church and voluntary gatherings for worship. The only known Welsh Separatist of the reign of Elizabeth was John Penry, who was executed in London on a charge of high treason in 1593, at the age of 30.

It was during the next century, the period of constitutional struggle, civil wars and revolution that Nonconformity appeared on Welsh soil. The first gathered church in Wales was formed at Llanfaches in Monmouthshire in 1639.[6] This was an Independent or Congregational church. The first Baptist church in Wales was established at Ilston (Glamorgan) in 1649.[7] After the Restoration of the Monarchy (1660) the government attempted to enforce conformity to the state church by a series of punitive Acts which came to be known as the Clarendon Code.

It was the resistance to these Acts which produced the descriptive category 'Nonconformist'.[8] These were the years of secret worship, of services 'in other manner than according to the Liturgie and practice of the Church of England', of extempore prayers—and of informers and punishment. All over Wales there are traditions of secret meeting places during this period of repression, some in the open air, others indoors like **yr ystafell dywyll** (the dark, windowless room), at Canerw in Llanboidy (Carmarthenshire), one of the farms associated with the ministry of Stephen Hughes.[9]

Those who attended such meetings or conventicles were liable to punishment; therefore there was a considerable degree of secrecy and the information that has come down to us is sparse. Some of the glimpses come as a result of the activities of informers. For example, the precise details of attendance at a conventicle held at the house of Ellis Owen at Llangybi (Caernarfonshire) on Sunday 23 April 1676 are known because two of those present, Amos John and Robert Parry, both of Clynnog in the same county, were there as spies, and gave full information to the neighbouring JPs.[10]

Various presentments to the authorities of the established church give names of individuals said to be Nonconformists. For example Jo.Price and John Morris, the church wardens of Llangennech (Carmarthenshire) in 1684 stated:

> There are several Nonconformists or dissenters in our parish, namely:- William Jones, alias Wm.John Rees. William fflemming. Anne David, alias Nicholas, wid. John Thomas. ffrancis David. Morris Dd.Thomas and his wife. who often frequent conventicles, as we are inform'd . . . We have observed one William fflemming and Morris David sitting at the reading of the creed and Gospel, and at the reading of Divine Service . . . [11]

Much later, when chapels were being built, the experiences of these years were sometimes recalled. For example when land was being acquired for the building of a meeting house in Henllan Amgoed (Carmarthenshire) in 1695 the representatives of the church, David John Owen of Llangan, John David Lewis of Eglwys Fair a Churig, Lewis Pryddroe of Egremont and Evan John Owen of Kiffig, were described thus:

> . . . being four actual members of the congregation of dissenting protestants that were and are wont to meet for the performing of religious worship and

divine service in the several and respective places of Pale, Canerw and Egremont in the aforesaid county.[12]

Nonconformity was numerically small in the second half of the seventeenth century. Nonetheless, some churches actually came into existence in the time of persecution, and documents survive to attest to this, for example, the register of the Baptist church of Rhydwilym (Carmarthenshire) which was founded in 1668.[13] Such books are rare, and very few of the early churches can claim the survival of a founding covenant, a statement of beliefs or a list of original members.

The Quakers became an organised Christian group in 1668 with the appearance of George Fox's *Rule for the Management of Meetings*. There were several groups meeting in Wales, particularly in Montgomeryshire, Merioneth, Pembrokeshire and Monmouthshire. Some of the people involved were of the landed classes. For example, it was claimed in 1669 that Quaker meetings were taking place in Meifod (Montgomeryshire) at the house of Charles Lloyd, gentleman, a Quaker. The numbers were said to be 50 to 60 and sometimes 100, 'Well horsed, sometimes by day, sometimes by night'.[14] The returns for the diocese of Llandaff for the same year include mention of Quaker meetings at the houses of Mr Robert Jones and Mr George Phillip in Shirenewton (Monmouthshire), and also a denunciation: 'Edward Webley of Shirenewton entertaines of the Quakers'.[15] The Quakers suffered more severely under the penal code than any other Christian body and in the 1680s a number of Welsh Quakers sought religious freedom in the new American colony of Pennsylvania.[16] In Wales itself the number of Quakers declined.

## Toleration for Nonconformists

Following a period which was, for the most part, characterised by intolerance towards Nonconformists, the position was changed radically by the accession of William and Mary in 1688. Following the Toleration Act of 1689, Dissenters could have their own ministers and build their own meeting houses. These were to be registered at the Quarter Sessions, the bishop's court, or the court of the archdeacon (a regulation which continued until 1852). For several of the Welsh counties the Quarter Sessions rolls are not extant for this period, but the evidence for registration may survive somewhere else. For example, there is a memo in the register of the Independents meeting at Haverfordwest (Pembrokeshire) that on 17 July 1691:

> . . . the Meeting House in St Thomas Green was appointed a place for Dissenting Protestants to meet about the exercise of Religion and it was then recorded according to the form of the Statute in that case made and Provided. . . . George Lewis was maior that year.[17]

This was the later Albany church.

It was also required that Nonconformist ministers should subscribe to 36 of the 39 Articles of Religion and take an oath of allegiance to the crown. Certificates had to be sent to the Quarter Sessions attesting the suitability of would-be Nonconformist ministers.

Despite the freedom of worship, Nonconformists—like Catholics—remained disadvantaged because of their religious affiliations. For example Nonconformist registers did not have equal validity with parish registers as legal testimony until 1840. The Test and Corporation Acts, which were not repealed until 1828, debarred them from certain public positions, and they were excluded from the universities of Oxford and Cambridge till the late nineteenth century. However as the Quarter Sessions papers of many of the counties show, some individuals overcame these disabilities by occasional conformity, that is occasional taking of communion in the parish church.

### A Change of Tempo

Following the achievement of toleration, chapels were built and there was a gradual advance of Baptist and Independent causes in the early eighteenth century, both denominations being stronger in south than north Wales.[18] The keeping of registers seems to have become usual by the middle years of the century. This was important since the only record outside the family of the existence of a child was the entry in the parish or some other register. The oldest Independent registers record baptisms and sometimes births. For example the earliest register for Llanedi Independent Church, Carmarthenshire (which provides the information that Llanedi 'New House' was founded about 1700 and the chapel built about 1712) begins in 1745.[19] However it includes a record of children born earlier. Two of them are children of John Rhyddrech (*sic*) of nearby Llannon parish, Mary born 27 February 1734 and David, 7 November 1737. Such retrospective recording is not unusual in the older registers. The Baptists of course did not christen infants, but they kept records of births.

The whole religious atmosphere was altered by the Revival of the eighteenth century which had its origins in the established church. It is associated with the Reverend Griffith Jones, vicar of Llanddowror, on the one hand and Methodism on the other. The original leaders of Welsh Calvinistic Methodism were Howell Harris, Daniel Rowland and William Williams, and of English Methodism—Wesleyan Methodism—the brothers John and Charles Wesley and George Whitefield. The aim of both groups of Methodists was to invigorate the spiritual life of the Church of England. Both groups were very successful in their itinerant ministry, the Wesleyans operating within areas where English was known, such as South Pembrokeshire, the Vale of Glamorgan and some of the coastal towns. The Calvinistic movement, which appealed to the Welsh-speaking majority, swept through the interior of the country, confirming the new tastes which had been created by Griffith Jones's circulating schools. However the authorities of the Church of England were intransigent opponents of their methods of evangelising and eventually both groups ordained their own ministers, thus becoming Nonconformists (the Wesleyans in 1795 and the Welsh Calvinistic Methodists in 1811). Calvinistic Methodism was found in all parts of Wales but it was particularly strong in parts of the north which had not been greatly affected by the old Dissent. And so the spiritual revival which had begun in the Church of England had led to a large numerical growth of Nonconformity.[20]

And yet, religious enthusiasm was not the whole story of Nonconformity in the eighteenth century. In parts of Cardiganshire and Glamorgan Arminianism had taken root; this was to develop through Arianism into Unitarianism. One of the Cardiganshire churches that was to follow this pattern was Wernhir founded in 1726. This congregation built the chapel at Llwynrhydowen in 1733. In Glamorgan the church at Cefncoedycymer founded in 1747 was to move all the way to Unitarian beliefs in due course.[21] In their philosophy and practice the Unitarians were a complete contrast to the Methodists.

## Increase of Churches and Membership

Expansion is the story from the late eighteenth century. Old religious causes (churches) increased their membership at this time, under the influence of zealous ministers and a growing population. New style Baptist and Independent ministers started taking the religious message out into the countryside. The nineteenth century was of course a period of phenomenal expansion of Welsh industry and there was an accompanying redistribution of the Welsh population together with in-migration. The growth of the industrial communities was paralleled by the growth of Nonconformity. The ministry of the Established Church in the industrial areas was hampered at first by the rigidity arising from the old parochial system; there were already parish churches in existence. While this should have been an advantage, if they were at some distance from the developing industrial communities it was counterproductive. The Anglican problem was compounded by the fact that many of the ancient Glamorgan parishes were very large.

Llanwonno (Glamorgan) was typical of this situation, with its ancient church situated at some distance from the growing townships of Pontypridd and Mountain Ash which lay in part within the parish. The situation in Llanwonno in 1851 can be appreciated from the religious census.[22] The incumbent commented 'The church being at a considerable distance from the Bulk of the inhabitants of the parish causes the attendance to be smaller than it should.' Of a total population of 3,253, only 56 people had been present at the one service of the day in the little upland church. According to another informant the usual number of attendants there was from 25 to 35, and there was no Sunday School. By contrast the Nonconformists were adaptable and chapels were built where there were people. There were already by 1851 one Particular Baptist, one Baptist, one English Wesleyan, one Primitive Methodist, three Calvinistic Methodist, and one Independent church in the parish, each offering a Sunday School as well as two services. Between them they could seat well over 1,500, by contrast with the 150 places which the vicar said were available at the parish church. (The other informant put the number at 80.) This adaptability of Nonconformity is the more apparent from the description of the buildings. One of the Calvinistic Methodist chapels dated from 1786, but by contrast, the Primitive Methodists met in a recently erected Temperance Hall; the remaining six chapels had been built since 1810, and three of them in fact in the previous four years. The comment of the minister of the Particular Baptist chapel built in 1840 was, 'The chapel is now too small, the congregation require a larger.' This was a process which was happening and was to continue to happen as industry and trade expanded and people were drawn by the magnet of employment prospects. It was still taking place in some areas in the early twentieth century as new economic enterprises took off and villages and townships proliferated. Where there were existing pre-industrial chapels they were enlarged and rebuilt, and many of these in their turn produced further offshoots. These churches were utterly of the minute, their lists of trustees and founder-members a mirror of the community. To quote a nineteenth century example, the following trustees took out a mortgage for £150 on 8 June 1878 towards the erection of a new Primitive Methodist chapel at Bargoed:

> Wm Nash of Fleur de lis, Mynyddislwyn, grocer, Tho Phillips of Aberbargoed, Bedwellty, platelayer, Jos Hughes of Cwmsyfiog, Bedwellty, collier, Jn English of Cwmsyfiog, collier, Wm Castell of Fleur de lis, collier, Hen Pope of Blackwood, collier, Wm Elliott of Tredegar iron works, carpenter, Charles Haytor late of New Tredegar, Bedwellty, collier, William Blacker of Bargoed, collier, Hen Wells of Bargoed, collier, Tho Jasper of Pontlottyn, Rhymney, collier and George Castell of Fleur de lis, collier.[23]

Surviving documents are a testimony to the way of life which centred on the chapels when industrial Wales was in its prime. This is not a claim that everyone went to chapel, but for thousands, the question 'Where do you go?' meant 'Which chapel do you go to?' It was in the world of the chapel that many talents were fostered and people found a role other than that in the often brutalising world of work. Chapel archives often include the following or similar material from the nineteenth and twentieth centuries: deeds; minute books of the church in general and of the Sunday School and chapel societies; financial accounts of the church and the various societies, including collections for foreign and home mission societies, the British and Foreign Bible Society and other non-local organisations; self-help devices such as savings banks and collections for the poor; matters pertaining to reading rooms, festivals, eisteddfodau, choirs, dramas and concerts.

In the late nineteenth century the place of many rural chapels in the community became sharpened by the emergence of politically militant Nonconformity—whose story can be read in other places.[24] In the longer term however the importance of the rural chapel is associated with the preaching services, Sunday Schools and festivals, and a new variant of folk culture focused on the meeting houses. Many chapels—as indeed many churches—have a special place in the lore of certain families because of an association over several generations.

## Capel

The great social and economic changes experienced in Wales during the late twentieth century have, predictably, affected the position of the Nonconformist churches and chapels. These changes and their implications are too vast for analysis to be attempted in this chapter. All that can be said here is that the gradual decline of the indigenous population of rural Wales and in-migration of people from different traditions has led to a decrease of potential members. In addition, the industrial communities which many nineteenth and early twentieth century chapels served are fast disappearing and the population of the urban areas has been redistributed.

Recently there has been an increasing consciousness that, in the changes and increasing secularisation (which seems to characterise our age), so much of the tangible evidence of Nonconformity might be lost by default. In 1986 this led to the foundation of 'Capel—the Chapels Heritage Society' which seeks to:

> . . . study, record and interpret the architecture and archives of Nonconformity in Wales, and to encourage their preservation.[25]

## Locating Nonconformist Records

Locating relevant records has tended to be one of the problems when on the trail of Nonconformist ancestors. Part of the explanation has been that some chapels seem to have very few archives, and that others have not yet reached the decision to deposit what they have for safe keeping in the local county record office or the National Library of Wales. In some cases the historical value of items such as annual reports, and of much twentieth century documentation, has not been recognised. Fortunately, however, there is an increasing realisation of the importance and interest of this material, and for this and other reasons more and more chapel records are being placed in the care of the experts. There is in any case already a great deal of original manuscript material relating to Nonconformist churches and chapels in the various repositories (and also printed books and papers, and microfilm copies of certain archives which are located outside Wales).

The search must begin by identification of the chapels with which one's ancestors may have been associated. The names of chapels in existence in the early twentieth century may be discovered from the Report prepared by the Welsh Church Commission, 1910.[26] Most denominations also publish Yearbooks. Data on the chapels in existence in 1851 was collected as part of the Census and this is available for study thanks to recent valuable editorial work.[27] The Census gives a date or approximate date of foundation. If it is hoped to use Baptist or Independent records for the period before about 1840, it would be useful (if it is possible) to establish whether the chapel was a mother or daughter church, since the records of the newer churches were often subsumed in those of the original.

One should make oneself familiar with the local county record office: with its schedules of documents, its lists of accessions, collections of books and pamphlets relating to the local area (including religious history), its publications, including newsletters and annual reports. It is also important to establish whether documents of the relevant denomination are more likely to be in one repository than another. The official repository of the Presbyterian Church of Wales (formerly known as Calvinistic Methodist) is the National Library of Wales. On the other hand it is the present policy of the Methodist Church in Wales (the Wesleyan Methodists) for churches and circuits to deposit their archives in the local county record office. It should be noted though that there is a holding of Wesleyan records at the National Library of Wales. In the case of these and the other main denominations, archives have been deposited by individual churches both at the National Library and local record offices. Society of Friends (Quaker) records for Wales are held at the Glamorgan Record Office, Cardiff.[28]

Identification of useful material will be greatly facilitated by a project which is well in hand at the National Library of Wales, namely a survey of Nonconformist chapels and records from the earliest period to the present day. It is concerned with archives held at the county record offices as well as those at the National Library. A computerised gazetteer including basic information on the location, denomination and date of foundation of all known chapels, together with a guide to records, will soon be available. It will be possible then to determine whether, for example, any of the following are known of for a particular church: registers, a 'church book', treasurers' accounts, annual reports, minute books of the Sunday school and societies, legal papers, plans and photographs, manuscript histories, information about charities and graveyard surveys. The gazetteer will include Welsh chapels outside Wales.

There are other means also by which the family historian can become familiar with Nonconformist sources and history. Inquiry could be made regarding projects recording chapels and chapel history under the aegis of the record office, the family history society or some other body. Local Heritage Centres such as the Pontypridd Historical and Cultural Centre at the former Tabernacl chapel (Glamorgan), museums such as Yr Hen Gapel, Tre'rddol (Cardiganshire) and the new Quaker

Museum (Tŷ Meirion) in Dolgellau (Merionethshire) should be noted; likewise, the Capel meetings and newsletters.

Transcripts of documents and articles of Nonconformist relevance can be found in the *National Library of Wales Journal,* the journals of the denominational historical societies, the journals of county societies and other learned bodies.[29] For an easy aid in the locating of articles having to do with Nonconformist history, one should turn to the lists of articles relating to the history of Wales published in the *Welsh History Review.* Amongst useful current features in the journals of the denominational history societies is the section 'Lloffion' (Gareth O.Watts) in the Baptist Transactions (*Trafodion Cymdeithas Hanes Bedyddwyr Cymru*) in which are listed publications relating to the history of the Welsh Baptists, and Baptist archives received at the National Library of Wales.

Researchers may wonder whether there is any material relating to Nonconformity in Wales at the Public Record Office or any other institution in England. There are at least two relevant classes at the Public Record Office: RG4 and RG5. RG4 is described as 'Registers, Authenticated: Main Series' and RG5 as 'Certificates'; an outline of the contents can be gained from the *Guide to the Public Record Office.* RG4, a very large collection, includes registers of births, baptisms, deaths, burials and marriages, from a large number of Nonconformist congregations in England and Wales (these are usually referred to as 'Non-Parochial Registers'). The registers in this category of churches in Wales have been microfilmed, and this material is therefore available for study at the National Library of Wales and many of the local county record offices. The Non-Parochial Registers Act 1840 had followed upon a Royal Commission to enquire into the state, custody, and authenticity of registers kept in churches and chapels other than those of the Established Church. Its effect was that the registers which had been certified, and came into the custody of the Registrar General, were now public records—and had equal validity with parish registers as legal testimony. The Births and Deaths Registration Act of 1858 provided for the authentication of some further Non-Parochial registers which had come to light, and their deposit in the General Register Office.

There are also other archives in RG4 including registers from two very distinguished Nonconformist institutions: Dr Williams' Library and the Wesleyan Methodist Metropolitan Registry. The certificates on which these registers are based comprise the contents of RG5.

The Methodist Archives and Research Centre are at the John

Rylands Library in the University Library of Manchester. There is also a Wesley Historical Society Library housed at Southlands College, Wimbledon, London.

Apart from original documents, there is other source material which can be usefully consulted by family historians at the National Library of Wales, the county record offices or the public libraries. The periodicals (in Welsh) which were a feature of the various denominations until very recently, and the local papers, are an important source of chapel news, and each number of the periodicals includes some notices of births, marriages and deaths. Particularly in the earlier years, the family news is not restricted to one denomination or indeed to Nonconformity. A summary of some of the family information in one issue of *Seren Gomer* (May 1822) will illustrate the usefulness of such a periodical to the researcher. It notes the marriage at Liverpool of Mr William Williams, Saddler, Amlwch, and Sara, the fourth daughter of Owain Williams, esquire, Castell Tyriccar, Amlwch, (Anglesey); the marriage at Swansea of Mr J.Jones, Tanner, and Ann the daughter of G.Jencins, esquire; and also six deaths: those of Mr Dafydd Thomas (Dafydd Ddu o Eryri) Waunfawr (Caernarfonshire), Mr T.Jencins, editor and publisher of the *Cambrian* (Glamorgan), two merchants of Holyhead (Anglesey), the wife of J.Daniel, the Carmarthen printer and bookseller, and the 12 year old daughter of a minister. Amongst the brief comments, the reader is told that Dafydd Ddu, poet and hymnwriter, aged 63, drowned on the way home from Bangor in a storm, while crossing the Cegin river by stepping-stones.

## Using the Records

It seems likely that family historians would approach Nonconformist records with two main aims in mind, identification of people from the past and compilation of biographical detail. To what extent can either of these aims be forwarded by looking at records associated with Nonconformity?

Let us begin with identification. The institution of civil registration and the decennial census in the early part of the nineteenth century, has resulted in the creation of a vast archive of data which can be used for the discovery of ancestors, which has nothing to do with church or chapel registers. Obviously someone researching in his home area would in the early stages have checked accessible material such as gravestones, chapel annual reports, memorial tablets, foundation stones and family

Bibles. Then the most efficient way of proceeding is through the data mentioned above.

For the period prior to 1837 the task of identification of ancestors is more difficult, and clues have to be sought in a variety of registers, amongst them any lists made by Nonconformist churches or ministers. As far as today's user is concerned, these registers or lists fall into one of two groups. The one consists of material deposited in the General Register Office following the Acts of 1840 and 1858, and now housed at the Public Record Office. As mentioned earlier, these documents can be studied on microfilm at the National Library of Wales (records for the whole of Wales) and at many of the county record offices (for the area). The other group consists of originals which are held in Wales (and which sometimes continued in use after the introduction of state registration in 1837). Further comparison of the lists of churches represented in the two groups is needed. It is clear that the lists are not mutually exclusive. It would appear that in some cases the registers were transcribed before the originals were sent to London. In other cases some of the information—that which pertained to people still living—was transferred to another working list retained by the minister or church. There were also congregations which seem to have ignored the legislation and retained the registers in their own custody.

Some of the features of these early registers, whether now in the Public Record Office or in Wales, can be looked at together. The earlier ones do not use purpose-printed books, and the nature of the information given varies. They may, for example, include a statement of beliefs signed by members, up-dated lists of members (people 'admitted to communion'), births and/or baptisms, burials, lists of members deceased, minutes of church meetings, memoranda relating to the building, contributions to charity, and lists of the households providing hospitality for visiting preachers. However, in the case of those churches founded more recently, predictably there are fewer entries in the registers and there is less ancillary information about the chapel.

The older registers are particularly interesting since they reflect the wide, though sometimes sparse, distribution of the membership of some of the early Nonconformist mother churches. The register of Henllan Amgoed chapel (Carmarthenshire) 'and the Meeting Houses connected therewith' for the period 1748-85 includes christenings from 36 parishes—one in Cardiganshire, the others in Carmarthenshire and Pembrokeshire. Such eighteenth century lists of baptisms drawn from a wide area should forewarn the researcher that, if there is a tradition of

Nonconformity in a family, the register of a church at some distance might be searched with favourable results. By the last decade of the eighteenth century the old Nonconformist bodies were launched in evangelisation. The baptisms reflect the spheres of influence of major churches and also some of the peregrinations of the ministers. Samuel Griffiths, minister of Horeb Independent church, Llandysul, recorded not only baptisms in his area of Cardiganshire, but also a few from Clydai in Pembrokeshire, his home parish. Some ministers recorded children baptised on more distant journeys in the register of their chapel. These stray baptisms will continue to foil family historians until there is a computerised index of the Non-Parochial Registers.

Fig 6-1 illustrates the distribution of local christenings recorded in the Capel-y-Graig, Tre-lech a'r Betws (Carmarthenshire) register for the period 1820-37. (The total christenings involve a wider area.) The numbers from each parish are shown: 111 from Abernant, 112 from Conwyl Elfed, 249 from Cilrhedyn, 58 from Cenarth, 294 from Clydai, 31 from Penrith, 100 from Llanfyrnach, 99 from Llanwinio, 132 from Meidrim and 553 from Tre-lech a'r Betws itself. Some comment, useful for researchers, emerges from these figures as it may sometimes appear that baptisms have not been recorded. If, for example, someone was looking for a believed Independent ancestor in the parish of Clydai (Pembrokeshire), he might seek a register for Llwynyrhwrdd chapel in that parish, founded 1808—and for this period he would not find one. The explanation is that baptisms at three daughter churches were still being recorded in Capel-y-Graig register: evidence for the usefulness of knowing the line of descent of the local churches!

The high number of Nonconformist baptisms is a reminder of the importance of the Nonconformist strand in our history. Moreover in Tre-lech a'r Betws far more of the parish-born children had a chapel than a church baptism in these years: that is, 553 chapel by comparison with 177 church baptisms.

From the early nineteenth century, standard format volumes tended to come into use. For example these are the printed headings under which early nineteenth century baptisms in many of the Calvinistic Methodist chapels of Anglesey are recorded: Number, Child's Name, Names of Father and Mother, Former Name of the Mother, Whether (formerly) Spinster or Widow, Father's Business or Profession, Parents' Residence, Father's Parish, Mother's Parish before Marriage, When Child Born, In what Parish Born, When Baptized, Where Baptized, By whom Baptized. The book in use at Penbryn Chapel, Bodedern

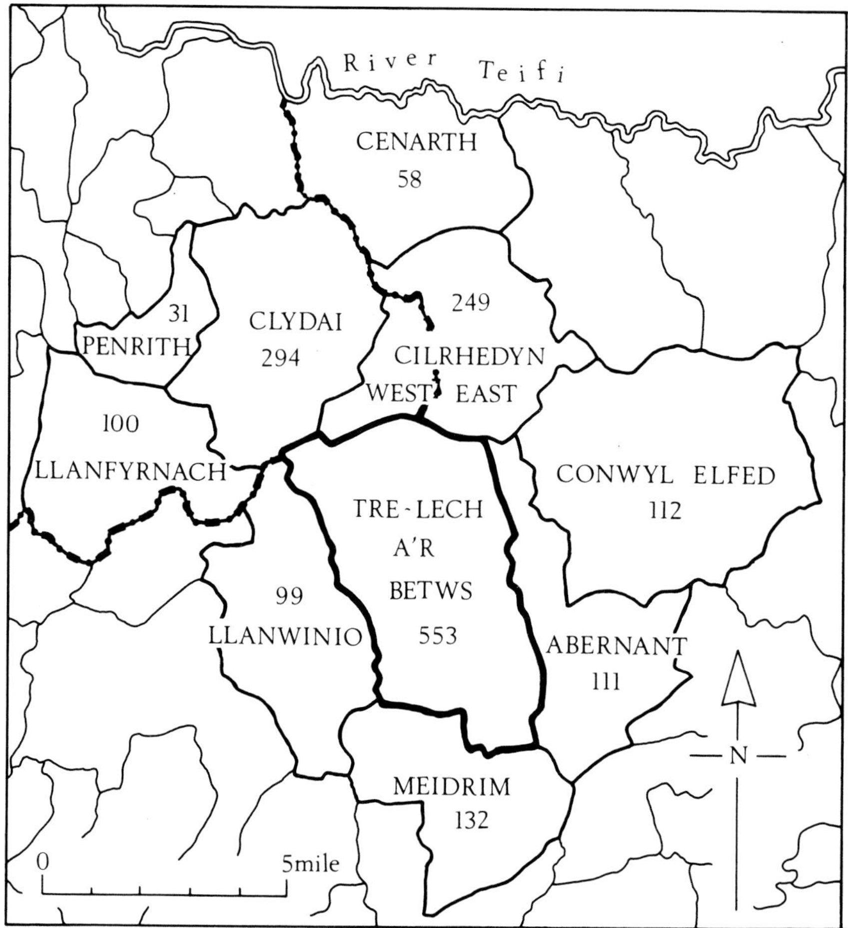


Fig. 6-1: Distribution of local christenings, Tre-lech a'r Betws

(Anglesey) had been printed by Enoch Jones, Llanerchymedd. The first entry refers to Evan the son of Hugh (shop-keeper) and Jane Edwards born 27 August 1811 and christened at Penbryn Chapel, on 1 September by John Elias. Hugh, John and Elin were subsequently born to the same family and christened at Penbryn Chapel. Amongst others christened were the children of David and Sarah Foulkes of Machynlleth (Montgomeryshire); and Edward son of Thomas Jones schoolmaster, Penyrallt, Bodedern (Anglesey) and his wife Mary. The last recorded baptism was 7 May 1837, and, for the period 1811-1837, 146 are listed.

The register of the Baptists of Brynsiencyn and Pencarneddi (Anglesey)[30] reminds one of the differing practices among Nonconformists and also of a contemporary custom. We are told that the chapel was founded about 1810 and that the register has been in the care of Thomas Owens, Deacon, throughout. It records:

> . . . naming their children according to the Manner of the Baptists and not Baptising them after the form of the Church of England and many Dissenters of the Age.

The first entry reads as follows:

> Jane Thomas, The Daughter of Thomas Jones by Elizabeth Jones his Wife was Born in the Place Commonly Called Ty'n Ddrain in the Parish of Llanidan, in Anglesey, on the 1st Day of July, AD 1811
> Witnesses
> WH Roberts
> Robert Francis
> Elinear Price Midwife
> John Morgans Minister

This form persisted with slight variations and a tendency to give further details about the mother. An entry of 24 December 1833 is more specific about the witnesses:

> These are to certify that Robert Prichard the son of John Prichard By Elinear Prichard his Wife Who was Daughter of Lot Prichard was Born in the Place Commonly called Lon las in the Parish of Llanidan . . . at whose Birth we were Present.
> Witnesses
> John Williams
> Wm Roberts
> Ann Williams Midwife
> John Davis Minister

For those churches that are represented, the value of these registers for the identification of people is considerable. They are a study in themselves.

As far as archives are concerned, our main subject is records which have emanated from the Nonconformist bodies. Space does not allow discussion at any length of the degree to which chapel-goers figure in the parish registers. The Registration Act of 1695 required notice of all births to be given to the incumbent or clerk of the parish. One finds examples of the clergyman noting births to Nonconformist parents and, occasionally, comment with regard to baptism. But it is difficult to assess at present how far this requirement was kept and when it fell into abeyance. In 1785 the stamp duty was extended to registration in Nonconformist registers, giving this record some official recognition. Another point to notice is that for a long period some practising Nonconformists baptised and buried in the parish church because of family tradition. Amongst such families were some Methodists. In families with one parent from church and the other from chapel children might be christened alternately by vicar and minister. As for marriages outside the church, there is virtually no evidence one way or the other for the period before Hardwicke's Marriage Act of 1753, except for the Quakers. Between 1753 and registration of chapels for marriage, which became possible in 1837, the marriage of Nonconformists took place in the parish church.

## A Case Study

For many researchers into family history, an important use of chapel records is to find out more about the names on a family tree. To discover a forebear in a Sunday School register, in the chapel orchestra, in a list of deacons or trustees, organising an eisteddfod or a Sunday School trip, defending the rights of the individual conscience, helping to found a church—or frequenting a conventicle—adds to the knowledge of that character. One of the joys of family history is to discover evidence of one's ancestors in their day by day living, over the generations, and to find mention of them in a variety of source material.

To get to know our ancestors, the information which comes from registration documents and the censuses needs to be amplified from elsewhere—and how our understanding and appreciation can be enhanced! To take one example, on the last day of December, 1914, the death took place in Park Terrace, Llansamlet (Glamorgan) at the age of 74 of Rees Thomas, and a few days later he was buried at Tabor chapel, Maes-y-bar, Llansamlet. In his working years he had been a collier. He was much loved by his family. But what more can we discover about him? A few pieces of paper and some books in the home of his great-grand-daughter make an admirable starting-point.

The memorial card which gives the date of Rees's death provides a clue for further investigation: 'Ganwyd yn Llangyndeyrn, Medi 2il, 1840' ('Born in Llangyndeyrn, 2 September, 1840'). So, migration from an area of sluggish economy in Carmarthenshire to one of the industrial growth-points in Glamorgan was part of the family experience. Investigation of parish and non-parochial registers, the census enumerators' returns and the birth certificate of Rees produced the following outline.

The parents, William Thomas and Margaret Rees, were married on 3 November 1829 at Llangyndeyrn (Carmarthenshire) parish church, William being able to sign his name in the parish register. The record of the baptism of their first child has not been found, but their second, third and fourth children were all christened at Salem, the local Calvinistic Methodist chapel. (No register has been discovered for 1840-41 when Rees may have been christened.) The note in this register of one of the christenings (in 1832) gives the information that William Thomas was a lime burner. He was still in Llangyndeyrn on 11 September 1840, since on that day he registered the birth of his son Rees at Carmarthen, but before census night 1841 he had departed for Llansamlet. Here he was quite soon joined by his wife and five children, and about 1844 their youngest child was born in Llansamlet.

By 1851 Margaret Thomas was a widow, her three eldest sons were colliers (aged 22, 19 and 17) her daughter aged 14 was at home, and Rees (11) and George (seven) were returned as 'Scholars'.

The later censuses show that Rees too became a collier, and it is clear from knowledge in the family that he was industrious and provided well for his dependants. But what sort of a person was he? Found amongst his possessions were a volume of *Y Gwyddoniadur* (the Welsh encyclopedia published between 1854 and 1878 by Thomas Gee), a volume on the history of Llansamlet: *Hanes a Hynafiaethau Llansamlet* (by W.Samlet Williams, 1908) and books of music, revealing him to have been a literate and musical man. His tomb-stone at Tabor continues the biography: 'Blaenor ffyddlawn, ysgrifenydd, ac arweinydd y gan yn yr eglwys hon, am dros ddeugain mlynedd' ('A faithful elder, secretary, and leader of the singing in this church for over forty years'). Tabor, like most of the industrial area chapels, bears the date of foundation. It was formed by members of nearby Methodist churches to serve the expanding industrial area, and it is clear from the obituary in the Calvinistic Methodist monthly magazine, *Y Drysorfa* (1915, p.419) that Rees was the first secretary of this new church. The obituary lists other voluntary offices he filled, including the secretaryship for nearly 40 years of the combined Methodist Sunday Schools in the parish of Llansamlet, and of the Llansamlet Singing Festival. He had been presented with a framed picture of himself, with suitable inscription, by this Cymanfa Ganu. The obituary says of the funeral:

> Yr oedd yn un o'r angladdau mwyaf lliosog a welwyd yn y rhanbarth. Canwyd ar y ffordd gan gantorion a chantoresau addoldai y cylch. [It was one of the largest funerals seen in the district. On the way the choristers of all the chapels of the area were singing.]

People remembered Rees Thomas with affection and respect and one of the competitions at a concert at Tabor, 13 November 1918, was for a poem in his memory.

He represented a particular type of family: his father a lime-worker, but able to sign his name; God-fearing people; Calvinistic Methodists; migrants to an area of economic growth; a widowed mother sending her children to school 20 years before the Elementary Education Act. His story illustrates the leadership which developed within chapel society in a South Wales industrial community. It also shows the importance of that society in developing gifts which were never expressed in a career. These gifts enriched the life of the locality. The details vary from person to person, but the life centring round the chapel, which was so important to Rees Thomas, was part of the ethos of nineteenth century Welsh industrial society.

So, to conclude, the search for family is more than a search for names. It is an opportunity to discover something of the society within which our ancestors lived.

## NOTES TO CHAPTER 6

[1] T.Rowland Hughes, *Cân neu Ddwy* (Denbigh: Gwasg Gee, 1948), p.35.

'Our numerous, big old chapels may not be beautiful to you my friend, but they made us, from these boxes came the inspiration of our yesterdays, if poor their appearance, if clumsy their look, Caersalem, Seion, Soar and Bethlehem.'

This poem pre-dates the interest in chapel architecture which has been quite a feature of local and historical studies in the second half of the twentieth century.

[2] K.O.Morgan, *Wales in British Politics 1868-1922.* (Cardiff: UWP, 1963), Appendix B: Comparative Statistics of Church and Nonconformist Communicants, 1905.

[3] Nonconformist: ' . . . especially after the passing of the Act of Uniformity of 1662 and the consequent ejection from their livings of those ministers who refused to conform, a member of a religious body which is separated from the Church of England; in modern use, usually = Protestant Dissenter.' *Oxford English Dictionary*, 2nd ed. (Oxford: OUP, 1969).

[4]Quaker: ' . . . one of the Religious Society of Friends, founded by George Fox (1624-91) . . . [Nickname (not adopted by themselves, and earlier applied to another sect) given them by Justice Bennet at Derby, because Fox bade him and others quake at the word of the Lord.] *Chambers Twentieth Century Dictionary*, new ed. (Cambridge: Chambers, 1983).

[5]The old Presbyterian Church which existed in England from the sixteenth century is not represented in Wales, though aspects of the presbyterian system influenced the Independents, Baptists and Unitarians and the word is used in describing some of their congregations in the eighteenth century.

[6]Gareth Watts, 'William Wroth (1570-1641) Father of Non-conformity', *The Congregational History Magazine* (1990).

[7]T.M.Bassett, *Bedyddwyr Cymru*, (Swansea: Tŷ Ilston, 1977).

[8]See note 3, above.

[9]J.E.Lloyd, ed., *History of Carmarthenshire*, Vol.2. (Cardiff: W.Lewis for the London Carmarthenshire Society, 1939). Also local information.

[10]Based on Thomas Richards, *Wales under the Penal Code: 1662-1687* (London: National Eisteddfod, 1925).

[11]National Library of Wales, Churchwardens Presentments, 1684, reproduced and edited by George Eyre Evans in *Transactions of the Carmarthenshire Antiquarian Society*, 10 (1914-5), 92-100.

[12]Henllan Amgoed Independent church, Chapel Archives.

[13]The 'Old Book' is at the National Library of Wales. T.M.Bassett. See note 7 above.

[14]Thomas Richards. See note 10 above.

[15]Thomas Richards. See note 10 above.

[16]Thomas Richards. See note 10 above.

[17]Pembrokeshire Record Office, DFC/C/8/1.

[18]See for example Glamorganshire: E.T.Davies, Glanmor Williams & Gomer M.Roberts, 'Religion and Education in Glamorgan 1660-c.1775' in *Early Modern Glamorgan*; ed. Glanmor Williams. Glamorgan County History, 2. (Cardiff: Glamorgan County History Trust Ltd, 1974).

[19]One of the Non-Parochial Registers; see later in the chapter.

[20]Geraint H.Jenkins, *The Foundations of Modern Wales 1642-1780*, (Oxford: Clarendon Press, 1987).

[21]D. Elwyn Davies, *They Thought for Themselves* (Llandysul: 1982). Aubrey J.Martin, *Hanes Llwynrhydowen* (Llandysul: Gomer Press, 1977). Gwyn A.Williams, 'The Merthyr of Dic Penderyn' in *Merthyr Politics: The Making of a Working-Class Tradition*. ed. Glanmor Williams. (Cardiff: UWP, 1966).

[22]Ieuan Gwynedd Jones & David Williams, *The Religious Census of 1851: A Calendar of the Returns relating to Wales*, Vol.1, South Wales (Cardiff: 1976). Also Ieuan Gwynedd Jones, Vol.2, North Wales. (Cardiff: 1981).

[23]West Glamorgan Area Record Office, D/D Wes/RV 32.

[24]K.O.Morgan. See note 2 above. Gwyn A.Williams, *When was Wales? A History of the Welsh* (London: Black Raven Press, 1985).

[25]Information about activities from County Record Offices or the National Library of Wales. National meetings are held twice a year; meetings are also held by regional branches.

[26] *Report, Evidence & Indexes of the Royal Commission appointed to inquire into the Church and other Religious Bodies in Wales* (London: 1910).

[27] Ieuan Gwynedd Jones & David Williams. See note 22 above.

[28] Formerly part of RG 6 at the Public Record Office.

[29] The main denominational journals are:

**Wales**:
Baptists—*Trafodion Cymdeithas Hanes Bedyddwyr Cymru*, since 1901;
Presbyterian Church of Wales. Calvinistic Methodists—*Journal of the Calvinistic Methodist Historical Society*, since 1914.
Welsh Independents—*Y Cofiadur*, since 1923.
The Methodist Church in Wales—*Bathafarn*, since 1946.
Unitarians—*Yr Ymofynydd.*

**General** (but including Welsh material):
United Reformed Church—*Journal of the United Reformed Historical Society.*
Wesleyan Methodists—*Proceedings of the Wesley Historical Society*, since 1893.
Congregationalists—*Transactions of the Congregational Historical Society*, since 1901.

[30] PRO: RG 4/3547.

# 7. The Surnames of Wales

Sheila Rowlands

No single aspect of research has been more responsible for family historians shying away from Welsh genealogy than the seemingly intractable problems posed by common surnames in Wales. Yet researchers who have only Welsh family lines prove over and over again that such problems are not always insuperable.

The proportion of those named Jones or Davies can be daunting. However, these names are not found in isolation but are attached to first names and to combinations of names in family groups which make them more easily identifiable, particularly in small communities. The population of Wales has always been relatively small and once a family has been traced to a parish through, for example, the census it is frequently possible to distinguish it from others with similar names.

## The Origins of Welsh Patronymic Surnames

Many family historians turn at an early stage to books on surnames, intending to learn the origin of their name (though it is doubtful whether, in so doing, many people learn much family history). It comes as a great shock to some researchers to find that the whole pattern of Welsh names is different from that in England. In the standard surname works of the past, you will learn that surnames in England can be divided into four basic types: those derived from a personal name (Bartram, Annis, Jackson); those derived from a location, either a placename (Clifton, Coleridge, Marston) or a topographical feature (Green, Hill, Bywater); those derived from occupation or status (Smith, Mason, Taylor); and those derived from nicknames or descriptions (Keen, Wellbeloved, Hardy).

Such surnames would have settled between the twelfth and fourteenth centuries in England, in response to the needs of growing towns and increasing bureaucracy. Since then individual names have proliferated or decayed, but they continue to reflect the great variety which were in use 600-800 years ago.

At the time that surnames were settling in England, a completely different picture can be drawn of Wales, most of which—outside the few settled towns—led a life largely unaffected by English social practices. In the greater part of Wales, the ancient naming system continued: by this system, children were identified or placed chiefly in relation to their father. This is, of course, comparable to the system which led to the adoption of surnames from personal names in England, but it was fundamental to the social structure of the Celtic areas of Britain and was not easily to be discarded. Parallels may be found in other European countries.[1]

The Welsh word for son is *mab* (often written as *map*) which is a cognate of the Scottish *mac*. A man called Rhys would be known as Rhys mab Owain (Rhys son (of) Owain). In the system of mutation of the Welsh language (see Chapter 9) *mab* becomes *fab*, and the initial soft 'f' sound (English 'v') would have been dropped in normal speech. This would produce Rhys ab Owain. *Ap* was used in conjunction with some initial sounds: Rhys ap Hywel, though firm rules did not always apply to personal names.

Moreover, a free Welshman would know not only his father's name, but those of his earlier male ancestors, and he would be able to recite his name as a patronymic string, thus: Rhys ab Owain ap Hywel ap Maredudd ap Gruffydd. This aspect of the development of names is mentioned in Chapters 1 and 18.

Daughters were known by their father's name: Gwenllïan *verch* (*ferch* in modern orthography) (daughter (of)) Rhys; the relationship was often shortened to *vch* or *vz* in documents and appears also as *ach*. Traditionally this led to women retaining their maiden names (that is, their father's name rather than their husband's) and this is reflected in many documents in both Welsh and English to quite late dates. Henry Adams of Manorbier in south Pembrokeshire names his wife Elizabeth Rhydderch as executrix in 1603.[2] In the same parish a century later, Mary Gibbon alias Jones, widow, refers to her sisters, Jane Cole alias Jones and Margaret Watkins alias Jones, as well as to her cousins, the children of Thomas Jones of Ambleston and Dorothy Cod his wife.[3]

Because of the very strong predisposition towards the use of male ancestors' names as a means of identification, the other main types of surname (by English standards) have never featured significantly. That said, such names do exist in Wales, though in far smaller numbers. There are surnames taken from Welsh places, from nicknames or personal descriptions and from occupations expressed in the Welsh language, and these will be considered briefly in this chapter. A much more detailed account of the patronymic naming system is to be found in *Welsh Surnames* by T.J. and Prys Morgan.[4]

The surnames which have descended to us as a result of the essentially patronymic Welsh tradition do not often represent truly Welsh forenames. Rather, they represent fashions in naming children a generation before a surname was taken. In Wales, as in England, a handful of Christian saints' names and Bible names have predominated since medieval times: John (and its derivatives, including Evan), William, Thomas and David (naturally popular as the name of the national patron saint) provide the bulk of surnames. Clergymen and clerks did not generally consider the Welsh versions of these simple names as acceptable officially; far less did they attempt to record anything which it was difficult to get the English tongue around. Our ancestors' names were recorded as David, William, John, etc, in parish registers, but among their families and friends they were known as Dafydd, Gwilym or Siôn, or by pet versions of their names.[5]

As is common in traditional societies, patterns may be found in the use of forenames in Wales. Certainly to the mid-nineteenth century at least, it was common for children to be named after their grandparents, their parents and their close relations, the exact sequence often varying according to circumstances.[6] Godparents were also honoured in this way, though it would be rare to find examples of named godparents except in family documents. The main value to the family historian is that the choice of forenames may sometimes be used to distinguish between different families with the same surname. However, the consequence has also been to reduce the pool of names from which surnames developed.

Older native names have survived to vary the stock: Morgan, Llywelyn (often anglicised to Lewis), Maredudd (Meredith), Hywel (Howells, Powell, and even responsible to some degree for the popularity of Hugh/es) and Gruffydd (Griffith/s). Some pet versions, or hypocoristic names, did evolve into surnames: Bedo, the popular form of Maredudd, has given rise to Beddoes; Guto (from Gruffydd) has led to Gittins; Dai and Dei, from David, developed into Day and its variants.

Names which have contributed very little to the pool of English surnames but which are found often in Wales came as a result of the late adoption of surnames: Francis, George, and James are examples of forenames which had a later popularity than most and became surnames through the patronymic system. Some less common Christian names are found through the same process, such as Clement, Julian and Timothy. The affection for biblical names as first names after the Reformation (particularly in nonconformist families), duly becoming surnames through the patronymic system, has resulted in Welsh (and not only Jewish as is often supposed) surnames such as Abraham, Benjamin, Ephraim, Isaac, Mordecai and Moses.

## The Adoption of Permanent Surnames in Wales

In due course, and under pressure from bureaucracy and outside influences, the patronymic system was dropped. The first to adopt fixed surnames were the wealthier classes, and the practice filtered through society at different levels from Tudor times on. The *ap* system survived in a shorthand form for some time: a man who might previously have been known as Dafydd ab Ifan could be known in the transitional period as David Evan; his son might be known as Thomas David and his grandson as Evan Thomas. All that is missing is the implied *ap*, and the patronymic system continued essentially unchanged. In some cases, indeed, the *ap* element did not quite disappear, but became attached to the name which followed it, ap Hywel becoming Powell, ap Harri becoming Parry, and ab Evan becoming Bevan. In no sense, however, can the second name be described as a surname at this stage. Late examples can be found: in Ciliau Aeron, Cardiganshire, in 1807, Sarah the illegitimate daughter of Jenkin David Evan Jenkin John was baptised.[7] Generally, though, such strings had reduced to two, or at most three, elements by this time.

The next stage of transition towards surnames of the patronymic type occurred when the second name was passed on, more or less unchanged, to later successive generations. Evan Thomas, the imaginary grandson above, might have had a son known generally as David Thomas. When David Thomas has a son known as William Thomas, we can usually assume that the surname has become settled in a family.

However, that a surname could seem fixed in a family yet still be liable to change is illustrated well by the example given at the start of Chapter 16. Indeed, several chapters of this book give examples of varying levels of patronymic development in real situations, the many possibilities of which a short chapter such as this can only touch on.

For examples of the various stages in development in an area with both native Welsh and anglicised social practice, the reader is referred to D. Elwyn Williams's article on Glamorgan surnames[8] which shows, with instances taken from title deeds, how individuals were known at different dates by gradually more 'modern' forms: for example, Thomas ap John ap Henry (1599); Thomas John ap Henry (1600); Thomas John Penrie (1602). The gradual loss of the *ap* form is illustrated: Howell ap Jevan's son was Mirick Howell (1581). Within the same family, children might bear different surnames: Thomas William (1748) had sons called David William and William Thomas.

Along with the settling of surnames at different times came the addition of the letter 's' to what was basically a forename. These forms appear earlier where surnames were taken early and transitional stages can be seen here, too. The 's' represents the possessive case, but also reflects a liking for this style of name in Wales which must be a direct descendant of the *ap* system. Thus, also in Glamorgan, Jenkin John (1759) had sons called John Jenkins, David John and Will John.[9] In other parts of Wales, the addition of 's' to what had been essentially a patronymic name came about in the eighteenth and nineteenth centuries.[10]

## The Time-Scale of Change

The whole process of adopting fixed surnames was completed at different times in different communities in Wales, evolving gradually and only rarely being the result of conscious decision, let alone legislation. Generally speaking, such surnames were taken earlier in the lowland areas, especially in the east and south of Wales, later in the upland areas; earlier among the gentry, later among labouring people. However, other factors were the degree of anglicisation and urbanisation in an area. The adoption of a fixed surname may vary from little (if any) later than in England (e.g., south Pembrokeshire, where English influence was strong from the twelfth century) to the middle years of the nineteenth century in parts of Caernarfonshire.

The clearest examples of the late formation of surnames through this system are to be found in Caernarfonshire in the 1841 and 1851 censuses: R.M. and G.A. Benwell give a number of examples of the names of families changing between censuses and of the children bearing the father's first name as their final name.[11] The children of Robert Williams of Llanbedrog bore the final name Roberts in 1841 and were Williams in 1851.In 1851, in Llanfihangel Bachellaeth, Ellis Williams had five children with the final name Ellis. Other types of record provide evidence: in 1862, the marriage took place in Llangïan, of Ellen Roberts, daughter of Robert Jones.[12] This timing may reasonably be described as at the very late end of normal, but it is by no means confined to the relatively remote area of Llŷn and examples from the mid and late nineteenth century are found occasionally in other areas.

The family historian should study the naming patterns generally in a family parish to judge whether or not a name can be described as a surname. In Llanrhystud in mid-Cardiganshire, neither at one extreme nor the other of the time-scale of change, surnames among small freeholders were settled by about 1780; this can be deduced by a study of the parish register and other parochial documents and by a parallel scrutiny of wills. A list of Cardiganshire Freeholders in 1760 includes William John Elusdan (his father was John Elystan); he is variously recorded in documents as William Siôn, William John and William Jones, but he signed as Jones and this is how his sons always appear in records.[13] (However, his daughter married as Jane William in 1772.) Other families of freeholder status have a similar pattern in this and nearby parishes, while labourers generally assumed a surname about a generation later. The ability to sign one's name and, indeed, actual appearance in written records affected the process; personal and informal documents may indicate that more than one name was in use even where the eventual surname seemed settled. For the majority of the population an arbitrary choice would be made by clergymen, clerks or officials, according to their own preference or prejudice, which might vary on different occasions.

The patronymic system may be unstable at different times in particular families. In the parish of Llansantffraid, Cardiganshire, which adjoins Llanrhystud, Alban Thomas, Gentleman, (actually, a freeholder) buried his infant children with the final name of Thomas. He died prematurely in 1742 and his sons who lived to grow up were known by the final name (in effect, surname, as it then became hereditary) of Alban.

Hard and fast rules are impossible, and it is up to family historians to consider not just their family in isolation, but to develop a sense of what is happening in other families in that community. Among the most useful contributions which could be made to this study would be statistical analyses of material in parish registers and other documents.

Figure 7-1 indicates the gradual change of form from patronymic name to surname in the case of two common names in northern Cardiganshire in the significant century or so before 1813.

It is ironic that the patronymic naming-system lasted so long yet was often forgotten quickly. Writers of parish histories in the late nineteenth and early twentieth centuries appear sometimes to be oblivious to the

| Period | JOHN | JONES | DAVID | DAVIES |
|---|---|---|---|---|
| | No. | No. | No. | No. |
| 1695-1736 | 101 | 34 | 83 | 10 |
| 1737-1753 | 27 | 9 | 23 | 4 |
| 1754-1759 | 28 | 37 | 48 | 13 |
| 1760-1769 | 73 | 88 | 74 | 24 |
| 1770-1779 | 49 | 88 | 52 | 28 |
| 1780-1789 | 38 | 169 | 49 | 49 |
| 1790-1799 | 10 | 213 | 22 | 73 |
| 1800-1809 | 2 | 220 | 9 | 88 |
| 1810-1812 | 0 | 80 | 3 | 29 |
| TOTAL | 328 | 938 | 363 | 318 |

Fig. 7-1: The change from John to Jones and David to Davies, based on marriages in Geneu'r Glyn Hundred, 1695-1812[14]

relative modernity of supposedly ancient family names. Newspaper obituaries of similar date may refer to the sudden appearance (often assumed to be from Scotland or Ireland) of a distinguished family, since its modern surname cannot be found in old records. Welsh families nowadays can be extremely particular about the exact spelling of their surname—whether or not it ends in an 's', for instance—but few ordinary Welsh people in the past had any such concern.

The patronymic system should be viewed by family historians as part of their Welsh inheritance; efforts made to understand its development in a given area may open new avenues for research. In what other system, in any case, does one find 100 or 150 years of genealogy encapsulated in a few names? For labouring families, little more may be found out about the individuals concerned when this stage is reached but, as other chapters indicate, there are more possibilities ahead for the fortunate researching relatively modest families.

## Surnames derived from Personal Characteristics

Adjectives have given rise to a number of well-known Welsh surnames, often describing the appearance of a person. Readers are once more referred to Chapter 9 to understand the process by which the beginning of words can change in Welsh, though there are many exceptions where these words are adopted as epithets and ultimately become surnames.

Examples of such epithets are:[15] *Bychan/fychan* (small or younger): Vaughan; *Coch* mutated to *goch* (red): corrupted in speech to Gough,

Goff, Gooch;[16] *Du* (black): Dee; *Gwyn* (white): Gwynne, Wynn; *Hir* (long or tall): Hier, Hire; *Llwyd* (grey or brown): Lloyd, Floyd; *Moel/foel* (bald): Voyle; *Sais* (English): Sayce. Names such as Vaughan and Lloyd were surnames in some areas relatively early—until modern times they were rarely used as forenames so were not interchangeable, as it were, between generations in the way that Dafydd and Rhys were. Really, these names cannot be dissociated from the patronymic system, for they were often added first to a patronymic name: Dafydd ap Rhys Fychan.

## Occupational Names

Welsh surnames of this type are unusual, not least because a largely pastoral society would have a limited number of occupations to act as useful distinguishing elements. Saer (Welsh *saer*—carpenter) is found, fairly reliably with this meaning, on the borders of Pembrokeshire and Carmarthenshire, where it has become Sear/s, but it may be often confused with the English Sayer (sawyer or a personal name) in the eastern Welsh counties. *Gwas* (servant) has led to Wace[17] and *Welsh Surnames* has examples of compounds found in documents, such as Wasmeir (servant of Mary—a devotional name). Crowther is shown[18] as from the Welsh *crythor*, the player of the *crwth* (a stringed instrument) though some surname books have it as derived from Middle English in what may be a borrowing from Welsh. The interesting Goyder (from *coedwr*—woodman) has been found in some Glamorgan parishes, while Meddick (from *meddyg*—doctor) still survives. Like the adjectival names these are perhaps more reasonably classed with epithets, occasionally found among the patronymic majority.

## Surnames derived from Welsh Place-names

Although these names are held by relatively few families, they form an interesting category, illustrating the possibilities of a more varied pool of names if the patronymic system had not prevailed so late.

Even before the social changes from Tudor times on, the more influential classes, particularly in north-east Wales, began to take the names of their estates as surnames. Mostyn, Nanney and Pennant are frequently quoted examples of this category.[19] For the most part, however, people bearing Welsh place-names in Wales were to be found in the anglicised areas where the patronymic system faded sooner; such names were also common in the border areas of England, reflecting an English naming-pattern describing someone who had left Wales.

This category of names has potential pitfalls, for the origins of a name are not always obvious. There is, for example, no place called Scourfield in Pembrokeshire, where it is a far from rare surname;[20] the family of that name came there from Westmorland and their name may be a variant of Schofield, common in Lancashire. Nor is the Marychurch family native to Pembrokeshire: its representatives can be traced back to St Marychurch in Glamorgan.[21] Genealogy can often throw light on the origins of less usual names even in Wales, so that the work of individual family historians, if rigorous standards are applied, have much to contribute to surname studies.

Nevertheless, the simplest explanation of surnames like Conway, Gower, Laugharne, Narbett (Narberth), Nash, Pembroke, Roch and Upton is that ultimately they arose from local place-names; it is unlikely that modern families with this type of surname are all descended from earlier distinguished or landowning bearers of the names. There is rarely continuity of documents to connect random sightings of such names through the centuries among ordinary families, and family historians should appreciate that surnames could be taken for other reasons than blood relationship, for example through adoption or apprenticeship.

## Non-Welsh Surnames in Wales

There is a much greater variety of surnames in border areas of Wales: that is, in the areas of greatest English influence. Some of these names are of such antiquity in Wales (and their early bearers, in any case, intermarried with Welsh women to such a degree that arguments about Welsh descent are unproductive) that they should not be considered alien, having in some cases been established in Anglo-Norman times. Indeed, for many family historians, they are as much part of Welsh genealogical research as more common patronymic names.

To take the earliest areas of settlement in south Wales first, the work on Glamorgan surnames by D.Elwyn Williams has already been recommended and the full range of possibilities are covered in that article.[22] Several helpful articles have appeared in issues of *Glamorgan FHS Journal* and its predecessor, the *South Wales FHS Journal*.[23]

Little has been written about surnames in Pembrokeshire, where Anglo-Norman settlement produced a stock of characteristic names which are undoubtedly non-Welsh in origin yet have too long a domicile to be ignored. Such names include Hood (de Hoda) traced back to a farm in the parish of Dartington in Devon and Canton (de Cantington), which has its earliest form in common with that of Cannington in Somerset. The popular assumption that many Pembrokeshire surnames are of Flemish origin can be discounted[24] and Scandinavian origins are even less likely, since the activities of the Norse invaders on this coast preceded the era of surnames. Many of these very typical local surnames are be found also in the West Country of England (and can be readily seen in the International Genealogical Index for, especially, Devon and Somerset) but it should be stressed that many of them appear in Pembrokeshire documents from medieval times onwards. In every century, traffic across the Bristol Channel brought in new names, or reinforced existing ones, along the whole of the coast of South Wales.

Some Pembrokeshire surnames come from local place-names: Carrow (from Carew), Martell, Picton, Trewent, and at one time these were even more varied: Corston, Lawrenny and Pelcam are just three to be found in medieval documents.[25] The background to many such names may be found in the classic *Non-Celtic Place-names*.[26] Some names reflect local dialect pronunciation; for instance, Hoplow becomes Hopla; Harlow: Arla; Gibbon: Gibby; Whittow: Whitta/Wittle/Vittle. The native Welsh name Cadogan (Cadwgan) becomes corrupted to Duggan. Some surnames, of which Cadogan and its variants are examples, exported to Ireland from Pembrokeshire via the Anglo-Normans, may have returned at any time in the centuries since. Unfortunately, once again it has to be stressed that there is no continuity of records for ordinary families.

The eastern border with England is another area in which a large number of unusual but settled names are to be found. David Peate (see Chapter 20) lists several of these. Useful articles are to be found on this topic in the journal of Powys FHS.[27] Such articles are able to consider a selection of names in depth, using genealogical methods and tracing a name to its earliest appearance in documents. Once more, it should be stressed that in this direction, individual researchers can contribute much to this subject.

Besides cross-border movement where a dilution of Welsh names would be expected, evidence[28] has recently come to light of what appears to be an English plantation or settlement in the lordships of Arwystli and Cyfeiliog in Montgomeryshire and Chirk, Chirkland and Denbigh in Denbighshire, all of which belonged to Robert Dudley, Earl of Leicester, by lease from the Crown.[29] Dudley was permitted by virtue of a licence from the Crown, dated 9 July 1576, to alienate away the lands in the above lordships in whatever way he wished, for a period of four years. It is during this period that a significant in-migration of English people occurred.

The documentary evidence for this is provided in a case of sheep-stealing trumped-up by two local Welsh men who clearly resented the English newcomers.[30] Their victim was John Thornhill who had moved to the parish of Llangurig in the lordship of Arwystli in 1576, together with John Bamford, Robert Hatfield, Henry Gregory and his wife Margaret, and Nicholas Bennett. They came from the communities of Thornhill, Bamford and Hatfield, which all lie in close proximity to each other in the Peak district of Derbyshire. A number of witnesses also testified to the innocence of John Thornhill. They were all Englishmen with family names of Bowring, Cottrell, Downes, Woosencroft, Wilson, Aston, Marple and Cowper.

Traditional surname books are sometimes able to throw light on the origins of such non-Welsh names, since they are often found in pockets in England as well as in Wales, though obviously they stand out more in the latter.[31] Many names in this category will have been formed from an English place-name, for which the appropriate reference book should be consulted.[32]

To find the origin of any family name, one must trace it back to its earliest appearance in writing, collecting dated examples of its use. Such a history of a name will often throw light on an earlier pronunciation as well as on its etymology.

## The Distribution of Welsh Surnames

It is only possible to skim the surface of this topic. An indication of the possibilities for research into the subject is shown in Fig 7-2, which illustrates the relative frequency of common names in contrasting areas.

From this it may be seen that a very small pool of names predominate in Cardiganshire, the top one (Jones) covering almost as high a percentage of the population as the top 10 names in a Cheshire parish (and even there some Welsh names appear). A more anglicised county such as Glamorgan has a wider spread of names, with the top 10 comprising a substantial percentage, though a smaller one than in Cardiganshire. Names of patronymic origin still predominate, but variants have taken on an independent existence in their own right: John and David as surnames are found in such large numbers that to group them with Jones and Davies would be misleading in Glamorgan by the

| **Cheshire** | | **Cardiganshire** | | **Glamorgan** | |
|---|---|---|---|---|---|
| 1800-09[33] | | 1813-37[34] | | 1813-37[35] | |
| | % | | % | | % |
| 1. Wright | 2.4 | Jones | 18.5 | Thomas | 8.8 |
| 2. Walker | 2.4 | Davies | 15.8 | Williams | 8.1 |
| 3. Dutton | 2.1 | Evans | 11.4 | Morgan/s | 5.8 |
| 4. Wilkinson | 2.1 | Thomas | 6.4 | David | 5.0 |
| 5. Davies | 1.9 | Williams | 5.0 | Jones | 5.0 |
| 6. Jones | 1.9 | James | 3.6 | Lewis | 4.9 |
| 7. Hassall | 1.6 | Morgan/s | 3.5 | Evans | 4.0 |
| 8. Smith | 1.6 | Jenkin/s | 3.2 | John | 3.7 |
| 9. Williams | 1.6 | Lewis | 2.8 | Jenkin/s | 3.7 |
| 10. Bowker | 1.4 | Griffith/s | 2.4 | Davies | 3.0 |
| TOTALS | 19.0 | | 72.6 | | 52.0 |

Fig. 7-2: A comparison of the incidence of surnames in Cheshire, Cardiganshire and Glamorgan.

nineteenth century. Another area where John and David exist in their own right as surnames is in Pembrokeshire. These can be seen emerging as fixed surnames by the late eighteenth century in the Dungleddy and Narberth hundreds, where Welsh influence was stronger. Searching for a family with the surname John can be very difficult in Pembrokeshire, yet as a surname it is rarely to be found in neighbouring Cardiganshire.

Phillips (and its variants) is an example of a patronymic surname which is found with great frequency in Pembrokeshire and western Carmarthenshire and which is far less common in other counties. As with other names of this type, it must reflect a greater popularity of the first name Philip a generation before surnames settled—the favoured spelling was Phillip in many eighteenth century Pembrokeshire parish registers.

The distribution of some other patronymic surnames is also relatively localised. Richard was a popular forename in early modern times and has given rise to a number of modern surnames: in the form Pritchard (from ap Richard) it is most commonly found in north Wales, particularly in Anglesey and Caernarfonshire; in southern counties, it has most frequently developed as Richards. Many other examples of the tendency for names to follow one form or another in different areas could be given.[36]

The greater variety of names in anglicised areas does not preclude a heavy dominance by the patronymic type: in the 1670 Hearth Tax, 46% of surnames in the English-speaking Pembrokeshire hundred of Castlemartin were patronymic in origin, suggesting a strong element of intermarriage with and influence by more purely Welsh parts.[37] Moreover, in the same area, less common Welsh forenames, such as Grono (Goronwy), Gwyther and Wogan survived as surnames; unusual variants of others, such as Loveling and Whelling (Llywelyn) helped to produce a more varied pool of surnames.

### Modern Names

American family historians are particularly inclined to describe an ancestor as, for example, William Hopkins Davies born in Wales about 1812. Few Welsh people from ordinary backgrounds had such a complex name at that time. The usual explanation is that during his lifetime the man was known as William Davies. Later and more sophisticated descendants have attached the maiden name of William Davies's mother to identify him, but it is unlikely that he adopted it himself. It is a useful convention to enclose the mother's name in brackets, e.g, William (Hopkins) Davies, since the genealogical importance of the middle name is not lost but the individual's real name is not altered permanently. Similar confusion is sometimes caused by initials: John T.Rees, emanating from Wales in the first half of the nineteenth century, probably left as John Rees, and his mother's name, beginning with 'T', has been interpolated.

Double surnames did develop in Wales in the later nineteenth and in the twentieth centuries. The sheer weight of common names meant much confusion in a growing population. Increasing sophistication made the ambitious see the need for something more distinctive. The mother's surname was frequently adopted, or that of another family member, and—since these names themselves came from a limited stock—such combinations as Jones-Davies or Rees-Williams emerged in fairly large numbers. Although such concoctions have sometimes been mocked as snobbish, they were often the result of sheer necessity. Young men entering the professions, the clergy, law and medicine in particular, were often urged to adopt a second name to distinguish themselves from the several others of the same name in the same academic group. John Davies, baptised thus in 1863, added his mother's maiden name of Alban when he entered the church, so spending most of his life as Revd John

Alban Davies. His brother, born 10 years later and reflecting the greater variety in naming as the nineteenth century went on, was christened David Alban Davies and chose to be known as such. His descendants in turn have hyphenated the two names, thus forming a 'new' surname.

The existence of a second forename element in a surname is a reasonable pointer towards another family line, the name of a mother's line being the most popular choice. Some double surnames, however, come from places or have a bardic connection. Nowadays, there is a definite trend in many quarters to adopt more distinctive Welsh names. The use of a middle family name is fairly widespread. Some names have been 'cymricised': Williams becoming Gwilym, Jones becoming Siôn, Hughes becoming Huws, and so on. This has the effect of differentiating individuals, as well as providing a satisfying authentic look, though really it is only another way of spelling an English (or Anglo-Norman) name. Others revive old Welsh names and adopt them, and one modern tendency is to revive the *ap* form even, illogically, amongst women. Gratifying as this is for the families concerned, overseas researchers may fall into the trap of believing that these are genuinely old surnames, though rarely do they predate the last two generations. The problems they may present will be for future generations of family historians to unravel.

## NOTES TO CHAPTER 7

[1]P.Hanks & F.Hodges, *A Dictionary of Surnames* (Oxford University Press, 1988) provides an overview of European names, though its section on Welsh names is brief. The same authors have produced *A Dictionary of First Names* (Oxford: 1990) and include a good many Welsh names.

[2]NLW St David's Probate 1603/ Henry Adams, Manorbier.

[3]NLW St David's Probate 1703/ Mary Gibbon, Manorbier.

[4]T.J.Morgan and Prys Morgan, *Welsh Surnames* (Cardiff: University of Wales Press, 1985; paperback, 1986). In these notes, this work is hereafter referred to as *WS*. It has superseded all previous writings on its subject and is essential reading for the Welsh family historian. The scholarly introduction should be read in full before consulting the alphabetical section, which includes a large number of Welsh names of all types, and their variants.

[5]The popular name John is Siôn in Welsh, which has no letter 'J'. Its pronunciation (with a long 'o') has led to the surname Shone, found in north-east Wales and the border area. The same basic name, with anglicised spelling and with an additional 's' (explained later in this chapter) developed into the commonest Welsh surname, Jones.

[6]An example, far from unique, of the result of such practice may be seen in the will of Jane Rees, Llanrhystud (NLW, St David's Probate, 1821), widow of Richard Rees, who names her grandsons Richard Williams, Richard Davies, Richard Isaac and Richard Evans; and her granddaughters Jane Jones, Jane Davies, Jane Lewis and Jane Isaac.

[7]NLW MS 1242B.

[8]D.Elwyn Williams, 'A short enquiry into the surnames in Glamorgan from the thirteenth to the eighteenth centuries', *Transactions of the Honourable Society of Cymmrodorion*, 1962.

[9]D.Elwyn Williams, see 8 above, p.55.

[10]The inevitable standardisation of names which resulted from the introduction of civil registration and other aspects of modern bureaucracy helped to fix such spellings finally.

[11]R.M. & G.A.Benwell, 'Interpreting the census returns for rural Anglesey and Llŷn', *Transactions of the Anglesey Antiquarian Society*, 1973. Other useful material on names in this area is contained in the same authors' 'Interpreting the parish registers and bishops transcripts for Anglesey and Llŷn', *Transactions of the Anglesey Antiquarian Society*, 1975, and in their 'Naming patterns in Gwynedd', *Gwreiddiau* Gwynedd FHS Journal, 1981.

[12]HO 107/1392; HO 107/2513, folio 369; Llangïan parish register; these three references were kindly drawn to my attention by Auronwy James, Penrhyn-coch.

[13]Cardiganshire Freeholders 1760, from *West Wales Historical Records*, iii (Transactions of the West Wales Historical Society, 1913); NLW: Llanrhystud parish registers, parochial records, St David's Probate.

[14]Unpublished work by John Rowlands, Aberystwyth, based on all surviving records of marriages in Geneu'r Glyn Hundred to 1812.

[15]*WS* has fuller details of the history of such names. A list of adjectival names and their variants may be found in Prys Morgan, *A Background to Wales* (Llandybïe: Christopher Davies, 1968), in the chapter on Welsh surnames.

[16]Whether such descriptions refer to hair colouring or to complexion is uncertain, just as with their English equivalents.

[17]T.E.Morris, 'Welsh surnames in the border counties of Wales', *Y Cymmrodor*, XLIII, 1932. The article concentrates on surnames of Welsh origin to be found over the border in English counties; some of its conclusions are now out of date.

[18]T.E.Morris, see 17 above, p.120.

[19]*WS* relates these in fuller detail.

[20]*WS* includes it in the list of Welsh surnames from Welsh place-names.

[21]Lewys Dwnn, *Heraldic Visitations of Wales* (ed. Sir S.R.Meyrick, Llandovery, 1846)

[22]D.E.Williams, see 8 above.

[23]J.Barry Davies, 'Welsh names and surnames', (Glamorgan FHS *Journal*, No.7, 1985, reprinted from South Wales FHS *Journal*, Vol.3, No.1, 1979) and 'Christian names in 16th-18th century Glamorgan' (South Wales FHS *Journal*, Vol.4, No.2/3, 1980); Wendy Cope, 'Some Oystermouth families: Webborn, Gammon, Bidder and Ace' (Glamorgan FHS *Journal* No.5, 1984) provides useful pointers to the origins of characteristic Gower surnames.

[24]B.G.Charles, *The English Dialect of South Pembrokeshire* (Pembrokeshire Record Society, 1982) makes it clear that the linguistic influence of Flemish settlers was less than is often assumed.

[25]E.g., Picton Castle Deeds, 13-14C.

[26]B.G.Charles, *Non-Celtic Place-names in Wales* (London, 1938).

[27]*Cronicl*, Journal of Powys FHS: E.Ronald Morris, 'Notes on some Montgomeryshire surnames' (No.4, 1982); Michael Faraday, 'Is your name Badland: the story of a Radnorshire surname' (No.9, 1984).

[28]I am grateful to Murray Chapman for providing me with the information in this and the following paragraph. The case cited is a good illustration of how valuable the records of the Courts of Great Sessions can be. (See Chapter 17, where they are discussed more fully.)

[29]PRO: C 66/1137/m.33.

[30]NLW: Montgomeryshire Court of Great Sessions Gaol Files, WALES 4/129—1, mm. 24-66.

[31]P.H.Reaney, *The Origin of English Surnames* (London, 1967, 1980) and (with R.M.Wilson) *Dictionary of British Surnames* (London, 2nd ed., 1976); Basil Cottle, *The Penguin Dictionary of Surnames* (2nd ed., 1978).

[32]E.Ekwall, *The Concise Oxford Dictionary of English Place-Names* (OUP, 4th ed., 1960); publications of the English Place-Name Society.

[33]Parish of Nantwich. From 'Population change and stability in a Cheshire parish during the eighteenth century', by Grace Wyatt, *Local Population Studies*, 43, Autumn 1989.

[34]Unpublished study by John Rowlands, Aberystwyth, based on all marriages in Cardiganshire 1813-1837.

[35]Information kindly supplied by Derek Habberfield from Glamorgan FHS Marriage Index, 1813-1837.

[36]Francis Leeson, 'The distribution of Welsh surnames', *Genealogists' Magazine*, XIX (1977). The author's tables are based on a count of surnames in *Returns of Owners of Land, 1873*; labourers are therefore excluded, but the general figures reflect observations from other sources.

[37]1670 Hearth Tax for Pembrokeshire, published in *West Wales Historical Records*, ix-xi (Carmarthen, 1923-6).

[38]*WS* has numerous examples of this, with material taken from many areas on the eastern border of Wales.

# 8. Place-names

Bedwyr Lewis Jones

People live in houses which have names. These houses are located in administrative units—in parishes, towns, counties, etc—which again have names. Inevitably, researchers into family history will from the outset find themselves dealing with place-names.

The name of a house which was once the home of an ancestor will naturally have a sentimental appeal for many but for the purpose of researching family history it is the names of parishes which are really important. It is on parish names, and not on habitation names, that the researcher should concentrate—at least, initially.

Parishes came into being in the Middle Ages as ecclesiastical units, consisting of a township or cluster of townships, each parish having its own church and clergyman to whom various ecclesiastical dues were paid. From the Elizabethan period onwards these ecclesiastical parishes acquired certain civil duties. The parish became the basic administrative unit. People were identified as So-and-So from Such-and-Such parish. Their births, marriages and deaths were recorded in parish registers.

The main concern of family historians is to be able to identify and locate parishes. In doing this there is one thing which has to be remembered, namely that until fairly recently the spelling of place-names, even in official documents, could vary considerably. This is true of all countries. It is especially true in Wales where Welsh place-names have often been recorded by persons unfamiliar with the Welsh language. CRICIETH in Caernarfonshire can appear as **Crickaeth**, **Crikeith**, **Krickieth**, **Criccieth**, etc., LLANFAIR CAEREINION in Montgomeryshire as **Llanvair in Krynion**, **Llanvair Caerinion**, **Llanvair Caerengion**, **Llanvair in Caerinion**, or just plain **Llanfair**; LLANBOIDY in Carmarthenshire as **Llanboydy**, **Llanbeyde**. etc. There is no way of providing researchers with a full list of possible variants nor indeed of drawing up a codified set of rules or principles of variation. All one can do is to recommend patience and caution, to urge them to copy parish names with pedantic accuracy, and to advise them, when in difficulty, to seek help from an archivist or someone else with experience in dealing with historical records rather than give reign to their own ingenuity. If researchers follow this advice at the outset they will be surprised at how quickly they acquire a 'sense' or 'feeling' in these matters, especially with post-1600 documents.

Parishes in Wales can have a Welsh and English name which are completely different. **Trefdraeth** in Pembrokeshire is one example; in English it has been known as ***Newport*** for at least 700 years. Other examples of similar, and not uncommon, dual naming are:

**Caergybi**: ***Holyhead*** in Anglesey
**Llandeilo Ferwallt**: ***Bishopston*** in Glamorgan
**Pen-y-bont ar Ogwr**: ***Bridgend*** in Glamorgan
**Y Drenewydd**: ***Newtown*** in Montgomeryshire

A Welsh name of a parish may in other instances have a well-established highly anglicized version such as ***Denbigh*** for **Dinbych**, ***Carmarthen*** for **Caerfyrddin**, ***Lampeter*** for **Llanbedr Pont Steffan**, ***Llantwit Major*** for **Llanilltud Fawr**, etc. All this may well seem confusing, especially to someone from outside Wales, but provided the researcher is aware of the possibility of the coexistence of a dual Welsh/English or anglicized naming pattern there is no real problem. Three reference works: *Welsh Administrative and Territorial Units* by Melville Richards (1969), *Gazetteer of Welsh Place-names* by Elwyn Davies (1975), *Parish Registers of Wales* by C.J. Williams and J. Watts Williams (1986), all list both the Welsh and the English or anglicized names of parishes.

More misleading, possibly, is the fact that in Wales, as in other countries, the same name may be borne by more than one parish. I have already referred to **Trefdraeth**: ***Newport*** in Pembrokeshire. **Trefdraeth** is also the name of a parish near Aberffraw in Anglesey; ***Newport*** is the name of a large town in Monmouthshire. There is a **Llanddeusant** in Anglesey and south of Llanymddyfri in Carmarthenshire; **Llantrisant** in Anglesey and outside Cardiff; **Llanwnda** outside Caernarfon and near Fishguard; **Cemais** in Montgomeryshire, inland from Machynlleth, **Cemais** or **Kemeys** in Monmouthshire near Caerllion, a **cantref** or hundred called **Cemais** in north Pembrokeshire, as well as a village called **Cemais** or **Cemaes** within the parish of Llanbadrig in Anglesey. Wrong identification of such place-names can lead to all sorts of subsequent difficulties but the problem can, in most cases, be avoided if researchers note down always, after the name of the parish, the name of the county or diocese to which the record or document which they are consulting refers.

Many, many Welsh parish-names, as the examples mentioned above will have indicated, begin in LLAN- (with an initial double **l** symbol representing phonetic ɬ). Originally the word **llan** meant an open space or clearing; it derives from the same root as ***land*** in English. In Welsh it came to mean a piece of land enclosed for a special purpose and more particularly a piece of consecrated land containing a church or chapel and a burial-ground. As a first element in place-names it can be equated with 'church' and is followed more often than not by the name of the saint to whom the church was dedicated. Some saints acquired more renown than others and as a result a number of churches were in time dedicated to them. Dewi or David, the patron saint of Wales, is the obvious example; the growth of his cult in the Middle Ages resulted in numerous churches in South Wales being called **Llanddewi**, i.e. **Llan** + **Dewi**, the church of David. Something similar happened in the case of other popular Welsh saints such as Cadog or Catwg, Illtud, Padarn, Teilo; in the case of the Irish saint Bride or Brigit, known in Welsh as Ffraid or Sanffraid; and particularly with the three universal saints Peter, Mary and Michael—in Welsh **Pedr**, **Mair** and **Mihangel**; hence the many instances in Wales of churches called **Llangatwg** (St. Cadog's), **Llanilltud** (St. Illtud's), **Llanbadarn** (St. Padarn's), **Llandeilo** (St. Teilo's), **Llansanffraid** (St. Bride's), **Llanbedr** (St. Peter's) and especially **Llanfair** (St. Mary's) and **Llanfihangel** (St. Michael's). Where this was the case it became customary to add a geographical description, often the name of a medieval administrative area, to **Llanddewi** or **Llanfihangel**, etc., to form the parish name. **Llanddewibrefi** is St. David's church on the river Brefi in Cardiganshire; **Llanddewi Felffre** (or **Llanddewi Velfre**) is St. David's church in the medieval commote of **Efelffre** in Pembrokeshire.

Some other examples are:
**Llangatwg** (**Llangattock**), without any qualifier, near Crucywel (or Crickhowell) in Breconshire; **Llangatwg Feibion Afel** (**Llangattock Vibon Afel**), St. Cadog's church patronized by the **meibion** 'sons' of Afel, east of Abergafenni in Monmouthshire; **Llanilltud Fawr** (Llantwit Major) and **Llanilltud Faerdref** (Llantwit Fardre), both in Glamorgan; **Llanbadarn Fawr** at Aberystwyth and north of Llandrindod in Radnorshire; **Llanbadarn-y-Creuddyn**, St. Padarn's church in the commote of Creuddyn, in Cardiganshire; **Llandeilo**, without any qualifier, in Carmarthenshire; **Llandeilo Tal-y-bont**, St. Teilo's church at Tal-y-bont, near Pontarddulais in Glamorgan; **Llansanffraid Glynceiriog**, St. Bride's church in the Ceiriog valley, in Denbighshire, south from Llangollen; **Llansanffraid Glyndyfrdwy**,

St. Bride's church in the Dee valley, near Corwen in Merioneth; **Llanbedr** or **Llanbedr-ar-Artro**, St. Peter's church on the river Artro, south of Harlech in Merioneth; **Llanbedr-y-fro** or **Llanbedr-ar Elái** (Peterston super Ely), St. Peter's church on the river Elái (Ely), in Glamorgan; **Llanfair-ar-y-bryn**, St. Mary's church on the hill, in Carmarthenshire; **Llanfair Pwllgwyngyll**, St. Mary's church in the township of Pwllgwyngyll, in Anglesey; **Llanfihangel Genau'r-glyn**, St. Michael's church in the commote of Genau'r-glyn in Cardiganshire; **Llanfihangel y Bont-faen** (**Llanmihangel**), in Glamorgan. Again, there is no real problem, provided the researchers are aware of the naming-pattern, and provided also that they note the full name of the parish. To note down **Llanfair** for **Llanfair-ar-y-bryn** or **Llanfair Pwllgwyngyll** or **Llanfair Caereinion** is insufficient and may well lead to endless and avoidable difficulties.

In identifying parishes two books (referred to earlier) will prove indispensable. The first is *Parish Registers of Wales*. It lists all the parishes existing in 1812, noting their standardized Welsh name, the English or Anglicized version of the name where this is applicable, and then the modern diocese to which the parish belongs. It also identifies new parishes created within older ones as a result of the growth of new centres of population. For example, it lists **Aberpennar** (***Mountain Ash***) in Glamorganshire and adds in the following line '< Aberdâr & Llanwynno 1863': this means that the parish of **Aberpennar** (***Mountain Ash***) was created in 1863 within the older civil parish of **Aberdâr** and **Llanwynno**. This kind of information will prove invaluable when dealing with industrial areas of Wales where population changes during the nineteenth century resulted in substantial modifications to the old parochial pattern.

The second invaluable aid is *Welsh Administrative and Territorial Units*, which provides a full list, in alphabetical order, of all the units of civil administration in medieval and modern Wales. It enables its user to locate a parish within its county, modern urban or rural district, medieval commote, etc. It also lists the townships—the smallest civil administrative unit - which were grouped together to form parishes. Should researchers come across a reference in a document from c.1600 to So-and-So from **Llysdulas** in Anglesey, by consulting Melville Richards' *WATU* (as the title is usually abbreviated) they will learn immediately that Llysdulas was a township within the ecclesiastical parish of Llanwenllwyfo in the civil parish of Llaneilian. For the researcher who manages to trace a family back to 1600 and earlier, this kind of information will be crucial. *WATU* is out of print at present but a copy will be available in record offices and public libraries.

After identifying a parish or township, i.e. ascertaining one of the usual forms of its name, researchers will need to locate it geographically. To do this they can turn to *A Gazetteer of Welsh Place-names* also referred to earlier. This gazetteer lists all Welsh towns, villages and parishes, notes the pre-1974 county in which they are situated, and adds a four figure National Grid reference. The National Grid is a simple system of lines, forming a square network, printed on Ordnance Survey Maps, and numbered in such a way that the position of any place can be pinpointed by means of a series of figures. For example, the position of Llanfair Caereinion in Montgomeryshire is given as '33/1006' (or in more recent grid references as SJ/1006). The two digits 33 (or the letters SJ), which come before the stroke /, indicate a general location within the overall national grid for the whole of Britain; they lead one to the relevant Ordnance Survey one-inch or 1:50 000 map sheet, and can be ignored provided one has the right area sheet. It is the four digits after the stroke which are important. The first two—in this case 10—refer to the vertical lines numbered along the top and bottom of the map; the last two—06 in this case—refer to the horizontal lines numbered along the vertical edges of the map. In the case of Llanfair Caereinion, take the OS sheet for north Montgomeryshire, find the line numbered 10 along the bottom and follow this north until it intersects with the horizontal line 06: you then have the exact location.

Once a parish has been located on a map, it is well worth-while noting the names of neighbouring parishes. The reason for this is simple: marriage links and changes of employment and habitation in the past tended to occur within a more limited area than is the case in our century. It follows that familiarity with the names of parishes within an area will often prove useful in tracing family connections.

The question of identifying and locating habitation names remains. There is no gazetteer of house names for a single Welsh parish, let alone for a whole county. Modern electoral rolls, postal directories from the second half of the last century, land tax documents from the eighteenth century will include most habitation names within a parish, but locating a house name is really a matter of looking at maps of the relevant parish. The best maps in this connection are either the pre-1939 2½ (1:25000) or 6 inch (1:10560) Ordnance Survey ones, and complete sets of both will be available at County Record Offices for their respective areas and at the National Library of Wales. If a careful search of these proves unproductive, library copies of the first—nineteenth century—one-inch Ordnance Survey maps are well worth consulting.

Habitation names vary immensely. Some are simple, uncompounded names such as **Bryn** 'hill'; **Glyn** 'dale, valley'; **Gors** 'marsh, fen'. The great majority, however are made up of more than one word element. Often they include a generic element such as **Bryn** followed by a descriptive qualifier—for example, **Brynhyfryd** from **bryn** 'hill' and **hyfryd** 'pleasant', or **Brynglas** from **bryn** and **glas** 'green, grass covered', etc. In other cases a qualifying word will precede the main generic element, as in **Pen-y-bryn** 'top of the hill', from **pen** 'top', **y** 'the' and **bryn**, or **Tan-y-bryn** 'below the hill', from **tan** 'below', **y** and **bryn**.

Listed below are some sixty or so of the more common generic elements together with a selection of typical qualifiers. In using the list, as indeed in seeking to understand all Welsh place-names, the researcher should always bear in mind that consonants at the beginning of Welsh words change or mutate in certain situations, according to a well-known phonological phenomenon called lenition. This is explained fully in Chapter 9. **Gors**, above, is an example. It is the mutated form of **cors**, with lenition of **c** to **g** at the beginning of a feminine noun following an unshown definite article **y**. In short, **cors** is 'marsh'; **y gors** is 'the marsh', but in the place-name the article **y** is dropped to leave mutated **Gors**. It is also worth remembering that **r** before a vowel at the beginning of a name may well be the attached remains of the definite article **yr**, as in **Rallt** from **Yr Allt** 'the hill', **Refail** from **Yr Efail** 'the smithy'.

In the list of common elements which follows, examples of these kinds of linguistic change will be indicated. No attempt has been made to cover the variety of personal names which so often follow a first generic element—for example, in **Boduan**, 'the residence of Buan', **Hendreforfudd** 'the permanent home which belonged to Morfudd', **Trefeilyr** 'the home of Meilyr'.

**allt**: 'wooded slope' in South Wales, 'hill' in North Wales—**Yr Allt** or **Rallt**, **Pen-rallt** 'top of the wooded slope/hill'
**banc**: 'bank'
**blaen**: 'end, upper reaches'—**Blaen-rhos** 'end of the moor'
**bod**: 'residence'. It occurs as a prefix, originally in North Wales often followed by a personal name, more recently over a wider area in names such as **Bodhyfryd** 'pleasant residence'; from **bod** and **hyfryd** 'pleasant'

**bont**: mutated form of **pont** 'bridge'—**Pen-y-bont** 'end of the bridge'
**bryn**: 'hill'
**cae**: 'field'—**Cae-hen** 'old field'; **Cae-mawr** 'large field'
**caer**: Either **caer** 'fort', or more often the shortened form of **cae yr** 'the field of' as in **Caermelwr** 'the field of the honey seller', **Caerodyn** 'the field of the lime kiln' (with **odyn** 'lime kiln')
**carreg**: 'stone', plural **cerrig**
**cefn**: 'ridge'—**Cefn-coed** 'wooded ridge', **Pen-cefn** 'end of the ridge'
**cil**: 'corner, nook'—**Cilcoed** 'nook by the wood'
**coed**: 'wood'
**craig**: 'rock'—**Pencraig** 'top of the rock'
**cwm**: 'valley'—**Blaen-cwm** 'upper reaches of the valley'
**dol**: 'meadow'
**erw**: 'acre'—**Yr Erw** or **Rerw** 'the acre'
**fedw**: mutated form of **bedw** 'birch tree'
**felin**: mutated form of **melin** 'mill'—**Felinesgob** 'the bishop's mill' (with **esgob** 'bishop'), **Tynyfelin** 'the farm of the mill' (with **tyn** 'small farm')
**fron**: mutated form of **bron** 'breast, hill-side, slope' — **Fronolau** 'sunny slope'; **Tan-y-fron** 'below the slope'
**ffynnon**: 'well'—**Tynyffynnon** 'small farm by the well'
**gelli**: mutated form of **celli** 'grove, small wood'—**Y Gelli**; **Penygelli** 'end of the wood'
**gilfach**: mutated form of **cilfach** 'corner, nook'
**glan**: 'edge, bank'—**Glan-gors** or **Glan-y-gors** 'edge of the marsh', **Glanrafon** 'bank of the stream', **Glan-traeth** 'edge of the shore'
**glyn**: 'glen, wooded valley'
**gors**: mutated form of **cors** 'marsh'
**hafod**: 'summer dwelling, shieling'
**hendre**: 'permanent home'
**llain**: 'strip of land'
**llan**: 'church'—**Tyn-llan** 'the small farm by the church'
**llwyn**: 'copse, grove'—**Llwyn-onn** 'ash grove'
**llys**: 'court, hall'
**maen**: 'large stone'
**maes**: 'open field'
**marian**: 'level, gravelly land'
**mynydd**: 'mountain'—**Trosymynydd** 'the far side of the mountain'
**nant**: 'valley, stream'—**Tyn-y-nant** 'the small farm in the valley/by the stream'

**pant**: 'hollow'
**parc**: 'field', especially in Dyfed
**pen**: 'end, top', usually as first qualifying element—**Pen-bryn** 'top of the hill', **Pen-cae** 'end of the field', **Pen-rhiw** 'top of the hill'
**plas**: 'big house'—**Plas Isaf/Uchaf** 'lower/upper big house'
**pont**: 'bridge'
**pwll**: 'pool'—**Tyn-pwll** 'the small farm by the pool'
**rallt**: **allt** preceded by article **r**, 'the wooded slope/hill'
**refail**: **efail** preceded by article **r**, 'the smithy'
**rhiw**: 'hill'
**rhos**: 'moor'
**rhyd**: 'ford'
**sarn**: 'causeway'
**tai**: plural of **tŷ** 'house'
**tal**: 'end', as first qualifying element—**Tal-y-bont** 'end of the bridge'
**tan**: 'below', as first qualifying element—**Tan-rallt** 'below the hill'
**tre(f)**: 'homestead, land belonging to a family'
**troed**: 'foot', as first qualifying element—**Troed-y-rhiw** 'foot of the hill'
**tros**: 'far side of', as first qualifying element—**Tros-y-gors** 'far side of the marsh'
**tŷ**: 'house'
**tyddyn**: 'small farm'
**tyn**: shortened form of **tyddyn**, often written **Ty'n**—**Tyn-llan** 'small farm by the church', **Tynymynydd** 'small farm on the mountain'
**waun**: mutated form of **gwaun** 'wet level land, moor'
**wern**: mutated form of **gwern**, 'land where alder trees used to grow, marshy meadow'
**ynys**: 'island, river-meadow'
**ysgubor**: 'barn'

# 9. Some Basic Welsh for Family Historians

M. Auronwy James

Relevant material written in Welsh (**Cymraeg**) may well be encountered during the course of tracing the history of a Welsh family. If the researcher is not familiar with the language, then the following outline of its history with some grammatical notes and a select word-list may be of interest and assistance.

The Welsh language belongs, with Breton and Cornish, to the Brythonic branch of the Celtic family of languages, being derived from the language of the Celts who came to Britain during the first millenium BC, though it may also have retained some elements of the language of their British predecessors. By the middle of the sixth century AD the language spoken throughout the island of Britain south of the Forth-Clyde line had evolved into Old Welsh. It was some centuries later that the language of the Anglo-Saxons who began invading Britain in the fifth century developed into Old English. Consequently, the meaning of the already well-established Welsh commonplace words and phrases, and in particular those associated with family life, are unrelated to their more recent English equivalents, and cannot be deduced from them.

The Welsh language is one of the most ancient living languages in Europe. The earliest examples of Welsh literature consist in the main of poems attributed to Taliesin and Aneirin. These poets of the sixth century pioneered a continuous tradition of literature which has lasted to the present day. The poets, being chroniclers of the times in which they lived, became versed in and preserved the genealogy of the princes and their descendants. This tradition was continued as late as the beginning of the seventeenth century, in particular by Lewis Dwnn, himself a poet, who presented his heraldic visitations of Wales mostly in Welsh.

Welsh was spoken throughout Wales and in parts of the English border counties up to the end of the sixteenth century when the translation of the Bible into Welsh in 1588 gave the people of Wales a standard language which helped maintain its use during the succeeding centuries. The western and northern parts of Wales are still predominantly Welsh in speech.

## Genealogical Sources in Welsh

As already indicated, many of the old manuscript pedigrees, as well as some published pedigrees, are in Welsh. The Welsh poems or **cywyddau** composed by the Welsh bards are also an important source of early genealogical information.

Church records and legal documents were kept in Latin or English until 1733, and in English thereafter. Nevertheless, a few Welsh words or phrases may be found in these records. A more deliberate use of Welsh has been made by some of the clergy from time to time, especially mid-eighteenth century, but these are rare exceptions. Church vestry minutes were likewise kept in English, irrespective of the language in which the meetings were held. Many of the Nonconformist churches, on the other hand, kept the minutes of their meetings in Welsh, and also some of their registers of christenings, baptisms and burials. However, gravestones in both the parish churchyards and Nonconformist chapel graveyards are frequently found to have Welsh inscriptions on them, some of which include an appropriate Welsh verse or an **englyn** (a particular kind of Welsh stanza) composed in memory of the deceased. Several collections of these gravestone **englynion** (mostly from north Wales) together with the customary inscriptions have been published recently.[1]

Wills were usually written in English, even when the testator did not understand the language, but a few have been written in Welsh. The Welsh ones from Cardiganshire were mostly made by poor people and were written by friends or neighbours who had had very little education. There are some well-written wills from Pembrokeshire circa 1770, as well as from other counties, with a considerable number of Welsh wills among the probate records of the diocese of Bangor, especially circa 1800, but, again, these Welsh documents are exceptional.

Of the published Welsh genealogical sources perhaps the most accessible are the biographical dictionaries. *The Dictionary of Welsh Biography down to 1940*[2] contains a complete list of earlier biographical dictionaries relating to Wales, including those written in Welsh, some of which may be identified by the word **bywgraffiadau** (biographies) or **enwogion** (eminent people) in the title. Numerous Welsh biographies (**cofiant**) have been published during the last hundred and fifty years, whilst the collected works (**gweithiau**) of poets often contain a short biography of the poet.

From about 1840 onwards Welsh denominational periodicals published in Wales and America[3] contained much information of use to the genealogist, including obituaries and notices of births, marriages and deaths. Such items were of great interest to emigrants and to their friends and relatives who remained in Wales. Many collections of Welsh letters have been preserved, and those to and from emigrants usually contain genealogical information. Obituaries and reports of weddings and funerals written in Welsh may be found in local newspapers, particularly those published since World War I.

Pedigrees and monumental inscriptions can probably be understood with the aid of the short glossary presented below. A greater mastery of the language would be required to read letters, obituaries and longer works such as biographies and church histories, though the following notes on Welsh grammar and how to use a Welsh dictionary may enable a novice to extract some of the genealogical relationships they might contain.

## Aspects of Welsh Grammar

In a simple Welsh sentence the verb usually comes first, followed by the subject and then the object of the verb, e.g., **priododd yr etifedd Ann** means 'the heir married Ann' (**priododd**, 'he married'; **yr etifedd**, 'the heir').

Adjectives usually come *after* the noun in Welsh, e.g., **plentyn ieuengaf** means 'youngest child' (**plentyn**, 'child'; **ieuengaf**, 'youngest'). In English the possessive (or genitive) case is indicated by the word 'of', or by an apostrophe, e.g., 'the cap of the boy', or 'the boy's cap'. In Welsh the possessor is named immediately after the object which belongs to him, e.g., **bedd Dafydd** means 'the grave of David'; **tŷ Dafydd**, 'the house of David' or 'David's house'; **mab Dafydd**, 'the son of David'. Another example of the genitive case is found in the expression: **Ann Robert gwraig Griffith Parry**, i.e., 'Ann Robert the wife of Griffith Parry'.

A similar construction shows the connection between a person or object and a place, e.g., **coleg y Fenni** is 'Abergavenny college' or 'the college at Abergavenny'; **Dafydd Cae-glas**, 'David of Caeglas'; **Siôn yr efail**, 'Siôn (John) of the smithy'.

Anyone who is not familiar with the Welsh alphabet is almost certain to have difficulty finding some words in a Welsh dictionary because the letters do not all appear in the same sequence as in the English alphabet. For example, **ch** is a letter of the Welsh alphabet rather than two separate letters, consequently in lists of words arranged alphabetically all those beginning with **ch** come in a group of their own after all the words beginning with **c** have been dealt with. A similar rule applies when **ch** appears in the middle of a word. For example, all words beginning with **cloc-** are arranged alphabetically and then followed by words beginning with **cloch-**. This results in **clociwr** (clock-maker) preceding **clochydd** (sexton).

Letters of the Welsh alphabet which do not appear in the English alphabet are: **ch**, **dd**, **ff**, **ng**, **ll**, **ph**, **rh**, **th**.

The letters are arranged in the following sequence:
**a**, **b**, **c**, **ch**, **d**, **dd**, **e**, **f**, **ff**, **g**, **ng**, **h**, **i**, (**j**), **l**, **ll**, **m**, **n**, **o**, **p**, **ph**, **r**, **rh**, **s**, **t**, **th**, **u**, **w**, **y**.

It should be noted that in alphabetically arranged lists **ng** usually comes after **g** (and not after **n**); e.g., **angau** (death) would come fairly soon after **agwedd** (attitude) rather than after **anffyddion** (unfaithful).

One of the greatest obstacles to using a Welsh dictionary effectively is encountered when a word has undergone mutation, because the mutated form is not listed. In Welsh the initial letter may be altered, depending on how the word is used in a sentence. For example, **t** may mutate to **d**, **nh**, or **th**, as in **tad** (father), **ei dad** (his father), **fy nhad** (my father) and **ei thad** (her father). **Tad** is easy enough to locate in a dictionary, but neither **dad**, **nhad**, nor **thad** may be found there; only the radical form of the word in given.

**Ei wraig** (his wife) is frequently found on tombstones, yet a dictionary will yield no such word as **wraig**, merely its radical, **gwraig**. Similarly, **Gorffennaf** (July) can lose its initial **g**, as in **y 5ed o Orffennaf** (the 5th of July).

Words beginning with a vowel are mutated by prefixing **h**; e.g., compare **pedair blwydd oed** (four years old) and **o'i hoed** (of her age); **ei annwyl fab** (his dear son) and **ei hannwyl fab** (her dear son). The vowels are: **a, e, i, o, u, w,** and **y** (although **i** and **w** can also occur as consonants).

The following table should enable the radical of a mutated word to be found.

| Initial letter of a mutated word | Initial letter of the radical |
|---|---|
| **b** | **p** |
| **ch** | **c** |
| **d** | **t** |
| **dd** | **d** |
| **f** | **b, m** |

| | |
|---|---|
| **g** | **c** |
| **ng** | **g** |
| **ngh** | **c** |
| **h** | the next letter (delete h) |
| **l** | **ll**; or restore initial g |
| **m** | **b** |
| **mh** | **p** |
| **n** | **d** |
| **nh** | **t** |
| **ph** | **p** |
| **r** | **rh**; or restore initial g |
| **th** | **t** |
| **a, e, l, o, r, w, y** (initial **g** is missing) | **g** + mutated word (i.e restore initial **g**) |

Consider the following words: **brawd** (brother); **ei blentyn** (his child); **chwaer** (sister); **ei Chreawdwr** (her Maker). The first is readily found under the letter **b**, whereas the second is derived from **plentyn**; the third comes under the letter **ch** whilst the last one is a mutation of **Creawdwr**. If it is not known whether the word is in its radical form or not, then assume, initially, that it is. If it cannot be found in the dictionary, then try and see whether it has been mutated. With the aid of the above table of conversions it may be possible to find the desired word. If the process does not yield a plausible solution, try prefixing the letter **g**, or delete an initial **h**.

Perhaps attention should be drawn to the fact that **glan**, 'shore, bank (of the river, etc)', and **llan**, 'church environs' both mutate to '**lan**'; and **glyn**, 'glen' and **llyn**, 'lake', both mutate to '**lyn**'. The context usually helps determine which to choose.

Another class of words which can cause some difficulty is the verb, since the end of the word may be altered to modify its meaning, e.g., **canu**, 'to sing', may appear as **canodd**, 'he sang', and the latter form is not listed in a dictionary. A Welsh grammar may be consulted for further details.

## Pronunciation

Welsh spelling is phonetic, with each consonant having one sound only. Welsh vowel sounds are 'pure' sounds, similar to those found in German or Italian. Stress (or accent) in Welsh usually falls on the last syllable but one: **gwel**ed, gwel**ed**ig, gweled**ig**aeth, gwelediga**eth**au. There are some exceptions in which the last syllable (ultima) is stressed, but the accent is often shown in such cases, as with **nacáu**, 'to refuse', and in some words borrowed from English such as **apêl**, 'appeal'. In the illustrative examples below, the pronunciation is that usually practised in England.

### Vowel sounds

Vowels may be long or short.

**a** long as in 'bar': **tad**, 'father'; short as in 'cap': **cant**, 'hundred'.

**e** long as in 'hair': **hen** (pronounced 'hane'), 'old'; short as in 'ten': **pen**, 'head'.

**i** long as in 'machine': **mil** (pron. 'meal'), 'thousand'; short as in 'pin': **dim**, 'nothing'.

**o** long as in 'more': **pob**, 'every'; short as in 'top': **ffon**, 'stick'.

**u** long 'ee' sound as in 'keen': **un**, 'one'; short 'i' sound as in 'thin': **pump** (pron. 'pimp'), 'five'. (In some parts of north Wales it is similar to the 'y' in 'myth').

**w** long as in 'food': **mwg** (pron. 'moo-g'), 'smoke'; short as in 'foot': **cwm**, 'valley'.

**y** this symbol represents two sounds:
1. Clear (similar to the Welsh **u**) as in 'myth'; long as in 'mean': **dyn**, 'man'; short as in 'bin': **bryn**, 'hill'.
2. Obscure, as in 'myrtle': **dynion** (pron. 'dunn-yon'), 'men'. Only the following one-syllable words have this sound: **y**, **yr**, 'the'; **yn**, **yng**, **ym**, 'in'; **fy**, 'my'; **dy**, 'your', and a small number of borrowings from English, such as **syr**, 'sir', **nyrs**, 'nurse'.

### Consonants

**b**, **d**, **h**, **l**, **m**, **n**, **p**, **ph** and **t** have the same sounds as in English.

**c** Always as in 'cap'.

**ch** As in Scottish 'loch', German 'Bach'; **bach**, 'small'.

**dd** As 'th' in 'the' or 'breathe'; **pridd**, 'earth'. For **dd** the symbol δ is often found in manuscript.

**f** Always as in 'of'; **afon**, 'river'.

**ff** As in 'off'; **fferm**, 'farm'.

**g** Always as in 'get'; **gardd**, 'garden'.

**ng** As in 'sing'; **angau**, 'death'. In a few words it is sounded 'ng-g' as in 'finger'; **dangos** (pron. dang-gos in some parts of Wales), 'to show'; and in place-names such as **Bangor** (Bang-gor).

**j** Occurs in words borrowed from English; the Welsh sound system originally did not include the sound of j or the -g- of Roger; the nearest sound in Welsh was **s** or **si**, so that John became **Siôn** and Roger became **Roser** or **Rosser.**

**ll** Produced by putting the tongue in the 'l' position and hissing; **llyn**, 'lake'.

**r** Trilled as in 'horrible'; **radio** (pron. rrahdio), 'radio'.

**rh** An aspirated 'r' as in 'rhinoceros'; **rhan**, 'part'.

**s** Always as in 'sit'; **nos** (long 'o'), 'night'.

**th** Always as in 'thick'; **cath** (pron. caa-th), 'cat'.

### Consonantal vowels

The letters **i** and **w** sometimes perform the function of a consonant.

**i** Like the 'y' in 'yes'; **iach**, 'healthy'.

**w** Like the short 'oo' sound in 'water'; **gweld**, 'see'.

### Combinations of letters

**si** is equivalent to English 'sh' in 'ship'; **Siôn** (pron. 'shorn'), 'John'.

**ts** is equivalent to English 'ch' in 'church'; **Tseina**, 'China'.

## Reading Welsh Manuscripts

When reading Welsh manuscripts, note should be taken of the difference between **d** and 'δ', the latter being usually the symbol used for **dd**. The name **Dafyδ**, for instance, should be transcribed as **Dafydd** (the Welsh for David) rather than **Dafyd**, and **wedi ei glaδu** as **wedi ei gladdu** (buried).

In old writings **f** may be found to be replaced by **v**, e.g., **vab** instead of **fab**, 'son (of)'. Also, **ph** may be found instead of **ff**, e.g., **corph** for **corff**, 'body'.

The following abbreviations are often found in pedigrees:

χ = **ch**
**-z** = **-ch** or **-erch**
**coz** = **coch**, red
**fh** = daughter and heiress
**m** = **mam**, mother
**Sr** = sir, a title for a clergyman
**Sr** . . . **marchog** = sir . . . knight
**vz** = **verch**, daughter

## GLOSSARY

**Numerals:**

1 **un**
2 **dau, dwy** (fem.)
3 **tri, tair** (fem.)
4 **pedwar, pedair** (fem.)
5 **pump, pum**
6 **chwech, chwe**
7 **saith**
8 **wyth**
9 **naw**
10 **deg, deng**
11 **un ar ddeg**
12 **deuddeg**
13 **tri (tair) ar ddeg**
14 **pedwar (pedair) ar ddeg**
15 **pymtheg**
16 **un ar bymtheg**
17 **dau (dwy) ar bymtheg**
18 **deunaw**
19 **pedwar (pedair) ar bymtheg**
20 **ugain**
30 **deg ar hugain**
40 **deugain**
50 **hanner cant**
60 **trigain**
70 **trigain a deg, deg a thrigain**
80 **pedawr ugain**
90 **deg a phedwar ugain**
100 **cant, can**
1,000 **mil**

**Days:**

**dydd Sul, Saboth** Sunday
**dydd Llun** Monday
**dydd Mawrth** Tuesday
**dydd Mercher** Wednesday
**dydd Iau; Difiau** Thursday
**dydd Gwener** Friday
**dydd Sadwrn** Saturday

**Months:**

**Ionawr; Ionor** January
**Chwefror; Chwefrol; Mis Bach** February
**Mawrth** March
**Ebrill** April
**Mai** May
**Mehefin** June
**Gorffennaf; Gorphenaf** July
**Awst** August
**Medi** September
**Hydref** October
**Tachwedd** November
**Rhagfyr** December

**a aned** who was born
**a anwyd** who was born
**a foddodd** who drowned
**a fu farw** who died
**a gladdwyd** who was buried
**ab** son (of)
**ach, -au** lineage; pedigree, -s
**aelod, -au** member, -s
**aer, -es, -esau** heir, -ess, -esses
**ail o Ionawr** second of January
**am** for; at
**am 8 mlynedd** for 8 years
**annwyl, anwylaf** dear, -est
**ap** son (of)
**ar y 7fed o Fai** on the 7th of May
**arf, -au** weapon, -s; plural arms (heraldic)
**arfbais** coat of arms
**arglwydd, -i** lord, -s
**argraffydd** printer
**arian** silver; money
**arweinydd y gân** precentor
**asiedydd** joiner
**athraw, -es; -on**; teacher (male, female); -s
**athro** teacher; professor

**baban** baby
**babandod** infancy
**bach** small
**bardd** poet
**bedydd** baptism
**bedyddiad**, **-au** baptism, -s
**bedyddiwyd** was baptised
**bedd**, **-au** grave, -s
**beddfaen** tombstone
**blaenor**, **-iaid** deacon, -s
**blwyddyn** year
**blynedd** years (after a number)
**bonheddig** noble; nobility; noble descent
**bonheddwr** gentleman
**brawd**, **brodyr** brother, -s
**brenin** king
**bu farw** he (or she) died
**bugail** shepherd; pastor
**bychan** little, junior
**bywyd** life

**cabden** captain
**caifn**, **ceifn** third cousin
**calan** first day (of month or season)
**Calan Gaeaf** All Saints' Day
**Calan Mai** Mayday
**capel**, **-i** chapel, -s
**capten** captain
**carreg**, **cerrig** stone, -s
**cefnder** first cousin (male)
**ceiniog** penny
**cerddor** musician
**claddedigaeth**, **-au** burial, -s
**claddfa** burial-ground
**claddwyd** was buried
**clochydd** sexton
**cof** memory, remembrance
**cofadail** monument
**cofio** to remember
**coffa** memory; memorial
**coffadwriaeth** remembrance
**colier** coal-miner
**collodd** he (she) lost
**collwyd** was lost
**corff A** the body of A
**corph** body
**cowper** cooper
**crydd** shoemaker
**crythor** fiddler
**curad** curate
**cyfarfu â'i ddiwedd** he met his end (died)
**cyfnither** first cousin (female)
**cyfreithiwr** attorney
**cyfyrder** second cousin (male)
**cyfyrdres** second cousin (female)
**cyffredin** common, ordinary
**cymynnu** bequeath
**cymynnwr** testator
**cyntaf** first

**chwaer**, **chwiorydd** sister, -s
**chwarelwr** quarryman

**damwain** accident
**darfodedigaeth** consumption, tuberculosis
**diacon**, **-iaid** deacon, -s
**dilledydd** clothier
**dim plant** no children
(y) **diweddar** (the) late
**diwethaf** last
**diwrnod**, **-au** day, -s
**dydd**, **-iau** day, -s
**Dydd Calan** New Year's Day
**Dydd Gwener y Groglith** Good Friday
**Dydd Iau Dyrchafael** Ascension Thursday
**Dydd Mawrth Ynyd** Shrove Tuesday
(y) **dywededig** (the) said

**ef** he, him, it
**eglwys**, **-i** church, -es
**ei annwyl wraig** his loving wife
**ei blant** his children
**ei blentyn** his child
**ei briod** his spouse

**ei fab** his son
**ei ferch** his daughter
**ei gŵr** her husband
**ei hannwyl ŵr** her loving husband
**ei mab** her son
**ei merch** her daughter
**ei phlant** her children
**ei phlentyn** her child
**ei phriod** her spouse
**eigion** depth, ocean
**enwyd** was named
**er cof am** in memory of
**er coffadwriaeth am** in memory of
**er serchus gof am** in loving memory of
**esgobaeth** diocese
**etifedd**, **-es** heir, -ess
**eto** again
**eu mab** their son
**eu merch** their daughter
**eu plant** their children
**eu plentyn** their child
**ewyllys**, **-iau** will, -s
**ewythr** uncle

**ffermwr** farmer
**fferyllydd** pharmacist
**ffyddlon** faithful

**gaeaf** winter
**ganwyd** was born
**gefail** smithy
**gefell**, **gefeilliaid** twin, -s
**glofa** colliery
**glöwr** collier
**gof** blacksmith
**gorchaifn** fourth cousin
**gorchaw** fifth cousin
**gordderch** concubine; illegitimate child
**gorffwys** rest
**gorffwysodd oddi wrth ei lafur** he rested from his labours
**gorphwys** rest
**gorwedd** to lie down
**gorwyr**, **-ion** great-grandchild, -ren
**gosodwyd** was placed
**gwanwyn** spring
**gweddillion** remains
**gweddw** single, solitary; widow
**gwehydd**, **gwëydd** weaver
**gweinidog** pastor, minister
**gweithiwr** worker
**gwniadwraig** seamstress
**gwniyddes** seamstress
**gŵr** man, husband
**gŵr Ann** Ann's husband
**gŵr bonheddig** gentleman
**gwraig** woman, wife
**gwraig David Jones** wife of David Jones
**gwreigan** poor or insignificant little woman
**Gŵyl Ddewi** St. David's Day, 1st March
**gwylmabsant**, **gwylfabsant** feast of patron saint
**Gŵyl Mihangel** Michaelmas day, 29th Sept.
**Gŵyl (San) Steffan** St. Stephen's day, 26th Dec.
**gynt o Gwm-bach** formerly of Cwmbach

**haf** summer
**heb** without
**hefyd** also
**hen**, **-af** old, -est
**hengaw** great-great-great-grandfather
**hi** she, her
**hoff** fond
**hon** this (fem.)
**honno** one spoken of (fem.)
**huned mewn hedd** may he (she) sleep in peace
**hunodd yn yr Iesu** he (she) died (lit. fell asleep) in Jesus
**hwn** this (masc.)

**hwy**, **hwynt** they, them
**hydref** autumn
**hynaf** eldest

**i** to, for
**ieuangaf**, **ieuengaf** youngest
**isod** below

**llafurwr**, **-wyr** labourer, -s
**lle** place; where
**llenor** literary person
**llog** interest (monetary)
**llong**, **-au** ship, -s
**llong-lywydd** ship's captain
**Llungwyn** Whitmonday
**llysdad** stepfather
**llysfab** stepson
**llysfam** stepmother
**llysferch** stepdaughter
**llystad** stepfather
**llythyrdy** post-office
**llywodraethwr** governor; executor
**llywydd** president

**mab**, **meibion** son, -s
**mab yng nghyfraith** son-in-law
**mab yr uchod** son of the above
**mabwysiedig** adopted
**maen** stone
**mam** mother
**mam-gu** grandmother
**mam honno** her mother
**mam wen** stepmother
**mam y rhain** the mother of these
**marchog**, **-ion** knight, -s
**marw** to die
**masnachwr** merchant; shopkeeper
**mawr** big, great
**meddiant**, **-iannau** possession, -s
**meddyg** medical doctor
**meistr** master
**merch**, **-ed** daughter, -s
**merch yng nghyfraith** daughter-in-law
**mhab** (see mab)
**mherch** (see merch)
**milfeddyg** veterinary surgeon
**mis**, **-oedd** month, -s
**modryb** aunt
**môr** sea
**mordaith** voyage
**morwr**, **morwyr** sailor, -s
**mwynwr** miner (lead, copper)
**mynwent** graveyard

**Nadolig** Christmas
**nai**, **neiaint** nephew, -s
**nain**, **neiniau** grandmother, -s
**nith**, **-oedd** niece, -s
**nod** mark
**Nos Calan** New Year's Eve

**o** from; of
**oddi wrth** from
**oed**, **oedran** age
**oedd** was
**offeiriad** priest
**olaf** last
**o'r dref hon** of (or from) this town
**o'r plwyf hwn** of this parish

**pais** coat (heraldic)
**pais arfau** coat of arms
**parchedig** reverend
**parchus** respectful; respectable
**(Y) Pasg** Easter
**plant** children
**plas** mansion
**plentyn**, **plant** child, -ren
**plentyn gordderch** illegitimate child
**plwyf**, **-i** parish, -es
**pregethwr** preacher
**priod** spouse
**priodas**, **-au** marriage, -s
**priododd** married
**punt** pound (money)

**rhieni** parents
**rhoddi** give
**rhyfel** war

**saer**, **seiri** carpenter, -s
**saer llongau** shipbuilder
**saer maen** mason
**serchog** affectionate; pleasant
**serchus** affectionate
**sir** county
**Sulgwyn** Whitsunday
**swllt** shilling
**syr** sir
**syrthiodd** fell

**tad**, **-au** father, -s
**tad-cu** grandfather
**tafarnwr** innkeeper
**taid**, **teidiau** grandfather, -s
**tanchwa** explosion
**teiliwr** tailor
**telynor** harpist
**teulu**, **-oedd** family, -ies
**tlotyn** pauper
**tref**, **-i** town, -s
**trefnu** arrange
**trwy ddamwain** by accident
**trysorydd** treasurer
**ty**, **tai** house, -s
**tyddyn** smallholding
**tylwyth** family, ancestry
**tyner** tender
**tyst**, **-ion** witness, -es
**tywysog**, **-ion** prince, -es

**uchod** above
**unig blentyn** only child
**urddo** ordain

**ŵyr**, **-ion** grandson (also grand-daughter), grandchildren
**wyres**, **-au** grand-daughter, -s
**wythnos**, **-au** week, -s

**y** the
**yma** here
**yma y gorwedd** here lies
**ymadawedig** departed, deceased
**ymadawodd â'r byd hwn** departed this life
**ymadawodd â'r fuchedd hon** departed this life
**yn y plwyf hwn** in this parish
**yn 52 mlwydd oed** 52 years old
**yr** the
**yr hon a** who (fem.)
**yr hwn a** who (masc.)
**ysbyty** hospital
**ysgol**, **-ion** school, -s
**ysgolfeistr**, **-es** schoolmaster, mistress
**ysgrifennydd** secretary
**ysgutor**, **-ion** executor, -s
**ysgwier** esquire

## NOTES TO CHAPTER 9

[1]Good examples are to be found in J. E. Hughes, *Englynion Beddau Dyffryn Ogwen* (Llandysul: 1979) and E. Jones, *Dagrau Gwerin* (Caernarfon: 1982). For other examples, see Chapter 23.

[2]J. E. Lloyd and R. T. Jenkins (eds), *The Dictionary of Welsh Biography down to 1940* (London: 1959).

[3]For example, *Y Cyfaill o'r Hen Wlad,* 1838-1933.

# 10. The IGI for Wales

Chris Pitt Lewis

## The IGI

The International Genealogical Index (IGI) is a computer-based index, containing details of the births (and parentage) and marriages of individuals in the past. Initially compiled for their own purposes by members of the Church of Jesus Christ of Latter Day Saints (LDS), better known as the Mormons, it has since been made available to the rest of us, and is now one of the family historian's most important tools.

It exists in two formats: on microfiche, in which form it is available in many public libraries, record offices and family history societies; and on compact disc (CD-ROM), in which form it is at the time of writing available only in certain LDS Genealogical Libraries in the USA. It is expected to appear in LDS libraries in the UK in due course.

This chapter describes the IGI by reference to the 1988 microfiche edition, and explains how to use its Welsh sections. Some information about the compact disc version is given at the end of the chapter.

## What it contains

Entries derive from two main sources: the 'Controlled Extraction Program', involving the systematic indexing of entire parish registers, and 'patron' entries supplied by individual members of the Mormon Church relating to their own ancestors.

The IGI includes a set of fiche called the 'Parish and Vital Records Listing' which explains what records have been included in the controlled extraction program for each county. It therefore indicates what is **not** included and should always be referred to if a search of the index does not reveal the required entry. There is also an 'Instructions' fiche, which contains valuable information about the arrangement and composition of the index.

In Wales, the Mormons have not been allowed to microfilm and index the parish registers, as they have in most English dioceses. Therefore, the Welsh IGI contains only a small number of entire registers. But this is less serious than it seems, because they have been able to microfilm and index the Bishop's Transcripts, and the majority of these are in the

IGI. It also contains most of the births and baptisms to be found in the non-parochial registers deposited in the Public Record Office; this in itself is a valuable feature.

It cannot be denied that the IGI contains less information for Wales than for some English counties. But it still contains a great deal, and it is not for that reason that successful searches in it are more difficult than in England. The reason lies in the nature of Welsh names themselves, and the difficulty of indexing them.

## How it is arranged (microfiche edition)

The IGI is arranged first by region, which in England and Wales means by the historic (pre-1974) counties. Monmouthshire will be found among the English counties, but it is indexed on the Welsh pattern described below. Within each county, events (births or baptisms and marriages; burials are not included) are listed alphabetically by name.

In England, of course, this means alphabetically by surname. Within each surname, the arrangement is by alphabetical order of given (that is, Christian) name, and within each given name by date. Thus, John Jones baptised or married in 1771 comes before John Jones baptised in 1772, who in turn comes before Joseph Jones baptised in 1624.

Many surnames have numerous variant spellings, and so the computer program sorts similar surnames together. By 'similar' the computer understands not only variant spellings but also similar sounding names, according to rules which are too complex to examine in detail here. For example, under Hayward will be found not only the obvious spelling variants (Haywood, Heyward, etc) but also the unconnected surname Howard. There is a cross-reference under each of the variants.

Given names, however, are not sorted in this way, so that, for instance, a parish register entry referring to Wm. Hayward will be found alphabetically after all the William Hayward entries, and Gulielmus Hayward somewhere between Griffith and Harriet Hayward.

In Wales it is not so easy, since, as explained in Chapter 7, for much of the period covered by the IGI most Welshmen did not have surnames. Worse still, you cannot tell from a single record whether William John and William Jones are using an hereditary surname or whether they are both just William ap John. Conversely, you cannot tell merely from a baptism register whether William the son of John Thomas will grow up to be William Jones or William Thomas, or indeed something else altogether. Any indexing system should take account of both the obvious possibilities (it cannot do much about the others), and this presents considerable difficulties, for both the indexer and the searcher.

## Indexing Welsh Names

When the IGI was started in 1968 its eventual scale (it now contains 118 million names worldwide) was not envisaged and it was not designed as a research tool for genealogists. A rule of thumb was adopted for indexing Welsh names which, in retrospect, leaves a lot to be desired

Each Welsh County (including Monmouthshire) has two indexes, the 'Given Name Index' and the 'Surname Index'. Every entry is indexed twice, once under the subject's 'given' or first name and once under his 'surname'. But what is his surname?

From 1 January 1813 the established church used a standard printed baptism register which had a column for the parents' surname. The IGI treats the name in this column as the child's surname, and indexes it accordingly.

Thus William the son of John and Mary Thomas was baptised at Llanelly, Breconshire, on 28 September 1817. He appears on the IGI thus:

In the Given Names Index (GN), indexed under William:
William (son of) John Thomas/Mary

In the Surname Index (SN), indexed under Thomas:
Thomas, William (son of) John Thomas/Mary

This is what one expects and presents no problem. The surname index works just as it would for an English county.

But before 1813 there was no surname column in the register. The typical entry might read: William the son of John Thomas and Sarah his wife was baptised. The IGI assumes, of course wrongly, that in all cases before 1 January 1813 the child took its father's Christian name as its surname. Thus, when William the son of John and Sarah Thomas was baptised at Cowbridge, Glamorgan, on 12 October 1783, he appears on the IGI as follows:

In GN, indexed under William:
William (son of) John Thomas/Sarah

In SN, indexed under John:
John, William (son of) John Thomas/Sarah

He does not appear in the surname index under Thomas.

Note that the computer has generated the entirely fictitious surname 'John', which does not occur in the original register. This 'surname' forms part of the computer database. Data was put into the computer from a form which contained a box for the child's surname. The computer operatives were instructed to enter the father's given name in this box, when dealing with the pre-1813 Welsh material. It can be removed only by re-inputting the data.

This happens even if the family obviously had a settled surname. There was a family in Carmarthenshire called Brigstock, originally immigrants from England, and Elizabeth, daughter of Lewis Brigstock and Elizabeth his wife, was baptised at St Clears on 26 June 1716. She appears on the IGI like this:

In GN, indexed under Elizabeth:

| | | |
|---|---|---|
| Elizabeth | (dau of) | Lewis Brigfloch/Elizabeth |

In SN, indexed under Lewis:

| | | |
|---|---|---|
| Lewis, Elizabeth | (dau of) | Lewis Brigfloch/Elizabeth |

There is no entry under Brigstock, or even under Brigfloch—never forget the possibility of a silly mistake by the transcriber!

The change in the indexing system on 1 January 1813 is nicely illustrated by adjacent entries in SN:

| | | | |
|---|---|---|---|
| Thomas, John | (son of) | Thomas Deane/Mary | C 28 Nov 1812. Pembrokeshire, Burton |
| Thomas, John | (son of) | James Thomas/Mary | C 24 Jan 1813. Pembrokeshire, St Ishmaels |

This explains a peculiarity of the surname index which is immediately apparent to the user. An English-style surname, such as Deane or Brigstock, may appear to have many baptisms after 1813, but hardly any before. The earlier baptisms are there, but they are indexed under the father's christian name. On the IGI essentially identical surnames, such as Jones and John, are indexed together in the surname index (see above). After 1813 Jones, which is the commoner surname today, is in the clear majority on the IGI, but before 1813 it hardly appears there at all, except for marriages. 'Jones', of course, was never the father's Christian name.

There is worse to come.

Early registers in Wales often give a string of patronymics, e.g:

Rachel dau. of Thomas John Charles of Glasgoed
(baptised at Panteg, Monmouthshire, on 25 March 1741)

Edmond son of John Thomas Lewis Bevan
(baptised at Bedwellty, Monmouthshire, on 29 March 1752)

These multiple names carry their owner's genealogy, but which are the important ones to index? The computer assumes that the first two are the important names, and totally discards the rest, which do not appear on the IGI at all. Thus the Panteg entry becomes:

| | | | |
|---|---|---|---|
| In GN: | Rachel | (dau of) | Thomas John/ |
| In SN: | Thomas, Rachel | (dau of) | Thomas John/ |

and the Bedwellty entry:

| | | | |
|---|---|---|---|
| In GN: | Edmond | (son of) | John Thomas |

and similarly in SN.

This may happen even if the last name is clearly the most important. There was a Thomas Plomer in eighteenth century Bedwellty, with an English-style surname. He had a son William, baptised on 5 February 1743, and it was apparently this William who had a son baptised in 1770, for in the register he is given an impressive Welsh-style triple name, complete with patronymic:

27 May 1770 baptised William son of William Thomas Plomer

The IGI blindly follows its rules, and loses the surname:

| | | | |
|---|---|---|---|
| In GN: | William | (son of) | William Thomas/ |
| In SN: | Williams, William | (son of) | William Thomas/ |

Although the above is the basic system, and applies to the vast majority of entries, it is not a hard and fast rule. A lot seems to depend on the intelligence or whim of the individual who made the original input into the computer. Many examples of multiple names can in fact be found in full in the index, and also some pre-1813 baptisms indexed under the 'correct' surname. Occasionally what seems to be the same event is indexed in two different ways from different inputs. The following names occur next to one another in GN (Cilybebyll and Neath are adjacent parishes in Glamorgan):

| | | | |
|---|---|---|---|
| Philip | (son of) | Rees John Gibbs/Margt | C 2 Mar 1806. Cilybebyll |
| Philip | (son of) | Rees John Gibbs/Margaret | C 2 Mar 1806. Neath |

They are in different parts of SN:

| | | |
|---|---|---|
| Gibbs, Philip | Rees John Gibbs/Margt | C 2 Mar 1806. Cilybebyll |
| Rees, Philip | Rees John Gibbs/Margaret | C 2 Mar 1806. Neath |

Sometimes, strange results can be produced. The entry quoted above from Bedwellty for Edmond son of John Thomas Lewis Bevan appears in SN under Thomas:

| | | |
|---|---|---|
| Thomas, Edmond | (son of) | John Thomas/ |

which is difficult to justify.

We have mentioned above how the computer program sorts similar surnames together. In the surname index for the Welsh counties the same system applies, and there are additional rules which ensure that the various derivatives of a single patronym are found together. Thus, under 'Owen' will be found Owen, Owain, Owens, and Bowen, as well as the Latin form *Audoenus*. It is worth mentioning that the common surname Lewis will be found under 'Louis', and is not, as it should be, indexed together with Llewelyn.

In the given name index obvious variants, such as John, Johannes and Jno, are indexed together. The treatment of Welsh and English equivalents is inconsistent; for instance, Dafydd and David are indexed together, but Griffith, Guto and Griffin are separate.

## The Treatment of Wills

There are also some highly confusing entries derived from wills, best illustrated by an example. Griffith Hitchings of St Nicholas, Pembroke, died in 1752, having made a will dated 25 September 1748 which was proved in St David's, 21 March 1754. The Will mentions (among others) his wife Mary, his daughter Jane, his son John, and John's children Elizabeth and Henry. This gives rise to the following entries in SN (there are corresponding entries in GN):

| | | |
|---|---|---|
| Hitchings, Griffith | Hitchings/ | M W |
| Hitchings, Griffith | Mary Mrs Hitchings | H M |
| Hitchings, Mary Mrs | Griffith Hitchings | W M |
| Hitchings, Mary Mrs | Griffith/ | F W |
| | | |
| Hitchings, Jane | Griffith Hitchings/Mary Mrs Hitchings | F W |
| Hitchings, John | Griffith Hitchings/Mary Mrs Hitchings | M W |
| | | |
| Hitchings, John | Mrs_John Hitchings | H M |
| Hitchings, Mrs_John | John Hitchings | W M |
| Hitchings, Mrs_John | | F W |
| | | |
| Hitchings, Elizabeth | John Hitchings/Mrs_John Hitchings | F W |
| Hitchings, Hennery | John Hitchings/Mrs_John Hitchings | M W |

All the entries are dated 25 Sep 1748, which may be twenty or thirty years later than the real date of the marriages and births concerned. All of them give the place as 'Pembroke St Nicholas', but this is the testator's residence and not necessarily the parish where any of these events took place. Most of them can be distinguished easily by the letter W for Will in the second column, for the type of event, but the thoroughly confusing items are the marriage entries for Griffith and Mary, and their son John and his unnamed wife, which have the letter M for Marriage in this column. At first sight these look like ordinary marriage entries taken from the parish register. They can be distinguished only by the use of the word 'Mrs' in the entry. This is an appalling trap for the unwary.

It will also be observed that there is no easy means of discovering the name of the testator from these entries, although once found, his entry (the first in the list above) has a distinctive form. Worse, there seems to be no means at all of discovering the date or court of probate, short of using the batch number to call for the original record.

In the 1988 edition, only St David's Wills appear in any quantity, affecting Cardigan, Carmarthen, Pembroke and part of Glamorgan; but it is possible that there are occasional will entries in other counties.

Frankly, these entries are more trouble than they are worth; it would have been better to have kept them out of the main part of the IGI in a separate index of their own.

## How to use the microfiche version

Despite all its complications, the IGI for Wales is not difficult to use. It just has to be used in the right way, and regrettably with more limited objectives than are possible for the English part of the index. The method is as follows.

### 1. To search for a specific baptism or birth after 1812

No problem. Use the surname index just as for an English county. Only if the event took place in an area where surnames are still unsettled at this late date may it be necessary to use the given names index.

### 2. To search for a marriage

No problem. Whether before or after 1813, these are indexed in the usual way for both parties in the surname index, under the apparent surname given in the register. For example, John Philip married Ann

Hitchings is indexed under Philip and Hitchings. However, beware entries derived from wills.

**3. To search for a specific baptism or birth before 1813**

For example, William Thomas known to be born in Cowbridge, Glamorgan, in 1783/4. Search the given name, not the surname index. Under William this lists children baptised with that name, throughout Glamorgan, in chronological order. Find the right years, and then look for those baptised in Cowbridge. If Thomas is a genuine surname, then you want one whose father's surname is Thomas. If it is likely that he is really William ap Thomas, then you want one whose father's first name is Thomas. Sometimes you will have to consider both possibilities.

If you are unsure of the date, your search will be a long one. For common Christian names, there may be dozens of entries each year. If you are unsure of both date and place, then your search will be almost impossible, except for an uncommon name. But remember that any surname not derived from a Christian name was uncommon in Wales, even Smith.

Whether you find the entry you want or not, always check the original register. This should of course be done when using any index, for all indexes are fallible, but it is doubly important with the Welsh IGI. Remember William Thomas Plomer. If you were searching for the name Plomer, you would not find him on the IGI, and if you were searching for a plain William Thomas born about the same time, you could be seriously misled.

This may sound complicated, but it is not. The basic system is actually quite simple to use, once you know the rules.

Once you have used it a few times, and become thoroughly familiar with it, you can (if you wish) try to be clever. You will find it is worth using the surname index for a pre-1813 baptism in three cases:

**a**. If you are dealing with a patronymic, you can use it as intended.

**b**. If you know the father's Christian name, it may be quicker to use the surname index. For example, William, known or assumed to be the son of John Thomas, born about 1783/4, should be indexed under the surname John. There will be a number of 'William John' entries in the index. Look for one whose father is John Thomas. This should be quicker than using the given names index, but unless you find what is clearly the right entry you will have to check the given names index as well in case it is an instance of indexing 'against the rules'.

**c**. You could look for all the children of (say) Rees Gibbs by searching the surname index under Rees and (just in case) under Gibbs, checking the father's name for every entry in the appropriate years. This is laborious, but possible if you are desperate.

**4. One name studies**

Not really possible for the period before 1813, but marriages are easily found, and you can check a lot of guesses using methods **b** and **c** above.

## Other Editions

New editions of the IGI are produced every few years to incorporate new material, and the above account is based on the 1988 edition. Earlier editions follow the same basic system, but there are differences of detail. It is always best to use the latest edition, which contains more material, and in the case of Wales the 1988 edition is far easier to use than any of its predecessors, so that the earlier versions should be avoided.

The CD-ROM version, initially, is based on the 1988 edition, and includes exactly the same material.

Future editions will undoubtedly see further changes. The compilers of the index are understood to be well aware of the problems associated with indexing Welsh names, and improvements can be anticipated, although some of the problems (eg, the 'dropping' of multiple names) cannot be cured without re-inputting large quantities of material, an expensive task which is unlikely to be undertaken.

The greatest improvement would certainly come if the Church in Wales could be persuaded to allow the Mormons access to the parish registers, and to microfilm them systematically, as has happened in many English dioceses, something which would be of benefit to all historians.

## The Compact Disc (CD-ROM) Edition

At the time of writing this is not available in the United Kingdom, and I have not been able to investigate its treatment of Welsh material. However, it uses the same database as the 1988 microfiche edition. Because of this, all I have said above about the treatment of Welsh names, and the contents of the index, must apply to it just as much as to the microfiche edition.

The difference is in the presentation of the material. It is accessed via a computer screen. All the IGI entries for Wales are held on a single compact disc.

The 'Birth and Marriage Index' displays the entries in a single alphabetical surname index, covering the whole of Wales. This is essentially the same as the Surname Index of the microfiche edition, and presumably contains the same fictitious surnames. With a common name, you will wish to narrow the field to a particular year, or to a particular locality or group of localities, and this can be done. A list can be displayed showing alternative surname spellings that could be searched, and the number of entries under each variant.

It is not clear from published material about the CD-ROM edition whether it can also be accessed by a Given Name Index, like the microfiche edition, or whether there are other means of searching for all children with a particular given name in a particular year or locality, regardless of surname.

A novel feature is the 'Parent Index'. This indexes all birth and baptism entries in alphabetical order of the father's name. For instance, entries where the father is 'John Thomas' will appear in the following order:

| *Parents* | *Child* | *Year* |
|---|---|---|
| Thomas, Jno/Mary | William Thomas | 1790 |
| Thomas, John | John Thomas | 1784 |
| Thomas, John | Christopher Thomas | 1790 |
| Thomas, John/Ann | Mary Thomas | 1785 |
| Thomas, John/Ann | Martha Thomas | 1786 |
| Thomas, John/Anne | Anne Thomas | 1784 |
| Thomas, John/Mary | John Thomas | 1789 |

The purpose of this is to enable family groups to be identified. For example, all children of John and Ann Thomas, even if baptised in diiferent parishes over a period of time, will appear in the same part of the index. Clearly, where the parents have common names, several different parishes over a period of time, will appear in the same part of unusual name is involved it should be relatively easy to identify a particular family.

This should be particularly useful for Welsh research, where it is almost impossible to put together pre-1813 family groups from the microfiche edition (see paragraph 3c in 'How to use the microfiche version' above). It also means, for example, that the entry for John, son of Thomas and Mary Deane, in 1812, quoted above can now be found under 'Deane', by using the Parent Index; and that it should at last be possible to use the pre-1813 Welsh IGI for One Name Studies.

The researcher using the compact disc version for the first time on

Welsh research would be well advised to get the measure of it first by trying to find an event known to be in the index, such as one of the examples quoted earlier in this chapter. This should help to understand it.

## Summary

This chapter has inevitably described the IGI in a rather detailed way. Do not be put off by this. The IGI for Wales will never be quite as easy to use as its English counterpart, but there is a mass of information in it, and it is not difficult to extract if you know how. There is no other source which provides such a ready means of tracing people who moved from one parish to another. For the microfiche edition, the basic method is very simple, and can be described in a single sentence. Use the surname index for births and baptisms from 1813 on, and for marriages at all times, but use the given names index for births and baptisms before 1813; and always try to check what you have found in the original Bishop's Transcript or register.

**Acknowledgements**

I must thank David Gardner and Geoffrey Mowlam, both of the Genealogical Society of Utah, the former for taking the trouble (some years ago) to explain to me how the index was compiled, and the latter (more recently) for providing me with general information on the CD-ROM edition. Needless to say, neither is responsible for any of the views expressed in this chapter, or for any errors or misapprehensions it may contain.

An earlier version of part of this chapter appeared in the Gwent Family History Society Journal in April 1982, and was later reprinted in an updated version in *Where to find the IGI*, edited by Jeremy Gibson and Michael Walcot and *The General Register Office and International Genealogical Indexes* edited by Jeremy Gibson (see Chapter 23 for details). These contain details of earlier editions of the IGI.

For general information about the IGI, reference should be made to the introductory fiches included in all sets of the IGI, and to articles by Alf Ison and Colin Atkinson reprinted in the two booklets mentioned above.

**Editorial note:** The 1992 edition of the IGI became available in the final stages of the production of this book, too late for the author to take account of it in his text. The CD-ROM version has also become available at several LDS Family History Centres in Britain.

# 11. Estate Records

David W. Howell

Large landed estates owned by aristocratic and gentry families were increasingly a feature of the Welsh countryside from late medieval times to the beginning of the present century. From the fifteenth century through to the seventeenth century there came about the gradual disintegration of the old tribal society and the adoption of primogeniture as the mode of inheritance of land, a process which facilitated the growth of large freehold estates owned by aristocratic and gentry families. The latter benefited in particular from the acquisition of Crown and monastic lands during the Tudor period. On the whole we can speak of a remarkable survival of old Welsh landed estates in the hands of the same families right down to the end of the nineteenth century, a feature remarked upon by the Welsh Land Commissioners of the 1890s.[1] Nevertheless, certain forces were at work which saw changes in the distribution of landownership and which affected the fortunes of individual families and perhaps whole sub-groups of landowners, like great landlords, esquires and lesser gentry. Our concern in the first part of this chapter is to trace, however crudely, the survival and organisation of the landed estates from the mid-seventeenth century onwards so that in the later stages we can more meaningfully assess the value of estate records for the family historian.

The Civil War of the mid-seventeenth century witnessed no thoroughgoing break-up of Welsh estates and redistribution of land nor a general extinction of the old county families. Although many Welsh royalist landowners were financially embarrassed by having to pay a fine to compound for their delinquency, by the extra burden of taxation levied by King and Parliament alike and by their tenants' failure to meet their rents, most managed to stave off sales. True enough, a few royalist lands were sold and such land entering the market led to the founding of new families as well as the enlargement of the patrimonies of existing ones: Colonel Philip Jones and his 'creatures' built up estates in south Wales while, in the north, parliamentary men like George Twistleton, Colonel John Carter, John Glynne, Colonel John Jones, and John Peck bought royalist lands. Some families, too, had so mortgaged their lands in the 1660s and 1670s as a direct consequence of Civil War debts that they had finally to sell out. Such casualties included the royalists Colonel Edward Lloyd of Llanforda (Denbighshire), whose estate was sold by his son to Sir William Williams in 1676, Bevis Lloyd of Carreg y Pennill (Denbighshire), who sold out to Chirk Castle in 1672, and Captain Ellis Sutton of Gwersyllt Issa (Flintshire), who sold out in or before 1684 to Sir Jeffrey Shakerley, a former royalist officer.[2]

## Growth by Marriage and Inheritance

Although from the late seventeenth century down to the mid-eighteenth century there was to occur no marked decline of the small estates belonging to the lesser gentry and freeholders, such as Prof. Habakkuk saw occurring in certain Midland counties of England where small estates were swallowed up by the large 'Leviathans',[3] there is no mistaking the relatively faster growth of the large estates in Wales over those years. One major factor in estate compilation throughout the earlier centuries was marriage to heiresses, and the years of the late seventeenth and early eighteenth centuries saw such marriages play an unusually crucial role, given the high level of failure of male heirs within all ranks of landed society in a large number of Welsh counties—Anglesey, Merioneth, Glamorgan, Breconshire, Montgomeryshire, Pembrokeshire and Carmarthenshire—as in English shires.[4] It meant that landowning families of all ranks rose in the landed hierarchy through carrying off heiresses, but there is no mistaking the superior advantage of the large owners in procuring the wealthiest heiresses. The Kilgetty estate came into Picton Castle's (Pembrokeshire) possession in 1685 through the marriage of Edward Philipps with its heiress Elizabeth Cannon.[5] In 1675 Sir John Wynn, 5th Baronet of Gwydir, married Jane, heiress of Watstay, and upon acquiring the estate he renamed it Wynnstay. Sir William Williams, 1st Baronet, (d.1700), besides inheriting the Chwaen Isaf estate and, as shown (see Fig 11-1), purchasing Llanforda from Edward Lloyd, acquired the Glascoed estate through his marriage with Margaret, daughter and co-heiress of Watkin Kyffin of Glascoed, Llansilin. Sir William Williams, 2nd Baronet, of Llanforda came by Plas y Ward through marrying Jane Thelwall, its heiress, and their son Sir Watkin Williams Wynn, 3rd Baronet, of Llanforda, succeeded to Wynnstay under the will of Sir John Wynn, Baronet, and assumed the surname of Wynn. He married in 1715 Anne, daughter and heiress of Edward Vaughan of Llwydiarth, and this union brought to the Wynnstay estate the combined properties of Glanllyn,

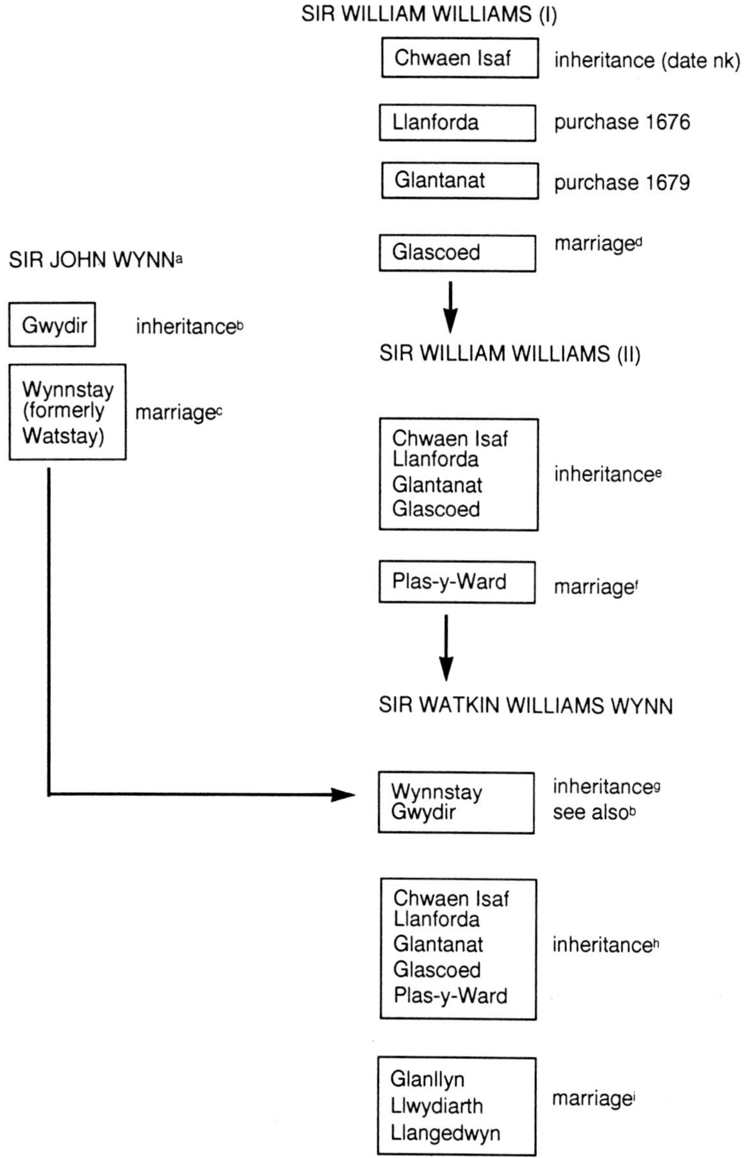


Fig. 11-1: Formation of the Wynnstay Estate c.1500-1740

Notes to Fig. 11-1

[a]5th and last Baronet of the direct Gwydir line; died 1719, aged 91.

[b]In 1674 after successive inheritance following a purchase by his great-great-grandfather (Meredydd of Cwm Penanmaen) who died in 1525. It should be noted, however, that the bulk of the Gwydir Estate went to the Duke of Ancaster by his marriage to Mary, sole heiress of Sir Richard Wynn (4th Baronet).

[c]By virtue of his marriage in 1675 to the heiress of Eyton Evans of Watstay.

[d]By virtue of his marriage in 1664 to Margaret, daughter and co-heiress of Watkin Kyffin of Glascoed.

[e]On the death of his father in 1700.

[f]By virtue of his marriage in 1684 to Jane, daughter and co-heiress of Edward Thelwall of Plas-y-Ward and great grand-daughter of Sir John Wynn of Gwydir.

[g]In 1719 after his cousin, Sir John Wynn of Gwydir. On taking the Baronetcy he assumed the additional surname and arms of Wynn.

[h]On the death of his father in 1740.

[i]By virtue of his marriage in 1715 to Ann, daughter and heiress of Edward Vaughan of Llwydiarth and Llangedwyn.

Llwydiarth and Llangedwyn. The Wynnstay estate by now had grown into a mammoth-like sprawl of properties across the counties of north Wales yielding a annual rental approaching £20,000.[6]

In Carmarthenshire, the Stepneys of Llanelli made good marriages; Sir John, 6th Baronet, married Eleanor, daughter and heiress of John Lloyd, Esquire, of Llangennech, while his son, Sir Thomas, 7th Baronet, became betrothed in 1741 to Elizabeth Eleonora Lloyd, heiress of Derwydd and part of Derllys. In 1751 Richard Vaughan of Golden Grove (who had in the scheming mind of the childless Ann Vaughan of Golden Grove been intended for the aforementioned Elizabeth Eleonora Lloyd but to no avail) married his second cousin Margaret Elizabeth, sole child and heiress of Charles Phillips of Llandybie, Llettygariad and Bremenda.[7]

One of the foremost early eighteenth-century Pembrokeshire families was the Campbells of Stackpole Court, a Scottish family who had acquired the estate at the close of the seventeenth century through the marriage of Sir Alexander Campbell of Cawdor, in Nairnshire, with the heiress of the Lorts of Stackpole. In 1725 John Campbell married Mary Pryse of Aberllefenni (Merionethshire), a match which brought to the Stackpole estate lands in Merionethshire, Montgomeryshire and Cardiganshire. In 1743 Thomas Pryse of Gogerddan (Cardiganshire), M.P., married Maria Charlotte, heiress of Rowland Pugh of Mathafarn (Montgomeryshire) and Rûg (Merionethshire). As a final example, George Rice of Newton (Dynevor), (Carmarthenshire), married in 1756 Hon. Cecil Talbot, daughter and only child of 2nd Lord Talbot of Hensol (Glamorgan).[8]

As mentioned, marriage-related inheritance did not only benefit the large owners in these years down to the mid-eighteenth century. Although the latter got the pick of the choicest heiresses, lesser landed families made good marriages and expanded their estates through such 'property deals'. In Carmarthenshire, the Gwynnes of Gwempa acquired Middleton Hall (Carmarthenshire), the Lloyds of Pantgilgane got Mountain Hall (Carmarthenshire), and the Lewises of Llysnewydd came by Colebrook (Carmarthenshire). Likewise in Cardiganshire, the Lloyds of Bronwydd acquired Penpedwast and Henllys (Pembrokeshire), the Johnes of Llanfair Clydogau got Hafod (Cardiganshire), the Lloyds of Ffosybleiddiaid came by Mabws and Ystrad Teilo (Cardiganshire), the Hughes of Hendrefelin acquired Aberllolwyn (Cardiganshire) and the Lloyds of Castell Hywel absorbed Crynfryn (Cardiganshire).[9]

A number of Welsh landed families also acquired property via indirect inheritance when, in the absence of direct male and, often, female heirs, property was devised to collateral relatives or friends: in so far as the large estates were concerned, we have seen how Watkin Williams, 3rd Baronet of Llanforda, succeeded to the seat of Wynnstay and other estates under the will of his kinsman Sir John Wynn, Baronet, in 1719; the Campbells of Stackpole unexpectedly came into possession of the Carmarthenshire Golden Grove estate upon the death of John Vaughan in 1804 under the terms of his will of 1786, and the Campbells thereby became the largest territorial magnates in west Wales.[10] A number of lesser families, likewise by sheer good fortune, were changed into owners of consequence: to cite but one example, in 1721 Richard Jones of Tregib (Carmarthenshire) inherited Taliaris in the same county from his great-uncle, David Gwynne.[11] We emphasise that, with female and indirect inheritance occurring from the late seventeenth to the mid-eighteenth century to such a significant degree, there were fewer estates and landed families in the 1760s than in 1700 and the average size of estates increased.

## Growth by Purchase

Besides marriage and inheritance, land changed hands through sales and purchase. Once again, large owners were in the best position to snap up properties of lesser gentry and small freeholders entering the market from the 1660s to the 1750s (owing to the burdensome land tax between 1692 and 1715 and to adverse economic conditions in the form of low agricultural prices and sluggish rents). And if the amount of property coming up for sale was greater in the early eighteenth century than in its later decades, there was still plenty of land up for sale in the late eighteenth century owing to the discomfiture of small owners arising from war-time taxation (the Seven Years' War, the War of American Independence and the French Wars at the close of the century) and the higher standard of living. Moreover, a number of large estates (mostly in part) were to enter the market from mid-century, so that the ability of large owners to hold on to land through elaborate strict settlements, easy availability of mortgages at low interest and also because of rising rents from the 1760s was not as effective in warding off sales as Prof. Habakkuk claimed.[12]

A large proportion of land up for sale was bought by wealthy landowners. A survey of the lordship of Ruthin (Denbighshire) observed: 'At the time of Richard Myddelton [d.1716] most of the freeholds of this lordship have gone into the hands of great men.'[13] Thomas Pennant mentioned 35 deserted seats in Merioneth in the early 1770s, 'most of them,' he observed, 'now swallowed up by our Welsh Leviathans'.[14] William Williams, a Caernarfonshire land surveyor, reflected in 1806:

> How melancholy it is to observe the immense number of withered mansions we meet in these countries (*sic*) where, in the past and better times opulency, hospitality and good neighbourhood dwelt and cheered the drooping spirit of the indigent . . . Now these adored residences have disappeared; harassed and oppressed annual lodgers are the present inmates . . . All those venerable habitations have sunk by marriages, purchases and etc. into one irrecoverable gulph; their possessors strangers, and those of opulency gone to enjoy themselves in the town.[15]

Around the same time Richard Fenton similarly observed of north Pembrokeshire:

> . . . like the vale of Llanstinan, in the vale of Trewern you meet at every mile a mansion degradingly altered, deserted or in ruins . . . which within the last century was the rendezvous of beauty, wit and festivity.[16]

Examples of great landlords who purchased small estates in their respective localities include Sir Edward Mansel of Margam (Glamorgan) between the 1660s and 1690s, the Wynns of Wynnstay (Denbighshire), the Myddeltons of Chirk (Denbighshire), the Bulkeleys of Baron Hill, the Baylys of Plas Newydd and the Meyricks of Bodorgan (Anglesey), the Philippses of Picton Castle and the Owens of Orielton (Pembrokeshire), the Vaughans of Crosswood (Cardiganshire) and the

Vaughans of Golden Grove (Carmarthenshire).[17] Thus Chirk Castle purchased Plas Is-clawdd in 1668, Ty Ucha in Llangollen Vechan in 1714, Issa Coed in 1724 and Lloyd of Ashton's Foxhall and Denbighshire estates in 1734.[18] In Pembrokeshire, the Philippses of Picton Castle purchased around mid-eighteenth century the estate of the Wheelers, part of Haroldston, the estate of Mr Summers of Haverfordwest and, in 1762, lands in Carew parish belonging to the financially embarrassed John Powell Cuny for £530. Viscount Lisburne extended his Crosswood estate in Cardiganshire between 1759 and 1795 by purchasing 16 properties costing just over £17,000. John Vaughan of Golden Grove purchased the Gellydywyll estate (Carmarthenshire) in 1778 and the moiety of Piode in Llandybie parish from the collapsing Morgan Gwyn Davies of Cwm.[19] In 1676 Sir William Williams, 1st Baronet of Llanforda (d.1700), purchased Llanforda and in 1679 he bought the Glantanat estate.[20] Sometimes, such purchases ruinously overstretched a family's resources. Instance the Campbells of Stackpole Court (Pembrokeshire): their financial position, already shaky, was worsened upon the purchase of the Bangeston estate (Pembrokeshire) in 1786 for £52,318 and of part of the encumbered Wiston estate in 1793 for £38,000. Such was his financial plight that Lord Cawdor of Stackpole was obliged to sell 10,000 acres in south-west Wales in 1802, the sale realising £123,900.[21]

Not only large owners purchased. Examples of south-west Walian squires, for instance, who were purchasers in the eighteenth century are numerous. In 1750 Thomas Lloyd of Bronwydd (Cardiganshire) bought for £2,000 the encumbered estate of John Laugharne, Esquire, of Llanrheithan (Pembrokeshire). In 1787, Thomas Lloyd, referring to his father's purchase, reflected: 'It was the ambition of the Day to covet many acres not to cultivate the few'.[22] In like manner, John Colby of Ffynone (Pembrokeshire) bought part of the encumbered Vaynor estate in 1787 for £4,202 and George Bowen of Llwyngwair (Pembrokeshire) was purchasing lands in the north of the county between the 1750s and the 1770s.[23]

By the end of the eighteenth century the large estates had grown ever more extensive at the expense of lesser properties, though we stress that there was no radical dispossession of the lesser gentry and freeholders at the bottom of the landed hierarchy. Moving into the nineteenth century, it is impossible to make a general statement about the changing distribution of landownership within the Principality. It seems, however, that a large proportion of the landowning families and estates of gentry and aristocratic status that were already established in the early 1800s were also to be listed in the Returns of the 'Second Domesday Book' of 1872-73. If we look at Caernarfonshire, then we see that of the 12 principal estates there in 1815 just two had been broken up by the 1890s.[24] Of course, land was changing hands consequent upon the very vagaries of human experience. In particular, for various reasons, (but especially the fall in prices after 1814), small owner-occupiers of freeholds of anything up to a 100 acres or so were forced to sell out in the early nineteenth century. Once again, their lands were usually snapped up by the neighbouring aristocratic and gentry families, a tendency which further concentrated landownership. Thus it was observed in 1882:

> Yet there is no part of the Kingdom in which small properties have been more extensively absorbed by the large landowners. The class of small Welsh owners who were numerous enough 100 years ago is comparatively limited now.[25]

Dr Cragoe has looked in detail at the Cawdor estate in Carmarthenshire (which came to the family in 1804, as we have shown) and observes: 'Right up to the 1880s they were keen to buy farms or small estates which abutted or intermingled with their existing holdings'. Indeed, he estimates that the Cawdor property in Carmarthenshire grew from around 35,000 to 50,000 acres across the nineteenth century.[26] The tendency from the late seventeenth century had been in the direction of the enlargement of estates so that in the 1870s Wales was essentially a country of large estates in the possession of a small number of landowners, estates of over 1,000 acres covering 60 percent of the total land area of the Principality.

## The Decline of Large Estates

These estates began to disintegrate from the 1870s consequent upon the selling off of outlying parts of the large estates. The extension of the franchise after 1867 weakened the political influence bestowed by landownership and outlying parts of estates were sold, too, because they were costly to manage. Despite agricultural depression from the late 1870s, in Wales (unlike England) pressure for land kept up capital values and so land was continually being sold, usually to tenants whose remarkable attachment to their holdings made them anxious to purchase. Sales of estates noticeably quickened after 1910, the impulse to sell arising partly out of fear of Lloyd George's proposed land taxes and, more importantly, because of the decline of status conferred by land ownership, particularly within a radical nonconformist Welsh social context. Disintegration of estates reached a dramatic level only from 1918, many owners now being heavily in debt. They could take advantage not only of the higher prices prevailing but also, as we have mentioned, of their tenants' anxiety to purchase their farms.[27] The *Montgomeryshire Express* remarked on 21 October 1919: 'Little short of an agrarian revolution is being witnessed in central Wales, where large tracts of territory are continually tumbling into the market'.

## Estate Administration and Records

Estates were mostly let out to tenant farmers, the landlords retaining in their own hands only a small home farm. During the course of the eighteenth century Welsh estate administration was rationalised and placed on a more organised footing so that landlords could make the most of their property. Sometimes stewards trained in the new techniques of management were appointed, but generally landowners, or their London accountants, endeavoured to instruct their stewards in the stricter methods coming into vogue at this time. In so far as rentals, among the whole range of estate records, are beyond question the most useful source for the family historian, the greater efficiency shown in drawing up rentals from the early eighteenth century on the part of stewards or agents is a vital factor for our consideration. John Vaughan of Golden Grove, pleased with the accurate accounting of Arthur Price, steward there between 1714 and the 1740s, and likewise with the accounts of John Phillips and Erasmus Saunders in the 1750s, harangued his chief agent, Lewis Lewis, in early 1756:

> I desire you'll be very exact now in your rent roll, to put everything down, I mean *the names of the old tenants, the tenements, the present tenants*, the old rents and improved rents now, in different columns with your observations, and the real value now according to the plan I sent you some time ago . . . I am surprised you will not do things methodically according to the plan I sent you which is the method used in passing accounts before Masters in Chancery, and with every agent but you.[28]

Similarly, James Lewes, Esquire, of the Gellydywyll estate (Carmarthenshire), chief agent to Thomas Pryse of Gogerddan (Cardiganshire), informed his employer in 1744 of the unsatisfactory work done by Evan Williams, a rent receiver:

> As I find Evan Williams is uneasy at the letter you wrote him on the subject of his accounting, I intend summoning him hither next week to set about the work. I am told that he intimates as if he was long since ready and willing but I give you my word that I never found him prepared to enter a point in a regular manner, for without a regular rental I am sure no manifest fair work can be done.[29]

It is stressed that this keeping of more regular accounts was a feature of the large estates. It is thus on these estates that we find the best runs of rentals, some large estate collections, indeed, having uninterrupted runs of rentals from some period in the eighteenth century down to the time of their disintegration early in this century.

Of crucial importance for the family historian, too, is the fact that on Welsh estates, particularly the large ones, families were often permitted to stay from generation to generation on the same holding, even when tenancy from year to year set in at different times from the end of the eighteenth century. It was stated of the Wynnstay estate before the Land Commission of the 1890s:

> The custom of continuous family succession in tenancy has always been a predominant feature of this estate. When there is a member of the family eligible to succeed, the preference is given to him or her ungrudgingly, and I cannot record any case where the widow was not allowed to succeed her deceased husband if she so wished, or, failing her, the son or other near relative.[30]

The continuity of tenancy, continued the agent, was particularly a feature among the Welsh-speaking tenants on the estate, 'who take as much pride in their heritage as if they were fee-simple owners of their holdings'.

Evidence for individual families residing long periods of a hundred up to three hundred years and more on the various Wynnstay estates was provided by the agent. The Land Commissioners heard evidence for other large estates concerning the continuance on farms by the same families. Thus Colonel W.E. Sackville West testified that on the Penrhyn estate (Caernarfonshire) about 167 farms had been held by the same families for 50 years or more. Similarly, Lord Stanley of Alderley provided an exact list of tenants' names, the tenancies they held and for how long they and their ancestors had resided on his Anglesey estate; some went back for over 50 years, a few for over 70 years. Out of 751 holdings on the Montgomeryshire estate of Lord Powis, 49 had been in the same family for 50-60 years, 50 for 60-70 years, 39 for 70-80 years,

22 for 80-90 years, 21 for 90-100 years, 46 for 100-110 years and 76 for periods of above 110 years.[31]

Furthermore, even if families did not always remain from generation to generation on the same holding it was frequently the case that they continued as tenants on the same estate. Dr. David Jenkins has shown for south Cardiganshire how the movement of a family between different size farms was a crucial way in which the change in size and requirements of the family over time were accommodated to the needs of the farm. The farmer was identified in the community mainly through membership of a particular kin group, and a vital role of kinship was its facilitating such family movements between farms of different sizes.[32] This was done, of course, with the co-operation of the landlord. Moreover, in difficult times of farming depression Wynnstay (and perhaps other estates) permitted failing tenants to move to smaller holdings on the estate.[33] We have mentioned the importance of kinship, and it was indeed the case that through intermarriage of families, some Welsh estates were virtually in the occupation of one family. John Gibson observed in 1879:

> These intermarriages go on from generation to generation and owners of estates in Wales, rather than rudely break up these clans, put up with the losses and inconveniences of a low state of cultivation.[34]

So the family historian may well find that even if one particular holding is suddenly vacated by a member of his family, then there is a good chance that the person concerned might be found farming another holding on the same estate.

The various collections of the large estates house valuable runs of rentals which can be of great use to the family historian. Of course, there will have to be previous research undertaken so that some sort of connection can be made between a particular farmer and a landed estate. If we know what unit of land our person farmed at the time of the tithe legislation of the 1830s then, by looking at the tithe maps, it will be possible to identify which estate owned it. Having once established a connection between a person and a farm on a certain estate, then the estate rentals may well provide a quick return, for the long runs of such rentals on many of the large estates will enable the searcher to identify quickly the farm holding and the name of the tenant in a particular year. We have thus been able by using this source to tie the man or woman concerned to a particular named tenement and so we can distinguish that person from others of the same name in the parish or locality. If successful in this first aim of pinpointing the tenant and his holding, the yearly runs of rentals will further allow us to find out when the tenant first came into the farm and who he succeeded and also when he left and who followed him as tenant. As we have stressed, the custom of continuous family succession in tenancy may well enable the searcher to discover names of his subject's relations, when they came and went, presumably 'leaving' when they died.

The best-organised series of rentals at the National Library of Wales is that for the huge Wynnstay estate and it can be fully utilised by working from the excellent volume: 'Rentals and Accounts' of the Schedule of Wynnstay Archives, 1980. In the words of the compilers, A.J. Roberts and G.C.G. Thomas, 'The rentals are preserved in an almost unbroken series from the time of Sir William Williams, 1st Baronet,(d.1700)'. The estate, we have discovered, comprised a big group of different estates that came together via marriage, inheritance and purchase (See Fig. 11-1). What the compilers of the rental archive have done is to describe the rentals twice over, so easing our working on the rentals in order to discover a known property and to trace it through successive rentals. To quote them again: 'For the searcher who wishes to trace a given property, or to find out what property Wynnstay owned in a given parish, or whether a person known to be living in a given parish was a Wynnstay tenant, an analytical list of rentals is provided, pp.37ff. In the analytical list, the separate estates or collections which made up the Wynnstay estate at different periods are isolated and the location of all their surviving rentals is given'.

If Wynnstay is a model carefully planned by the staff of the National Library, other large estate collections there, too, boast valuable runs of rentals, notably those of Powis Castle, Chirk Castle, Tredegar Park, Nanteos, Dunraven, Gogerddan and Picton Castle. Thus the Nanteos estate has good runs of rentals from 1771 down to the early 1920s; the Picton Castle archive houses rentals from 1710 onwards through the eighteenth and nineteenth centuries; and the rentals for the Powis Castle estate begin in 1745 and continue through to 1927. In like manner, local county record offices contain important estate collections, not least the marvellous Cawdor/Vaughan collection at Carmarthen Record Office. Rentals are a valuable item of this last archive, comprising different collections like those of Llanarthney, Llandovery, and Llandeilo and Llandybie with their long runs of years.

Rentals of Chief Rents owed to a lord of the manor can serve a similar purpose as estate rentals; they, too, enable the searcher to identify a

Fig. 11-2: Wynnstay, Denbighshire

By permission of the National Library of Wales

person with a particular place and, if a good run of such rentals exists, to ascertain any changes in his or her position. However, rentals containing Chief Rents are much rarer; they are, of course, tied into the manorial economy and the latter was mainly a feature of areas like Montgomeryshire, the border marches, Monmouthshire, Glamorgan and south Pembrokeshire, being absent in the area of the old Principality of 'Welsh' Wales. To take but a couple of examples, the Wynnstay estate records carry an excellent run of Chief Rents of the manor of Cyfeiliog (Montgomeryshire) payable to the owner of the Wynnstay estate, and the Powis Castle collection likewise has a rich treasure of manorial records for Montgomeryshire: tenants' names and the tenements they held in the different parishes and townships are all included in these lists of Chief Rents so that a particular person can be tracked down fairly quickly.[35]

## Leases

If rentals are the most valuable item for the family historian contained in estate collections, other types of document are also helpful. Leases can be an important follow-up to rentals. Whereas leases for lives were disappearing from counties in north Wales from the end of the eighteenth century, in south Wales, according to Walter Davies in 1814, such leases were much more widespread.[36] Indeed, as late as 1849 leases for lives were still often granted to tenants in the south-western counties of Wales, although by mid-century throughout Wales the usual tenancy was from year to year.[37] Leases for lives can fill out the information contained in rentals, providing as they do the names of the lives in the two—or three—life lease and these, crucially for the family historian, were usually those of the wife and children or other relatives, such as nephews and uncles. Certain large estate collections will, conveniently, provide a schedule of leases: thus in the Cawdor/Vaughan collection (MS 103/8057) there is an 'Old Rental' covering the parishes of St.Ishmaels, Llangendeyrn and Kidwelly which provides details of early eighteenth-century leases with the names of the lives, and similarly, MS 103/8056 of the collection comprises a 'Schedule of Leases of the Golden Grove Estate in the years 175 (*sic*)' which relates to the late seventeenth and early eighteenth century; again, in the Picton Castle estate collection there are a number of separate schedules of leases ranging over the eighteenth and nineteenth centuries.[38]

## Estate Surveys

Other estate records can also assist the family historian, providing as they do a name, a date and a location, the three essential pieces of information in this field of historical inquiry. Thus estate surveys are useful documents and the family historian is lucky once again, as with rental compilation, that the drive towards improvement in estate administration led to a crop of estate surveys being carried out in the late eighteenth century. Specialist surveyors and cartographers were hired to undertake this work.[39] A good example of a Pembrokeshire estate survey is that relating to the estate of Harcourt Powell drawn up in 1778, a survey which provided the names of the tenants of each holding.[40] Akin to the estate survey are the 'particulars' of estates up for sale from the eighteenth century onwards. For example, in the Pembrokeshire County Library, Haverfordwest, there is a document entitled 'Particulars of the Llanstinan, Martel and Ford Estates in co. Pembs.' which, although undated, relates to the early 1780s and contains a list of the farms in their respective parishes, the tenants' names, the rents and the terms of the leases. From the opening years of this century there are available the sale catalogues relating to the break up of the landed estates. There are many such catalogues at the National Library of Wales, as for example those of the Buckland, Kinmel and Crosswood estates, and they provide the names of the tenements and the tenants.

## Other Sources

Another source for the family historian among the estate archives is the marriage settlement and other forms of settlement. Such settlements will name the living descendants who are meant to inherit. Marriage settlements occurred widely among landowning families and an index is available of those settlements contained in the various estate archives housed at the National Library of Wales. Wills are another form of settlement and these, too, are to be found among estate records. Marriage settlements and wills were the two common means by which descent of land was fixed in advance and these are considered in detail in a separate chapter.

We have already seen how estate collections contain manorial Chief Rents. Manorial records housed in the different estate collections will also provide names of resident freeholders and of tenants of the non-resident ones who were fit to serve on juries at the leet court of the manor. Thus in the Cawdor/Vaughan estate collection there is 'A true list of all the names of the landlords, tenements and tenants within the parish of Abernant, May 1, 1767' from which the jury at the court leet of the manor of Elvet (Carmarthenshire) could be drawn. A similar list is provided for the parish of Trelech-ar-Bettws, 18 April 1762, appertaining to jury service at the same manor court of Elvet.[41] So, once again, the family historian is provided with names, precise locations and a date.

Leases have already been discussed as an important supplement to rentals. Another form of title deed was the 'Abstract of Title' of a landowner to a particular property he has acquired, which includes details of the land like names of the previous owner, the date of transfer and the precise location.

So far, nothing has been said of the value of estate records for revealing information about landless people. Once again, it was the large estate with its more organised administration which kept detailed home farm accounts. Account books of servants' wages paid by the year are available in many estate collections; a good example is the 'Account Book of Servants' Wages at Mostyn, 1737-1782' housed in the Mostyn papers at the Library of the University College of North Wales, Bangor.[42] Mostyn servants, whose individual names and type of employment are entered, continued in service at the mansion and its home farm over a run of years, a few like William Lloyd, 3rd husbandman, and John Roberts, stable boy and then head groom, for up to nine or 10 years, so that the family historian can keep a certain individual in focus over a short period of time. Numbers employed at the mansion and home farm varied over the years: in 1767, 18; in 1768, 23; and in 1774, 25. In addition, home farm accounts carry weekly accounts of labourers working by the day on the home farm. For example, the Nanteos (Cardiganshire) estate collection contains a broken run of home farm labourers' wages: between 5 and 11 March 1832 there were in all some 47 different people working (ten of whom were females), some up to six days, others just for one. Their names and occupations like carpenter, gardener, carter or simply 'labourer' are provided. If we look at the Nanteos Labourers' Account for 16 to 22 March 1840 we find that in some instances the same names as those in the 1832 Account are listed, such as John Morris, carpenter, John Samuel, gardener, John Walters and Isaac Bonsall, labourers.[43] Of course, the fact that these individuals were not associated with a specific property on a one-to-one basis as a farmer with a farmholding means that any attempt at identifying them and then, perhaps, tracing them over a run of years, is less easily done, particularly when we bear in mind the serious problem posed by commonality of surnames in Wales.

## In Conclusion

Estate records can be of great use to the family historian, especially rentals and leases. Names, places and dates are available, and such data are particularly valuable in the years before the Census Returns starting in 1841. However, we must end on a cautious note; the family historian will need some luck if he or she is going to benefit from estate collections, for records are likely to have survived in a systematic, extensive form only for the large properties. Although such estates had grown larger over the course of the eighteenth century, it was nevertheless the case that in the 1870s large estates, covering upwards of 3,000 acres, occupied just over 44 per cent of the total area (excluding waste) of the Principality.[44]

### Acknowledgements

I have received generous advice and information in writing this chapter from Mr Daniel Huws, Mr R.W.MacDonald and Mr Alwyn Roberts of the Department of Manuscripts, National Library of Wales, and Mr Clive Hughes, Pembrokeshire Archivist.

## NOTES TO CHAPTER 11

[1]*Report of the Royal Commission on Land in Wales and Monmouthshire.*, P.P., xxxiv (1896), p.238.

[2]D.W.Howell, 'Landlords and Estate Management in Wales' in J.Thirsk, ed., *The Agrarian History of England and Wales*, vol.V.ii, *1640-1750: Agrarian Change*, (Cambridge University Press, 1985), pp.254-8.

[3]H.J.Habakkuk, 'English Landownership, 1680-1740', *Econ. Hist. Rev.*, x (1940).

[4]D.W.Howell, 'Landlords and Estate Management in Wales', see 2 above, pp.259-60.

[5]NLW, Picton Castle papers: marriage settlement of 1685.

[6]For a pedigree to show the descent of the Wynnstay estates see NLW, Schedule of Wynnstay Archives, 1980, vol. i: Rentals and Accounts; P.R.Roberts, 'The Decline of the Welsh Squires in the Eighteenth Century', *NLW Jnl.*, 13 (1963-4), p.163.

[7]D.W.Howell, *Patriarchs and Parasites: The Gentry of South-West Wales in the Eighteenth Century*, (Cardiff: UWP, 1986), pp.20-1.

[8]NLW, Derry Ormond MS 16; P.R.Roberts, 'The Decline of the Welsh Squires in the Eighteenth Century', see 6 above, p.170; T.M.Humphreys, 'Rural Society in Montgomeryshire in the Eighteenth Century' (Unpublished Ph.D. thesis, University of Wales, 1982), p.62; W.R.Williams, *The parliamentary history of the principality of Wales*, (Brecknock, 1895), pp.47-8, 100; J.O.Martin, 'The Landed Estate in Glamorgan, *circa* 1660-1760' (unpublished Ph.D. thesis, Cambridge University, 1978), p.304.

[9]D.W.Howell, *Patriarchs and Parasites*, see 7 above, p.26.

[10]D.Williams, *The Rebecca Riots*, (Cardiff: UWP, 1955), pp.5-6.

[11]F.Jones, 'Taliaris', *Arch. Camb.*, ccvii (1968), pp.160-1.

[12]D.W.Howell, *Patriarchs and Parasites*, see 7 above, pp.32-9.

[13]NLW, Ruthin MS 2084.

[14]NLW, NLW MS 2352 B, fo. 28, cited in F. Jones, 'An Approach to Welsh Genealogy', *Trans. Cymm*, (1948), p.430.

[15]NLW, NLW MS 821: Survey of Caernarvonshire.

[16]R.Fenton, *A historical tour through Pembrokeshire*, (London, 1811), p.558.

[17]D.W.Howell, 'Landlords and Estate Management in Wales', see 2 above, p.263.

[18]NLW, Chirk Castle MSS F. 10,166, E. 395(i), E. 3236; W.M.Myddelton, ed., *Chirk Castle Accounts, 1666-1753* (Manchester, 1931), pp.56-7, 127, 133.

[19]D.W.Howell, *Patriarchs and Parasites*, see 7 above, pp.40-1.

[20]NLW, Schedule of Wynnstay Archives, 1980, vol. i: Rentals and Accounts, pp.56-7.

[21]Carmarthen R.O., Cawdor/Campbell MSS, boxes 234 and 253; Cawdor MSS box 2/68.

[22]NLW, Bronwydd MS 5016.

[23]NLW, Williams and Williams MS 7417; Owen and Colby MSS 254, 1101; Llwyngwair MS 858; F.Jones, 'Pentre Ifan and Llwyngwair', *Pembs. Histn*, no.6 (1979), pp.48-9.

[24]*Report of the Royal Commission on Land in Wales and Monmouthshire*, p.238; D.W.Howell, *Land and People in Nineteenth-Century Wales*. (London: Routledge & Kegan Paul, 1978), pp.23-4.

[25]*Select Committee on Agriculture*, Parliamentary Papers, v (1833), Evidence, Q. 5821; Royal Commission on Agriculture, Parliamentary Papers, xv (1882), *Report*, p.7.

[26]Mathew Cragoe, 'The Tory and Anglican Gap in Welsh Historiography: The case of Carmarthenshire, 1832-1885', (unpublished D.Phil. thesis, Oxford University, 1991), pp.32-3.

[27]J.Davies, 'The End of the Great Estates and the Rise of Freehold Farming in Wales', *The Welsh History Review*, vol.7, no.2 (1974), pp.186-212. J.H.Davies 'The Social Structure and Economy of South-West Wales in the Late Nineteenth Century' (unpublished M.A. thesis, University of Wales, 1967), p.154.

[28]Carmarthen R.O., Cawdor/Vaughan MS102/8029: letter of 21 Feb. 1756, (author's italics).

[29]NLW, *Gogerddan* MSS.

[30]*Royal Commission on Agriculture in Wales and Monmouthshire*, Parliamentary Papers, xli (1895), Q. 70, 030.

[31]J.E.Vincent, *The Land Question in North Wales* (London: 1896), pp.160-70.

[32]David Jenkins, *The Agricultural Community of South-West Wales at the turn of the Twentieth Century* (Cardiff: UWP, 1971), pp.176-77.

[33]D.W. Howell, *Land and People in Nineteenth-Century Wales*, see 24 above, p.62.

[34]John Gibson, *Agriculture in Wales*, (London: Hodder & Stoughton, 1979), p.5.

[35]For example, Wynnstay R.76: 'W.W.W. Rental, 1821'.

[36]W.Davies, *Agriculture of South Wales*, (London: 1814), vol.i, pp.170-3.

[37]*Report of the Royal Commission on Land in Wales and Monmouthshire*, p.281.

[38]NLW, Picton Castle MSS 1074-1091, 1141-5, 1263-75, 1276-1283, 1284-1288, 1289-1322, 1750, 1887-1889.

[39]M.C.S.Evans, 'The Pioneers of Estate Mapping in Carmarthenshire', *The Carmarthenshire Antiquary*, xiii (1977), pp.52-64.

[40]The survey of the Greenhill estate of Harcourt Powell is housed at the Pembrokeshire county library, Haverfordwest; see also Carmarthen R.O., Cwmgwili MS 223 for mention of Richard Jones' survey of Cwmgwili in the mid 1780s.

[41]Carmarthen R.O., Cawdor/Vaughan MSS Box 64/6611.

[42]University College of North Wales, Bangor, Mostyn MS 6508.

[43]For example, Nanteos MSS A.14, A.29, A.32, A.33, A.39, A.43 and A.44; see also NLW, Picton Castle MSS 1854: List of labourers and their families employed at Picton Castle, 16 December 1823.

[44]For a break-down county by county of such a coverage of the large estates see D.W.Howell, *Land and People in Nineteenth-Century Wales*, see 24 above, pp.20-3.

# 12. Maritime Records

Lewis Lloyd

## The Emergence of 'Maritime Wales'

An extensive coastline of seven to eight hundred miles and a mountainous or corrugated hinterland ensured the importance if not the primacy of sea communications in the lives of the inhabitants of Wales and, not least, an intricate relationship with the people of Britain's sister isle of Ireland to unremembered times.

Apart from the maritime significance of the sites of chambered tombs, enclosed hut circles, Iron Age hill forts and early Christian enclosures (**llannau**), evidence of seafaring during the Dark Ages and mediaeval times is, as one might expect, scanty and unreliable. However, bardic references and persistent legends do afford glimpses at aspects of a largely unknowable past.

The first hard evidence of what may be called 'Maritime Wales' comes from the Tudor period when the 'dominion' or colony of Wales (with parts of the Marches) was progressively annexed to the English realm from 1536 to 1543. The Tudors and their officials recognised the importance of maritime trade and sea power in what was generally a stable and expansive period. In the 1560s, Wales was brought within the ambit of the English customs system with the immediate object of the suppression of piracy in the Bristol Channel and elsewhere.

The early modest expansion of merchant shipping along the coasts of Wales was recorded thereafter in the Welsh Port Books and the Port Books of Chester and other English ports.[1] In addition, Welsh merchants prospered in, and Welsh seamen sailed from, such ports as Bristol and London on military expeditions and voyages of discovery. Others engaged in the developing slave trade from West Africa to North America. Richard Ameryck (ap Meurig) of Bristol, merchant, was closely associated with the Cabots and it has even been suggested—imaginatively—that 'America' is derived from his corrupted Welsh patronymic.[2]

Welsh captains, such as William Midleton of Llansannan, Denbighshire, and Thomas Prys of Plas Iolyn, served under Francis Drake in the New World and Welshmen were soon numbered amongst the piratical brethren of the Spanish Main. The most notorious Welsh pirate was

'Black Bart' (**Barti Ddu**), Bartholomew Roberts (1682?-1721/2) of Pembrokeshire. His exploits soon overshadowed those of his mentor and compatriot, Howell Davis. So, like their West Country cousins, the Welsh were ubiquitous in all forms of maritime enterprise from at least the Tudor period onwards. No less than ten of the crew of 85 of Captain Cook's *Endeavour* in 1770 on the expedition which resulted in the discovery and claiming of Australia ('New Wales') were probably Welshmen.[3]

Meanwhile, during the seventeenth and eighteenth centuries, maritime Wales from Chepstow to Connah's Quay advanced steadily, though modestly, in association with Ireland and such ports as Bristol, Chester, Liverpool and London. The period is not well documented but in the mid-eighteenth century two important publications were added to the Port Books. *Lloyd's List* was a twice-weekly publication full of information of interest to ship-owners and others (including reports of captures by privateers of British vessels during the American War of Independence, 1775-1783), and *Lloyd's Register of Shipping*, an annual publication listing vessels, masters, when and where such vessels were built, destined voyages, owners (often as 'Capt.& Co.') and other details.

The quickening pace of the Industrial Revolution in Britain during the closing decades of the eighteenth century was clearly reflected in the expansion of maritime trade and of shipbuilding throughout the British Isles. In Wales, the growth of the extractive industries (coal, iron ore, lead ore, copper ore and slate, principally) provided the true basis for the expansion of shipping and maritime trade. Documentation increased from 1786 with the introduction of statutory Shipping Registers. These registers, maintained by the Customs in select Ports of Register, are prime sources of information regarding vessels (tonnages, dimensions, rigs, etc), masters (including changes of masters) and ship-owners or shareholders.[4]

## The Nineteenth Century Expansion of Maritime Wales

The dramatic expansion of Maritime Wales from the late eighteenth century, during the Napoleonic Wars (1793-1815), is a complex subject which has been studied with increasing enthusiasm and commitment during the last two decades. The extractive industries of Wales provided the catalyst for the expansion and the most intense phase coincided with the British economic miracle which commenced in the 1850s and continued until the late 1870s. The main south Wales coal ports expanded mightily, subject to economic fluctuations, from the 1830s and 1840s and, prior to the First World War, Cardiff and Barry were the two leading coal-exporting ports in the world. Swansea was developed from the 1840s principally for the importation of copper ore and other non-ferrous ores destined for the smelters of the Swansea-Neath district.

The main south Wales ports developed as cosmopolitan centres, though many of the master mariners, mates, seamen and engineers were drawn from the seafaring communities of south-west Wales (south Cardiganshire and Pembrokeshire) whilst others hailed from north Wales. The ports and associated havens and creeks of Cardigan Bay developed more modestly as did the ports of the north coast of Wales and Anglesey. For example, Aberystwyth harbour was improved in the 1840s to facilitate the export of lead ore and the importation of North American timber and other commodities. The exportation of roofing slates was the staple trade of Gwynedd, from the late eighteenth century onwards, from Port Penrhyn (Bangor), Port Dinorwig (Y Felinheli), Caernarfon, Porthmadog (Port Madoc) and Aberdyfi. The fleets of these ports and others were composed largely of schooners and smacks of local construction which were owned by a wide range of shareholders in each locality as the statutory Shipping Registers indicate. However, in most of these there are a few prominent family enterprises like the brothers Davies of Menai Bridge, Thomas Jones & Son, Ropemakers, Aberystwyth, William Jones & Son, Timber Merchants, Pwllheli, and Humphrey Owen & Son and John Owen, Timber Merchants, Caernarfon. Vessels owned by such prominent firms included North American timber carriers and global traders. In short, many of the lesser ports of Wales were not confined to coastal and short-sea trading.

Seafarers were, of course, a mobile group of men and boys. They moved quite readily from one small Welsh port to another and from the smaller Welsh ports to the great coal ports of south Wales and to Liverpool, Bristol, London and overseas. This presents problems and challenges for the family historian. Whilst the mariners of the lesser Welsh ports were mainly local men a few exotic names are encountered: Aberystwyth (Delahoyde, Doughton, Clayton, Riddell or Riddle), Aberdyfi (Godfrey, Julian, Peters), Barmouth (Barrow, Martin, Barnett, Garnett, Lowe) and Caernarfon (Hudson, Barlow, Barlow-Prichard). Yet the common Welsh surnames predominated and English and other incomers were quite readily assimilated by such tightly-knit Welsh communities, in most cases.

Movement from one Welsh maritime centre to another is well-illustrated in regard to Captain Griffith Dedwydd (1706-1783) of Nevern (Pembrokeshire) who married the heiress of Gorllwyn Fawr, Llanaber (Merionethshire), in 1747 and became the ancestor of one of Barmouth's most distinguished seafaring families. He was also an early Calvinistic Methodist. Other Welsh mariners settled in the West Country, in Ireland (Captain William Jones of Pwllheli commanded the brigs *Union* and *Suir* of Waterford in the early nineteenth century) and in such major ports as Bristol, Liverpool, London and even Newcastle. Many had distinguished careers as commanders of famous clippers, windjammers and steamers (Captain John Prichard who commanded Cunard's *Mauretania* was a native of Caernarfon).

A number of Welsh mariners settled overseas after making a 'pier-head jump' (deserting) at such ports as San Francisco and Port Phillip (Melbourne).[5] It should be remembered also that master mariners' wives commonly sailed with their husbands on global voyages during the first few years of marriage. For example, Sir Lewis Casson's mother, a daughter of Captain Lewis Holland Thomas by his wife Winifred, was born in Valparaiso in the 1840s.[6] A few single women served as stewardesses aboard Welsh-owned ocean-going vessels in the nineteenth century. So seafaring was not an exclusively male preserve.

In short, the expansion of Maritime Wales is an engrossing story in its more intimate and global senses; it is or should be of great interest to many family historians. As will be seen below, British maritime expansion in the nineteenth century resulted in a considerable increase in the recording of individual seafarers in the form of registers of masters and seamen and other sources of information. The decline of Maritime Wales and of British merchant shipping generally need not detain us here.[7]

## Sources of Information Regarding Welsh Seafarers

Relatively few Welshmen volunteered for service in the Royal Navy prior to the First World War so the Merchant Service will be concentrated upon here.[8] The main sources for seafarers in the Merchant Service are essentially the same for Wales as for England. The general sources, such as parish registers, census returns, gravestones and memorial inscriptions and so on, demand no more than brief attention, whereas the specialised sources call for more extended comment.

**General Sources**

By general sources I mean those sources of information which are common to all family historians in Wales as in England. Gravestones and memorial inscriptions were commonly beyond the means of poor families and since many seamen were heads or members of poor families many were unrecorded in this regard. However, the cemeteries situated in the coastal districts contain numerous gravestones and memorials to local seamen. Some inscriptions are especially poignant in that they relate to several members of a single family who died together by shipwreck, or to young boys who died at sea or who died of fever in the notorious South American ports (such as Santos, Brazil) or elsewhere. Grieving parents sometimes recorded the loss of sons at sea by giving the position of the vessel, in terms of latitude and longitude, that is, information furnished to them by the ship-owners, when they fell overboard or when their mortal remains were consigned to the deep. Welsh and English language newspapers contain many graphic and harrowing accounts of shipwrecks and losses of individual seamen.

Parish registers contain much information relating to seamen and their families from about 1750 onwards when male occupations are commonly recorded. However from the early nineteenth century records of baptism diminish, since a high proportion of Welsh seamen were Nonconformists, so the searcher must turn in many cases to the records of the various nonconformist sects.

Census returns relating to seamen present their own problems because many men were absent from home when the census was taken. In such cases, it is usually possible to trace their families if certain facts are already known. Thus, for example, where the head of the household is recorded as 'Ann Williams Seaman's Wife' (or 'Master Mariner's Wife') the seafaring husband may be identifiable. Some seamen who were absent from home on the census night may well have been recorded aboard vessels moored in one of the numerous harbours, great or small, within the British Isles, but their location may be difficult. In other cases, where vessels were at sea or in foreign ports all over the world, masters and seamen were simply unrecorded, though they may be traced in Crew Lists and Agreements and in the various Registers (see below).

Probate records (wills, administrations and accompanying inventories) can provide useful information relating to seamen, especially master mariners. This is particularly true regarding inventories of the personal estates of master mariners as these commonly include their shipping investments (e.g. two 'shares' or 2/64ths of the schooner *Betty*, an 'ounce' or 1/16th of the smack *Jenny*, and suchlike—with valuations). Of course, such investments were by no means limited to seafarers in the eighteenth and nineteenth centuries or to people, including women, of the coastal districts of Wales.

In short, a good deal of information relating to seafarers and their families can be gleaned, in most cases, from these and other general sources. It is usually advisable to proceed from the more to the less familiar sources.

## Specific or Specialised Sources

Christopher T. and Michael J. Watts have produced a most useful booklet *My Ancestor was a Merchant Seaman: How can I find out more about him?*[9] which provides a wide-ranging survey of specialised and non-specialised sources relating to merchant shipping and seamen. These range from 'Trade and Taxation' (including Port Books and Shipping Returns) to miscellaneous material such as Trinity House Petitions, the records of shipping and marine insurance companies and the extensive collections in the National Maritime Museum at Greenwich, in Liverpool and other major ports. It is necessary here to concentrate upon the principal sources: official registers of apprentices, seamen, engineers and masters and Crew Lists and Agreements (Articles). However, certain other sources should be mentioned and briefly commented upon.

### a. Disbursement Books, Account Books, etc

These private records relating to individual vessels, were kept by masters to satisfy shareholders regarding expenditure (harbour dues, the costs of maintenance, repairs, and provisions, wages and payments to apprentices, etc) and, sometimes, income (freights), and are fortuitous survivors especially for the eighteenth century. From time to time, profits were distributed amongst the shareholders as dividends and some of these records may still survive amongst family papers, though a number are preserved in public archives in Wales. For example, in the Area (Meirionydd) Record Office of the Gwynedd Archives at Dolgellau there are three disbursement books plus other related accounts.[10] The disbursement books relate to two sloops called *Unity* of Barmouth (1781-1799), to the brig *Susannah* of Aberdyfi (1816-1825) and to the *Jane Brown* of Barmouth (1840-1851), a slate trader between

Caernarfon, Bangor and London. Disbursements of the sloop *Amity* of Aberdyfi (1803-1809),[11] like those of the sloops *Unity* of Barmouth, have been published in full with editorial comments by this writer, and those of the brig *Susannah* are the subject of a short study[12] which demonstrates the value of such records to family historians and others. These and similar as yet unpublished records contain a substantial amount of detailed information, essential background materials for family and maritime historians, since they provide invaluable insights into the operation of coasting vessels and the nature of seafaring for periods when documentary evidence is otherwise quite scanty. Family historians are well advised to ascertain whether any such records exist for their own districts, whether in private hands or public archives.

### b. Secondary Sources: Books and Articles

Since the early 1970s there has been a distinct revival of interest in the maritime history of Wales. This revival was led in Gwynedd by Aled Eames and others with the unstinted support of the Gwynedd Archives and Museums Service under the direction of Bryn R. Parry, the County Archivist. Interest soon spread to other parts of Wales. It has been sustained, since 1976, by the appearance of fifteen volumes (to 1992) of *Maritime Wales/Cymru a'r Môr*. These annual volumes already contain a huge amount of information of interest to family historians. Other pertinent articles may be found in the journals of the Welsh county historical societies. Some fuller studies are listed in the Select Bibliography. Like the published disbursements already noted, these studies, articles and books, can be said to be essential background sources (at least) for family historians since they range generally beyond the confines of economic, business and transport history.

### c. Trinity House Petitions

Apart from its familiar public responsibilities regarding the supervision of lighthouses, buoys and pilotage around the British coasts the Corporation of Trinity House had various charitable funds at its disposal. To benefit from these funds, seafarers or their dependents had to make formal application—by way of a Petition to Trinity House—providing details of their circumstances. Surviving petitions[13] cover the period from 1780 to 1854 (the Merchant Shipping Act). Their value as a source for family historians is well conveyed in an article in the journal of the Dyfed Family History Society[14] with reference to Evan Evans of New Quay (Cardiganshire) in 1845, aged 60:

> He went to sea at the age of 15 in 1799 and was employed in the Merchant Sea Service for 44 years. His first vessel was the *Nancy*, a sloop of 63 tons built in Devon in 1792, a local coaster; the second was the *Sea Horse*, another local ship.
>
> In 1801 he was mate aboard the 40 ton sloop, *Betsey*, built in Cardigan in 1797. By 1807 he was serving on board HMS *Delight* in the Napoleonic Wars and may have volunteered to serve rather than being press-ganged as he became a Petty Officer. He saw service in the Mediterranean and was still in the Navy in 1812, aboard HMS *Le President*, captured from the French. After leaving the Navy when the war ended, he purchased a 12 ton sloop which he named *Delight* . . .

This and much more detailed information was recorded in his Petition which further illustrates their value as a prime source for family historians despite the difficulties in relation to common names such as Evan Evans, John Jones and so on. As a rule, the more detailed the information the greater the chance of distinguishing seafarers (and others) who bore such names.

## d. Lloyd's Registers and Lists

As noted earlier, *Lloyd's Registers of Shipping* and *Lloyd's List* date back to the eighteenth century and contain much relevant information. Reprints of the *Registers* and *List* (to the 1820s) may be studied in the National Library of Wales, Aberystwyth, and in the Guildhall Library, London (including later issues of *Lloyd's List*). In fact, Lloyd's records were transferred to the Guildhall Library some years ago.

For their own corporate purposes, Lloyd's of London introduced a Register of Masters in 1869. Active masters with certificates of competency or of service were listed in a printed volume in 1869 along with details of their place of birth, where and when they gained their certificate(s), their previous commands and so on. Thereafter, masters may be traced in large leather-bound manuscript volumes arranged alphabetically a few years at a time. Searching may be arduous but it can be very worthwhile.

## e. The Statutory Shipping Registers from 1786

These official (Customs) Registers have been referred to already, but one or two points should be made here. They illustrate the wide range of shareholders in shipping between the gentry and the poor both within and beyond Wales and list masters, including changes of masters, apart from recording significant details of each vessel. Sadly, some of the early volumes for Welsh ports and for Chester have not survived, though the Registers for Gwynedd (Beaumaris from 1786, Caernarfon from 1840 and Pwllheli, 1838-1851) are complete as are those for Chepstow.[15] Surviving Registers, apart from current ones, have been transferred in recent years to more accessible locations, e.g, the Gwynedd Registers from Holyhead and Caernarfon Customs to the Gwynedd Archives at Caernarfon. They are certainly important sources for family historians.

## f. Registers, Crew Lists and Agreements (Articles)

Without doubt registers of apprentices, seamen, mates, master mariners and engineers, together with Crew Lists and Agreements (Articles), are the most useful records for family historians. A series of Merchant Shipping Acts in the nineteenth century, which were consolidated in 1854 and 1894, introduced a welter of regulations under the auspices of the Board of Trade. Most of the resulting records remain in the Public Record Office at Kew, though Crew Lists and Agreements have been dispersed—some are retained by the PRO whilst others are at the National Maritime Museum, Greenwich, in local archives (including the Gwynedd Archives at Caernarfon, Llangefni and Dolgellau) and others have been transferred to the Memorial University, St.John's, Newfoundland.

### Apprentices' Indentures

In 1823, masters of vessels of over 80 tons (which exempted most coastal vessels) were required to carry a quota of indentured apprentices. To encourage compliance indentures had to be filed—from 1835, either with local Customs or with the Registrar General of Shipping and Seamen (RGSS) in London and, from 1844, those filed with local Customs had to be forwarded quarterly to the RGSS.

An Index of Apprentices was compiled by the RGSS from the 1820s. It is subdivided into London and Outports (Class BT 150, PRO, Kew) and the entries in each volume are sorted according to the first letter of the apprentice's surname. Entries relate to the month (and year) of registry, the port of registry, date of the indenture, name of the apprentice, his age and the term for which he was bound (commonly three to five years), the name and residence of the master and the name and tonnage burthen of the vessel. Although indexes survive from 1824 by no means all the indentures have been preserved. The PRO decided to cull these and other records, retaining those for every fifth year with the rest being destroyed. For further details see Watts and Watts, *My Ancestor was a Merchant Seaman*.[16]

As noted above, Disbursement Books refer to apprentices. Two apprentices of the brig *Susannah* of Aberdyfi, relatives of the master, Captain Roger Peters, junior, subsequently gained rapid promotion aboard that vessel in the early nineteenth century. Apprenticeship under a competent and considerate master mariner was clearly an advantage but it was limited commonly to those whose parents could afford the premiums demanded. Many Welsh seamen were obliged to sign as boys and seamen and to save money from their meagre wages to study for their mates' and masters' tickets ashore; that is, to advance the 'hard way' (or as 'hard cases').

## The Register of Merchant Seamen[17]

The first point to make is—be prepared for disappointments. Pursuant to the Merchant Shipping Act of 1835, a registration scheme was introduced to facilitate the manning of the Royal Navy. Merchant seamen had good reason to be suspicious of such schemes and, besides, a high proportion of them were illiterate and, for various reasons, a number gave false names and other false or inaccurate information (though this was much less common where men registered in the smaller ports of Wales as elsewhere). The Registrar in London had great difficulty in compiling an Index[18] and many entries are unreliable; yet it was 'a landmark in the history of British seamen' since it made 'the final distinction between the Royal Navy and the Merchant Navy'.[19] Despite the limitations vital information can be gleaned from this Register and Index. The same can be said of the Register based upon new regulations introduced in 1844 whereby every British seaman leaving the UK had to have a valid Register Certificate or 'Ticket'. At Caernarfon, seamen were registered at the Custom House and were warned about making false declarations in August 1845.[20] By 1852, 148,465 names were on the Register, of whom nearly 95,000 were liable for service in the Royal Navy.[21]

These Register Tickets (Alphabetical Register of Seamen's Tickets) are of great interest since the Register includes a list of 'Reported Voyages' garnered from the Crew Lists and Agreements (below) to which the searcher can refer for additional information. The gaps in census returns in relation to seamen mentioned earlier may be filled by these means. However, in October 1853, the ticket system was abolished as it had proved difficult to enforce in the face of resistance from seamen. Finally, a new register was commenced in 1853 which listed seamen alphabetically (Register of Seamen, Series III), though this was discontinued after 1857. Thereafter, the careers of merchant seamen may be traced, with difficulty in many cases, in the now dispersed Crew Lists and Agreements.

In resisting registration schemes, it may be said that our seafaring ancestors (amongst others) made it difficult for future family, economic and labour historians to trace careers of boys, ordinary and able seamen and boatswains in the merchant marine, though such thoughts never crossed their minds at the time! They had their reasons for being suspicious of such registration schemes.

## Registers of Masters, Mates and Engineers[22]

Here the searcher is on firmer ground. An Alphabetical Register of Masters, compiled by the Registrar General of Shipping and Seamen, relates to the period from 1845 to 1854, that is, from the commencement of examinations of competency for masters and mates. These examinations were voluntary and restricted initially to service on foreign-going vessels but they were made compulsory in 1850, subject to exemptions for long service where 'Certificates of Service' (signified in the registers by 'S' followed by the number of the certificate). 'Certificates of Competence' (signified, for masters, by 'C' followed by the number) for masters, mates and engineers soon became universally required for those engaged on foreign-going vessels and vessels employed in the 'Home and Coasting' service. The suspension or withdrawal of certificates or 'tickets' became, of course, a powerful disciplinary device. This remains so today for officers serving in the much reduced British merchant fleet.

## Crew Lists and Agreements (Articles)

These records are truly remarkable in scope and detail since they relate to the men who commanded and manned the huge British merchant fleet during the second half of the nineteenth century to the eve of World War II. They are (or should be) a prime source for economic, maritime, labour and family historians since no other large-scale activity is better recorded. Having said that, a significant proportion of these records may be studied by only the most assiduous searchers because of the dispersal policy adopted some years ago by the Public Record Office due to the remarkable volume/tonnage of these records. The situation is outlined below. Dispersal was preferable to the main alternative, wholesale destruction.

Crew Lists date from 1835 when the Merchant Shipping Act provided for the filing of Crew Lists and other documents with the Register Office of Merchant Seamen, the precursor of the Registrar General of Shipping and Seamen (RGSS). From these the Registrar abstracted the service profiles of individual seamen.

The Crew Lists from 1835 to 1844 were of two main types: Schedule C, Crew List (Foreign) and Schedule D, Account of Voyages and Crew for Home Trade (Half Yearly Return). The former were the responsibility of masters of foreign-going vessels, that is, vessels proceeding beyond certain defined limits of the UK and continental Europe; and the latter Lists were half-yearly returns made by masters of vessels engaged in the home and coasting trades, including fishing vessels. Schedule D returns of voyages and crew(s) for the preceding half year were to be lodged within 21 days of the end of June or December. These Lists (1835-1844) were then filed according to the port of registry (Beaumaris, Aberystwyth, Caernarfon—from 1840, Chepstow, etc) by ship's name, not number.

Additional Lists were introduced: Schedule A, Agreement for Foreign Trade ('Articles' in common parlance). Each agreement constituted a contract between the master and crew, subject to extensive discretionary powers vested in masters, and it had to be filed within 24 hours of the vessel's return to a UK port where the crew were commonly 'paid off' and discharged. The Schedule B agreement related to the home and coasting trades and these agreements were to be filed within 30 days from the end of June or December in each case. In addition, a Crew List had to be filed on sailing by masters of foreign-going vessels (Schedule G). Many vessels made both foreign-going and home and coasting trade voyages—an added complication for hard-pressed master mariners. Some masters clearly found this mounting paper work irksome, but they had no choice in the matter. However, these Crew Lists and Agreements afforded some protection for seamen with regard to their wages and conditions of service.

In 1857, each vessel was given an Official Number on registration and these numbers were retained so long as each vessel survived on active service. These records are a remarkable source of information but, from the early 1860s, their location is problematic. The Crew Lists and Agreements to about 1861 remain in the Public Record Office at Kew, but the Lists and Agreements (plus Logs) from about 1861 to 1938 are now widely dispersed. Sample years are retained by the PRO and collections are held at the National Maritime Museum, Greenwich, in some county or other local archives and a substantial proportion now reside in the Memorial University, St.John's, Newfoundland. Bryn R. Parry, the Gwynedd County Archivist, with a team of energetic assistants, 'rescued' a remarkable collection of these records pertaining to vessels registered in Gwynedd (the three former counties of Anglesey, Caernarfon and Merioneth). For most other parts of Wales searchers must first locate relevant Lists and Agreements and their quest may well result in correspondence with the keepers of such records in Newfoundland.

Finally, what do the Crew Lists and Agreements and related documents, including Official Logs, contain of interest to family historians in addition to lists of names and the basic conditions of maritime service? In general, they list names (many seamen signed by mark), ages (or natal years) and places of birth (towns or parishes, and countries for many foreign seamen), i.e, of masters and crews. Some of this information is not strictly reliable and some seamen, though not many, deliberately disguised their true identities. The Lists also name the vessel in which masters and crewmen had last served so it is possible, in some cases, to trace an individual's career backwards from one vessel to another; when they were discharged from such vessel and where; when and where they signed on the vessel in question; and when and where they were discharged or 'paid off' at the completion of an engagement or otherwise lawfully discharged due to sickness, death, by agreement with the master or due to the sinking of the vessel (a not uncommon reason for discharge). Desertions were also recorded (San Francisco and Melbourne were popular locations).

For foreign-going vessels, the Agreements or Articles stipulated the general nature of the 'employment' in terms of primary destination and maximum duration (commonly nine months, a year, eighteen months, though sometimes three years). Both types of Agreement record the number of the master's certificate (Certificates of Competence or Service), but not their monthly wages. Typically this would have been about £8 for a schooner master in 1900. Mates' certificate numbers were recorded as were their monthly rates of pay. Royal Naval Reserve numbers were also recorded where appropriate. Seamen were rated as boatswain, able seaman (AB), ordinary seamen (OS) and 'boys', and their monthly rates of pay were stipulated. Boys on Welsh schooners were quite commonly appointed cooks, a rather daunting prospect for them and the rest of the crew! Seamen also served as cooks, and stewards and stewardesses are occasionally encountered aboard Welsh vessels.

Wages were commonly settled in respect of foreign-going vessels at the end of an engagement in a UK port. In the meantime, masters doled out cash to seamen for the purchase of tobacco, items of clothing, etc, afloat (from the 'slop chest' when some masters charged inflated prices) or ashore, so the balance of wages owing when a man was finally 'paid off' was often quite small. When men signed on, many received a month's wages in advance of joining the ship though a few pocketed the money and promptly disappeared. Responsible married seamen and men with dependent relatives (aged parents, etc) commonly arranged 'allotments' from their wages to be paid each month by the owners. Such payments meant quite a small 'balance' payable at the end of a period of service. Both types of Agreement (for foreign-going or home and coasting voyages) operated as contracts between masters and men, but a master's authority at sea was quite formidable. If a man signed on as an AB and was found by the master to be unequal to that rating the master could reduce the man's wages accordingly (to those of an OS). Some masters were notoriously tight-fisted, as newspaper reports of magistrates' court hearings of seamen's claims for unpaid wages indicate. Seamen who refused duty were commonly imprisoned by magistrates where no adequate reason for refusal was established.

The Agreements also cover the vital matter of provisions (salt beef and pork, ship's biscuit or 'hard tack', water, tea, coffee, flour, etc). Detailed 'Scales of Provisions' were laid down on a daily basis monotonously rotated each week, though a common undertaking was that the provisions be 'Sufficient without waste'—three words which signified a customary parsimony on the part of ship-owners. Some masters made money 'on the side' by purchasing poor quality provisions at a discount not revealed in their accounts (disbursements). Aboard the ocean-going and coasting vessels of nonconformist Wales 'No Grog' was a common stipulation written into the printed standard-form contract (articles). In general, crewmen were bound to carry out all lawful instructions of the master in a prompt and seamanlike manner. Wilful disobedience commonly resulted in seamen being clapped in irons and subsequent imprisonment, but seamen were not entirely without redress against masters in respect of unpaid wages, ill-usage and so on.

In general, Official Logs provided for foreign-going vessels are disappointing as regards their contents though there are notable exceptions.[23] When a man died at sea or overseas the master recorded the fact, the apparent cause and the dead seaman's effects, which were often pitiable. Such effects were commonly purchased by the dead man's shipmates for considerably more than they were worth in the hope that the money would benefit the man's dependents. A dead man's 'allotments' from wages generally ceased when the owners were apprised of his death, and families were usually thrown upon parish relief.

In short, Crew Lists and Agreements contain a wealth of information concerning mariners in the Merchant Service, but the tracing of individuals by family historians in these records from 1861 onwards can prove difficult owing to their wide dispersal. Yet the effort can be thoroughly worthwhile.

## In Conclusion

Families played a conspicuous part in the expansion of Maritime Wales during the eighteenth and nineteenth centuries when whole communities became committed to the opportunities and the harsh imperatives of seafaring. For the family historian at least the natural course is to begin with the familiar, that is, with surviving family lore and legend, discharge papers of family members, information derived from gravestones, memorial inscriptions, parish registers and census returns, newspaper reports and so on. In many cases, mariner-ancestors will thereby assert their own claims to the searcher's attention, as it were, since seafarers were by no means confined to the coastal districts of Wales.

When the non-specialised and readily accessible sources have been thoroughly investigated, the quest can then be extended to the labyrinth of more specialised and official sources. The scope of such subsequent studies may well be global. There will be disappointments in attempts to trace individual seamen, especially those with common Welsh names, but the expansive nature of this aspect of family history will generate its own excitements and satisfactions. I have certainly found this to be so.

**NOTES TO CHAPTER 12**

[1]E.A.Lewis, *The Welsh Ports Books, 1550-1603* (Cardiff: 1927). The Port Books are in the PRO, Kew.

[2]David B.Quinn, 'Wales and the West', in *Welsh Society and Nationhood, Historical Essays Presented to Glanmor Williams* (Cardiff: 1984), pp.90-107. See also Arthur Davies, 'Prince Madoc and the Discovery of America in 1477', *The Geographical Journal*, Vol. 150, No.3 (Nov.1984), pp.363-372, for interesting speculations concerning mariner John Lloyd and the Americas (pre-Columban).

[3]John Thomas, 'Captain James Cook, and "New Wales"', *Transactions of the Hon.Society of Cymmrodorion*, 1969 Part II, pp.336-345.

[4]Grahame Farr, 'The Statutory Ship Registers of the Welsh Ports', *Maritime Wales/Cymru a'r Môr*, No.1 (1976), pp.47-50. Some Welsh vessels were registered at Chester, London and elsewhere.

[5]Public Record Office, Melbourne, Victoria: *Deserters from Vessels*, Vol.I (at Geelong) and Vol.II (at Melbourne—Port Phillip), 1852-1923. Deserters are also recorded in Crew Lists and Agreements (Articles).

[6]Lewis Lloyd, 'Captain Lewis Holland Thomas of Caeffynnon Hall, Talsarnau', *Maritime Wales/Cymru a'r Môr*, No.4 (July 1979), pp.89-95. Capt.Thomas, commander of the brig *Laura Anne* (146 tons) of Liverpool traded extensively in the Pacific at this time. See also No. 14 (1991), pp. 25-53.

[7]See Aled Eames, *Machlud Hwyliau'r Cymry/The Twilight of Welsh Sail* (Cardiff: 1984).

[8]For a general survey of service in the Royal Navy see Christopher Lloyd, *The British Seaman* (London, Paladin 1970).

[9]Christopher T. and Michael J.Watts, *My Ancestor was a Merchant Seaman: How can I find out more about him?* (London: Society of Genealogists, 1992).

[10]NLW Deposit 289B.

[11]Ibid.

[12]Lewis Lloyd, *The Brig 'Susannah' of Aberdyfi* (Privately published by the author)

[13]These documents are now held by the Society of Genealogists who have published a calendar, *The Trinity House Petitions* (London: 1987)

[14]S.C.Passmore, *Dyfed Family History Society Journal* Vol.3 No.5 (Dec.1989). Evan Evans's first application was unsuccessful as he was 'only 60'. Lieut.J.Fauriel Barrett, R.N., took up his case in 1849. Susan Passmore also cites the application of widow Ann Jones whose husband had died in January 1852 from an injury received aboard his vessel the *Ocean* of Cardigan.

[15]Grahame Farr. See note 4 above, p.49. Some Registers are in the PRO, Kew.

[16]Watts & Watts. See note 9 above, pp.13-14

[17]Watts & Watts. See note 9 above, pp.14-17. For information concerning ordinary seamen post-1870 searchers should contact the Registrar General of Shipping and Seamen, Llantrisant Road, Llandaff, Cardiff, CF5 2YS.

[18]But see the PRO *Alphabetical Index to Seamen and Register of Seamen*, Series II, 1835-1844.

[19]Christopher Lloyd. See note 8 above, p.251. Yet, until 'Continuous Service' was introduced in 1856, sailors in the Royal Navy were signed on for single voyages so Admiralty Records can contain information relating to men who were essentially merchant seamen. See also Watts & Watts (note 9 above), pp.9-11 for 'Military Connections'.

[20]*Carnarvon & Denbigh Herald*, December 21, 1844, and August 9, 1845.

[21]Christopher Lloyd. See note 8 above, p.251.

[22]Watts & Watts. See note 9 above, pp.27-29. There are three consolidated indexes to the various Registers in the Reference Room at the PRO, Kew.

[23]See Lewis Lloyd, *Pwllheli—The Port and Mart of Llŷn* (Harlech: 1991), Appendix III (5) the *John Arthur Prichard* (14185), pp. 302-310.

# 13. Wills and Other Records of Inheritance

Gareth Haulfryn Williams

Among all the types of historical records which the family historian consults, perhaps none exceeds the last will and testament in its ability to cast a sudden ray of light onto a host of relationships and family connections otherwise unrecorded—and the further back in time one reaches with one's family researches the more valuable, since the more obscure, such information becomes. Similarly, of all the records preserved in official archives of state, courts of law and local administration, civil and ecclesiastical, none touches so immediately on personal concerns and few refer to such a wide spectrum of the population of bygone years. This chapter deals with records preserved either in the course of the administration of the laws of inheritance or with records which in other ways deal with the process of inheritance.

## Wills

Of these records, the one of paramount interest to the genealogist is the will and testament. Technically, a will broadly deals with landed property and rights to that property and a testament to other, moveable, possessions, but here for simplicity the term 'will' is used to denote both. To understand the strengths and weaknesses of wills as a historical source, it will be useful briefly to examine the process of will-making. Nowadays, the responsible person will often consult a solicitor and prepare a will in middle life, long before the shadow of the cemetery hovers over him, but until the middle of the last century, will-making was very much a last minute tidying up of personal affairs, often days or hours before death; a good description of the philosophy is that of Montaigne:

> I warrant you there is none will set his hand to [a will] til the Physician have given his last doome and utterly forsaken him.[1]

Dangerous journeys to foreign parts might make a man far-sighted enough to put pen to paper: in 1638 Rees Griffith of Cricieth wrote in his will that he intended to travel overseas 'if service I cannot obtain at

London or some other place within the Realm of England', and made his will for the convenience of his family, should the worst come to the worst, although in the event he lived another nine years[2]—but such foresight was rare. Sometimes things were left so late that a scribe could not be summoned in time and then an oral will—or nuncupative will as it was called—could be legally valid. Except in the case of the literate yeomen and gentry, the parish priest was usually called upon to act as scribe. In 1636, the vicar of Clynnog recorded what happened on one such occasion:

> being sent for to haste and administer holy Communion one Kadwaladr ap Hughe Griffith, I omitted to bring . . . my pen ink or paper for to make his will . . . whereon and here made his personall will before the persons subscribed.[3]

In such circumstances, it is not surprising that will-making was regarded as a religious duty and indeed, until 1858, it was the Church and not secular authority which was responsible for the granting of probate so that the deceased's goods could be distributed. This religious ethos is exemplified in the diplomatic—or standard phraseology—of wills, and the remarkable consistency of wording of virtually all wills over at least three centuries throughout Wales—and England—suggests that clergymen had access to precedent books to guide them.

Let us now turn to the structure typical of the standard form of will. It starts 'In the name of God Amen' and after giving his or her name, parish and, if one is lucky, the house or farm name, the testator (or will-maker) will note his mental and physical state: 'sick in body but sound in mind' is a common phrase, important as wills of those not deemed sane would be invalid. The first bequest (*Imprimis*) is of the testator's soul to his Maker, and his or her body to be buried. This clause can be of great interest and should be examined: if the phraseology is extended and devout in tone, it may point to a testator's nonconformist allegiance which will open other avenues of research; and sometimes the parish church or churchyard specified may not be that of residence, which should suggest an examination of that parish's registers for baptism or marriage entries. Sometimes too the location of the grave can hint at unsuspected family relationships (e.g. 'adjacent to the grave of my sister X'). Charitable bequests then follow, usually of a small sum for the reparation of the parish church and the cathedral, sometimes for the relief of a parish's poor; mention of parishes other than the testator's own again gives the family historian clues about origins and antecedents.

The next section is probably of most direct interest in the context of this book, for a number of bequests normally follow to the children and, if one is lucky, grandchildren, nephews, nieces, uncles, aunts and so on, usually organised in a hierarchical way, male before female and elder before younger. One should not be surprised if only small bequests are made to older children: this is probably an indication that they have already received settlements or portions upon marriage, and indeed can be a useful pointer to marriage dates. It is necessary to be a little cautious about terminology: 'brother', 'sister', 'uncle' and 'aunt' often include 'brother-in-law' and so on; and 'cousin' (or 'cozin') can refer to any reasonably close relative, even by marriage, of the same generation. The term 'cousin german', although normally used for 'first cousin', is often used to mean anyone of acknowledged but slightly distant relationship. Up to the eighteenth century, married women often retained their 'maiden' name, whether in fact it was a patronymic, or a true surname such as Holland, Spicer or whatever. In wills of the eighteenth century and earlier care should be taken not to read 'natural son' as meaning 'illegitimate son' for what was more natural than birth within wedlock? Testators, especially in a rural society, were however surprisingly open about including bequests (usually of a lesser value) to illegitimate offspring, termed 'base' children. Where patronymics were still in force among the bulk of the populace but the gentry had adopted surnames, a gentleman's child given a patronymic name must be suspected of being illegitimate even if not stated to be so.

Patronymics, of course, have a wider use, as they give evidence of ancestry, especially where three or more generations are listed—e.g. David ap John ap Harry. With the restricted number of common given names, patronymics can also be misleading: there could be several David ap Johns in one parish. A will may however allow the right David ap John to be identified through the names of relatives who appear in the document. It should also be remembered that from 1650 to 1850 increasingly patronymics, while still active, may be anglicised in documents, so that David ap John (or Dafydd ap Siôn) may be rendered as David Jones—but his son might be William Davies.

The will may proceed to list bequests to friends and associates—often of money to buy a mourning ring, or of a suitable object such as a book or trinket—and also note down any debts owing by or owed to the testator. Such details may not be of strict relevance if one is interested in a testator's family, but it should never be overlooked that these lists of names could be of vital importance to anyone whose family was living in the vicinity at the time.

Finally, overseers or guardians may be appointed to care for a young family's welfare and education and one or more executors are named, usually including the spouse. These persons had substantial duties in the case of a large estate or a young family, and their status is usually named, being friends, in-laws or brothers of the testator. The will would then be signed by the testator, but a mark (a cross or rudely-drawn initials) would suffice if he or she were illiterate; however, given the death-bed context, some literate testators understandably struggled to make even a shaky mark. On the other hand, if one finds a fluent and elegant signature one is at least entitled to suspect a high level of education, and this could point the genealogist in the direction of lists of university graduates or members of the Inns of Court. Finally at least two, and often six or seven, witnesses would sign, or make their mark on, the completed document. Beneficiaries were barred from signing, but often distant relatives or in-laws were included in the list, as usually was the scribe, who would often add 'clerk' or 'clericus' after his name, denoting an ordained Churchman.

A further element in some wills is the provision for inheritance of land, and often the details of that land's purchase is given. This can be very interesting, but should never be taken as an indication of the testator's total land-holding; the chances are that such references are only to recent acquisitions, not already disposed in settlements of land, to be discussed briefly later.

If a testator recovered, or if he untypically prepared a will when not at death's door, there would be time for a change in circumstances—the birth of additional children, deaths (or indeed disagreements) within the family circle, or the acquisition of property—and thus a change of mind. A testator could revoke an earlier will, and this should be borne in mind when wills are found in private archives without associated probate documents. Alternatively, additional clauses, called a 'codicil', could be made, to add to or alter the provisions of the substantive will.

## Probate and the Associated Documents

Once a testator has died, it is the duty of the executor to obtain legal permission (called probate) to administer the estate, after which a will is said to have been proved. If someone dies leaving an invalid will (i.e, one unsigned, unwitnessed or otherwise unacceptable) or without making a will at all, he or she is said to have died 'intestate'. In such cases, the next-of-kin has to obtain letters of administration to distribute the estate according to certain rules. Before 1858, probate and administrations were granted by the established Church, which no doubt looked on it as both a spiritual duty in the care of souls and as a source of revenue, as fees were payable. Since it could be a lucrative business, the right to grant probate was held by a number of different Church bodies, depending on the location, and the situation in parts of England is very complex. In Wales, things are much easier for the family historian, as wills were normally proved in the appropriate Bishop's Consistory Court, at Bangor, Chester, Hereford, Llandaff, St. Asaph and St. David's. The choice of Consistory Court was dictated by the diocese in which the testator's parish was located. The only exceptions were the Archdeaconry of Brecon in St. David's diocese (which included Breconshire, nearly all Radnorshire and Kerry and Mochdre in Montgomeryshire); and the 'peculiar jurisdiction' of the parish of Hawarden, which had the right to grant probate in that one parish.

It was, however, open to executors to seek probate at superior courts in London (the Prerogative Court of Canterbury or PCC) or, in the case of parishes in Chester diocese (Hawarden, Holt and the parishes of Maelor Saesneg), at York (the Prerogative Court of York or PCY). In theory at least, if a testator had substantial property in more than one diocese, probate had to be granted by the PCC or PCY; if property was in the archdioceses of both York and Canterbury, PCC took priority. In fact, few North Wales wills were proved at these courts, and even Glamorgan and Monmouthshire wills are relatively uncommon there, although more executors there opted for PCC probate than did their North Walian cousins. It seems that the greater landowners and the gentry with relations practising law in London took most frequent advantage of this option, even when the location of their estates did not dictate it. Welsh men and women resident, or dying, in London, often appear among lists of PCC probates, and if a search in Wales for a well-to-do ancestor's will is fruitless it is well worth consulting the printed indexes for PCC which are available for most periods in the largest public or college libraries. It is of course worth searching any relevant English probate court accumulations if there is a suspicion that an ancestor had trading, professional or marriage connections over Offa's Dyke.

Finally, it must be remembered that during the Interregnum,

ecclesiastical courts were abolished, and between 1653 and 1659, wills had to be proved at a civil court in London (although a few appear somehow to have been proved at Llandaff); in fact, although Welsh wills are not uncommon during that period in the London court records (maintained as part of the PCC series of records), many executors waited in the not unfulfilled hope of a restoration of local probate courts, in 1660, and proved wills after that date although testators had long since died.

An examination of a collection of probate records and parish registers suggests that many wills were proved within two or three months, and most within a year, although others might be proved only when a later death occurred in the family which cancelled the direct line of inheritance; one gets the suspicion at times that executors only sought probate when they could not avoid it, and this may account for the many people 'missing' from probate records. Non-residence of the clergy, a lack of local 'peculiars' and the poor roads all contributed to a higher level of avoidance of probate in much of Wales than in lowland England.

On 12 January 1858, civil jurisdiction took over from the Church authorities and a number of district registries were established, broadly speaking at the locations of the previous church courts. After 1926, these were all of equal status, and wills were proved and administrations were granted at any, at the convenience of the executor. Fortunately, all deceased persons whose estates figured in the registries' activities are listed, by year, in alphabetical order in printed Calendars of Probate available at the National Library of Wales, 1858-1972, and (for years 1858-*circa* 1938) at the County Record Offices at Caernarfon, Cardiff, Carmarthen, Dolgellau and Ruthin and many English county record offices. The latest date available varies from office to office. (A full set of the Calendars is available at Somerset House in London.)

The records of the Probate Courts include registered copies of wills proved, original wills or loose paper copies going back to the mid to late sixteenth century (PCC from 1383) except for Bangor, where a fire destroyed those prior to 1635; and also a host of associated documents. Most interesting, since they allow one to enter a deceased ancestor's house and roam his fields or workshop in the imagination, are the inventories of goods: they set the person in context, and give indications as to his or her substance—and they list the names of the friends or neighbours who drew up the inventory, called 'appraisers'. Where loose wills survive, these inventories are usually filed with them, but not with register copies of wills. The survival of PCC inventories is disappointing, and those available are not conveniently indexed, but a prolonged search could be useful. Incidentally, a great deal of doubt has been cast on the validity of 'probate valuation', the suggestion being that prices given are unrealistically low in order to minimise payments for probate, which were on a sliding scale according to the value of estates. While this might be true today, recent work on Welsh seventeenth century inventories shows a realistic correlation between market prices and values quoted in probate documents, and often a painstaking attempt to be accurate and comprehensive on the part of the appraisers.

Acts of administration, for persons dying intestate, name the administrator and may give his or her relationship to the deceased: that in itself is interesting, and they also confirm that no will is available to the researcher. Bonds by administrator or executors, pledging themselves to observe the provisions of a will, produce an inventory or return an original will needed as evidence of title to land, can fill in some gaps; and where a will was disputed, the record of probate court procedure (usually in Latin until the mid-eighteenth century) may well provide some invaluable information on family feuds! Sometimes executors were unwilling to act, and a revocation of executorship, nominating a replacement, can reveal the name of another relative. Finally there are occasionally informal notes which give a little human interest to an often matter-of-fact legal process: for example, Thomas Jones, vicar of Llanarmon near Pwllheli, wrote:

> You shall understand that ye pore woman Margaret vz David is seanty two years ould and not able to undertake such a long journey to come herselfe to Bangor, and I hope you will grant me ye favour as to let Doctor Gwynne (who will be there ye next Sabbath day) give her an oath to administer truly and justly: and if you doubt in anything I will undertake to keepe ye Court harmelesse.[4]

## Using Probate Records

Unlike most official records of earlier centuries, wills are almost always written in English; some early ones, and some up to 1733 written by well-educated men and clerics, are in Latin, but this is rare. The note on a will that probate has been granted was in Latin up to the same date, but only the date of probate is of interest and this can be easily interpreted (although beware of abbreviations such as '7ber'—which means September, and not July). Notes of court proceedings up to the mid-eighteenth century will be in Latin too, but most other documents should cause no problem.

A very few wills and inventories in Welsh are to be found. Early ones are usually poorly written and bear evidence of a lack of availability of any competent scribe. Following the success of the circulating schools in the eighteenth century which taught people to read and write in Welsh, there is a slight increase in the number of Welsh documents, couched in a more literate Welsh—and a small but continuing tradition of Welsh wills continues up to the present. Words for objects and concepts not readily translatable are often given in Welsh in otherwise English wills and inventories, but a dictionary should solve most problems. English-language documents also occasionally present problems because of unfamiliar spellings or the use of words borrowed from the dialect of adjacent English-speaking areas, and reference to a dialect dictionary may be of help. Try saying the word out loud in a Welsh accent to yourself if spelling is the problem! If confusion still reigns, and you do not understand Welsh, ask someone who does: spelling and even grammar may have been heavily influenced by the writer's lack of fluency in English.

There is little difficulty in locating extant collections of wills in Wales, even if some travelling is involved, since those of all ecclesiastical probate courts in Wales (i.e. those prior to 1858) are at the National Library of Wales, except for those of a very few border parishes in Hereford diocese, which are to be found at Hereford County Record Office. Those of PCC are at the Public Record Office, and of PCY at the Borthwick Institute, York. The registered copy wills of post-1858 district registries in Wales have also all been transferred to the National Library of Wales; Montgomeryshire wills, however, were normally proved at Shrewsbury, and these registered copy wills are available at the Shropshire Record Office. Original copies of wills remain at the appropriate District Registries.

Finding a pre-1858 will you need is more difficult, since indexes are not comprehensive and the amount of work involved means that it will be many years before they are complete. The best runs of printed indexes are for PCC wills and of course the post-1858 calendars already mentioned are comprehensive. For wills in the National Library, printed indexes only exist for Bangor records (to 1700), and for Brecon records to 1600, although work continues apace, and the staff may be able to help by referring to manuscript indexes being prepared by a project team. The National Library has recently issued a free leaflet on probate records at the Library which is well-worth obtaining from the Keeper of Manuscripts (but remember to enclose return postage if writing.)

The Church of Latter-Day Saints has recently completed a microfiche index to Welsh diocesan wills, which gives the testator's name and address and the names of any relatives mentioned. Entries are sorted by diocese and then by year (of granting of probate). These can be useful, but care must be taken as they are far from free of errors of transcription, and place-names have often been sorely mis-rendered. Copies of the fiche for the appropriate dioceses are available at all the local record offices in Wales, and a complete set is to be seen in the National Library.

## Other Sources for Wills and Estates of Deceased Persons

Occasionally, the probate registry failed to preserve a copy of a will or record of grant of administration among the official records, and there are problems too with poor or incorrect indexing. English probate clerks often made appallingly incorrect transcriptions of Welsh personal and place names, and sometimes idiosyncratic spellings by the original testator can cause problems as well, if one relies on an alphabetical index. When a search of the apparently appropriate records draws a blank, there is always the chance that the copy of a will or the letters of administration have been preserved among family papers by the executors. Sometimes, to avoid the fees or because circumstances had changed, thus rendering a will meaningless, or when a will had been mislaid, probate was never sought. To locate such records, which from the point of view of a family historian are equally as valid a source as probate records, one could search any extant family collection in the appropriate record offices. Some offices in fact maintain indexes of these 'stray' wills. This is mainly applicable to the families of upper-class, landed descent, but large estates often absorbed small estates or single freehold farms and along with deeds of title came many wills relating to comparatively humble families. In Wales, such chance survivals are not very common, but the craft of family history often depends on such apparently forlorn hopes. It should also be remembered that wills often lead to family acrimony, and in a more litigious age, especially from the mid-eighteenth to the mid-nineteenth centuries, many disputes in Chancery hinged on the disposition of estates after a contested will, the records remaining in family archives. The family collection of estate documents can therefore often yield more than deeds and accounts and can make up for probate court deficiencies on occasion. Charities benefiting from a will also preserved copies, and the family historian should always seek these out too.

From around the mid-nineteenth century, more and more people had sufficient substance to make a will, and simultaneously solicitors' practices increased their business among the prosperous farming class and the business community. There was a boom in the probate business of solicitors at this time, and all record offices hold large accumulations of records relating to the solicitors' work in administering estates on behalf of executors. Files of papers relating to individual testators' estates survive by the thousand and, as well as wills, letters of administration and accounts, they often include much other interesting material. A few large landowners used English solicitors in centres such as London or Chester, but most Welsh solicitors' practices were local, based on the catchment area of a market town.

## Deeds of Settlement

While this chapter does not basically deal with deeds of title, one particular type of land transaction is so tied up with matters of family inheritance that it should briefly be mentioned here. The novice may often wonder that the will of a rich landowner may make no reference to landed property. This is because, as has been said, a will was a last-minute tidying-up of affairs, and land was too valuable to be left unassigned until such a time. Parents of betrothed couples also wanted to make sure that dowries of land or money stayed within the family. Succession to land was therefore usually ordained by grants of title to land from parents to the new husband either before or immediately after marriage, or on the birth of an heir. Sometimes fathers made over their lands to unmarried sons during their lifetime, with a proviso that they themselves had use of the land for life. These documents supplement the information gleaned from wills and allow a fuller picture to be gained of a family's total substance; and they often name relatives deceased before a will came to be made. As such they are worth searching for in estate papers and as they were deeds of title they should have been passed over to the purchaser if the land was sold, perhaps centuries later, so that they can turn up in unexpected places. The family historian will need to research the comparatively modern ownership of lands once in his own family's possession and then enquire whether recent owners have deposited their deeds in the local record office.

## The Scope of Inheritance Records

Since wills, and documents such as settlements, deal with property, landed or moveable, they naturally relate to persons of substance. Much work remains to be done on the demographic aspects of will-making in Wales and only generalised remarks can have any authority. Many more men than women figure as testators—perhaps in a ratio of 5:1 in the period before the Married Women's Property Acts (1870 and 1882). The greater the spread of wealth and freehold land in an area, the greater the proportion of the population making a will; the more landless labourers and poor tenants there were, the smaller was such a proportion. Rich farming areas with prosperous tenants, such as the South Wales lowlands, seem to yield a greater proportion of will-makers to non will-makers than the poverty-stricken smallholdings and small tenanted farms of much of Snowdonia. In seventeenth century Caernarfonshire, something like 50% of surviving wills came from the top 5% of society. As the distribution of wealth increased into the nineteenth century, more people made wills, since there was a new business, professional and trade class: perhaps something like 60% of all searches in the post-1858 calendars in North West Wales yield results, and this was an area of relative poverty, where one might expect many estates to be not worth the trouble of seeking probate.

For all the drawbacks of an essentially unrepresentative cross-section of society provided by wills, they are nevertheless some of the most exciting documents a family historian can find. In Wales, where many early records have been lost, they assume an almost unassailable importance, especially in the years before the dawn of the nineteenth century, with its great bureaucratic record-keeping institutions and plethora of extant genealogical source material. Moreover, of all the documents you may examine, wills are the most truly personal; in them, you find your ancestors talking to you.

Once one has a little experience of the phraseology and lay-out of wills, such as outlined above, there should be few problems for the researcher. No one, however, should venture into the world of probate records without the aid of Jeremy Gibson's comprehensive (and incredibly cheap) *Probate Jurisdictions: where to look for wills*.[6] As well as maps, dates for which documents survive, and lists of indexes, there is an invaluable glossary. Equally useful are two McLaughlin Guides.[7,8] Since all three together will cost very little, the reader will be well advised to invest in them. A.J. Camp's *Wills and their Whereabouts*[9] (now out of print) is a useful alternative.

**NOTES TO CHAPTER 13**

[1]Quoted in Leonard Owen, 'A Seventeenth Century Commonplace Book', *Trans. Hon. Soc. Cymmrodorion*, 1962, p.31.

[2]NLW Bangor Probate Records 1647/25.

[3]NLW Bangor Probate Records 1636/26.

[4]NLW Bangor Probate Records 1664/64.

[5]Most estates have deposited their records in either the local County Record Office, the National Library of Wales or the University College Library, Bangor. Estates can often have lands in several areas, and records may not be deposited in what would appear initially to be the most likely place. The local County Record Office, if it does not hold the records, will probably know if and where they are available.

[6]Jeremy Gibson, *Probate Jurisdictions: where to look for wills*, 3rd ed. (Birmingham: Federation of Family History Societies, 1985)

[7]Eve McLaughlin, *Wills before 1858* (Aylesbury: privately published).

[8]Eve McLaughlin, *Somerset House Wills from 1858* (Aylesbury: privately published).

[9]Anthony J Camp, *Wills and Their Whereabouts* (London: Society of Genealogists, 1974).

# 14. EDUCATION RECORDS

David A. Pretty

Few aspects of Welsh history have attracted greater attention than the development of the educational system. With the completion of the 'ladder' linking elementary and secondary schools to the university colleges at the end of the nineteenth century this achievement became a symbol of national pride. Naturally enough it also provided a theme which has inspired pietistic homage. Apart from the specialist studies, we have an extensive list of unpublished theses that concentrate mainly on the growth of education within a county framework, or else highlight the particular contribution of a key pioneering figure. Local studies usually trace the history of an individual school, sometimes in order to mark the centenary of its foundation. Taken together, they provide a clear indication of the value traditionally placed upon education in Wales. Even so, the majority tread a well-beaten track in that they place precise emphasis on religious issues or administrative matters. In the case of the latter the impact of a succession of Education Acts are discussed in copious detail and make bleak reading. Unfortunately for the family historian they evince little interest in the personal side and reveal few names. For one reason or another, one is often left with the impression that an educational structure was constructed without pupils: a teacher's dream but a genealogist's nightmare!

Over the centuries the progress of popular education in Wales has followed a well-defined course. At the same time its direction was strongly influenced by two distinct traditions—the religious and the secular. Which school a pupil attended, however, depended initially on his place in society. Class origins became the crucial factor that governed educational opportunity and determined both the character and the content of the curriculum. From the middle of the seventeenth century the religious motive achieved prominence as shown by the desire to save the souls of the poor. Charitable endeavour provided the initiative behind the supply of schooling for the lower classes; the main aim was to immerse the children in Biblical knowledge. Long regarded as the preserve of the socially ambitious upper and middle classes, the secular tradition took some time to secure predominance under the aegis of the state. Of course, both elements had always combined to some degree.

But with the rise of nonconformity the religious issue aroused bitter sectarian rivalry that characterised education in Wales until the close of the Edwardian Age. Outside the state system there existed a flourishing private sector. The infinite variety of quality private schools that dotted most towns and villages reflected the aspirations of those intent on social elevation and worldly success. Wealthier parents sent their children to boarding schools in England.

The inter-relationship between religion and education became evident during the years of Puritan rule when the Act for the Better Propagation and Preaching of the Gospel in Wales was passed in 1650. In accordance with its design at least 60 free schools were established, chiefly in market towns along the border. Both sexes received instruction in a course of learning that had a strong Puritan bias. The names of 74 schoolmasters and ushers who were appointed during the years 1650-3 are known, but not the scholars.[1] Because of the political situation the schools did not take deep root and by the time of the Restoration in 1660 they had all disappeared.

Existing grammar schools were left untouched because their educative value was already well appreciated. Prior to the Tudor period many of the Welsh squirearchy had sent their sons to be educated in English grammar schools, notably those in the border towns of Oswestry, Shrewsbury and Hereford. Under the new order that followed the political Acts of Union 1536-43 the Welsh gentry class, in general, seized on the opportunities afforded by equal citizenship to seek advancement in government, law and the church. Consequently, a number of grammar schools were to be endowed by high-minded individuals in Wales itself. Beginning with Christ College, Brecon (1541), a string of establishments followed in the reigns of Elizabeth and James I: among them Bangor, Beaumaris, Carmarthen, Cowbridge, Hawarden, Llanrwst and Ruthin. The grammar school at Cowbridge was founded by Sir Edward Stradling of St Donat's in 1609. Unlike the prestigious English grammar schools, the early registers and records of pupils who attended the Welsh schools have not survived. Indeed few primary sources are available for the period leading up to the eighteenth century. One of the earliest documents is the David Hughes, Beaumaris, school roll of 1785-1869.[2] Individual school histories usually chronicle the names of headmasters, assistants and ushers. Typically, only the names of the brightest scholars and those guilty of various misdemeanours are recorded for posterity! A register of scholars attending Bishop Gore's Swansea Grammar School between 1851 and

1894[3] includes information about admission, progress and conduct of pupils, their parents' names and occupations, and home address.

Modelled on their English counterparts they trained boys in grammar, the classical languages and religious precepts. Education was through the medium of English. Fees were charged and those pupils who came from outside the locality were boarded at the school. In many cases a quota of 'free places' were earmarked for deserving pupils from poor backgrounds. All in all, the basis was thus laid for a system of secondary education in Wales, even though the actual numbers who attended the 30 or so endowed schools were extremely limited by modern standards. In the course of time the grammar schools attracted their clientele from the emergent middle class, in particular merchants, farmers and professional people keen to ensure that their sons made their way in the world. Responding to such pressures, the trustees of the grammar schools were obliged, by the nineteenth century, to choose between the traditional classical curriculum and a diversified commercial course more in tune with the needs of the local middle classes. This clash of interests often led to fierce disputes over the future of such schools. Beaumaris Grammar School was involved in much controversy when efforts were made to change its elitist character. Its designation as a county school in 1895 heralded the final victory for the forces of progress.

The great landowners still looked beyond the confines of Wales for an elitist education for their sons. As they became increasingly anglicised, this close identification with all things English found no better preparation than in the famous public schools of Eton, Harrow, Westminster and Winchester. Westminster School maintained a close connection with North Wales; the first Marquess of Anglesey and five of his sons attended the school. The registers of Winchester College, likewise, record the names of the sons of upper class landed families from Caernarfonshire, Denbighshire and Glamorgan.[4] With no centre for higher education as yet in Wales, they went on to the universities of Oxford and Cambridge, thus maintaining a tradition that was at least two centuries old. Particularly after the foundation of Jesus College in 1571, the Welsh element at Oxford substantially increased. Altogether, some thousand Welsh students were enrolled at the constituent colleges of Oxford and Cambridge between 1571 and 1621. This flow continued, with many of the entrants winning scholarships from the grammar schools. *Alumni Oxonienses* and *Alumni Cantabrigienses* provide a record of the members of both universities from the earliest times to the end of the nineteenth century. Available for consultation in the reference section of most major libraries, they supply information as to parentage, birthplace and year of birth, often with the student's academic career and subsequent achievements. Familiar Welsh surnames immediately catch the eye: Davies, Howell, Lewis, Lloyd, Owen, Parry, etc. For example:

> LEWIS, GRIFFITH THOMAS. Adm. Pens. at SIDNEY, Oct 1, 1893. S. of David, Calvinist minister, of Trehiddian, Carmarthen. B. Feb 3, 1873 at Pilrhoth, Carmarthen. School, Llandovery College (Mr O.Evans). Matric. Michs.1893; exhibitioner; B.A. 1896; M.A. 1900 Assistant master at Pembroke Dock School 1896. Head Master of Tregaron School, 1897-1933.[5]

Alternatively, others flocked to the Inns of Court in London to receive a thorough grounding in the legal profession. Once again, registers and admittance books testify to a flourishing Welsh connection, with son often succeeding father.

Against this, one must consider the sensibilities of the Nonconformists who were debarred from the Anglican grammar schools and English universities. No better stimulus could be found for the establishment of nonconformist academies in Wales. Ironically, it was a fellow of Jesus College, Oxford, who opened the first academy for dissenters at Brynllywarch, Glamorgan, in 1662. The rapid growth of nonconformity over the next two centuries led to a proliferation of private academies and theological colleges run by various denominations: principally Carmarthen, Abergavenny, Brecon, Pontypool, Trefeca and Bala. The high standard of liberal education they imparted earned them a deserved reputation and it is not without significance that they became the nursery of some of the foremost preachers and politicians of their day.

The provision of education for the lower classes, meantime, reflected an intrinsically religious conception of philanthropic work. Individual benefactors now gave way to established agencies. The remarkable Charity School Movement of the seventeenth and eighteenth centuries found its direct roots in Puritanism. It was an ejected Puritan minister in London, Thomas Gouge, who had the inspiration to set up the Welsh Trust in 1674. Allied to the distribution of religious literature was the provision of schools for teaching poor children to read. Details are sketchy but the reports of the Trust list 87 schools in 1675 and 71 three years later. Up to 2,000 children are said to have been taught each year. The use of English as a medium of instruction proved counterproductive and with Gouge's death in 1681 its worthy activities came to an end.

Before long the same spirit manifested itself in the foundation of the Society for the Promotion of Christian Knowledge (SPCK) in 1699. Anglican in origin and London based, it maintained close associations with Wales through the support of Welsh lay patrons like Sir John Philipps and Sir Humphrey Mackworth. During the opening decades of the eighteenth century the SPCK played a leading role in both religious and educational activity, distributing books and establishing schools.

By 1737 the SPCK had sponsored 96 schools in Wales, not to mention another 61 schools set up by independent endowment. Whereas most could be found in the southern counties, the 10 charity schools endowed by Dean John Jones in North Wales epitomised the enthusiastic support of the Anglican clergy. Children were taught mainly the 3Rs (reading, writing and arithmetic) with added emphasis on scripture knowledge. Although Welsh was the preferred medium of instruction in some North Wales schools, the English language predominated elsewhere despite the monoglot nature of most communities. For various reasons the SPCK never came near to fulfilling its ambitious aim of providing schools throughout Wales. Poverty proved a major deterrent to regular attendance; children were compelled to go around begging for food. If a system of popular education was to flourish in eighteenth century Wales it had to take heed of the prevailing linguistic and social circumstances and adapt schooling to the situation as it existed.

In the annals of Welsh education the name of Griffith Jones, rector of Llanddowror, stands foremost in the ranks of heroes. His vision and pragmatic genius for organisation enabled him to succeed splendidly in what he set out to do. Aware of the high level of illiteracy that persisted among the mass of common people he was driven by a religious duty, early in the 1730s, to embark on an educational crusade. Thus began the Circulating Schools Movement that penetrated every corner of Wales. As a teacher in one of the early SPCK schools, Griffith Jones had surely noted its failings. His plan was simple but effective. Schools would be open to young and old alike for a period of usually three months, this being the time considered necessary to instruct people to read the Bible in their native tongue. Nothing else was to be taught. By employing itinerant teachers and utilising the local parish church, Griffith Jones found that he could achieve rapid progress at the minimum cost. Potential problems associated with the social condition of the people were overcome by holding schools during the winter months and running evening classes. In fact, it was estimated that two-thirds of those who received a free education were adults.

Each year, subscribers to the Circulating Schools Movement were issued with an annual report called *Welch Piety* (which can be consulted at the National Library of Wales, Aberystwyth). The statistics they published indicate the astonishing nature of his achievement. Even after the death of Griffith Jones in 1761, the movement continued to flourish under the supervision of Madam Bridget Bevan, one of his principal patrons. Between 1736 and 1776, the period covered by *Welch Piety*, 6,321 schools were established and 304,475 scholars taught. Even allowing for duplication (schools often returned to the same place to hold a second session, and not all scholars were fluent the first time round), it is probably true to say that half the population of Wales at this time attended a circulating school. Few nations in Europe could claim such a high rate of literacy. Consistent with Griffith Jones's attention to detail was the instruction given to teachers to keep a methodical list of names, places of abode, ages, calling, and progress of all the men, women and children who were taught by them. It is a tantalising thought for the family historian that such a store of information should now be lost forever.

The collapse of the movement upon the death of Madam Bridget Bevan in 1779 left a vacuum in the sphere of education. Once the parallel religious revival made rapid headway in North Wales the need for schools occupied the attention of Thomas Charles of Bala as he assumed the leadership of Calvinistic Methodism. Failure to revive the principle of the circulating schools in the 1780s compelled him to turn progressively towards the alternative idea of Sunday Schools. Unpaid teachers undertook the task of instructing adults and children in the Scriptures. The phenomenal growth of the Sunday schools at the turn of the century, and their adoption by other denominations, guaranteed the preponderance of Nonconformity in Wales. The consequent demand for Welsh Bibles was embodied in the story of Mari Jones, a sixteen year old girl who walked over 25 miles to Bala in 1800 to purchase her copy from Thomas Charles. An old family Bible, well prized over generations, can often be a valuable source of genealogical material.

With justification, the Sunday Schools came to be regarded as the people's 'college'. They offered a continuing education that was democratically organised and free from class distinction. As in the case of the Circulating Schools Movement, scrupulous regard was paid to organisational detail; attendance registers were kept and accurate figures compiled. The Sunday School Register of Moriah Chapel, Caernarfon, 1813,[6] gives the name, age, address, names of parents and, in the case of adults, their occupation: for example, Hugh Hughes, aged 22, Heol y Llyn, son of William Hughes, carpenter. The progress of each individual was regularly assessed, with a full record of what he had learnt by memory. Each denomination then proceeded to publish annual reports, brimful with statistics, based on chapel, district and county.

Accelerating migration from the countryside to the South Wales coalfield brought the Sunday Schools to the new industrial towns, along with the moral values they embodied. By their very nature, however, the scope of the instruction they offered was severely limited. Large scale economic developments soon presented a formidable challenge to educationalists. One answer was provided by the Works School system, whereby paternalistic employers of labour built and equipped schools for working class children. While the schools established by Sir Humphrey Mackworth in the 1700s were the first in the field, the heyday of the Works Schools came between 1810 and 1870. Industry and school went hand in hand in the form of the ironworks school, tinplate works school and colliery school provided by proprietors like the Guest and Vivian families of Dowlais and Swansea. Thirty two colliery schools were opened in Glamorgan after 1860; several in the Rhondda Valley were maintained by contributions from the workmen's wages. Instruction for the most part was confined to the orthodox 3Rs and religious instruction, although some schools offered a wider curriculum. The quality of each institution, by and large, depended on the character of the schoolmaster. Most of the Works Schools declined with the advent of the state system of elementary education in the 1870s.

Elementary education throughout most of the nineteenth century was complicated by religious rivalry; church and chapel vied for control in the belief that schooling would determine the sectarian allegiance of the child. Members of the SPCK had formed the National Society in 1811 with the specific intention of educating the poor in the principles of the Established Church. Beginning with Lord Kenyon, who erected and maintained the school at Penley, Flintshire, the Anglican gentry proved generous in the provision of land and money. Insofar as they would be employed to stem the Nonconformist tide the clergy, likewise, became fervent supporters of National Schools. In this respect, Dean J.H.Cotton made an outstanding contribution in the diocese of Bangor. The Annual Reports of the National Society, plus various official Government Reports, chart their rapid spread throughout Wales: from 30 (1814), 146 (1833), rising to 685 by 1870. Based on the monitorial system, National Schools provided an inexpensive method of mass education in the 3Rs reinforced by moral training and inculcation of Anglican doctrines. What is more, pupils were compelled to attend Church on Sundays, although this rule was later relaxed in the face of Nonconformist opposition.

Understandably, this situation stirred great anger amongst the Nonconformists, most of whom were content to have their children taught in the Sunday Schools. Although the answer was at hand, in the form of undenominational schools set up by the British and Foreign Schools Society, they showed little interest at first. In South Wales there was even opposition to the government grants introduced in 1833. Consequently there were only some 16 British Schools in the whole of Wales by the 1840s. It needed the intervention of Hugh Owen to goad the Nonconformists into action; hence the turning point marked by his *Letter to the Welsh People* in 1843. On his advice the Revd John Phillips became the British Schools Society's agent in North Wales in that year. Another decade was to pass before the Revd William Roberts, followed by David Williams, undertook the same mission in the South. Working hard to make up lost ground they achieved much despite the formidable obstacles in their way. By 1870 the number of British Schools in Wales stood at 302, served by a supply of teachers trained mainly at the Bangor Normal College opened in 1858. Given the religious background, the competition between both societies had intensified the bitter sectarian conflict and caused an unnecessary duplication of educational effort. Schoolmasters frequently complained of children moving from one school to another.

Things were made worse with the publication of the infamous Education Report of 1847. Three English commissioners, backed by Anglican assistants, had surveyed the state of elementary education in Wales with an eye for colourful detail. Most parish schools were in a dismal condition; Trefeglwys Church School, Montgomeryshire (held in the church tower) being a typical case:

> The master, who is only 20 years of age, has not been trained. He has been a teacher since he was 14 years of age. He was meanly dressed, and complained very much of his poverty . . . His knowledge of English is imperfect . . . he has no method either in teaching or governing his pupils, who are in bad discipline.[7]

Few doubted its educational content, but the overt attack on the morals, language and religion of the people provoked a storm of protest that widened the sectarian divide. Since then, the 'Treason of the Blue Books' has figured prominently in the historiography of Welsh education. The castigation of the Welsh language, however, merely underlined the low status accorded to it within the day schools. Parents recognised that a knowledge of English was indispensable to social advancement and were prepared to consent to a regime that not only elevated English to the medium of instruction but also deliberately ostracised their native tongue. Suppression of the language by means of the 'Welsh Not' (a piece of wood suspended around the neck of a pupil which signified he or she had been caught speaking in Welsh, which constituted a punishable offence) became commonplace in the schools of rural Wales. A period of national revival in the 1880s heralded a change of attitude. The Welsh language gained recognition as a specific subject, but only gradually did the principle of bilingualism seep into the schools of Wales.

Direct state intervention could not be long delayed. The 1870 Education Act set out to fill the gaps left by the two voluntary societies and pave the way towards a national system of education. School boards were elected to remedy any deficiencies. As it happened, this fuelled sectarian enmity still further as both sides fought for the control of local boards on church versus chapel lines. Added to this was the shameless self-interest often shown by rate-conscious farmers keen to keep down expenditure on board schools. All in all, hotly contested triennial campaigns received extensive coverage in both the denominational and local press—listing names, sectarian affiliation and sometimes occupation. Those returned in the first round of elections in 1871 are noted in R.H.Mair's book, *The School Boards: Our Educational Parliaments* (London: 1872). Transcending all points of dispute is the ultimate success achieved by the 1870 Act; each locality was now provided with an efficient school. Controversy flared up once more with the passing of the 1902 Education Act which placed all schools under the control of the county council. After that date all board schools and surviving National and British schools continued as council schools. With a single local education authority responsible for both primary and secondary schools, sectarian dissension soon gave way to the quest for true equality of opportunity that finally came with the 1944 Education Act and the implementation of the comprehensive system in Wales after 1953.

Since 1833, increased state control had meant more education decrees and official reports. In place of the old system of grants the 1862 Revised Code of Regulations brought in a system of payment by results which linked financial help to examination performance and regular attendance. It was now in the interest of headteachers to see that scholars attained maximum attendance and for this purpose they kept school registers. Legislation to compel parents to send their children to school was introduced in 1876, although compulsory full-time education for all children between the ages of five and 10 did not become mandatory until a further act in 1880. (This turned out to be something of a myth in rural areas.) Every school board and management committee had to pass bye-laws to enforce attendance. In 1877 the Education Department also issued Revised Regulations for Certificates of Age, School Attendance and Proficiency in the 3Rs to enable both managers and employers to determine whether a pupil was qualified to leave school and take up employment. Subsequent Acts raised the school leaving age to 12 (1899) and 14 (1918).

Those admission and attendance registers that survive usually date from the 1870s, although a few go back to the early '60s and even the late '50s. There is no set pattern and the degree of information shows variation from one register to another. The most basic type gives only the name and address of the pupil. Others can be very informative genealogically since they list the date of birth, name and occupation of parents, date of admission and withdrawal from school. Considering the high incidence of common Welsh surnames this source can often provide an invaluable starting point for the researcher. But the degree of reliability is sometimes open to question; in the manner of things names and dates can unfortunately be wrongly transcribed. In the case of an illegitimate child the names of the grandparents might be under the heading of parent. Even an approximate birthdate, however, is something from which to work and it can always be corroborated using other sources.

From 1863 headteachers were also required by the Education Department to keep a school log book. For the family historian they present a rich and intimate source of intelligence although some headteachers were far more forthcoming than others in their entries. As a record of daily events they deal with every aspect of school life, and school managers, staff and pupils are named for a multitude of reasons: visits, absence, lateness, ailments, death, misbehaviour, punishments, expulsions, progress, scholarships, etc. Fortunately, the majority of log books have now been deposited in the local record offices, although some might still be in private possession, in particular the local clergyman.

National or British school committee minute books that pre-date 1860 are extremely rare.

Published local studies can be interesting, informative and well illustrated. They invariably contain a separate chapter on education with reminiscences of 'schooldays' and vivid extracts culled from the log books. Not all the names cited, however, would find immediate acceptance in the family tree. Take for instance these entries:

> Bessie Jones caned for being disobedient. Very rude and unmanageable afterwards, threatening to knock her teacher down and running after her with a poker in her hand[8].

> Half day holiday owing to the father of Francis Evans coming to school and creating a disturbance.[9]

In addition, local histories often print old photographs of long-forgotten classes going back as far as the 1870s, appended (occasionally) with the names of the teacher(s) and pupils. Special brochures written to celebrate an individual school's centenary can offer excellent material. *A Short History of Llandebie National School 1851-1951* by T.H.Lewis is one of the best of its kind, replete with names, dates, photographs and direct quotations from the log books. Specific mention is made in such cases of past pupils who earned subsequent fame. On the occasion of its centenary in 1974, Llanddaniel Primary School in Anglesey was especially proud that one pupil had achieved high office with the National Aeronautics and Space Administration in the USA.

Innumerable biographies and autobiographies of eminent Welshmen (women are a rarity in this respect) provide a further line of enquiry. Those fortunate to live in an age which placed a high premium on scholarship record their early schooling in evocative language. A strong devotion to gifted schoolmasters is often blended with treasured memories of fellow pupils, a theme subsequently carried forward into college days. Fittingly enough, W.J.Gruffydd's biography of Owen M.Edwards's early life (1858-1883) lays great emphasis on the scholastic progress of a man who turned out to be one of Wales's foremost education administrators. Individual chapters abound with the names of teachers, contemporary pupils and students. Another literary classic that deserves mention is *Edrych Yn Ôl,* the autobiography of the distinguished Welsh historian, R.T.Jenkins (1881-1969).[10] Both his own education and subsequent period as a secondary schoolteacher are stylishly recounted with a characteristic interest in people.

Outside the state sector, and too often overlooked, were the hundreds of private schools of every description: dame schools, ladies' seminaries, preparatory schools, navigation schools, academies, grammar schools, collegiate and 'university' schools—that took both day and boarding pupils. One only has to peruse local trade directories and newspaper columns to be surprised by the vast assortment of advertisements. For those who could afford the fees, select education was readily available in all major towns. At one time or another every village in Wales must have boasted a private school. Needless to say, the tradition of sending children to fashionable boarding schools in England also continued. Whereas the advertisements name the proprietor and various specialist tutors, acquiring a list of pupils is especially difficult. One avenue of approach would be to consult the census returns. The larger boarding schools were enumerated in separate schedules and under each institution is listed the name, age and birthplace of the pupils in residence. Because reputations rested on academic achievement, proprietors made certain that their pupils' success gained maximum publicity wherever possible. Holt Academy, near Wrexham, filled half a page of *Baner ac Amserau Cymru* each June in the 1870s with the names of its students (drawn from most Welsh counties) and the results they achieved in the Midsummer Examination. Neither should we forget the handful of public schools in Wales: for example, Monmouth, Rydal and Llandovery. The admission registers of Llandovery College are available from 1866, also a list of free scholars 1848-1890.[11]

Secondary education in the form of the grammar schools went through a period of transformation in the latter half of the nineteenth century. Under the terms of the Endowed Schools Act of 1869 new schemes were promoted to place the schools within the reach of children of all classes. Local wrangling among interested parties delayed the process. The inception of a scholarship scheme in 1879 helped gifted boys to proceed from the elementary schools to the grammar schools. Details of scholarships, exhibitions and prizes won can be found in the *North Wales Scholarship Association Reports, 1879-1894*.[12] Meanwhile, proposals on the future of the grammar schools made in the Aberdare Report (1881)[13] were embodied in the Welsh Intermediate Education Act of 1889. A network of publicly funded, non-denominational secondary schools for boys and girls was set up under the control of the county councils who acted as local education authority. By 1902, 95 county schools had been established in Wales, including Pontypridd, opened in 1896 with 105 boys and 66 girls, the majority being children of managers, tradesmen and workmen. Notwithstanding their unsectarian character, they still maintained the academic traditions of the old grammar schools at the expense of commercial and technical education.

The few individual histories that have been published show that there is ample scope for detailed research into the wealth of secondary school records, viz. Wilfred Harrison, *Greenhill School, Tenby, 1896-1964*, A.Mór O'Brien, *The County School for Boys, Pontypridd, 1896-1973*. Anniversaries have also provided an opportunity for recording history and achievement as, for example, the *Cyfarthfa Castle Grammar School Golden Jubilee Booklet 1913-63*. Included among the records are school log books, admission registers, attendance registers, pupils' examination results, lists of school prefects, school fees books, school magazines, scrapbooks of newspaper cuttings and photographs of various school groups.

As the principal driving force behind the British schools, the secondary schools movement, and now the university college, Hugh Owen well deserved the title 'Father of Welsh National Education'. The opening of the university college at Aberystwyth in 1872 was the realisation of an idea first advanced in the early fifteenth century. The majority of students came from lower middle class backgrounds and the college had to struggle to survive. Following the recommendations of the Aberdare Report two new colleges were to be established at Cardiff (1883) and Bangor (1884). As a result, Wales could boast a complete educational structure at the close of the nineteenth century. Swansea (1920) and Lampeter (1972) were later additions to the federal structure, although St David's College, Lampeter, had existed as an Anglican theological college since 1827. Bearing in mind that only a very small percentage of secondary school pupils went on to higher education, there is a far greater chance of extracting personal information from admission lists, tutors' registers, records of individual students, college calendars, college magazines, etc, in that each college has its own archives. The histories of the university colleges at Aberystwyth, Bangor and Lampeter have all drawn on a substantial collection of printed and manuscript sources housed in the individual colleges.

Education records are legion. By today, each county record office in Wales has amassed a vast array of primary sources and it is here that the start should be made. Having established the locality and type of school, there is every chance that the researcher will strike gold if the relevant log books, admission and attendance registers remain available for scrutiny. Among other miscellanea to have possibly survived it may be worth noting attendance officers' report books, children's progress books and punishment books. Printed handlists in the record offices catalogue the extensive volume of school records that have been merely touched upon in this chapter. A special publication, *Guide to Research No. 2: History of Education*, can be purchased from the Gwent County Record Office. Each list of accessions is constantly updated as new material is deposited. Unfortunately, there are some schools whose records are incomplete or are unaccounted for. Then again, a few schools have chosen to retain their records, while certain items may still be found in private hands. All things considered, the sheer mass of education records dating from the second half of the nineteenth century offers great promise. Although possibly intimidating at first sight, the family historian should certainly not be discouraged from tracking down names; the main fascination lies in the basic detective work.

**NOTES TO CHAPTER 14**

[1]Thomas Richards, *A History of the Puritan Movement in Wales* (London: 1920).

[2]Gwynedd Archives Service, Llangefni. David Hughes Charity MSS

[3]Glamorgan County Record Office, Cardiff. Education Records, Secondary Schools.

[4]Geraint Dyfnallt Owen, *Elizabethan Wales* (Cardiff: 1964), p.206

[5]J.A.Venn, *Alumni Cantabrigienses*, p.162.

[6]Gwynedd Archives Service, Caernarfon. Moriah Chapel Records.

[7]*Report of the Commissioners of Inquiry into the State of Education in Wales* (1847), Vol III, p.163

[8]K.Kissack, *Monmouth: the Making of a Town.*

[9]Meirion Davies, *Glynogwr and Gilfach Goch: A History.*

[10]W.J.Gruffydd,*Cofiant O.M.Edwards* (Aberystwyth: 1937) and R.T.Jenkins, *Edrych Yn Ôl*, (Clwb Llyfrau Cymraeg Llundain: 1968).

[11]W.Gareth Evans, *A History of Llandovery College* (Llandovery: 1981).

[12]*North Wales Scholarship Association Reports*, available for consultation in the Library at the University College of North Wales, Bangor.

[13]*Report of the Committee Appointed to Inquire into the Condition of Intermediate and Higher Education in Wales*, (HMSO: 1881).

# 15. Parochial Records

John Rowlands

## Introduction

Those with experience of family history research in both an English and a Welsh context will know that the chances of tracing ancestors back into (say) the eighteenth century using the main sources for research—parish registers, wills, civil registration and the census—are far greater in England than they are in Wales. The poor survival rate for parish registers, the small stock of surnames, the survival of the patronymic system of naming and the influence of nonconformity, all conspire to make life difficult for the Welsh researcher.

When presented with the block to further progress which can stem from this, researchers are forced to turn to other less familiar sources. One such source which can certainly yield fascinating details about the sort of lives our ancestors might have lived, and which will occasionally give information of direct genealogical importance, is often overlooked. This source is known as parochial records, which are the records of the civil administration of a parish. While they will have been held for safe-keeping for centuries in the parish chest alongside the parish registers, they are not (as is often supposed) ecclesiastical records in any sense. Rather they are civil records relating to everyday matters in a parish as they affected all the inhabitants, irrespective of social status or religious affiliation.

## The Origins of Parochial Records

Prior to the Reformation, responsibility for local administration of community affairs fell variously on the manorial courts and on the parish, with the great religious houses assuming an especial role in the relief of the poor. In the sixteenth century, with the dissolution of the monasteries and a general decline in the manorial system, those responsibilities began to be increasingly (and formally) devolved to the parishes.

By the beginning of the seventeenth century responsibility for the administration of local affairs had been placed squarely on parishes. Those responsibilities were progressively modified and extended by various Acts over the next 200 years. The net effect of all this was that if a community wanted to build a school or needed to mend a road it was to local and not national resources it would look; if it needed to settle a dispute or help someone fallen on hard times, it was to local wisdom or benevolence that it would turn.

All these acts of construction, charity, etc, did not come about by accident; they needed a local administrative organisation to bring them about. That organisation was the General or Open Vestry which was in theory a meeting open to the whole of the parish. In practice it was usually confined to the principal inhabitants who met under the chairmanship of the parish priest as and when required. In some parishes a small number of the more important people would be delegated to handle the financial affairs of the parish; this they did in a Closed or Select Vestry.[1] These came into increasing prominence after the Napoleonic Wars when, as a result of a succession of bad harvests and the pressure of soldiers returning from the Wars, the scale of poor relief rose dramatically.

As their name implies, these meetings were normally held in the vestry of the parish church, although they might often be held in (or adjourned to) the house of a prominent local person, or even the local inn. Even though from its name the Vestry Meeting might seem to be an arm of the Established Church, dissenters of all sorts could, and often did, play a full and effective part in the decisions which were taken; not least because they too could be affected financially by those decisions.

The Vestry Meeting made decisions which affected the whole community and had powers to levy rates and to appoint officers to carry out its decisions. It is the record of those meetings together with the many other records which stemmed from them which make up the Parochial Records.

## The Nature and Location of Parochial Records

Most of the documents which are to be found in the parochial records stem directly from decisions taken at the Vestry Meeting. The documents of greatest use to the family historian among those likely to be found in the parochial records for a parish fall into the following categories:

Vestry Minutes
Rate Assessment and Collection
Churchwardens' and Overseers' Accounts

Settlement and Removal
Concern about commitments to the County Militia
Apprenticeship Records
Bonds of Indemnity
Control of Vermin and Strays

Most of the parochial records for Wales have now been deposited either at the National Library of Wales or at the appropriate County Record Office. As yet there is no published guide to what has survived for individual parishes, or to where they have been deposited. Unfortunately, the neglect which has resulted in the poor survival rate for parish registers has also affected parochial records and many parishes have no surviving records until quite late. However, as a rule of thumb it would be sensible to look for parochial records for a parish at the place where their parish registers have been deposited. The best book to consult for this information is *Cofrestri Plwyf Cymru/Parish Registers of Wales*.[2]

## Vestry Minutes

As with most other minutes, these are usually only a brief note of the items which were decided upon at the Vestry Meeting. People are named, decisions are recorded, and the minute is signed by those present. However, it is the multitude of other records which stem from those decisions which offer most for the family historian.

Many vestry minutes can be of interest in their own right and in particular when they firmly establish the authority of the vestry meeting within the parish. This includes authority over the select vestry as can be seen in two items from the minutes of a select vestry held at the Castle Inn, Angle (Pembrokeshire), in 1819:

> 2d: David Rees having appeared before the Vestry to request they should grant him (by way of a loan) two pounds from each of the farms in the Parish to enable him to purchase a small vessel to procure a livelihood for himself and family, and to liquidate this debt he will fetch the culm every year for the Parish, and do any other jobs the Parishioners may wish to employ him in, and will deposit in Mr Palmer's hands half of the Profits arising from the Vessel till the debt is paid off.
> 3d: The Vestry are of the opinion they are not competent to give the claimant an answer to his request, and do therefore direct the Overseers of the Poor to call a General Vestry for Tuesday at 4 o'clock pm for them to decide upon.[3]

**Rate Assessment and Collection**

Lists, particularly those which establish the existence of individuals in time and place, are a joy for family historians. Where those lists have been drawn up regularly (possibly annually) and give an insight into continuity and change within a parish, this is especially so.

There is no better context to search for such lists than where the collection (or payment) of money is involved and this applies right down to parish level. The power to levy rates brought with it a requirement to assess upon whom within the parish the burden of paying rates should fall and the amount each person who was liable should pay. The lists of those so assessed—and perhaps one-third of householders may have been exempt at certain times—often name the farm or other property with which they are connected. The amount for which individuals are assessed can give a clear picture of relative status within a parish.

These characteristics of continuity, change and status can be seen in the poor rate assessments for a group of farms in the parish of Llanrhystud (Cardiganshire) given in Fig 15-1. In this it can be seen when widows take over a farm on the death of their husbands. In the case of my own family at Pantyrhogfaen we can see not only continuity of tenure over a large part of the eighteenth century, but also clear evidence of the settling of the surname Rowland(s) over the three generations of Rowland William, Daniel Rowland and William Rowland (at Nantcennin). The last of these had secured the tenancy at Nantcennin before the death of his father and, as a result, the tenancy of Pantyrhogfaen passed to Evan Edwards on the death of Daniel Rowland.

| Name of Farm | 1738 (Names only) | 1773 @ 12d | 1788 @ 12d | 1812 @ 5/- |
|---|---|---|---|---|
| Pantyrhogfaen | Rowland William | Daniel Rowland 1/6 | Daniel Rowland 1/6 | Evan Edwards 7/6 |
| Rhydlas Ucha | Evan Evans | David Evans 2/- | Mary Evans 2/- | Widow Evans 10/- |
| Rhydlas Issa | Thomas Lewis | William Evans 2/6 | William Evans 2/6 | David Benjamin 12/6 |
| Glanperis | David Morris | David Jenkin 5/- | William Jones 5/- | William Jones 25/- |
| Nantcennin | John David Evan | Widow 2/6 | Jenkin David 2/6 | William Rowland 12/6 |

Fig. 15-1: Poor Rate Assessments for a group of farms, Llanrhystud, Cardiganshire[4]

Until the early part of the eighteenth century the demand for rates was usually a modest one and collected as a single levy. Over the next century, however, the burden of relieving the poor increased dramatically. In many cases this resulted in separate demands being made for a General or Church Rate (which was needed for the upkeep of the fabric of the church and for other minor parish activities) and the Poor Rate. At times of particular difficulty, perhaps as a result of a bad harvest or during times of war, more than one Poor Rate would be levied within a year as the calls for relief grew. In Fig. 15-1 it can be seen that, between 1788 and 1812 (at this latter date Britain was at war with Napoleon) the scale of the Poor Rate had increased five-fold.

Sometimes difficulties in collecting the rate will be recorded and this can be an indication of financial problems or family illness. Occasionally such a record can provide direct genealogical information, as is the case with the assessment and collection records for the parish of Llanrhystud for 1752. This shows Mr Owen Morrice and Stephen Edward being assessed at 2s:6d; yet at the year end Widow Morrice and Stephen Edward were in arrears for that sum.[5] As the registers for the parish have not survived for this period this incidental record gives a lead to the latest date to look for events in the life of Owen Morrice.

## Churchwardens' and Overseers' Accounts

The use of rates for the upkeep of the fabric of the church and other parish facilities was recorded in Churchwardens' Accounts. Those rates used for the relief of the poor are contained in the Accounts of the Overseers of the Poor. Both these series of accounts can be of great interest and value to family historians.

In the case of the upkeep of the church, the tradesmen who received payment for the multitude of odd jobs which needed to be done (such as replacing lost tiles, mending the leading, repairing windows or the churchyard wall, etc) can all be named, along with the amount they received. These entries can be both illuminating and amusing.

Thus we have the following entries in the Churchwardens' Accounts for the parish of Carew (Pembrokeshire) in 1738:[6]

> Pd: Thos Cod and Simon Davies for washing the Church & pointing part of him and Cleaning the leads . . . 17/-
> Pd: The Clerk for mending a hole in the Church yard wall & his wife for Cleaning the Church after washing . . . 1/6

Items such as these not only name regular tradesmen but also show that even the Clerk and his wife were not too proud to turn their hands to other tasks.

Later that century—in 1770—we have the following item which shows that Thomas Cod (or possibly his son) was still in business:[7]

Pd: Thomas Cod for Glaseing the windows & maso[n]ing work & plumer work rendering the leads . . . 2/11/8
Pd: Thos Cod since the storm for mason work as particulars you shall see his notes . . . 12/8

While in that same year three minor items clearly illustrate that mistakes can occur even in the best regulated of societies:

For a pees of Rope for the bell . . . 1/-
More Rope for the bell 2½ fatham . . . 1/2
For splicing the bell Rope In two places . . . 2d

Within most accounts, however, there will be one item of direct religious significance. It was accepted that the parish (as a whole) would provide bread and wine for the Communion in the parish church four times a year, namely at Christmas, Easter, Whitsun and on All Saints' Day.

## Settlement and Removal

Records relating to settlement and removal are frequently to be found among parochial records. Understandably, parishes were concerned to ensure that parish relief was only given to those paupers who were their responsibility. Legal responsibility for a pauper was known as settlement and individuals could gain this either by renting property to an annual value of £10 or more, by paying the poor rate, by being employed in a parish for a year or more, by serving as a parochial officer, or by undertaking an apprenticeship within the parish. A wife automatically took the place of settlement of her husband, and children usually took the place of settlement of their father. In the case of an illegitimate child, however, settlement was determined by its place of birth. It is important to realise that it was the last qualifying act which determined the place of settlement.

Where someone resident within a parish needed relief (or was heading that way) but was believed to be the responsibility of another parish, then the vestry minutes are likely to record a decision to take that person before the justices to be examined as to their legal place of settlement. Needless to say, such references abound in vestry minutes and those for Llanrhystud in 1781 record the following typical item:

> Ordered likewise that the Overseers of the Poor of this Parish apply for an order of removal against David Morgan now an inhabitant of this Parish, and effectually to remove him and his Family to their proper and legal settlement.[8]

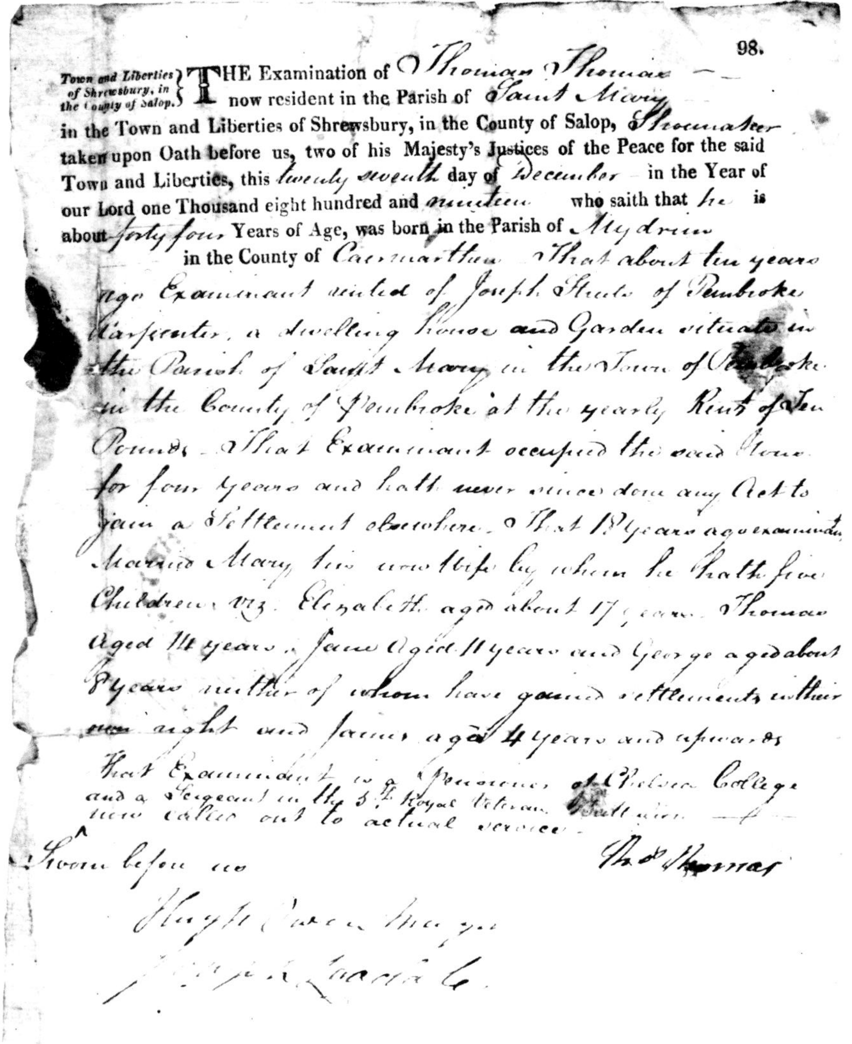

98.

Town and Liberties of Shrewsbury, in the County of Salop. THE Examination of Thomas Thomas now resident in the Parish of Saint Mary in the Town and Liberties of Shrewsbury, in the County of Salop, Shoemaker taken upon Oath before us, two of his Majesty's Justices of the Peace for the said Town and Liberties, this twenty seventh day of December in the Year of our Lord one Thousand eight hundred and nineteen who saith that he is about forty four Years of Age, was born in the Parish of Mydrim in the County of Caermarthen That about ten years ago Examinant rented of Joseph Steele of Pembroke Carpenter, a dwelling house and Garden situate in the Parish of Saint Mary in the Town of Pembroke in the County of Pembroke at the yearly Rent of Ten Pounds That Examinant occupied the said House for four years and hath never since done any Act to gain a Settlement elsewhere. That 18 years ago Examinant Married Mary his now Wife by whom he hath five Children viz. Elizabeth aged about 17 years Thomas aged 14 years, Jane aged 11 years and George aged about 8 years neither of whom have gained settlements in their own right and James aged 4 years and upwards

That Examinant is a Pensioner of Chelsea College and a Serjeant in the 5th Royal Veteran Battalion now called out to actual service.

Sworn before us

Thos Thomas

Hugh Owen Mayor

Joseph Loxdale

Fig. 15-2: Examination as to settlement (Thomas Thomas)

By permission of Dyfed County Archives

Of far greater value than the vestry minute, however, is the record of the examination as this can contain a great deal of genealogical information. A good example of this is to be found in the parochial records for the parish of St Mary, Pembroke, which are at the Pembrokeshire Record Office. In 1819, Thomas Thomas, then resident in Shrewsbury, was examined before two Justices of the Peace. As a result it was established that he and his family had a legal settlement in the parish of St Mary, Pembroke. The examination setting this out is shown in Fig 15-2, the full text of which reads as follows:[9]

> The Examination of Thomas Thomas now resident in the Parish of Saint Mary in the Town and Liberties of Shrewsbury in the County of Salop, Shoemaker, taken upon oath before us, two of his Majesty's Justices of the Peace for the said Town and Liberties, this twenty seventh day of December in the Year of our Lord one Thousand eight hundred and nineteen who saith that he is about forty four Years of Age, was born in the Parish of Mydrim in the County of Carmarthen. That about ten years ago Examinant rented of Joseph Streets of Pembroke, Carpenter, a dwelling house and garden situate in the Parish of Saint Mary in the Town of Pembroke in the County of Pembroke at the yearly rent of Ten Pounds. That Examinant occupied the said House for four years and hath never since done any Act to gain a Settlement elsewhere. That 18 years ago Examinant married Mary his now wife by whom he hath five Children, viz: Elizabeth aged about 17 years, Thomas aged 14 years, Jane aged 11 years and George aged about 8 years neither of whom have gained settlements in their own right and James aged 4 years and upwards. That Examinant is a Pensioner of Chelsea College and a Sergeant in the 5th Royal veteran Battalion now called out to actual service.
>
> Sworn before us Thomas Thomas
>
> Hugh Owen Mayor
>
> Joseph Loxdale

This single document gives the information shown in Fig. 15-3. It can be seen that although Thomas Thomas was born in Meidrim (Carmarthenshire) and probably completed an apprenticeship (possibly elsewhere), it was his rental of property in Pembroke when aged about 34 which determined his legal place of settlement. It would appear that in this instance the Churchwardens at Shrewsbury were safeguarding their position in case something happened to Thomas Thomas who had been called to actual service with the reserve. Students of British history will recall that this was a time of civil unrest, and that the Peterloo Massacre occurred in 1819.

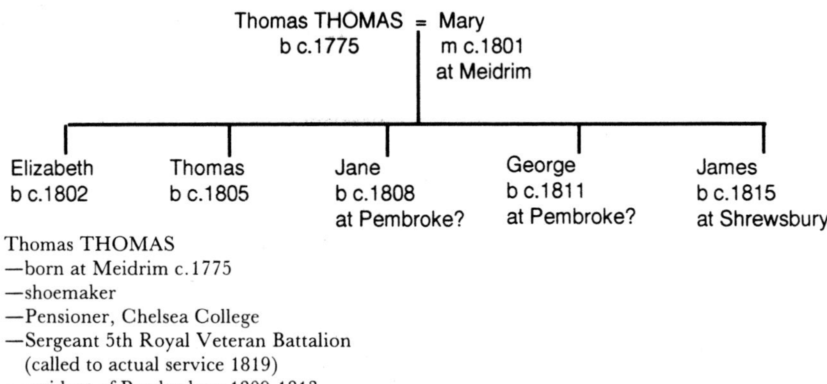


Thomas THOMAS
—born at Meidrim c.1775
—shoemaker
—Pensioner, Chelsea College
—Sergeant 5th Royal Veteran Battalion
(called to actual service 1819)
—resident of Pembroke c.1809-1813
(rented property in the parish of St Mary, Pembroke, from Joseph Streets, carpenter)
—he signs the Examination

Fig. 15-3: Family Tree and Biographical Information from Examination

Armed with a decision of this sort from the justices, a pauper (or a dead pauper's family) could be physically removed from the parish except where they were too ill to travel or the decision was challenged. Needless to say, decisions to seek the removal of a pauper (or pauper family) abound in the vestry minutes but the human misery which must often have resulted from those decisions can only be imagined. This point is very well made by David Williams in his *History of Modern Wales*, in which he writes:

> The harshness of the old poor laws was most evident in the provisions for the removal of those likely to become chargeable to the parish. Expectant mothers of illegitimate children were obviously in this position and it was doubly important that they should be removed, for the settlement of a child would be determined by the place of its birth. As the poor creatures concealed the fact as long as possible, their removal was often carried out in circumstances of gross indignity and brutality and in 1814, a woman, removed from Bedwellty to Haverfordwest, gave birth to a child on the way . . .[10]

Much of society's attitude to the poor is embodied in an Act of 1697[11] which required that every member of a pauper family should:

> . . . wear upon the shoulder of the right sleeve of the uppermost garment . . . in an open and visible manner . . . a large Roman P together with the first letter of the name of the parish . . . in red or blue cloth.

In the middle of the eighteenth century this requirement was still being enforced (by the parish) and resisted (by paupers) as shown in the vestry minutes of Llanrhystud in 1746 when, after agreeing to buy woollen cloth and flannel for clothing for Mary Rice, the minute ends ominously with:

> And moreover 'tis required that the officers put the Badge on the Uper Garment of each of their paupers on pain of 20s fine.[12]

The juxtaposition of these two items seems to have been of some significance as in 1752 we have:

> Ordered and agreed that Mary Rice a pauper be not further relieved by the said Parish she refusing to wear the Badge and Guilty of severall misdemeaners but that the overseers Doe pay her w[ha]t appears to be Due her to this day.[13]

Whether or not Mary Rice continued her battle is not known. I like to think so and I like to think she won, because late in 1752 we have:

> . . . ordered . . . that the sum of six pence by the week be paid by the Overseer of the Parish unto Mary Rice.[14]

## The County Militia

The obligation to provide men for the County Militia was a constant cause for concern for parishes, second only to their concern about the cost of relieving the poor. Under successive Militia Acts Lord Lieutenants were required to raise a specific quota of men for service locally (and sometimes further afield) in support of the regular army. The pre-nineteenth century quotas for individual counties are interesting in that they give some idea of relative populations. The Militia Act of 1761, for example, specifies county quotas as follows: Anglesey, 80; Brecknock, 160; Cardigan, 120; Carmarthen, 200; Carnarvon, 80; Denbigh, 280; Flint, 120; Glamorgan, 360; Merioneth, 80; Montgomery, 240; Pembroke, 160; Radnor, 120; Monmouth, 240.[15]

If sufficient volunteers were not forthcoming the able-bodied men of a parish could be balloted to make up the quota. As parishes might be required to support (at least in part) any dependents of a man chosen by ballot, the burden could be considerable where a man had a large family. It was very much in the interests of a parish, therefore, to avoid the need for a ballot by paying for a substitute—usually a single man, often from another parish—to serve on its behalf. Because of this, parishes often established quite complicated arrangements for raising money with which to purchase the services of a substitute should a ballot become necessary. At Llanrhystud in 1810, for example, the Vestry agreed that those men in the parish who did not pay the general rate should pay on a sliding scale (according to their means) either to purchase a substitute or, if no suitable person could be found, ' . . . in order that it may fall as light as possible on the Balloted person whose Lot it may happen to be drawn.'[16]

Sometimes, however, a parish would await the outcome of the ballot and react with a mild form of panic when the result was contrary to its interests. This appears to have been the case in Llanrhystud in 1765 when two men already receiving parish relief had been balloted. A vestry minute refers to their plight and records that:

> Agreed and ordered then at a publick vestry that the sum of fifty shillings be immediately levied (in the same manner as the poor rate) . . . in order to hire substitutes to serve in the Militia of the County in the room of Jenkin David Thomas and Rees John . . . [17]

## Apprenticeships

Many parishes attempted to arrange an apprenticeship for their pauper children as a means of providing an opportunity for them to become employable and, hence, no longer be a burden to the parish. However, we have seen elsewhere that an apprenticeship gave a legal settlement within a parish and it was in the interest of a parish, therefore, for the Overseers to place their pauper children with a master in an adjacent (or distant) parish. This was probably very much to the advantage of the apprentice master—and in particular the less scrupulous ones immortalised by Charles Dickens—as the degree of supervision would be greatly reduced.

There can be no doubt that the Dickensian picture of the ill-treatment of paupers was soundly based on fact. The minutes of a Select Vestry for Angle in 1821 record that the mother of a pauper apprentice challenged the treatment being meted out to her daughter as follows:

> 2d Jane Williams having appeared before the Vestry to lodge a complaint against Mr Eynon for ill treating her daughter his parish apprentice and the vestry find upon enquiry there is some foundation in the complaint, they are unanimously of the opinion it should be laid before the Parish with as little delay as possible and do therefore direct the Overseers of the Poor to call a General vestry on Monday the 27th Inst at 6 o'clock pm.[18]

This would seem to have been a very courageous act by Jane Williams because, in this instance, she was not only taking on a master but one who was also a member of the Select Vestry! This was probably also the reason why the Select Vestry referred the matter to the General Vestry. However, it appears that her courage achieved its reward as early in 1822 the Select Vestry recorded the following entry:

> 3d. Mr Eynon having refused upon repeated application to refund the sum of one pound fourteen shillings given to him on his receiving an apprentice to clothe her, but which apprentice has since been returned upon the Parish, Mr Smith one of the Overseers of the Poor is therefore directed to employ an Attorney to recover the same.[19]

## Bonds of Indemnity

Mention has been made above of the particular threat which mothers of illegitimate children—and therefore the children themselves—could pose for a parish. It was a common practice from the middle of the eighteenth century for fathers of illegitimate children to enter into a bond of indemnity with the mother's parish whereby they would bear the cost of supporting the child should it become chargeable to the parish. These bonds clearly had a long-term importance for the parish and, as a result, they often survive in parishes which otherwise have few parochial records. Once again, where they do survive they can offer a great deal of valuable information to the family historian.

An example of this is a Bond of Indemnity entered into in the parish of Llanfihangel-ar-Arth (Carmarthenshire) in 1811[20] which names not only the child and where (Gwyddgrug House) she was born, but also the unmarried parents and their respective fathers. This gives the family tree shown in Fig. 15-4.

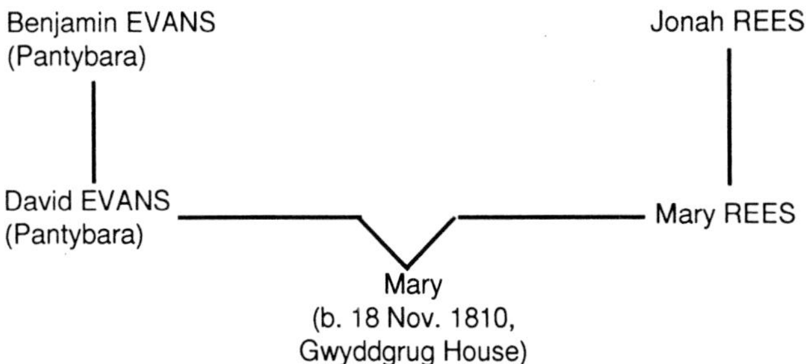


Fig. 15-4: Family Tree from Bond of Indemnity

## The Control of Vermin and Strays

Other activities which engaged the attention of the parish concerned the control of vermin and stray animals. These activities involved people within the parish in a variety of ways and their involvement is faithfully recorded in many vestry minutes.

The activity resulting in the greatest reference to individuals within the parish was undoubtedly the extermination of vermin. Payments were made out of parish funds for killing foxes, badgers, polecats, hedgehogs and many other vermin, and the people receiving payment were usually named in the Churchwardens' Accounts.

In the parish of Laugharne (Carmarthenshire) the Churchwardens' Accounts for the year 1803[21] show payments for killing 43 hedgehogs (at 2d each), five bitch foxes (1/6), two dog foxes (1/-), four owls (2d), three polecats (4d) and one badger (6d). There is plenty of evidence from other parishes to suggest that this level of activity was not exceptional. With about a thousand parishes in Wales it can readily be seen that the assault on the vermin population—and in particular hedgehogs—was a considerable one. Set against modern attitudes it is difficult to understand why hedgehogs should appear on the list in the first place, but several myths have long been associated with them in country communities.

Of interest (and value) to the family historian, however, is the fact that those accounts name William Lister, Margaret John, John Bevan, Powell's servant, Jane Raymond, George Powel, William Skyrme, Thomas Wilkins, William Howell, David Watt, a man at the Hills, William Morris, William Bevan, William Rees, Henry Thomas and Walter John as being active on this front. While it would be reasonable to assume that these were all poorer people within the parish, interestingly enough William Skyrme (who killed a bitch fox) is described as 'Esq and Huntsman', showing that even the better off were not averse to making an honest shilling from the parish.

Pembrokeshire people will have no difficulty in understanding repeated references in the Churchwardens' Accounts for Carew[22] to payments for killing fitchens (1622, 1738, 1770). The use of this word for the polecat is local to Pembrokeshire (and certain other areas) and is still in use today.

Stray animals were also a preoccupation of the parish and many found it necessary to construct a pound to control them. It was a common practice to put the operation of the pound out to local tender having first specified the charges which could be made for redeeming stray animals.

The names of those constructing or repairing the pound or tendering for its operation frequently appear in Vestry Minutes.

## In Conclusion

Although the examples I have used have been taken from south-west Wales, the general points they relate to could have been illustrated by examples from the majority of the surviving parochial records for parishes throughout Wales. If the parish you are interested in has records which survive, you could well find that a dip into them will pay handsome dividends. The least they will give is a colourful backdrop to the lives of your ancestors.

### NOTES TO CHAPTER 15

[1] Select vestries are known to have existed since the seventeenth century but the basis of their right to govern is obscure. It is sometimes maintained that they were not subject to any form of control or audit but this is not borne out by the evidence of the examples given in this chapter. The Vestries Acts of 1818 and 1819 (Sturges Bourne Acts) established more firmly the position of the select vestry and led to a significant increase in their numbers.

[2] C.J.Williams and J.Watts-Williams, *Cofrestri Plwyf Cymru/Parish Registers of Wales*, (Aberystwyth: NLW, 1986).

[3] Vestry Book, 15 November 1819 (NLW, St David's Diocese, Parochial Records, Angle Vol.2).

[4] Poor Rate Assessments (Various) 1738-1812 (NLW, St David's Diocese, Parochial Records, Llanrhystud).

[5] Church Rate Assessments, 1752 (NLW, St David's Diocese, Parochial Records, Llanrhystud Vol.1).

[6] Churchwardens' Accounts, 1738 (Pembrokeshire Record Office, St David's Diocese, Parochial Records, Carew HPR/68/33). [Note: This is a particularly good example of the type of record which may be found among Parochial Records.]

[7] Churchwardens' Accounts, 1770 (Pembs RO, St David's Diocese, Parochial Records, Carew HPR/68/33).

[8] Vestry Book, 22 June 1781 (NLW, St David's Diocese, Parochial Records, Llanrhystud Vol.2).

[9] Examination as to Settlement, 27 December 1819 (Pembs RO, St David's Diocese, Parochial Records, St Mary's Pembroke, HPR/24/50).

[10] David Williams, *History of Modern Wales*. (London: Murray, 1965), p.201.

[11] 8 & 9 Wm.III, c.30 (1696-7). I am unsure how the Overseers coped with the similarity of many Welsh parish names when giving the initials for individual parishes.

[12] Vestry Book, 4 November 1746 (NLW, St David's Diocese, Parochial Records, Llanrhystud Vol.1).

[13] Vestry Book, 1 January 1752 (NLW, St David's Diocese, Parochial Records, Llanrhystud Vol.1).

[14] Vestry Book, 9 November 1752 (NLW, St David's Diocese, Parochial Records Llanrhystud Vol.1).

[15] 2 Geo.III, c.20 (1761).

[16] Vestry Book, 12 Sept 1810 (NLW, St David's Diocese, Parochial Records, Llanrhystud Vol.7).

[17] Vestry Book, 17 Oct 1765 (NLW, St David's Diocese, Parochial Records, Llanrhystud Vol.1).

[18] Vestry Book, 24 August 1821 (NLW, St David's Diocese, Parochial Records, Angle Vol.2, p.10).

[19] Vestry Book, 11 January 1822 (NLW, St David's Diocese, Parochial Records, Angle Vol.2, p.15).

[20] Bond of Indemnity, 8 June 1811 (NLW, St David's Diocese, Parochial Records, Llanfihangel-ar-Arth, Item 30).

[21] Churchwardens' Accounts, 1803 (Carmarthenshire Record Office, St David's Diocese, Parochial Records, Laugharne PR 165).

[22] Churchwardens' Accounts, 1622, 1738 & 1770 (Pembs RO, St David's Diocese, Parochial Records, Carew HPR/68/33).

# 16. The Welsh at Law

Chris Pitt Lewis

Records of legal proceedings form a vast body of material, from the twelfth century to the present day, much of it dealing with ordinary people, not just the rich. All of it is potentially of interest for the wider family history; much has direct genealogical value, and may solve problems that are otherwise insoluble. In Chancery in 1684, Thomas Williams, a baker from Abergavenny, laid claim (unsuccessfully) to the Llechdwnni estate in Carmarthenshire, stating that he was the son of William Thomas, son of Thomas Bowen, son of Morris Bowen of Llechdwnni who had died in 1639. Thomas Bowen, he alleged, had been in London when his father died, and so was deprived of his inheritance.[1] Many cases will give similar details. The problem is to find them among the sheer mass of unindexed material involved.

In Wales, the Great Sessions provide us with a relatively manageable series of records, described in the next chapter. But they were not the only Courts used by the Welsh.

## WELSH COURTS

### 1282-1542[2]

Before 1282, independent Wales had its own laws, the codification of which was traditionally attributed to King Hywel Dda (d. 949/50). The best known features of these laws were partible inheritance (the inheritance of a man's lands equally by all his sons, legitimate and illegitimate alike, instead of by the eldest legitimate son as in England), and *galanas*. This was the payment of blood money; a murderer and his family would pay for his crime by a money payment to the kindred of his victim. No records survive of legal proceedings in the independent Principality.

In 1282 Edward I conquered the Principality of Wales and two years later established the legal framework of his rule by the Statute of Rhuddlan. The conquered lands were organised as the shires of Anglesey, Caernarvon, Merioneth, Cardigan and Carmarthen. Royal Governors (Justiciars) were appointed for the north and south, and they administered royal justice in 'Great Sessions' in each county. The scope of the Laws of Hywel Dda was limited; serious crimes were to be tried by English law, but the Welsh (but not English settlers) could continue to use their own law in cases concerning inheritance and land. A very few Great Sessions records for this period (from Anglesey, Caernarvon and Merioneth) survive and are at the PRO.[3]

None of this applied to the March. Since the late eleventh century, the Welsh Princes had been confined to the north and west; the south and east of Wales became the preserve of the Anglo-Norman Lords of the March. Each of the Marcher Lordships, though nominally subject to the English Crown, was for practical purposes independent; 'the King's writ runneth not in the March'. The Lord held his own courts, with the same powers as were exercised in England by the King. Each Lordship had its own custom; in practice this meant a variable mix of English and Welsh law. Some Lords held separate courts for their English and Welsh subjects.[4]

Records of these Courts have survived only by chance. By far the most complete are the series of Court Rolls for the Lordship of Dyffryn Clwyd, from 1294 on, in the PRO.[5] There are stray records of many other Courts, some of which have been published.[6]

Flintshire was an anomaly, neither part of the Principality nor of the March. For administrative purposes it was attached to the County Palatine of Chester, and had its own Great Sessions, for which a largely complete set of records from 1284 to 1542 and inquisitions post mortem to 1642 are with the Chester records at the PRO.[7]

### 1542-1830

The March was abolished by Henry VIII. The Acts of Union of 1536 and 1543 attached some Marcher Lordships to the neighbouring English counties and created seven new counties from the rest. The Great Sessions were extended to six of these counties, as described in the next chapter, but not to Monmouthshire, which became subject to the Courts at Westminster. This is the origin of the myth that Monmouthshire was an English county. At the same time Welsh Law, including partible inheritance, was abolished, and ordinary English Law applied to all of Wales.

The Great Sessions were not the only courts with jurisdiction in Wales in this period. Firstly, they were supervised by the Council in the Marches, sitting in Ludlow, until it was abolished in 1689. The judicial records of this Council, alas, are lost. Secondly, several of the English Courts at Westminster heard Welsh cases, as described below.

The Great Sessions were abolished in 1830, and thereafter all Welsh cases, like those in England, became subject to the Courts at Westminster.

## ENGLISH COURTS[8]

### Court of Chancery

This arose from the right of the subject to petition the King in Council to do justice in cases where the courts were unable or unwilling to assist. The Common Law was rigid; form was more important than justice. To take an example: if a man mortgaged his land to secure a debt, and was a day late in repaying the debt as agreed, at Common Law he lost his land forever, though it might be worth far more than the debt. This was inequitable; the King's conscience could not allow it to stand. So he let the mortgagor redeem his land by late payment, with interest. A parallel system of justice thus grew up, known as Equity. From the late fourteenth century the administration of Equity was normally delegated by the King and his Council to the Chancellor, sitting in the Court of Chancery.

It is the records of Chancery and the other courts of equity which are most likely to help the family historian. There are two reasons for this. Firstly, many of the cases with which they dealt involved questions of inheritance, and contain specific genealogical information. Secondly, they took evidence in the form of written depositions. As well as fascinating information about the facts of the case, these depositions frequently include personal details, including the age, of the witness.[9]

Welsh cases up to 1558 have been separately calendared.[10] After that, we are dependent on general calendars and finding aids.[11] An indispensable source is the Bernau Index, which indexes very many Chancery records for the seventeenth and eighteenth centuries, including the names of all litigants 1714-1758.[12]

### Court of Requests/Court of Star Chamber

Despite the role of the Chancellor, the King in Council retained his prerogative to do justice, on request, in cases where he thought fit, and out of this prerogative grew the Court of Requests and the Court of Star Chamber. Established by Henry VII, they fell into disrepute under Charles I and were abolished; but until then they were popular and well-used courts. Star Chamber in particular was frequently resorted to by Welsh litigants, and there is a published calendar of Welsh cases.[13]

**Court of Augmentations**
From 1536-1553 this court dealt with the disposal of monastic property in both England and Wales after the dissolution of the monasteries. There is a published calendar of Welsh cases.[14]

**Court of Exchequer**
The Exchequer's role was originally to collect and account for the royal finance, and in fulfilling this it spawned a Court which claimed jurisdiction in any case affecting the royal finances. It came to hear a wide variety of civil cases, on the basis that the plaintiff's dispute with the defendant made him less able to pay his taxes or dues to the King. Originally it was a common law court, but in Elizabethan times it also developed an equity jurisdiction, probably as a result of the abolition of the Court of Augmentations. As such, it had jurisdiction in Wales and was a popular court for Welsh litigants. It dealt with similar cases to the Chancery, and its records can be equally valuable.

There are published calendars of Welsh cases in the equity side of the Exchequer up to 1625.[15]

Like Chancery, the equity side of the Exchequer took evidence by written depositions. There are two series of these: Barons' (or Town) Depositions, where the witness attended the Court in London, and Depositions by Commission (or Country Depositions), where the evidence was taken by Commissioners in the witness's home county. It is reasonable to assume that most Welsh deponents are in the Country series, and the Bernau Index is thought to include all Country deponents down to 1800.[16] The Society of Genealogists has a card index of Exchequer Country Deponents in Wales 1714-1770.

**Court of the Duchy of Lancaster**
This Court of equity sat at Westminster and had jurisdiction over any tenant of a Lordship of the Duchy of Lancaster, both before and after the Act of Union. In Wales, this includes Monmouth and the Three Castles, Caldicot, Kidwelly and Iscennen. It should not be confused with the Palatine Court of Lancaster, which operated only in Lancashire. Theoretically it still exists, although it has not sat since 1835.

**Court of King's Bench/Court of Common Pleas**
These Courts sat at Westminster and administered the Common Law in both criminal and civil matters. In principle, they only had jurisdiction in Monmouthshire after 1543 and in the rest of Wales after the abolition

of the Great Sessions in 1830, though there are a few Welsh cases in the Middle Ages. In addition, the Judges went on circuit administering justice locally according to the Common Law in the Assizes. Monmouthshire formed part of the Oxford Circuit from 1543, and when the system was extended to the rest of Wales in 1830, new circuits for North and South Wales were established. The common law courts are much less likely than the courts of equity to yield direct genealogical information; and in the nineteenth century local newspaper reports of cases will usually be more informative than the court records themselves.[17]

**Supreme Court**
This court was established in 1875 to replace the earlier Courts of Common Law and Equity. Only a selection of cases has been preserved.

## LOCAL COURTS[18]

**Quarter Sessions**
County Justices of the Peace met quarterly and heard criminal cases; they also exercised many administrative functions which were taken over by the County Councils in 1889. Their records are a mine of information about the county and its inhabitants. JPs were first appointed in Wales in 1541; but only in Caernarvonshire do the surviving records go back so far.[19]

**Borough Courts**
Many Boroughs had the right to hold a Court of Record; and many also acquired the right to hold their own Quarter Sessions. The records, where they survive, may be held locally, rather than being deposited at the County Record Office.[20] Boroughs whose local courts were still active in the early nineteenth century included Beaumaris, Brecon, Cardiff, Cowbridge, Denbigh, Haverfordwest, Monmouth, Newport (Mon), New Radnor, Pembroke, Swansea, Usk, and Welshpool; there were others. These, indeed borough records in general, are worth investigating for information about townsfolk, particularly in the smaller boroughs, where the chances of a householder or tradesman being mentioned are very high.

**Manorial Courts, etc**
See Chapter 11: Estate Records.

**NOTES TO CHAPTER 16**

[1]PRO, Mitford 338/339, 28 Nov 1684; quoted by Francis Jones in *Carmarthenshire Antiquary*, Vol XX (1984), p.41.

[2]R.I.Jack, *Medieval Wales*, (London: 1972), in the Sources of History series, is a very readable introduction to record sources for medieval Wales in general.

[3]WALE 4, 16 and 20.

[4]R.R.Davies, *Lordship and Society in the March of Wales 1282-1400*, (Oxford: OUP, 1978) pp.149-175 gives a general account of Marcher courts.

[5]SC 2/215/64-221/2.

[6]Too many to list here. Refer to P.H.Jones, *A Bibliography of the History of Wales*, 3rd ed., microfiche (Cardiff: 1989) and to county historical journals.

[7]CHES 30.

[8]The records of all these Courts are in the PRO (Chancery Lane). See *Guide to the Contents of the PRO*, vol 1 (HMSO, 1963) for full details.

[9]For general guides, see R.E.F.Garrett, *Chancery and other Legal Proceedings* (Pinhorns, 1968), and *An Introduction to Chancery Proceedings*, PRO Leaflet No.32.

[10]E.A.Lewis, *An Inventory of the Early Chancery Proceedings concerning Wales*, Board of Celtic Studies History and Law Series (HLS), no.3 (Cardiff: 1937). 85% of the cases listed are between 1536 and 1558. See also W.Rees, *Calendar of Ancient Petitions relating to Wales (13th to 16th century)* HLS no.28 (Cardiff: 1975).

[11]Listed in PRO Leaflet 32 (see note 9).

[12]Available on microfilm in the Society of Genealogists and through Mormon genealogical libraries. Described in detail in three articles by Guy Lawton, in *Family Tree Magazine*, vol.8, nos.2, 3 and 4 (Dec 1991-Feb 1992). See also *The Genealogists' Magazine*, vol.18, no.3 (Sept 1975) and *Family Tree Magazine*, vol.6, no.11 (Sept 1990).

[13]I.ap O.Edwards, *A Catalogue of Star Chamber Proceedings relating to Wales*, HLS no.1 (Cardiff: 1929). This may not be complete—see its introduction for the method of compilation. Some Star Chamber and Requests cases are included in Bernau's Index (Lawton, note 12 above).

[14]E.A.Lewis & J.C.Davies *Records of the Court of Augmentations relating to Wales and Monmouthshire*, HLS no.13 (Cardiff: 1954). This also includes details of leases of former monastic property granted down to 1603.

[15]E.G.Jones *Exchequer Proceedings (Equity) concerning Wales, Henry VIII to Elizabeth*, HLS no 4 (Cardiff: 1939). Also T.I.Jeffreys Jones, *Exchequer Proceedings concerning Wales in tempore James I*, HLS no.15 (Cardiff: 1955). Both of these volumes abstract the Bill (the Plaintiff's statement of his case); the second also abstracts the Defendant's Answer. They give the PRO references for the relevant depositions, orders, etc, but do not give further details. The introduction to the second volume contains a useful account of the Court's procedure and documentation.

See also PRO Information Leaflet no 96, *Equity Proceedings in the Court of Exchequer*.

[16]See Lawton in *Family Tree Magazine*, vol.8, no.4 (Feb 1992) (note 12 above).

[17]David T.Hawkings, *Criminal Ancestors: A Guide to Historical Criminal Records in England and Wales* (Alan Sutton, 1992) gives a comprehensive account of the records of criminal courts at all levels, as well as prison and transportation records and bankruptcy. See also: *Assize Records*, PRO Information Leaflet no 26; and Deirdre Beddoe, *Welsh Convict Women* (Barry: Stewart Williams, 1979) which has a list of Welsh women transported to Australia, and traces their stories.

*The Welsh Assize Roll 1277-1282*, HLS no.7 (Cardiff: 1940), is a political document connected with Edward I's conquest.

[18]Extracts from many of these records have been published. See note 6 above.

[19]J.S.W.Gibson, *Quarter Sessions Records for Family Historians*, 3rd ed. (FFHS, 1992) briefly lists the main classes of surviving Quarter Sessions records, their whereabouts and finding aids. Also J.R.S.Phillips, *The Justices of the Peace in Wales and Monmouthshire 1541-1689* (Cardiff: 1975) has a list of JPs in that period.

[20]For example, Monmouth (split between the Town Museum and the County Record Office), and Bangor (at University College, Bangor).

# 17. The Records of the Courts of Great Sessions for Wales

Murray Ll. Chapman

## Introduction

A vast amount of information exists amongst the records of courts of law which will be of great interest and use to family historians and genealogists. The records, which concern all strata of society, are voluminous and, because of this, finding out what they contain can be a problem.

There are some pitfalls in their use for there were many legal fictions which make some of the records, when taken at face value, not to be what they seem. Some of them are also written within the strait-jacket of common form.

This chapter concentrates on the records of the Courts of Great Sessions (hereafter referred to as G.S.) and has confined itself to describing those records which may be of interest to family historians and genealogists. Inevitably, in doing so, a description of some of the legal processes in the court needs to be given together with a description of some of the legal fictions.

The major problem with the records of the G.S. is that there are no calendars, and information on their contents is hard to come by. All that is available is a list of the various rolls, files and books.[1] Nevertheless, the Powysland Club, the oldest county historical society in Wales, is undertaking the work of calendaring the criminal proceedings for the Montgomeryshire G.S. in close co-operation with the National Library of Wales.[2] As a result of work being undertaken on this project all the examples given in this chapter are taken from that particular court and largely from the earlier files for which draft calendars have already been prepared.

## The Courts of Great Sessions

The G.S. in Wales were established by statute in 1542 as part of the programme to create union with England. These courts were peculiar to Wales and they embodied certain Welsh procedures and practices at law which had existed hitherto such as the process known as *concessit solvere* in civil actions to recover debts.

The courts dealt with the following proceedings:

(i) Common Law
—Civil, i.e. disputes between individuals.
—Crown, i.e. prosecution by the Crown of individuals.
(ii) Equity, i.e. disputes between individuals in which the common law offered no remedy.

A G.S. was established in each of the Welsh counties, except for Monmouthshire, and these were grouped into the following circuits (see Fig 17-1):

**Chester**: Denbighshire, Flintshire, Montgomeryshire
**North Wales**: Anglesey, Caernarfonshire, Merionethshire
**Carmarthen**: Cardiganshire, Carmarthenshire, Pembrokeshire
**Brecon**: Breconshire, Glamorganshire, Radnorshire

Monmouthshire was attached to an English Assize circuit (Oxford) since its inclusion in one of the Welsh circuits would have made one of them unbalanced in size with four instead of three counties. It was also the county nearest to the central courts in London.

The G.S. were abolished in 1830.

## The Jurisdiction of the Court

The jurisdiction of each G.S. was coterminous with the boundary of each county. In other words, the G.S. for, say, Montgomeryshire had jurisdiction only within that county. This was true for criminal and civil proceedings but for chancery proceedings the jurisdiction extended to the area of each circuit.

On the face of it, this would suggest that if an offender committed a crime in Montgomeryshire and crossed the border into an adjacent county, he or she would escape out of the court's jurisdiction. This apparent defect in the system was reduced in effect as a result of action taken by the Council in the Marches of Wales. The Council was established during the reign of King Henry VII to administer the Marches and Principality of Wales. The jurisdiction of the Council thus extended over all the Welsh counties, including Monmouthshire, and the English counties of Cheshire, Shropshire, Worcester, Hereford and Gloucester (see Fig 17-1), although as time went on its jurisdiction was reduced until it was finally abolished in 1689. The Council would

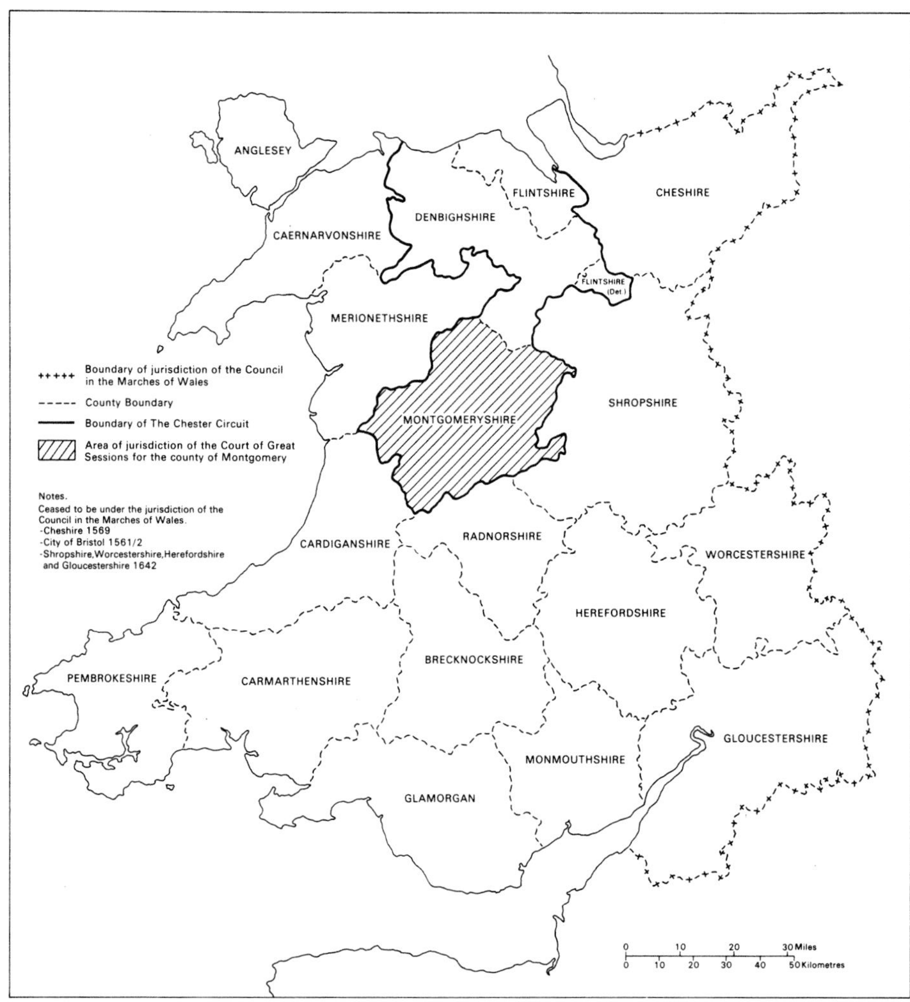


Fig. 17-1: The Jurisdiction of the Council in the Marches of Wales

apprehend offenders who tried to evade justice by crossing borders and either try such persons themselves or deliver them to the appropriate G.S. Offenders could also be removed from one county to another by writ of *habeas corpus*.

Each G.S. maintained its own records for the criminal and civil proceedings, whereas the chancery records were filed circuit by circuit. Indeed, this is how the records continue to be maintained.

As each court was separate each developed its own rules and, understandably, there are some differences in the type and form of records kept by each court.

## The Records

All the records of the G.S., which cover the period 1542 to 1830, are held in the National Library of Wales, Aberystwyth, having been transferred there from the Public Record Office, London, some in 1909 and the main body of records in 1962.

The official court language for the records was generally Latin up to the year 1732, after which it was replaced by English, although during the Commonwealth period 1651-1660 English was used. Interestingly, the wording of the documents of common form is the same be they in Latin or English.

The entries in the Plea Rolls are recorded in the official court language in court hand. The Gaol Files, on the other hand, are recorded in secretary style writing for the earlier records and the official court language was used for all documents of common form. Examinations and petitions were always written in English.

The records are rife with abbreviations which, in some cases, are so brief that only the first letter of each word is given. A list of some of the abbreviations which were used extensively in the records of the criminal proceedings together with their expansions and meanings has been prepared by the Powysland Club and is available for reference in the Manuscripts Department of the National Library of Wales.

The main records which would be of interest to family historians and genealogists are described in the following sections.

## Civil Proceedings

Civil proceedings concerned disputes between individuals, the majority of which were for debt. Other actions included disputes over property, defamation, trespass and the detention of goods. The greatest volume of business in the court was that of civil proceedings and this grew to such an extent that Parliament was petitioned for there to be a second or puisne justice, which was granted by statute in 1576, (18 Eliz. c.8). The Chief and Second Justice sat *en banc*, i.e. together. They did not sit separately to consider different cases. In addition, certain property transactions were enrolled in the court by means of processes known as Fine and Recovery.

## Docket Rolls

Where Docket Rolls or books survive, they are the only quick way into the records for researchers since they are an index to the records, but in themselves do not provide information of use to the family historian and genealogist. Each Docket Roll covers a number of sessions. The rolls record very brief details of the fictitious actions of fines and recoveries relating to the conveyance of property; the names of the parties involved and the property in question are noted. The greatest part of the Docket Roll is taken up in recording the civil actions, noting the names of the litigants to a dispute, the nature of the dispute and the initials of the solicitors acting for each party.

## Plea Rolls

These are the primary records of civil proceedings and a separate roll was prepared for each sessions. The Plea Rolls contain the following:

—Recoveries, being part of the fictitious processes of Recovery for property transactions.
—Pleadings in civil actions which had reached the stage of issue; i.e. each party had agreed to the matter being tried by a jury.
—List of attorneys and on whose behalf they were acting.

Until about the middle of the reign of Queen Elizabeth pleadings in criminal actions were also enrolled in the Plea Rolls together with presentments by the various indictment juries.

The greatest proportion of entries are pleadings in civil actions which are all in common form. They record the names of the parties to a dispute, their status, place of abode and brief details of the nature of the dispute. The names of the attorneys acting for them are also stated.

The Plea Roll, as its name suggests, records the plea of the plaintiff and the answer of the defendant. If the matter went to trial the following additional details would be provided:

—previous attempts for the matter to be tried but, for want of a sufficient number of jurors, had to be postponed. The names of the jurors that were present would be stated.
—the date and place where previous trials were attempted.
—the names of the impanelled jurors who actually tried the case.
—the verdict of the jurors including their award for damages.

The pleadings are of great interest for they can provide a wealth of genealogical material relating to the devolution of land and also in some cases which concern themselves with disputes over a deceased's estate. In some proceedings, and there are a small number of these, challenge pedigrees would be entered. The purpose of this was to show that the sheriff or coroner, who were the only officials empowered to summon jurors, together with their wives were related to one or other or both parties to the dispute and could not, therefore, act impartially. Pedigrees showing relationships as far as the sixth degree were recited. It was a tactical ploy to delay the trial for the Justice would have to appoint persons, usually two, called Elizors to summon a jury. The pedigrees entered in the Plea Rolls are simple and unsophisticated, being recorded in narrative form. The entering of challenge pedigrees appears to have ceased by the end of the seventeenth century, or became very infrequent.

Fig 17-2 sets out a challenge pedigree (given in chart rather than narrative form) which shows the relationship between the plaintiff, the sheriff and the two coroners for Montgomeryshire concerning a dispute between William Kyffin and Charles Vaughan together with his wife, Margaret, over some lands in the townships of Bodfach and Globwlch, Montgomeryshire, and which was tried in April 1630.[3]

The number of Plea Rolls which survive for each G.S. is given in the Appendix.

## Fines (Feet of Fines)

The files of fines record the fictitious legal process of Fine concerning the conveyancing of property. The procedure could be used to record the sale of land, conveying it into trust (usually marriage settlements), and disentailing. The files of fines are extensive and provide the names of the parties involved in the transaction as well as details of the land being conveyed. The information given is less than would be obtained from deeds but the fines may survive where estate papers have been lost.

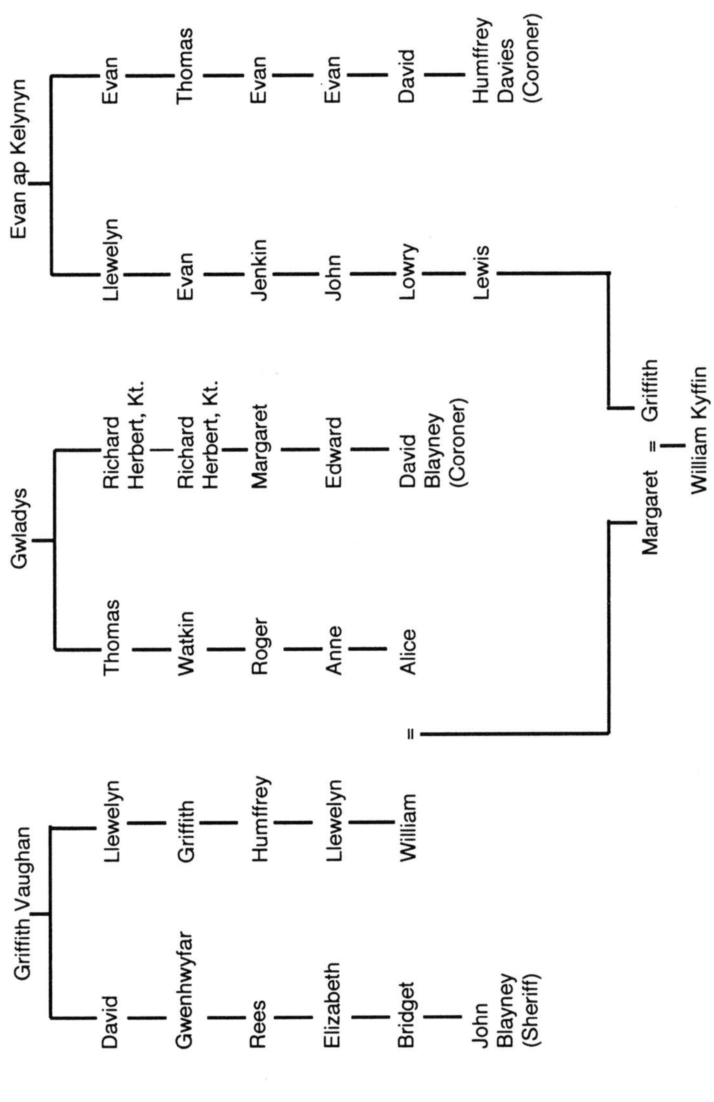


Fig. 17-2: Example of Challenge Pedigree (in Chart Form)

## Writs

The most common of the writs is that of *venire facias* to summon a jury to try the matter in dispute although other process writs may be filed amongst them. The parties to a dispute would apply for the issue of a writ of *venire facias* after pleadings had been completed and challenge pedigrees, if any, had been entered. A file of writs exists for each sessions being tied together by a cord.

The writ would normally be directed to the sheriff and the names of those summoned and those impanelled in a trial jury are recorded in a schedule attached to the writ in question. The verdict of the jury together with the amount of damages it awarded are included as an endorsement on the back of the schedule. The writs, therefore, provide brief details of the dispute and its outcome in the event of the details on the Plea Roll being lost.

## Prothonotary Papers

A bundle of papers for each sessions was kept by the Prothonotary being spiked and filed (strung) simply as a means of keeping them together. The papers principally comprise the declarations made by the plaintiff and the answer of the defendant and include supplementary information in support of an action, e.g. copies of leases and bonds. They also include schedules of costs. The Prothonotary Papers are important since they also record disputes which never reached issue and thus do not occur in other records of the court.

The most interesting papers in this file to genealogists are the challenge pedigrees which are given in chart form. It is highly probable that there are more challenge pedigrees on these files than in the Plea Rolls since a great many civil actions never went to trial. The challenge pedigrees would only be enrolled in the Plea Rolls in those cases that went to trial. However, the files of Prothonotary papers do not survive as well as the Plea Rolls for the earlier period.

## Chancery Proceedings

Equity covers all matters and disputes not covered by the common law. There has been some uncertainty as to when the G.S. acquired equitable jurisdiction for the records of the chancery proceedings in the G.S. only survive from the late seventeenth century.

Chancery courts were re-affirmed and established in the Welsh counties in 1535 by statute, (27 Hen. VIII, c.26), being 'An Act for

Laws and Justice to be ministered in Wales in like form as it is in this Realm'. Section 9, in particular, dealt with this. It would appear that with the establishment of the G.S. in 1542, the chancery proceedings were conducted, as a matter of convenience, by the Justice as he went his circuit. Although it was strictly a separate court, its business inevitably soon became part and parcel of the work done by the G.S.

The earliest known reference to a chancery action in the G.S. is a letter dated 5 November 1578 from Sir John Throckmorton, Kt., Chief Justice of Chester, to the Justices of the Peace for Montgomeryshire requiring them to commit David Lloyd ap John ap Ieuan ap Owen to gaol until he obtained bail in £40.[4]

The chancery proceedings are, perhaps, the most interesting of all the G.S. records to family historians and genealogists since the actions heard included disputes over wills, money, marriage settlements and property. The main set of records comprise the pleadings, and other records include Bill Books and Decree and Order Books. All the records are filed circuit by circuit, as noted earlier.

There were no trial juries for actions in chancery and following the submission of the pleadings in writing, one or both the parties would apply for a decree to be issued, in which the Justice would consider the matters in dispute and give his judgement.

## Bill Books

The Bill Books, where they survive, provide the quickest means to finding out what is contained in the records. The Bill Book records the date each Bill of Complaint was submitted and by whom.

## Decree and Order Books

Where Decree and Order Books survive, they will provide information on the progress of each action. When a case was determined a decree was issued which sets out the details of the case as presented by both the complainant and defendant as well as the judgement. The Decree and Order Books are therefore a convenient means to finding out the outcome of a dispute in the event that it progressed to this stage. The information contained would be a précis of the various pleadings and could contain information of interest to the genealogist and family historian.

**Pleadings**

These are the most important records of the chancery side of the court. The pleadings were divided by the Public Record Office into two sets: the paper pleadings and the parchment pleadings.

An action would commence with the aggrieved party, usually called the complainant, but sometimes the Orator or Oratrix, submitting a Bill of Complaint. There would then be an exchange of pleadings, all in writing, as shown in Fig 17-3.

| Stage | By the Complainant | By the Defendant |
|---|---|---|
| 1 | Bill of Complaint | Answer |
| 2 | Replication | Rejoinder |
| 3 | Surrejoinder | Rebutter |
| 4 | Surrebutter | — |

Fig. 17-3: Exchange of Pleadings

It was a requirement that the Answer of the defendant be submitted whilst the court was in sessions which was during the time that the justice went his circuit. However, it was possible for the defendant to submit his Answer when the court was not sitting by means of obtaining a commission of *dedimus potestatem*, usually abbreviated to *ded. pot.*

The pleadings could cease at any stage and most ended after the defendant had put in his or her Answer. A great majority never went before the Justice for judgement since a Complainant may have been satisfied by the Answer given by the defendant and had no need to pursue the matter further. If it did progress further, once all pleadings had been entered, issue was then said to be joined.

There were other written submissions such as the Defendant entering an Exception instead of an Answer, setting out that the matter was deficient in the law for answer. Also, a Bill of Reviver would be submitted where proceedings had lapsed, usually by the death of one of the defendants.

The paper pleadings comprise the drafts of the various written submissions set out in Fig 17-3. Additionally, amongst the papers are copies of Commissions of Dedimus Potestatem requiring appointed commissioners to take the Answer of the defendant. Lists of questions to be ministered to the defendants are sometimes also to be found. The parchment pleadings are the final and engrossed versions of the paper pleadings but it should be noted that a large number of the paper pleadings were never engrossed and prepared on parchment.

The information contained in the pleadings is of great interest to both the family historian and genealogist, particularly in cases involving disputes over wills. Schedules of property and valuations may be given in such cases. Fig 17-4 shows the sort of genealogical information which can be derived, being a dispute over a legacy in which the Complainants, the three grandchildren of the testator, submitted their Bill of Complaint on 20 August 1750.[5]

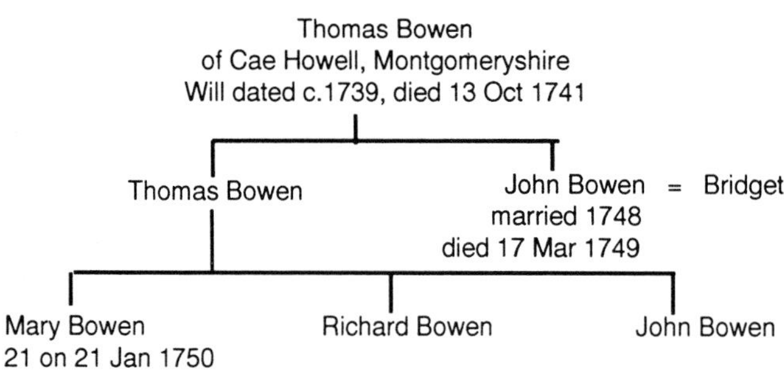


Fig. 17-4: Example of genealogical information derived from Pleadings

Thomas Bowen, by his will, left £10 apiece to each of his grandchildren when they became 21 years old and appointed his son, John, as sole executor of his will. John Bowen died on 17 March 1749 leaving his wife, Bridget, who obtained Letters of Administration of her husband's estate since he left no will. Bridget submitted with her Answer schedules of all the live and dead stock as well as an Inventory of the contents of the house which were valued by appraisers. She also submitted a schedule of her husband's debts, so demonstrating that there were no funds available to satisfy the legacy of Thomas Bowen to his grandchildren.

An indication of the extent of extant chancery pleadings in the G.S. is given in the Appendix.

## Criminal Proceedings

Criminal proceedings concerned disputes between the State and individuals. The records comprise a bundle of documents for each sessions with the documents of common form written on parchment and the rest on paper. The largest of the documents was normally used as wrapper. Collectively, they have become known as the Gaol Files. A list which indicates the extent of the extant files is also given in the Appendix.

Unlike the various files of civil records the gaol files contain a great variety of documents and each file may comprise: calendar of prisoners, lists of officers (*Nomina Ministrorum*), Quarter Sessions' records, examinations, recognizances, lists of jurors, schedules of prisoners, indictments, presentments, petitions, process writs, coroners' inquests and other miscellaneous correspondence and papers.

In simple terms, during the existence of the G.S., the law recognized two categories of criminal offences:

| | |
|---|---|
| (i) Felony | Murder, homicide (manslaughter), treason, arson, rape, burglary, theft of goods worth one shilling or more. |
| (ii) Misdemeanour | Trespass, riot, rout, affray, illegal assemblies, entries, ejectments, extortions, contempts, theft of goods worth less than one shilling. |

Felony was a capital offence which could lead to a convicted offender being hanged, whilst misdemeanours could be punished by the offender being whipped, put in the stocks, imprisoned, fined, mutilated or a combination of any of these.

## Calendar of Prisoners

This document is one of the largest in the file and thus was used as a wrapper. Consequently it is much damaged, making it very difficult to read. It lists all the prisoners to be brought to the G.S., including those on bail and bound for their good behaviour, which represented the majority. For example, of the 62 prisoners listed in the calendar for the Montgomeryshire G.S. held at Newtown on 2 September 1566:[6]

8 were detained in gaol as a result of previous convictions.
5 were convicted and sentenced to be hanged.
1 was to remain in gaol and not to be hanged since she claimed to be pregnant.
7 were sentenced to be hanged but were then reprieved to remain in gaol.
41 were bailed.

The total number, excluding those to be hanged, who thus remained in gaol was 16.

Each entry in the calendar provides details of the prisoner; their name, social status and place of residence. Sometimes details of the offence would be given and who committed him or her. The pleadings, trial jury's verdict and judgement are also given although these are usually in very abbreviated form. In the event of the prisoner being bailed, the names, status and place of abode of the sureties to the bail would be given. Invariably, the sureties would have family connections with the prisoner.

### Nomina Ministrorum

This document, because of its size, was also used sometimes as the wrapper to the file. It lists, for the county, all the justices of the peace, chief stewards of the lordships and manors, coroners, foresters, escheators, maiors and bailiffs of the boroughs and liberties, chief constables of the peace for each hundred and bailiffs of each hundred.

### Quarter Sessions' records

Quarter Sessions' records were returned into the G.S. as a result of them being lifted out of that lesser court by means of a writ of *certiorari*. The actions under consideration either did not fall within the competence of the Quarter Sessions or there was an appeal against the decision made there. The details provided state where the Quarter Sessions were held, when and before whom. The names of the Quarter Sessions' jurors are also listed, together with details of the indicted person and the matter in question. Normally, this concerned an indictment (formal charge) or recognizance (bond).

### Examinations

Examinations are written records of what suspects and witnesses said before a justice of the peace when they were interrogated. The justice of the peace was required by statute (2 & 3 Mary c.10) to write down and sign the examination.

A large number of the examinations are missing but those that survive provide a contemporary account of life during the period of the court. The survival of these records is particularly good for some of the G.S., with the earliest examination being dated about 1560. This makes such records superior to those of the English Assize Courts for which examinations rarely survive any earlier than the mid seventeenth century.[7]

Details contained in the examinations can describe the dress of people, their work, eating and sleeping habits and their means of travel as well as a great deal of interesting incidental information. The examinations were, of course, prepared for the purpose of giving evidence in the court and would have been read to the jury. As an example of the type of material contained in the examinations the following is a summary of an examination taken at 'Tyen in Lloyn', Montgomeryshire, on 19 June 1563 before Edward Herbert, Esq., JP, concerning the alleged theft and killing of a sheep:

> Alice verch David of the parish of Llangadfan, widow, aged 60 years, said that upon Wednesday night, the 13 January 1563 she saw the son of Howell ap Morris holding a fire brand and a candle in his hands lighting the daughter of Howell ap Morris and a maid servant washing puddings [sheep's entrails] in a brook adjoining Howell's house. Alice called her daughter to see what was happening who did so accordingly. Lowry verch Llewelyn, aged 25 years, the daughter of Alice, confirmed that she obeyed her mother.[8]

From another example it has been possible to prepare the rudimentary genealogical chart given in Fig 17-5. This relates to the suspected murder of Johanne Oakley of Winnington, co. Salop on 1 October 1651.

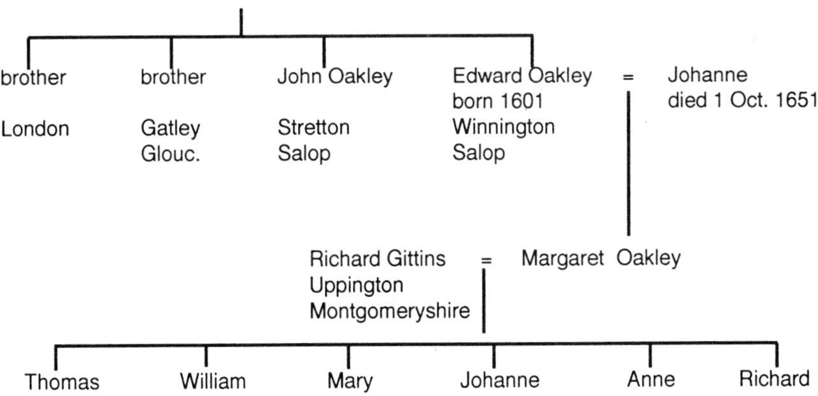


Fig. 17-5: Example of genealogical information from an Examination[9]

Some odd names will arise which will prove to be a nightmare for the genealogist such as Thomas Bromall alias John Sais alias Edward Phillips of Llanfair Waterdine, Salop, who occurs in the May 1571 G.S. for Montgomeryshire.[10]

## Recognizances

A recognizance was a bond entered into by an accused person to enforce their attendance in court to answer the charge laid against him or her. The penal sum for default of appearance was usually £40, although this did vary according to the seriousness of the offence. Sureties to the recognizance, usually two, would be required. Recognizances were also entered into by persons who prosecuted the accused to ensure that they, too, would attend the court, and by witnesses to give evidence against the accused.

The recognizances give details of the person who became bound for their appearance and details of the sureties. It was not unusual for members of the accused's family to act as sureties.

## List of Jurors

There are several lists of jurors within the files which are of great interest. During the period of the G.S. it was a requirement for each juror to hold land to the value of 40 shillings per annum or goods to the value of £40. Subsequently, these values were increased with the passage of time.

Originally, there were five different types of jury as follows:

|  |  |
|---|---|
| —Grand Jury or Jury for the body of the county<br>—Second Jury or Jury for the hundreds<br>—Jury for the boroughs and liberties | To consider Bills of Indictment and to make presentments. |
| —Trial Jury | To try cases. |
| —Jury of Matrons | To determine if a woman convicted of felony was pregnant or not. |

Members of the grand jury appeared to have been composed of the gentry of the county. This did not necessarily mean that they could all write, for some of the early records are subscribed by some of the grand jurors making a mark. A justice of the peace seems to have always acted as the foreman to this jury.

The second jury appears to have comprised members of the lesser gentry and members of the yeoman class and, again, it seems that a justice of the peace usually acted as its foreman.

The members of the jury for the boroughs and liberties were the freemen of the boroughs and liberties. They would normally consider bills of indictment for offences relating to infringements of the rights of their liberties and misdemeanours committed there.

From the mid seventeenth century the jury for the boroughs and liberties and the jury for the hundreds disappeared leaving the grand jury only to consider each bill of indictment, i.e. determine if there was a charge to be answered.

Lists of names survive from which trial jurors were selected and, in particular, record those that were sworn to serve, those that were sick, excused, fined for non-appearance or challenged either by one of the suspects, who was about to take his trial, or by the potential juror himself who claimed that he had to give evidence on the Crown's behalf at one of the trials.[11]

The jury of matrons was called after a woman pleaded that she was pregnant after having been convicted of a felony by a trial jury. It was the duty of the matrons to check this claim and return whether or not they found her pregnant. If she was found to be pregnant her hanging would be deferred and she would be kept in gaol until the next sessions when her case would be reviewed again. Indications are that, having been successful in claiming benefit of belly, very few were then sent to be hanged at subsequent sessions.

## Schedules of Prisoners, their Offences and Pleadings

When a trial took place, a jury would be sworn to consider as many as twelve or even more cases at one time. There has been much debate as to how the jurors were able to remember all the details of each case and come to a verdict after due deliberation. It appears that the trial jurors may have been handed a schedule giving details of the name of each offender and details of their offences. A copy of the schedule would be kept by a clerk of the court and perhaps the Justice to record the pleadings and the jury's verdict. The schedule is written in English, usually in court hand, with the pleadings and verdict given in very abbreviated Latin. The schedule is useful in providing details of offences committed by the prisoners who were actually tried at the sessions.

## Indictments

The indictment is the formal charge against a person. Initially, it would be called a Bill of Indictment and would be submitted to one of the juries considering these, (grand, second or jury for the boroughs and liberties), who would hear the prosecution's evidence and consider whether or not there was a case to answer. If they did, the bill would be returned *billa vera* (true bill) in which case the person was said to be indicted and, if not, they would return the bill *ignoramus* (we are ignorant) in which case the suspect would go free. During the early period of the existence of the G.S. the ignoramus bills were cut up in little pieces and thrown away.

The indictment gives the name, status and place of abode of the person and details of the offence. It is not unusual to find a number of indictments amended. This was not due to the scribe, who drew up the indictment, making a mistake but rather it indicates a process of plea bargaining. Examples of plea bargaining include the charge being reduced to a less serious one or, perhaps, any accessories to an alleged offence being deleted. More often than not, the suspect would confess to the amended indictment in the hope that in saving the court's time, and being seen to co-operate with the court, the Justice would pass a more lenient sentence.

The indictment also includes the names of the prosecutor and witness, usually as an endorsement, and sometimes the pleadings, verdict and judgement, albeit in abbreviated form. Sometimes the expression, *legit ut clericus* (he read as a cleric) would be included, indicating that the convicted person had been successful in claiming benefit of clergy—a legal fiction. There were certain offences for which it was possible for this legal fiction to be employed, e.g. homicide (manslaughter), but not murder. All the convict would have to do was to read a passage from the Bible—Psalm 51—which, understandably, became known as the 'neck verse'. If the convict could read then this would, in theory, prove that he was a cleric and he would be handed over to the church authorities to be dealt with under canon law, for which there was no death penalty. In practice, the convict would be set free after having his thumb branded, for benefit of clergy could only be claimed once.

### Presentments

Presentments (*Veredictum*) of the three indictment juries comprise a list of misdemeanour offences as well as presenting the inhabitants of various administrative areas for not keeping roads and bridges in repair.

### Petitions

A petition would usually be submitted by a person wishing to be released from his recognizance or to be released from gaol. The petitioner would normally state that he was a poor man having no manner or means to support his family due to the great expense of his bond or not being able to earn his living whilst confined in gaol.

**Informations or Articles of Misdemeanour**

These would be submitted by either an individual or a group of persons against an offender, especially a persistent one. Sometimes this would list all previous offences and court appearances and usually concluded by asking the court to bind the trouble maker for good behaviour towards the King or Queen's liege people or for the court to examine the offender.

**Process Writs**

There were a variety of process writs, the purpose of which was to ensure that a suspected offender was given due notice and brought to the court to answer the charges laid against him or her. The issuing of the various writs culminated in the offender being outlawed in the event that he or she did not appear in court.

Each writ records the names of the offenders, their status and place of abode. A court clerk sometimes noted on the writ at which G.S. they were indicted for their offences.

**Coroners' Inquests**

The coroner's inquest continues to this day in very much the same form as at the establishment of the G.S. Inquests were held on persons whose deaths were unusual or thought not to be by natural causes. The coroners were required to return the inquests into the G.S. The numbers of inquests on each file varies considerably and it is rare for there to be more than twelve.

Each inquest records when, where, and before which coroner the inquest was held and, of course, upon whom. The names of the jurors who, in theory, were from the same township and the three adjacent townships are also listed. Details of the circumstances leading up to the death of the person would be provided with precise times being stated as well as the cause of death. The coroner always signed the inquest and, sometimes, so did the jurors although most of them were only able to do this by way of a mark.

Inquests considered such events as murders, homicides and suicides, which the jury returned as being at the diabolical instigation of the devil or the person being of unsound mind, thereby saving the deceased's estate from being forfeited to the Crown. Drowning whilst crossing rivers and streams or whilst bathing, falling out of trees whilst picking fruit or cutting branches, freezing or burning to death, accidental shootings, being run over by a cart or plough, and dying whilst held a prisoner in gaol were some of the other causes of death considered by coroners' juries. Where the jurors considered death to be due to natural causes they would state that it was *ex visitaceone dieu* (by the visitation of God) or *ex divine visitaceone* (by divine visitation). It also returned verdicts of misfortune for death as a result of an accident.

For example, Thomas ap David of Dolgadfan, Montgomeryshire, was accidentally shot dead on 23 June 1577.[12] At 3.00 p.m. he, together with other neighbours, gathered together that Sunday afternoon and 'did sett marke or xii^e^ score prycke' for archery. Rudderch ap John shot an arrow to the mark which, by misfortune and against his intentions, hit Thomas ap David, who was above the mark, under the left ear causing his instant death.

## Miscellaneous Correspondence and Papers

There are, amongst the early files of the G.S., a number of letters, orders and other papers from the Council in the Marches of Wales concerning the trial of felons which they had apprehended or who had appealed to them, and these occur until the abolition of the Council in the Marches of Wales in 1689. There are also some stray papers which relate to civil actions, and in some of the files these may be substantial.

**NOTES TO CHAPTER 17**

[1] The Public Record Office *List and Indexes* IV and XL and the National Library of Wales' copy with typescript additions provides a basic list of the records. Mr Glyn Parry, Department of Manuscripts, National Library of Wales, has written a short pamphlet and is presently preparing a revised list of the records.

[2] The Powysland Club jointly with the National Library of Wales is publishing in 1993 a transcript of the six surviving Gaol Files of the Commonwealth period 1650-1660 for the Montgomeryshire Court of Great Sessions.

[3] NLW, WALES 24/154A m.28

[4] NLW, WALES 4/129-3 m.65

[5] NLW, WALES 12/1

[6] NLW, WALES 4/125-4 mm.67-68

[7] Only one English Assize circuit, the North Eastern, has examinations which survive any earlier, and then only from 1613. The best preserved examinations in the courts of Great Sessions are those for the Chester circuit.

[8] NLW, WALES 4/125-1 m.44

[9] NLW, WALES 4/154-2 mm.5-7 and 10-22

[10] NLW, WALES 4/127-1 m.87

[11] Sometimes, the Justice would prosecute a trial jury for returning a perverse verdict; see Murray Ll.Chapman, 'A sixteenth-century trial for felony in the Court of Great Sessions for Montgomeryshire', *Montgomeryshire Collections* 78, (1990), 167-70.

[12] NLW, WALES/128-5 m.28

## APPENDIX

### COURT OF GREAT SESSIONS LIST OF PLEA ROLLS, CHANCERY PLEADINGS AND GAOL FILES

| COUNTY | PLEA ROLLS | | CHANCERY PLEADINGS | | | | GAOL FILES | |
|---|---|---|---|---|---|---|---|---|
| | | | Parchment | | Paper | | | |
| | Period Covered | No. of Rolls | Period Covered | No. of Boxes | Period Covered | No. of Boxes | Period Covered | No. of Files |
| Chester Circuit | | | 1751-1830 | 6 | 1730-1830 | 12 | | |
| — Denbighshire | 1542-1830 | 529 | | | | | 1545-1830 | 454 |
| — Flintshire | 1542-1830 | 549 | | | | | 1542-1830 | 503 |
| — Montgomeryshire | 1542-1830 | 566 | | | | | 1554-1830 | 458 |
| North Wales Circuit | | | 1728-1830 | 13 | 1693-1830 | 14 | | |
| — Anglesey | 1576-1830 | 449 | | | | | 1708-1830 | 56 |
| — Caernarfonshire | 1550-1830 | 168 | | | | | 1622-1830 | 68 |
| — Merionethshire | 1553-1830 | 190 | | | | | 1702-1830 | 56 |
| Brecon Circuit | | | 1690-1830 | 81 | 1690-1830 | 1 | | |
| — Brecknockshire | 1542-1830 | 450 | | | | | 1559-1830 | 484 |
| — Glamorganshire | 1542-1830 | 559 | | | | | 1542-1830 | 497 |
| — Radnorshire | 1542-1830 | 548 | | | | | 1542-1830 | 502 |
| Carmarthen Circuit | | | 1689-1830 | 12 | None | — | | |
| — Cardiganshire | 1543-1830 | 449 | | | | | 1542-1830 | 256 |
| — Carmarthenshire | 1542-1830 | 462 | | | | | 1542-1830 | 250 |
| — Pembrokeshire | 1542-1830 | 521 | | | | | 1547-1830 | 385 |

The above table only concerns itself with the surviving records during the period of the existence of the Court of Great Sessions, i.e. 1542-1830. Plea Rolls do exist prior to 1542 for a number of Welsh counties which were 'shired' as a result of the Edwardian Conquest of Wales.

The table is only for the purpose of indicating the extent of available records and the periods for which they survive. It therefore only shows the earliest and latest files. In some cases, there are very large gaps of missing records, e.g. although the earliest Gaol File for Caernarfonshire is shown as 1622, it is a solitary one with a large gap until the beginning of the eighteenth century when a more complete run of records survive. The numbers of files and rolls indicate the survival of the records, clearly demonstrating that the preservation of the records for the North Wales Circuit is poor.

The lists available in the Manuscripts Department, National Library of Wales, should be consulted to determine exactly what records survive.

# 18. Printed and Manuscript Pedigrees

Michael P. Siddons

In common with many other nations, the Welsh preserved with care the genealogies of their rulers, and the earliest surviving genealogical manuscripts contain these royal pedigrees. We cannot tell when they were first written down, and they were probably transmitted orally for many centuries. The possibility of accurate oral transmission of rulers' pedigrees over long periods was confirmed in the Pacific islands where there were populations which had migrated centuries ago from a common source to widely scattered islands and which had had no further contact. In many cases the royal lines from different islands converge backwards to common ancestors referred to independently by the same names and at the same periods.[1]

The Welsh were recorded as early as the twelfth century by Giraldus Cambrensis as being particularly devoted to their pedigrees: 'Even the common people know their family-tree by heart and can readily recite from memory the list of their grandfathers, great-grandfathers, great-great-grandfathers, back to the sixth or seventh generation'.[2] The kindred was an extremely important unit in Welsh law, and was invoked for the inheritance of land, for the settlement of disputes, the compurgation of witnesses, and the payment and exaction of compensation.[3] It was in fact a legal necessity to know one's pedigree. From the fourteenth century on, the Welsh poets in their praise-poems and elegies took every opportunity to extol their patrons' ancestry, and in some cases gave the male-line ancestors for many generations. Iolo Goch, in his poem composed in the latter part of the fourteenth century on the pedigrees of Owain Glyndŵr, recites Owain's male-line pedigree, with some omissions, and then gives other distinguished ancestors by female lines.[4] Lewis Glyn Cothi, in his poem in the mid-fifteenth century on the pedigree of Dafydd Goch ap Maredudd of Stapleton, takes Dafydd's pedigree back for 17 generations to Rhodri Mawr (King of Wales, d.877), albeit with a mistake after the sixth generation.[5] Even when, with the introduction of English law, the knowledge of one's pedigree was no longer legally necessary, the Welsh attached great importance to ties of kinship. This is illustrated in the numerous 'challenge pedigrees' presented to the Great Sessions of Wales which are discussed in Chapter 17. This continued strong attachment of the Welsh to their ancestry has provoked amused and sometimes exasperated comment. Major Francis Jones quotes a number of amusing anecdotes concerning this tendency of the Welsh, of which one of the most striking is the case of John Jones of Coedymynydd, who in the 1640s protested to Thomas Mytton, general for North Wales, against being subjected to taxation for his lands, which, he maintained, descended to him directly from Dyfnwal Moelmud, King of Britain about 2400 years previously. His protest was accompanied by a detailed pedigree.[6] Gwenogvryn Evans, writing in 1899, tells how:

> A considerable section of the community takes a most astonishing interest in this subject of pedigrees, and a student not nursed in the firm faith of a descent from a follower of the Norman Bastard, or a Welsh Royal tribe, finds himself frequently in a most embarrassing position. The writer has found it difficult to swallow his soup with grace as he listened to a 'descendant of Rhodri Mawr wondering' if there was no way of recovering *some* of the family estate, which was so extensive in the year 946.[7]

Welsh law made a great distinction between the free man and the unfree, which was maintained for many centuries, and indeed there were echoes of this distinction even in the sixteenth century. Although the proportion of bond to free was less than in countries which adopted the feudal system, it appears that in the eleventh and twelfth centuries the proportion of bondmen of various classes was relatively high, even perhaps a majority of the population, but this proportion fell in the thirteenth and fourteenth centuries to perhaps a third of the total. Bondmen were tied to the land, to the ownership of which until a later date they had no hereditary right, and could be bought and sold with the land. The free man considered himself to be a nobleman, and the terms used in Welsh and Latin to denote a free man are those used for noblemen. The free man was a man with a pedigree, and his status and rights depended on his pedigree. The bondman was 'a man without a pedigree'.

Foremost among the rights of a free man were those to land. Title to land depended on descent from the founder of a kin-group. In the important late mediaeval surveys this is usually called a **gwely** (bed) or **gafael** (holding), and is often called after the founder of the group. In the *Record of Caernarvon*, a survey of land rights and dues made in 1352, there were for example in the township of Gloddaith, in the commote of Creuddyn, three free **gwelyau**, *Gwely Iorwerth ap Madog*, *Gwely Bleddyn ap Madog*, and *Gwely Gwyon ap Madog*, called after the sons of Madog ap

Mabon Glochydd.[8] The sole heir of *Gwely Iorwerth ap Madog* was Madog Fychan [ap Madog, son of the aforesaid Iorwerth ap Madog]. The heirs of *Gwely Bleddyn ap Madog* were Llywelyn Chwith [ap Heilin, son of Bleddyn ap Madog aforesaid] and Cynwrig ap Madog ap Heilin.

This land was not held in absolute right, and could not be sold or left by will. At the holder's death his rights in the land were divided equally between his sons or grandsons. Failing such, they went to his male heirs in the agnatic (male) line, as far as his second cousins. If there was no heir within the limit of fourth degree (second cousins), they escheated to the lord. Because the holder of land was not its absolute owner, gifts of land to religious institutions were often made with the assent of the male relatives of the donor, in order to avoid disputed title. For example, Maredudd ap Robert, lord of Cedewain, made a grant *c.*1216-17 to the nunnery of Llanllugan 'with the assent and good will of my sons Owain, Gruffudd and Hywel, my brother Trahaearn, and my nephews Cadwgon, Maredudd, Hywel and Owain'.[9] There are cases in the mediaeval surveys where daughters appear to have inherited land. For example, the sole heir to *Gwely Wyrion* (of the grandsons of) *Ithel* in the township of Bryn-bras in the commote of Eifionydd in 1352 was Gwenllian the daughter of Gronwy ab Iorwerth.[10]

The partible descent described above led within a few generations to a large number of free men, each with his claim to 'noble' status, but with smaller and smaller holdings. R.R.Davies quotes the example of Iorwerth ap Cadwgon (*fl.c.*1220), whose estate had been subdivided by 1313 among 27 direct male descendants.[11] The contrast between the 'noble' status claimed and the economic situation of these free men became ever more glaring.

Henry VII's charters to the principality of North Wales, and to several other lordships of North Wales in the early sixteenth century, followed by the Acts of Union of England and Wales of 1536-43, introduced English law into Wales, and, among other things, formally abolished the custom of partible succession. There were many instances where individual Welshmen had already found means of ensuring the passage of their estates to their heirs intact, and there was an increasing desire on the part of landowners to be allowed to do this.[12] However, even after this formal abolition in many parts of Wales the system of partible succession lingered on, due to native conservatism, for some time.[13]

Kinship played an important role in other domains, among which were the maintenance of public order by responsibility for the individual's behaviour, and defence of his rights and honour. Compensation for murder (*galanas*) was exacted from the murderer and his kindred up to the fifth cousin, the paternal kindred being expected to pay more than the maternal, and the sums paid diminishing with the distance of the relationship. The compensation was distributed along similar lines to the victim's kindred. The Welsh language has terms expressing kinship as far as ninth cousins.[14] The amount of compensation varied with the status of the victim. In cases of debt, the debtor's word should be supported by the sworn oaths of six relatives, four from his father's kin, and two from his mother's kin.

Although the distinctions between free and unfree were maintained, and efforts made to enforce them, in practice they became blurred, due to various factors, including the effects of the Black Death in the mid-fourteenth century, the transition from a military to an agricultural society, and the effects of partible succession leading to a large number of freeholders with rights to a very little land, many of whom sold their rights to their better-off neighbours, with the build-up of substantial estates on the one hand, and the creation of a mass of landless freemen on the other. C.A.Gresham describes how the descendants of a prominent freeholder in Pennant sold most of their holdings to the Clenennau estate between 1492 and 1540.[15] Many examples are found in the genealogical manuscripts of descendants of distinguished ancestors who sold their land to more prosperous freeholders, often relatives, and many are described as tinkers, fiddlers, etc.[16]

Heraldry came into Wales much later than into England and other countries of Western Europe. Apart from the princely families there is very little evidence of Welshmen bearing arms before 1350, and it is only in the fifteenth century that the use of coats of arms became widespread.[17] The bards who had previously taken little note of heraldry then added it to their repertoire, and until the decline of the bardic order in the late sixteenth and early seventeenth century, when this role was taken over by the largely English-educated and orientated gentlemen-antiquarians, were to a large degree the guardians of Welsh heraldry.

Most of those Welshmen who bore arms early on were men who had frequent dealing with the English, the earliest of all being the princes of the Houses of Gwynedd and Powys, and some Welshmen who served the English Crown, particularly in a military capacity, often as far as Scotland and France, or great marcher lords. Among those who served the Crown was Sir Rhys ap Gruffudd, a descendant of Llywelyn the

Great's minister, Ednyfed Fychan, whose arms were recorded at a tournament in 1334, while the arms of Hywel ap Meurig, of a family which had already served the de Bohun family in the Marches, were recorded *c.*1280. The arms of the principal Welsh princely dynasties appear to have been based on the English royal arms.

After the conquest Wales did not form part of the realm. That part which was not included in the Principality, which was the apanage of the [English] Prince of Wales, was divided up into numerous marcher lordships, whose lords enjoyed regalian rights within their lordships. The Welsh were left much to their own devices by the English heralds until the mid-sixteenth century, when the first deputy herald, Gruffudd Hiraethog (d.1564), was appointed. They paid little attention to the generally accepted heraldic conventions, such as not placing colour on colour, or metal on metal, and many examples can be found particularly of Gules on Sable recorded from houses or churches. Similarly they often quartered coats of families from which their descent was not through heiresses, and seldom differenced their arms to indicate the different branches of a family. The most striking characteristic of Welsh heraldry, however, was the systematic retrospective attribution of coats of arms to persons who lived long before the days of heraldry, and indeed often to persons who never lived at all. Retrospective attribution of arms was not in itself a Welsh invention, but was widespread in Europe in the late middle ages. Some 175 coats have been recorded of the knights of King Arthur, and many of the Saints have had arms attributed to them, as also the Trinity. Richard II bore the royal arms impaled by those attributed to Edward the Confessor.

In contrast with other countries, large numbers of Welsh families claimed descent from a relatively small number of far-distant 'patriarchs'. When a descendant of one of these 'patriarchs' adopted a coat of arms, such as, for example, Lleision d'Avene, lord of Afan in Glamorgan, whose arms are recorded in the Parliamentary Roll of *c.*1312, and who descended from Iestyn ap Gwrgan (eleventh century), it was argued that these arms must be those of Iestyn, and thus were also the arms of others whose male descent was from Iestyn. It mattered little that the arms adopted were almost certainly based on those of Lleision's overlords, the Clares, lords of Glamorgan. In the same way Gruffudd ap Nicolas of Dinefwr adopted in the first half of the fifteenth century arms including ravens, in an allusion to the ravens of his supposed ancestor Owain ab Urien (sixth century). By the same reasoning as in the case of the descendants of Iestyn, the very numerous families claiming descent from Urien subsequently bore the same arms.

The result of this practice is that whereas in England the bearing of a coat of arms is a declaration of the family from which the bearer descends, the bearing of one of the traditional Welsh coats is a proclamation of the far-distant 'patriarch' from whom he descends, and says little about his immediate family. This is often a help from a genealogical point of view, but since for example the descendants of Elystan Glodrydd occupy many pages in the pedigree books, it is only a limited help. Sometimes groups of families descended from a 'patriarch' have adopted arms attributed to an intermediate ancestor, thus splitting up the descendants into several groups. This can be seen with the descendants of Tudur Trefor, where different coats are found for Elidir ap Rhys Sais, Iddon ap Rhys Sais, Cynwrig ap Rhiwallon, Jonas ap Gronwy, and others. In some instances different coats of arms were attributed to several successive agnatic ancestors, and their descendants sometimes quartered them all. It cannot be emphasised too strongly that the fact that a particular family bore a certain coat of arms does not mean that all families of the same name bore the same arms, or were descended from the same patriarch. This will easily be understood after consideration of the origin of Welsh surnames (see Chapter 7).

The Welsh gentry were enthusiastic in their display of heraldry, and many-quartered shields were carved over fireplaces, or on porches, of houses all over Wales, and on the many heraldic pedigree rolls which were compiled from the late sixteenth century on. The quarters displayed included many of pre-heraldic and often unhistorical heroes, such as Brutus, said to have been descended from the Trojans, and to have been the first King of Britain, Beli Mawr, and others, as well as of the patriarchs mentioned earlier, many of whose coats are repeated by the entry of more quarterings through marriages. One extreme example of this enthusiasm was the shield of 323 quarterings registered with the College of Arms in 1894 by Lloyd of Stockton in Shropshire.[18]

The English heralds carried out heraldic visitations of parts of Wales, recording, as well as coats of arms, a variable amount of genealogical information. The book of William Ballard, March King of Arms, contains among other things what appears to be a record of his visitation of South Wales and the adjoining march in about 1480-90, and William Fellow, Lancaster Herald, visited South Wales and Herefordshire for Clarenceux King of Arms in 1530. Fulk ap Hywel, Lancaster Herald, had a commission in 1550 from Edward VI to visit Wales, but was degraded and executed for counterfeiting Clarenceux's seal, and his visitation was not carried out. Visitations were made of Flintshire in 1670, and Monmouthshire with Herefordshire in 1683. A visitation was to have been made of Denbighshire in 1670 but did not take place. Many Welshmen recorded their pedigrees and arms in visitations of the English counties where they were living.[19] Some of these pedigrees are very long, and this suggests that they took them with them when moving to England. A good example is that of John ap Rees alias Price of Kingston-upon-Thames, Surrey, who recorded his pedigree at the heraldic visitation of Surrey in 1623, tracing the line 12 generations back to Gwaithfoed of Ceredigion, and also giving several collateral lines.[20]

Gruffudd Hiraethog was the first of many deputy heralds appointed by the kings of arms for the whole or part of Wales.[21] Deputy heralds were also appointed for different counties of England, but there was an added need for them in Wales, owing to the language, and the different background and social structure. Gruffudd Hiraethog was succeeded by Lewys Dwnn, who was appointed in 1586, and by such notable genealogists as David Edwardes and Hugh Thomas in South Wales and Thomas Chaloner, the Randle Holmes and Griffith Hughes in North Wales. The first two named above, Gruffudd Hiraethog and Lewys Dwnn, were traditionally trained bards, and their writings, together with those of some of Gruffudd's pupils such as Wiliam Llŷn, Wiliam Cynwal and Simwnt Fychan, are particularly valuable. The later deputy heralds were mostly English-educated, though also Welsh-speaking, gentlemen-antiquarians. This association with the heralds led the practice of Welsh heraldry gradually closer to that of English heraldry, and this process was accelerated under the gentlemen-antiquarians, even if the old ways were not easily given up.

Dr. Peter Bartrum has published a series of important articles on the Welsh genealogical manuscripts.[22] Of the surviving genealogical manuscripts the earliest were originally written in the ninth and tenth centuries, and several others in the twelfth and thirteenth centuries. They contain the pedigrees of the rulers of various Welsh dynasties, including the lesser ones, such as those of Morgannwg and Gwent, together with those of some ancient heroes and saints and some other prominent families, and are taken back in some instances to the Dark Ages. In some cases the original manuscripts have not survived and we have only later copies, sometimes themselves made in the late fifteenth or sixteenth centuries.

As well as copying the work of their predecessors, the bards of the fifteenth and sixteenth centuries compiled a great quantity of new pedigrees of the gentry families. At first most Welsh pedigrees were of the *Achau'r mamau* (pedigrees of the mothers) type, where the male line pedigree of the subject is given in a string of patronymics, followed by the pedigrees of the mothers in all directions, with little attention being paid to collaterals, and often also to the subject's children. On occasion the pedigree takes the opposite form, and the descendants of a particular person are given in all directions. Some very early pedigrees are lists of names, X the son of Y the son of Z, and so on. Later writers, however, gave the names of the children and their marriages at least for the later generations. Gruffudd Hiraethog was the first Welsh genealogist to introduce the tabular pedigree. He and Lewys Dwnn in particular visited all parts of Wales, while the work of most of the other bardic genealogists was more limited in the area covered. The manuscripts of Wiliam Llŷn, Wiliam Cynwal and Simwnt Fychan treat mostly North Wales families, those of Rhys Cain of Oswestry and his son Siôn Cain North Wales and especially Mid-Wales, and those of Dafydd Benwyn South-east Wales. The bards all wrote in Welsh, except the Cains, some of whose work was in English, and for the most part, apart from Lewys Dwnn, their pedigrees were written in narrative form. It must be admitted that the writing, particularly that of Gruffudd Hiraethog and Lewys Dwnn, is extremely untidy and difficult to read without practice. The writing of the gentleman-antiquarians presents, on the whole, no special problem.

We are fortunate that when the old bardic order was declining in the late sixteenth and the early seventeenth centuries the last bards were on friendly terms with the new gentlemen-antiquarians who appeared, and this ensured the survival of much traditional material. Many of the bards' manuscripts came into the hands of the gentlemen-antiquarians. George Owen of Henllys was a friend of Lewys Dwnn and appears to have made a transcript of Lewys Dwnn's visitation manuscript, including that for North-east Wales, of the original of which only a fragment has survived. Most of the genealogical manuscripts of Gruffudd Hiraethog came to his disciple Wiliam Llŷn (d.1580), who left all his manuscripts and rolls in his will to Rhys Cain (d.1618), whence they came to his son Siôn (d.1650). Robert Vaughan of Hengwrt (d.1667) was a friend of Siôn Cain, and the latter's collection came to him, as well as many other important manuscripts. This great collection passed in 1859 to the Wynnes of Peniarth, and is now the Peniarth collection of manuscripts at the National Library of Wales.

From the mid-sixteenth century many pedigree rolls, or 'cards' as they were often called, were compiled by bards and later by deputy heralds and others. These were mostly painted with coats of arms, and showed the pedigrees of the subject, and often distinguished collateral relationships, such as to the Tudors, the Earls of Pembroke, or other noble families. The early rolls were somewhat untidily arranged, with lines branching out irregularly, but became more sophisticated from the latter part of the sixteenth century. Those compiled by Wiliam Llŷn and Wiliam Cynwal and some by Rhys Cain are in Welsh, but most of the others are in English. Among the compilers of these rolls were Thomas Jones of Tregaron ('Twm Siôn Cati') (d.1609), Randle Holme, Hopkin ab Einon and his son Walter Hopkins (*fl.*1630-40) and Rhys Cain's son Siôn Cain. Many of these rolls are now in the National Library of Wales, the British Library, and various county record offices, particularly that of Glamorgan at Cardiff.[23] Others are in private hands.

In the seventeenth century the first attempts were made at comprehensive collections of pedigrees covering all Wales, by Peter Ellis (d.1637) and Jacob Chaloner (d.1631), followed by Robert Vaughan of Hengwrt, Griffith Hughes (*fl.*1634-65), Owen Salesbury of Rûg and John Salesbury of Erbistock (compiled *c.*1630-77, David Edwardes (d.1690), William Lewes (d.1722) and Hugh Thomas (1673-1720).[24] The last of these great compilations was the Golden Grove Book (*c.*1765), now in the Dyfed Record Office at Carmarthen, which incorporated much of the work of David Edwardes and William Lewes, including large sections of David Edwardes's work without even changing the cross-references.[25] Although they set out to cover all Wales, they were all more complete either for the families of North or for those of South Wales. The families were grouped together under the names of the patriarchs, or ancestor figures, from whom they claimed descent. The compilers of all these collections made a strenuous attempt to trace the lesser branches of the families followed, and they were all written in English except the collection of Robert Vaughan. The latter, Griffith Hughes and Peter Ellis wrote their pedigrees in semi-tabular form with marginal links to indicate descent. The others all wrote in drop-line pedigree form.

Dr Peter Bartrum has edited most of the early material in a series of publications which make it unnecessary for the non-specialist to consult the original manuscripts. Indeed, in order to avoid further wear of the manuscripts it is desirable that the originals should be handled as little as possible. Dr Bartrum's chief publications are: 1. *Early Welsh Genealogical Tracts*[26] (*EWGT*), which presents the earliest texts. 2. *Welsh Genealogies 300-1400*[27] (*WG 1*). 3. *Welsh Genealogies 1400-1500*[28] (*WG 2*). In the last two works the pedigrees are presented in drop-line form, arranged in alphabetical order of the patriarchs from whom the families descended, with immigrant families or *advenae* placed under their surnames. All marriages are cross-referenced where possible. At the end of those lines of descent in *WG 1* which are continued in *WG 2*, a letter, e.g. A, B, C, is placed, and this letter is used in *WG 2* to indicate where the descent continues. Comprehensive indexes are provided of place-names, and personal names arranged in *WG 1* by period, and *WG 2* by region. The personal names indexes give the sources where each person in each pedigree is first mentioned, thus giving a guide to how nearly contemporary is the evidence. In *WG 2*, the genealogies are brought down to the generation born in the early 1500s, and many of the persons included lived until nearly 1600. This work includes in addition many immigrant families not included in *WG 1*, and Welsh families which attained prominence later than the period covered in *WG 1*. In addition, as well as more detailed studies of some of the texts published in *EWGT*, Dr Bartrum published two articles on the Welsh Tribal Patriarchs, where the genealogies of 77 of these ancestor figures are examined.[29]

The pedigrees which have been printed fall into several groups, namely:

1. Those contained in individual manuscripts.
2. Regional collections based largely on the traditional manuscripts, but brought up to date and with corrections.
3. Regional collections based on original research.
4. Studies of individual families.

Of the first group the most important is probably the visitations of Lewys Dwnn, the deputy herald.[30] Unfortunately much of this work is copied from copies of Lewys Dwnn's manuscripts, and the copying is careless, so that there are a number of errors in transcription. However, it is a very valuable work, especially in view of the difficulty for the inexperienced in reading the original. Other manuscripts which have been published include 'Llyfr Silin' (NLW MS 1666B), containing pedigrees of Powys and North Wales families, which was edited from a copy of a copy;[31] 'Llyfr Cedwyn' (1633), a transcript of a lost manuscript, of which the Montgomeryshire pedigrees were published;[32] 'Llyfr Baglan', written 1600-07 by John Williams and covering mostly families in Monmouthshire, Breconshire and West Herefordshire;[33] and the pedigrees of south-west Wales contained in the first two volumes of the *West Wales Historical Records*,[34] and taken from the Dale Castle Manuscript.

Collections in the second group include G.T. Clark's *Limbus Patrum Morganiae et Glamorganiae*,[35] covering Glamorgan families, and J.E. Griffith's *Pedigrees of Anglesey and Carnarvonshire Families*.[36] Both these contain many inaccuracies in the early periods, but are brought down to the time of writing, and are very valuable for the more recent period. A number of county histories, while not being concerned only with pedigrees, contain many of them. They include Theophilus Jones's *History of Brecknockshire*[37] and J.A. Bradney's *History of Monmouthshire*,[38] the latter drawn not only from the traditional pedigrees brought up to date, but also the fruit of much record research. J.Y.W.Lloyd's *History of Powys Fadog*[39] and the *Montgomeryshire Collections*[40] contain many such pedigrees. Others include the volumes of the Harleian Society's publications devoted to heraldic visitations, especially of Shropshire and Herefordshire, but there are many others which contain Welsh pedigrees.

A recent regional study based largely on wills and bringing the descents down to the present day is that of Prof.T.Ceiri Griffith on the area of South Caernarfonshire.[41]

Many individual pedigrees have been published in the volumes of *Archaeologia Cambrensis*, the *Transactions of the Honourable Society of Cymmrodorion*, and the county antiquarian and local history society journals. Francis Green published pedigrees of a number of Pembrokeshire families, including the Wogans.[42] Major Francis Jones has published a large number of pedigrees in the *Transactions of the Honourable Society of Cymmrodorion* and other journals.

It is not possible to list all the Welsh genealogical manuscripts, but a brief indication will be given of the possibilities. Many of those manuscripts in the Welsh language are described in Gwenogvryn Evans's report, including the Peniarth, Llanstephan and Mostyn collections, now in the National Library of Wales;[43] and Edward Owen's catalogue of manuscripts relating to Wales in the British Museum is also very helpful.[44]

**a.** The principal collection in the National Library of Wales is the Peniarth Collection. This contains most of the surviving manuscripts of many of the principal genealogists from the fifteenth century on, such as

Gutun Owain, Gruffudd Hiraethog, Wiliam Llŷn, Wiliam Cynwal, Siôn Cain, and Robert Vaughan of Hengwrt, together with the manuscript of Lewys Dwnn's visitation of North-west Wales. This library also has a transcript of the Golden Grove Book,[45] together with transcripts of David Edwardes's Cardiganshire and Carmarthenshire collections from the Bodleian Library,[46] the copy mentioned above of the collection of Owen and John Salesbury and numerous manuscripts by lesser-known genealogists, such as Richard Parry of Cwrt Gilbert (NLW MS 1598D, an early seventeenth-century manuscript containing pedigrees of Monmouthshire, Breconshire and Herefordshire families), Isaac Hamon's early 18th century collection of Gower and other Glamorgan pedigrees,[47] several transcripts of the Taicroesion MS, containing pedigrees of Caernarfonshire families,[48] and many others which are listed in the catalogue of manuscripts. The Alcwyn Evans MSS (NLW MSS 12356-88) include a number of volumes rich in pedigrees of families of south-west Wales. There are also a large number of pedigree rolls, and a photocopy of a very valuable collection of genealogical evidence of all kinds, mostly concerning Pembrokeshire families, compiled by Francis Green. The National Library has also a large collection of microfilms of genealogical manuscripts which are held in other libraries, particularly the British Library.

**b.** The British Library. The Harleian Collection in the department of manuscripts of this library contains a large number of Welsh genealogical manuscripts, many of them having come from the Randle Holmes of Chester, the Chaloners or Hugh Thomas. Among other important manuscripts are Lewys Dwnn's visitation of the three counties of South-west Wales,[49] and George Owen's pedigrees of North Wales and Radnorshire,[50] probably copied from Lewys Dwnn. A large collection of pedigrees and evidences for South Wales and Montgomeryshire by H.J.T. Wood is now in the British Library (Add. MSS 39707-56), and of these twelve (39745-56) contain collections of pedigrees arranged by counties and taken largely from the Golden Grove Book.

**c.** Major Francis Jones has compiled a report on the Welsh manuscripts in the College of Arms,[51] and has also related the history of the Protheroe Collection of Welsh genealogical manuscripts in the College.[52] This contains many volumes from George Owen of Henllys, George William Griffith, David Edwardes of Rhyd-y-gors, William Lewes of Llwynderw, and others and was built up generation by generation from the late sixteenth century until the early eighteenth century, and is very valuable for South Wales, and especially for south-west Wales, but much less so for North Wales. Most of the material in the Protheroe Collection was copied into the Golden Grove Book, of which, apart from the original, several transcripts, complete or partial, exist elsewhere. Among other Welsh material in the College of Arms are three volumes in the Vincent Collection, Nos. 135-7.[53] Nos.135 and 136 are in the hand of Augustine Vincent (d.1626), and No.137 is in that of Jacob Chaloner.

**d.** Cardiff Central Library. Important genealogical manuscripts in this library include Simwnt Fychan's manuscript of the late sixteenth century, containing heraldry and pedigrees;[54] Dafydd Benwyn's pedigree book,[55] with South Wales pedigrees; and Griffith Hughes's collection of Flintshire pedigrees[56] from the first half of the seventeenth century.

**e.** The library of the University College of North Wales, Bangor, contains a volume of pedigrees by Wiliam Cynwal from *c.*1570;[57] and the Taicroesion Book of Pedigrees, by John Ellis, *c.*1723.[58]

**f.** The Bodleian Library, Oxford. The principal manuscripts which concern us here are Richard Williams of Llywel's Breconshire Collection, 1644-5[59], and David Edwardes of Rhyd-y-gors's collections for Cardiganshire, Montgomeryshire and Radnorshire, Carmarthenshire, and Monmouthshire.[60]

**g.** Swansea. The William Bennet MS, belonging to the Royal Institute of South Wales, Swansea, are at present kept in the Library of University College, Swansea. This collection covers mainly Gower families and was compiled in the early seventeenth century.

Many scathing comments have been made on the untrustworthiness of the traditional Welsh pedigrees, even by people with close experience of them. J. Gwenogvryn Evans's remarks have often been quoted:

> when a pedigree reaches back beyond the third generation of the time in which it was originally drawn up, unless supported by independent documentary evidence, the work of even the most honest of men cannot be trusted.

He goes on to say, after quoting a pedigree by Gutun Owain which began with 'Adam son of God': 'It does seem as if reason took its leave of every genealogist, sooner or later.' But then continues:

> Nevertheless, from the middle of the fifteenth century to the end of the seventeenth, we have the continuous evidence of the manuscripts of successive bards, who were also professional genealogists.[61]

Among the features of Welsh pedigrees which attracted most scorn were these descents from God, and the total lack in most cases of any dates or evidence to support the descents. Gruffudd Hiraethog was a notable exception in that he quoted many of his authorities.

Mistakes did of course occur. The traditional pedigrees were all in manuscript form, and had to be copied. At each copying some misreadings would be made, which would pass into the next copies and so on, so that the texts became corrupted. Misidentifications were made between persons of the same name. In a pedigree where as often happened two names alternated over a number of generations, as for example Dafydd ap Rhys ap Dafydd ap Rhys, one pair of names might be omitted or added. And of course some deliberate attempts were made to concoct a pedigree or to provide a distinguished descent where none existed.

We must however bear in mind that these pedigrees were compiled at a time when the ways in which things were looked at were very different from those of today. Descents which we find impossible to accept were firmly believed in, and consequently recorded, and it was not thought far-fetched to show a descent from Adam, and thence from God. For the most part independent record evidence does not exist which would allow us to put the traditional pedigrees to the test, but in spite of Gwenogvryn Evans's remarks most people who have had much experience will agree that in those cases where such evidence does exist, they stand up in general very well to the test, and are shown to be remarkably accurate.

Many lesser branches, especially those with no heirs, are not recorded in the traditional pedigrees. Many other well-established families of freemen also do not appear. For example none of the numerous progeny of Iorwerth ap Cadwgon mentioned above appear in the pedigrees, and there are many persons named as the heirs of free *gwelyau* in the late mediaeval surveys who cannot be found there. This may again be owing to lack of heirs, but may also be because they lost their land and were forgotten.

For those persons unfamiliar with Welsh pedigrees, there are certain points which it is helpful to bear in mind.

**i.** The absence of surnames. The subject of Welsh surnames is dealt with elsewhere in this book. In most of the period covered by the manuscript pedigrees a large majority of the Welsh used no surnames, but were called by their Christian name, followed by *ap*, or *ab* before a vowel (son of), or *ferch* (daughter of), then their father's name, e.g. Dafydd the son of Rhys would be called Dafydd ap Rhys. Sometimes a string of such patronymics would be given, e.g. Dafydd ap Rhys ap Hywel ab Owain, this example covering four generations. In some manuscripts a long string of patronymics is given without any *ap*. Many people were given epithets such as *Goch* (red), *Gwyn* or *Wyn* (white), *Llwyd* > Lloyd (grey), *Fychan* > Vaughan (usually younger). These were at first personal, but later became surnames. They cannot therefore be taken as necessarily fixed family names, and cannot always be relied on.

**ii.** The importance of place-names, especially names of houses and farms. The lack of surnames results in a large number of people bearing the same names, and this leads to much confusion among persons unfamiliar with Welsh pedigrees. As a result, the association of the name with a place-name is of great help in identification. If we suppose that there are two persons with the Dafydd ap Rhys ap John, we have a much better chance of distinguishing them one from the other if we can say that one was Dafydd ap Rhys ap John of Pen-lan, and that the other was of Treowen. This means that an index of place-names is usually more useful than one of family names. Some of the general compilations mentioned above have place-name indexes, for example the Golden Grove Book and Robert Vaughan's Book.

**iii.** The pedigrees in the general compilations are usually grouped together under the patriarchs from whom the families claimed descent, and some of them give the name of the patriarchs from whom the wives descend. Coats of arms can often give a clue as to the patriarch under whom a family should be sought. But they can at times be misleading. In some instances families claimed descent from, and used the attributed arms of, an ancestor from whom their descent is no longer accepted. An example is the Blethin family of Shirenewton, Monmouthshire, one of whom was William Blethin, Bishop of Llandaff in the late sixteenth century. This family descends from Rhydderch ab Iestyn, which Iestyn was formerly taken to be Iestyn ap Gwrgan, but is now accepted as Iestyn ab Owain ap Hywel Dda. The Blethins bore the arms of their supposed ancestor, Iestyn ap Gwrgan. At other times, people bore the arms of their mother's, instead of their father's, family.

**iv.** In the early pedigrees in the *achau'r mamau* form women are given as mothers, rather than wives, and so their marital status is not clear.

Illegitimacy is often expressed in the work of Gruffudd Hiraethog and his pupils by the letter 'c' above the individual's name.

v. Wives and daughters are often not given Christian names in the manuscripts, but are simply referred to as 'the daughter of . . . '. In some pedigrees these blanks have been filled in later, with inconsistency between different manuscripts. In earlier centuries more than one son or daughter was often given the same name, and it cannot always be taken for granted that if marriages are found for two siblings of the same name it was the same person who married twice.

vi. It is always wise when using the traditional pedigrees to try to find a source as nearly as possible contemporary for each generation, since the incidence of errors is always greater the further back one goes from the time at which the pedigree is compiled.

vii. It is wise to take pedigree evidence as a signpost to be followed rather than as proof of a particular descent, and wherever possible to check the accuracy of the pedigree against independent evidence at every step. One important help is the system of numbering the generations adopted in *WG 1* and *WG 2*. A significant discrepancy in the generation numbers can draw attention to the need to look again very carefully at the pedigree concerned.

**NOTES TO CHAPTER 18**

[1]Thor Heyerdahl, *American Indians in the Pacific* (London: Allen & Unwin, 1952), p.35.

[2]Giraldus Cambrensis, *The Description of Wales*, book I, chapter 17. This passage is found in Gerald of Wales, trans. Lewis Thorpe, *The Journey Through Wales: and, The Description of Wales* (Harmondsworth: Penguin, 1978), p.251.

[3]For the social structure and the importance of kinship in Welsh society, see R.R. Davies, *Conquest, Coexistence and Change: Wales 1063-1415*. History of Wales Vol.2 (Oxford: Clarendon Press, 1987), 115-29, and A.D.Carr, *Medieval Anglesey* (Llangefni: Anglesey Antiquarian Society, 1982), chapters V, VI.

[4]D.R.Johnston, *Gwaith Iolo Goch* (Cardiff: UWP, 1988), no.VIII.

[5]E.D.Jones, *Gwaith Lewis Glyn Cothi 1837-39* (vol.I, Cardiff: UWP, 1953), no.59.

[6]Francis Jones, 'An Approach to Welsh Genealogy' (hereafter referred to as AWG), *Trans Cymm.*, 1948, 393; John Jones's letter is printed in *Arch. Camb.* VIII, 3rd series (1862), 143-7.

[7]J.Gwenogvryn Evans (ed.), *Reports on Manuscripts in the Welsh Language*, 2 vols. in 7 parts (London 1898-1910), vol.I. part II, Peniarth, p.vi.

[8]H.Ellis, (ed.), *Registrum vulgariter nuncupatum, The Record of Caernarvon* (London, 1838), p.1. The pedigree is found in P.C.Bartrum, *Welsh Genealogies A.D. 300-400* (Cardiff: UWP, 1974), Mabon 1.

[9]Richard Morgan, 'An Early Charter of Llanllugan Nunnery', *Mont. Coll.*, vol.73 (1985), 116-19.

[10]H.Ellis, see 8 above, p.42.

[11]R.R.Davies, see 3 above, p.120.

[12]Examples are quoted in R.R.Davies, see 3 above, pp.423-4.

[13]Glanmor Williams, *Recovery, Reorientation and Reformation: Wales c.1415-1642* History of Wales, Vol.3 (Oxford: Clarendon Press, 1987), pp.242-3, 274.

[14]These relationships and the terms used to express them are shown in a table in NLW, Peniarth MS 283, 79v.

[15]C.A.Gresham, *Eifionydd: a study in land ownership from the medieval period to the present day* (Cardiff: UWP, 1973), pp.8-11.

[16]Examples of men who sold their lands are given on pp.161, 1385, 1432, 1446, of the Golden Grove Book; those who are no longer classed among the gentry include Evan and David Morgan, and their cousin Evan Lloyd of Llanrhystud, descendants of Elystan Glodrydd, who are described respectively as shopkeeper, alehousekeeper and glover (*ibid.*, p.294), or David John Walter, a tailor and jockey, who married Sarah Bwmp (*ibid.*, p.78).

[17]The subject of Welsh Heraldry is treated in detail in the present writer's *The Development of Welsh Heraldry* (Aberystwyth: NLW, Vol.I 1991, Vols II and III to be published in early 1993). Only a brief outline will therefore be given here. Readers unfamiliar with heraldry in general will find a recent study useful: Thomas Woodcock and J.M.Robinson, *The Oxford Guide to Heraldry* (Oxford: OUP, 1988).

[18]Illustrated in Thomas Woodcock and J.M.Robinson, see 17 above, pl.25.

[19]The heraldic visitations of many counties have been published by the Harleian Society.

[20]*Visitation of Surrey* (London: Harleian Society Publications 43), 182-4.

[21]For the Welsh deputy heralds see *The Development of Welsh Heraldry*, Vol.1, pp.313-21.

[22]Peter C.Bartrum, 'Notes on the Welsh Genealogical Manuscripts', *Trans. Cymm.* (1968 (part I)), pp.63-98; 'Further Notes on the Welsh Genealogical Manuscripts', *Trans. Cymm.* (1976), pp.102-118; and 'Notes on the Welsh Genealogical Manuscripts (part III)', *Trans. Cymm.* (1988), 37-46.

[23]I am compiling a list of Welsh pedigree rolls.

[24]Details of these compilations will be found in the articles referred to in note 22.

[25]'The Golden Grove Book', in three volumes with an index, the property of the Earl Cawdor, deposited at the Dyfed Record Office, Carmarthen.

[26](Cardiff: UWP, 1966).

[27]8 vols. (Cardiff: UWP, 1974).

[28]18 vols. (Aberystwyth: NLW, 1983).

[29]'Pedigrees of the Welsh Tribal Patriarchs' *NLWJ*, XIII (1963), pp.93-146, and the same continued in *NLWJ*, XV (1967), 157-66.

[30]S.R. Meyrick, (ed.), *Heraldic Visitations of Wales and Part of the Marches*, 2 vols., (Llandovery, 1846).

[31]'Llyfr Silin', *Arch. Camb.* 15, fifth series (1887-91) 214-24.

[32]'Llyfr Cedwyn', *Mont. Coll.* 8, pp.399-420, and 10, 1-44.

[33]Cardiff Central Library, Baglan MS 2, edited by J.A. Bradney as *Llyfr Baglan 1600-7* (London: 1910).

[34]*West Wales Historical Records: Transactions of the Historical Society of West Wales*, I (1912), 1-96, and II (1913), 1-103.

[35]G.T. Clark, *Limbus Patrum Morganiae et Glamorganiae* (London: 1886).

[36]J.E. Griffith, *Pedigrees of Anglesey and Carnarvonshire Families* (Horncastle: 1914; facsimile reprint Wrexham: Bridge Books, 1985).

[37]Theophilus Jones, *A History of the County of Brecknock* (originally published 1805-09; Glanusk edition, 4 vols., Brecon: 1909-30).

[38]J.A.Bradney, *A History of Monmouthshire*, 4 vols. (London: 1904-33). The final volume, covering the hundred of Gwynllwg, is being prepared for publication by the South Wales Record Society.

[39]J.Y.W.Lloyd, *History of Powys Fadog*, 6 vols. (London: 1881-7).

[40]*The Montgomeryshire Collections*, the journal of the Powysland Club.

[41]T.Ceiri Griffith, *Achau ac Ewyllysiau Teuluoedd De Sir Gaernarfon* (Chwilog: The Author, 1989).

[42]*West Wales Historical Records*, e.g. the Wogan family, in VI (1916), 169-232, and VII (1918), 1-26.

[43]J.Gwenogvryn Evans, see 7 above, respectively vol.I, part II; vol.II, part II; and vol.I, part I.

[44]Edward Owen, *A Catalogue of the Manuscripts Relating to Wales in the British Museum*, 4 parts in 1 volume (London: 1900-22).

[45]NLW, Castell Gorfod MS 7, vols. I-XVIII.

[46]*Ibid.*, vols.XIX-XXI.

[47]Castell Gorfod MS 8.

[48]NLW MS 828D, 1216E, 1517E.

[49]BL, Egerton MS 2585.

[50]Egerton MS 2586.

[51]Francis Jones, *A Catalogue of Welsh Manuscripts in the College of Arms* (London: Harleian Society Publications, 1988).

[52]AWG, pp.459-66.

[53]Louise Campbell and Francis Steer, with index and notes by Robert Yorke, *Catalogue of Manuscripts in the College of Arms, Collections*, I (1988), 364-6.

[54]Cardiff MS 3.8.

[55]Cardiff MS 4.265.

[56]Cardiff MS 2.1 (Cardiff MS 10 in J.Gwenogvryn Evans, see 7 above, vol.II, part I, p.133).

[57]Bangor MS 5943.

[58]Bangor MS 13564.

[59]Bodleian Library, Additional MS A 281.

[60]Bodleian Library, Additional MSS C 177, C 178 and C 179 respectively.

[61]J.Gwenogvryn Evans, see 7 above.

# 19. Migration: Some Perspectives

W. T. R. Pryce

Migration, in reality a multifaceted phenomenon, is the term for movements of people—individuals, families, groups—from one permanent place of residence to settle and live permanently elsewhere. Usually such movements take place at significant stages in the life cycle of an individual—on marriage, when a new job is taken up, when children are born, on retirement, or, perhaps, following the death of a partner. It is self-evident, therefore, that migration is a topic of central importance and significance to the family historian.

## The nature of migration in the context of Wales

This chapter is concerned with the patterns and processes of internal migration: that is, movements that occur within an unitary nation state. In international scholarship the terms 'emigration' and 'immigration' are applied to transfers of people between nation states. These latter movements are considered separately in Chapter 20.

Although the Welsh are a distinctive nation in their own right, and, although the country is, in many respects, identifiable as a different place from England, at the present time Wales is not a separate state in constitutional terms. Therefore, it is in accordance with the internationally accepted fact that the country of Wales is an integral part of the United Kingdom, that migration is considered in this chapter. Hence, movements between Wales and elsewhere in the UK are referred to as 'in-migration' or 'out-migration' rather than as 'immigration' and 'emigration' (Fig 19-1).

Whilst at the most basic level of understanding migration is interpreted as the movement of individuals and/or families, it can also be seen as giving rise to a whole series of changes. For this reason, social scientists regard the phenomenon of migration as a process that alters the nature of the communities losing people by out-migration and brings about changes in places swamped by large numbers of new arrivals. And, of course, movements that result in a change of social and cultural milieu can, and do, have deep effects on the migrants themselves. Prolonged and sustained population movements have, in the past, led to

| | |
|---|---|
| **migration** | movements of individuals/families *within a unitary nation state* involving a permanent change of domicile. |
| **migrants** | individuals/families moving to a new permanent place of domicile *within a unitary nation state.* |
| **in-migration** | movements of new people arriving in a community. |
| **in-migrants** | persons/families involved in in-migration. |
| **out-migration** | movements of people who leave a community. |
| **out-migrants** | persons/families who leave their hitherto permanent home for a new permanent domicile elsewhere. |
| **emigration** | movements of individuals/families leaving a nation state to take up permanent residence *in another nation state* which, for British emigrants, means a foreign country overseas. |
| **emigrants** | persons/families involved in emigration. |
| **immigration** | movements of individuals/families *from a foreign country* who arrive and settle in a nation state, taking up permanent residence - in the case of Britain from countries overseas. |
| **immigrants** | persons/families involved in immigration. |

Fig 19-1 Key Terms in Migration Studies

profound changes in the social make-up of a country, region, town or rural parish.

Thus, the population geography of Wales in the pre-industrial conditions of the eighteenth century was to be changed, fundamentally, by the first commercial developments of the Denbigh and Flint coalfields in north-east Wales after *c.* 1750, the opening up of the slate mines and quarries of Gwynedd in the early nineteenth century, and by the very substantial exploitation of the south Wales coalfields from the 1860s onwards. In 1801, when the first census was taken, 12 per cent of the population of Wales (587,245) was enumerated in the county of Glamorgan. By 1911, the Welsh population had increased spectacularly to reach 2.4 millions, and now Glamorgan, on its own, accounted for a massive 46 per cent of the total.

Not only did migration bring about substantial shifts in the population geography of the country as a whole, it induced many changes in the sending societies, and eventually brought profoundly different conditions in the receiving societies. Many of the migrants to the valleys of Glamorgan and west Monmouthshire came from rural communities. And, they brought with them into these new growing industrial townships, many features of a previously rural way of life—the family pigsty(!), the tradition of cultivating a small plot of ground for subsistence crops, their rural ways of life and institutions in the form of the Sunday school, their chapels, and the rich independent cultural life and social activities that were integral to religious nonconformity (REES, 1975).

The published census reports contain much evidence for a whole series of massive population shifts affecting the whole of Wales. Although no birthplace data were collected by the official census until 1841 (and then only on a very crude basis of 'Were you born in this county or elsewhere?'), from other sources, such as Poor Law records, it is clear that migration was widespread and had been occurring over previous generations. But the late nineteenth century saw the development of a whole series of mass movements of the people. In 1851 the census began to collect more specific details as to where people had been born. Despite the availability of this information in the census enumerators' books, we have to wait until 1861 before the publication of birthplaces, county by county. Thence, the census made available a whole succession of birthplace returns, decade by decade, down to 1911; and, again, but for the last time, in 1951.

Fig 19-2 presents details of long-distance movements to specific locations within Wales, expressed as proportions of the residential population. Counties accommodating a higher proportion of migrants than in Wales as a whole are shown in bold type. Thus, the iron- and coal-mining districts of Glamorgan and Monmouthshire recorded substantial numbers of in-migrants throughout the period 1861-1911, as, indeed, did Denbigh and Flint in north-east Wales. In contrast, much of the rural west continued to lose people by out-migration and this is reflected in the low proportions in Cardiganshire and Carmarthenshire that had originated elsewhere.

By the mid-twentieth century—1951 is the last year for which the census authorities produced birthplace information county by county—there is clear evidence that substantial shifts had occurred in the direction and flow of migration. Now, as the final column of Fig 19-2 shows, north-east Wales and virtually all the rural areas returned high percentages of persons that had been born elsewhere: the south-east, which, in the later nineteenth century, had experienced very heavy industrialisation and the mushrooming growth of new urban

**LONG DISTANCE LIFE-TIME MIGRATION, 1861-1951**

Migrants born outside (a) the county of enumeration, and (b) contiguous counties

Per cent of enumerated population

| | 1861 | 1871 | 1881 | 1891 | 1901 | 1911 | 1951 |
|---|---|---|---|---|---|---|---|
| | % | % | % | % | % | % | % |
| **WALES** | 11.9 | 12.2 | 15.6 | 18.4 | 18.5 | 17.4 | 19.0 |
| Anglesey | 7.5 | 7.0 | 9.5 | 9.6 | 11.3 | 8.6 | **22.8** |
| Brecknock | 9.1 | 10.5 | 9.7 | 11.1 | 12.7 | 12.3 | 14.7 |
| Caernarfonshire | 5.2 | 6.6 | 9.5 | 10.6 | 12.7 | 9.9 | **26.2** |
| Cardiganshire | 3.0 | 4.1 | 4.6 | 5.9 | 8.9 | 8.9 | **23.0** |
| Carmarthenshire | 4.0 | 4.2 | 4.4 | 4.8 | 5.1 | 7.4 | 10.0 |
| Denbighshire | 6.7 | 8.3 | 9.8 | 10.7 | 12.2 | 9.2 | **22.0** |
| Flintshire | 10.5 | **12.7** | **17.8** | **15.2** | 17.6 | 14.9 | **31.0** |
| Glamorgan | **23.1** | **17.6** | **24.6** | **27.8** | **25.7** | **24.6** | 16.8 |
| Merionethshire | 3.4 | 6.0 | 7.7 | 7.5 | 8.6 | 8.0 | **27.3** |
| Monmouthshire | **16.7** | **27.0** | **22.9** | **25.4** | **18.8** | **26.3** | 18.6 |
| Montgomeryshire | 4.6 | 5.8 | 7.1 | 7.1 | 8.3 | 7.0 | 16.6 |
| Pembrokeshire | 9.5 | 9.6 | 11.0 | 11.8 | 13.4 | 12.6 | **25.0** |
| Radnorshire | 5.2 | 6.2 | 6.9 | 8.0 | 13.7 | 11.2 | **23.5** |

*Source*: based on the birthplace tables in the published census reports, 1861-1951.

Fig 19-2

communities, now recorded substantially lower proportions of in-migrants.

The nature of migration, and the role that it has played in the evolution of modern Wales, has been the subject of much discussion amongst researchers. Some have suggested that these massive shifts of population led eventually to the erosion of the Welsh language and our distinctive culture. Others have pointed out that the overall effects of the movements of the people stimulated by industrialisation have been to reinforce and enrich regional cultures. Such key topics, which have figured very prominently in the published researches of developmental economists, geographers and historians, are beyond the scope of the present chapter. Readers interested in these themes, which in themselves are of considerable relevance to family historians, should consult the published studies of THOMAS (1986, 1987), P.N.JONES (1969, 1988), I.G.JONES (1980) and PRYCE (1988, 1990), listed in the end-notes to this chapter.

**Migration in Great Britain: is Wales different?**

Throughout much of rural Britain population continued to grow rapidly in the eighteenth century, mainly, on the evidence of parish registers, by births exceeding deaths. By the 1830s, every community was beginning to record highest-ever numbers. In many rural districts peak populations were recorded in the early 1840s. After this decade rural communities everywhere—especially in upland Britain—began to decline and the decreases were to deepen progressively. Population pressures in these communities meant that new opportunities had to be sought elsewhere, and these 'push factors' led to the development of out-migration, especially of the young. And it was the growing towns and emergent new centres on the coalfields that were to become their destinations. The main exceptions to these prevailing trends were those rural areas where lead and mineral workings were able to offer employment for the children of farm labourers and servants. But throughout the nineteenth century in much of rural Wales and the border counties, like the rest of upland Britain, out-migration was the dominant trend.

In a very real sense, therefore, it was from the countryside that towns and cities were able to gather their populations. Whilst the population of England and Wales grew fourfold between 1801 and 1911, the largest increases were recorded in towns whose populations increased nine times. By 1901 a century of rapid urbanisation was over. Now, as census reports confirm, nearly 80 per cent of the people were living in urban communities, compared with some 30 per cent in 1801 (LAW, 1967; LAWTON, 1968). Britain—and especially Wales—had become the world's first fully urbanised society.

The problems generated by sustained migration from the countryside soon became a major talking point in public life. In 1885 E.G. Ravenstein published his famous paper 'The laws of migration' in the *Journal of the Royal Statistical Society*. This very important analysis confirmed that the impact of migration was to be found everywhere throughout the country. Great tracts of upland and lowland Britain had functioned as 'sending areas' in the migration process: from these rural districts the population was being progressively dispersed. The new industrial communities of northern and midland England, central Scotland, south-east England, the quarrying districts of Gwynedd and the valleys of south Wales had emerged as the principal destinations for large numbers of migrants (Fig 19-3). But, in reality, all the countries and regions of Britain were caught up in a series of interlocking migration streams that, ultimately, were to focus on these 'counties of absorption'. For these basic geographical reasons the migration history of Wales cannot be understood outside the British context in general.

Fig 19-3 Counties of Absorption (named and shaded) and Counties of Dispersion (unshaded), 1881, as identified by Ravenstein
*Source:* based on E.G. Ravenstein (1885), 184, map 6.

Many, many research studies have confirmed Ravenstein's original interpretations that the great bulk of all these movements were achieved in a step-wise manner. Thus, a single migrant/migrating family tended to halt, principally to take advantage of job opportunities, at intermediate locations between the place of birth (recorded in the census enumerators' books) and where he/she was enumerated in subsequent censuses. Alternatively, as Ravenstein himself pointed out, as each migrant moved on to the next location (often indicated in the census enumerators' books by the birthplace of children), his/her place was then filled by someone else following behind in the same migration stream (Fig 19-4). A whole series of interconnected links of this nature, extending outwards and backwards over a wide area, have been identified.

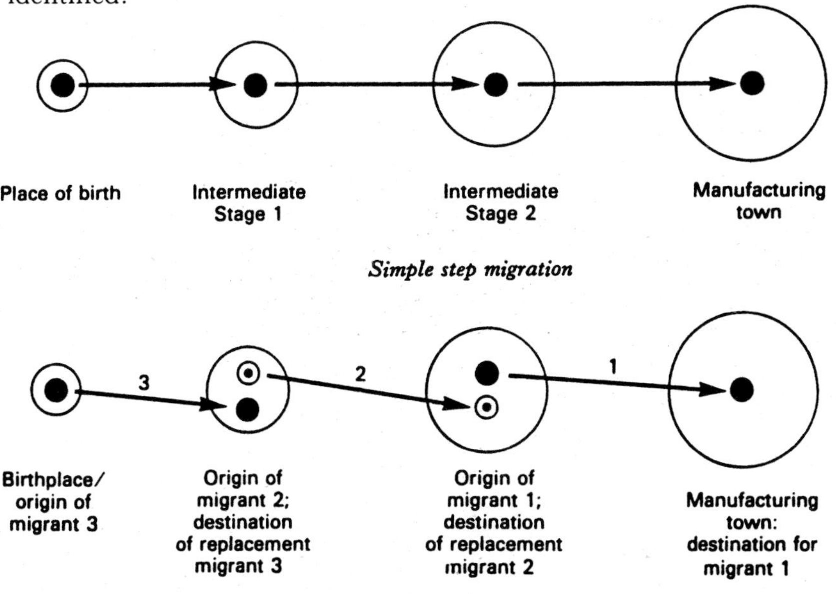


Fig. 19-4: Some Patterns of Migration

Large numbers of people continued to move from the countryside towards the growing towns and industrial areas; and, in the aggregate, these involved many thousands of detailed moves. All these movements gave rise, as Ravenstein explained, to a series of ripples that culminated in 'a series of wave-like motions', extending throughout the whole of

Britain and reaching the remotest of areas. Ravenstein's conclusions were based on the detailed analysis of census data but all the general trends that he identified were confirmed later in Redford's important study *Labour migration in England* (1926)—a book that explored the nature of movements for the earlier period between 1800 and 1850, using different sources, including Poor Law records.

E.G.Ravenstein is universally recognised as the pioneer founder of scientific research into migration. Since his time a vast and scholarly literature has grown up on this important topic. Because space constraints preclude even a basic presentation of the main findings, a number of the key concepts are presented in the Appendix to this chapter. From time to time in attempting to trace back an ancestral line every researcher seeking to complete a family history comes across 'gaps' in the written record. Many of us have experienced the growing feelings of frustration that grow and grow once we have 'lost the scent', as it were, of this or that ancestor. Knowing where next to search in order to pick up the trail again is vital. Knowledge of migration theory and the predominant migration trends within a particular community, occupation or region can suggest new approaches.

1. The majority of migrants go only a short distance
2. Migration proceeds step by step
3. Migrants going long distances generally go to one of the great centres of commerce or industry
4. Every migratory current has a counter-current
5. The natives of towns are less migratory than those of rural districts
6. Females are more migratory than males within the county of their birth, but males more frequently venture beyond
7. Most migrants are adults: families rarely migrate
8. Large towns grow more by migration than by natural increase
9. Migration increases as industries develop and transport improves
10. The major direction of migration is from the rural areas to towns
11. The major causes of migration are economic

Fig 19-5 Ravenstein's 'Laws of Migration', 1885
*Source:* based on E.G. Ravenstein (1885)

Ravenstein's eleven 'laws of migration' (Fig 19-5) are of great practical use in family history: (1) they offer valuable insights as to conditions in past times; and (2) each can serve as a working hypothesis when we are searching for data to fill in a missing link in a family lineage as we pass back in time. Nevertheless, despite their undoubted usefulness, and their general applicability, it is important to remember that Ravenstein's ideas were derived from the specific time context of the later nineteenth century.

## Region trends

So far, this chapter has been concerned with theoretical explanations and background. This final section will draw on a number of case studies to illustrate general migration trends within the various regions and localities of Wales. In addition, aspects of the movement of the Welsh people into England during the nineteenth century will be examined.

In England, the foundation of the Cambridge Group for the History of Population and Social Structure in 1964 gave a tremendous uplift to local studies, especially in the detailed analysis of data recorded in parish registers. Welsh scholars did not begin to explore aspects of the historical demography of their own country until much more recently (HARPER and SUNDERLAND 1986). This is very different from the situation in England where, for more than a generation, there has existed a strong involvement in local population studies, an established range of interests manifested in the continued publication of such influential journals as *Local Population Studies* (founded in 1968) and *The Local Historian* (formerly *The Amateur Historian*). Nevertheless, the scene is not all gloom and doom, because, fortunately, there now exists a growing range of important local and regional studies of migration trends in Wales that are of considerable relevance to family historians.

## Population movements in north Wales

As we have seen, in recent years many of the research studies concerned with migration have tended to be applied to understanding the impact that industrialisation and the growth of towns has had on the indigenous culture of Wales, specifically linguistic aspects (CARTER 1986). In the north, two regions, both of which experienced significant changes, have received detailed attention.

It has long been assumed that slate quarrying in Gwynedd evolved to become one of the most Welsh of industries. Despite the long-running strife between quarry owners and their workers, the quarries continued to recruit labour locally (R.M.JONES 1981). Many men, whilst working in the quarries, continued to be involved on the land, especially pastoral farming—that traditionally most Welsh of occupations. Despite the widespread acceptance of these explanations for the continued Welshness of Gwynedd's quarrying communities, somewhat surprisingly, it was not until very recently that migration trends to these very same communities have been examined closely, especially during the developmental years for quarrying.

Drawing on a variety of statistical sources, Dr P. Ellis Jones has shown that in-migration to the quarrying districts of Caernarfonshire was strongest in the first four decades of the nineteenth century; with further influxes in the 1860s and 1870s. But cyclical trends in house building were to bring depression to the quarrying districts. This led to difficulties locally and, starting in the 1840s, to variable flows of out-migrants from these same communities, including the emigration of skilled quarrymen to Pennsylvania and Vermont.

By analysing birthplace data from the census enumerators' books of 1851 and 1871, Jones confirmed that it was the largest of the quarries that exerted the strongest 'pulls' on migrants; but the majority of quarrymen had been born in nearby townships in Caernarfonshire itself; or in one or other of the neighbouring counties. Moreover, because the sons of migrants tended to follow their fathers into the quarries, eventually a situation was reached whereby 60 per cent of all quarrymen had been born in the quarry-working districts. Therefore, migration was substantially of a short-distance nature, thus confirming aspects of Ravenstein's 'laws' mentioned earlier. Long-distance movements were of no great significance, accounting for less than three per cent of all life-time migrations. But, what is of very great interest, especially for family historians, is the fact that amongst these longer-distance migrants many came from Merseyside and Manchester. From the high incidence of Welsh names, it seems clear that, in reality, these were Welshmen who had been born in England but they had decided to return home to work in the expanding quarrying industry (P.E. JONES 1989, 626). Here, therefore, we have a very interesting example of a distinctively Welsh migration stream that had been generated by the maintenance of links with the homeland—in effect, a splendid example of chain migration, a series of personal responses to the sending out of messages by people who shared a common background and ethnic identity.

Jones concluded that it was the regional patterns of migration to the quarries that have helped to sustain the distinctive character of the slate-quarrying communities that have grown up in rural Caernarfonshire. Because the migrants came from a short distance they shared the same 'common attributes and values' of the host community, so enriching the Welshness of these districts, in cultural as well as in linguistic terms.

The mineral-bearing zone and the adjacent coalfield in Denbighshire and Flintshire is the other region in northern Wales which experienced profound changes as a result of industrialisation. Readers do not need to be reminded that it was here that occurred some of the earliest industrialisation anywhere in Britain.

The region, which approximates to the present-day county of Clwyd, had an estimated population of some 59,700 in 1750. This increased rapidly to nearly 80,000 in 1801, reaching 134,000 in 1851. Thereafter, in demographic terms, north-east Wales was to experience decline. Much of the growth had been achieved through in-migration, first to the metallurgical and textile industries of Flintshire, later to the inland collieries of Denbighshire; and then to the iron smelting and clay-goods industries around Wrexham and Mold. Birthplace information from systematic samples of 3,187 household returns made for the 1851 census reveals that 84 per cent of the population had been born locally. A further 12 per cent were migrants from surrounding counties. These dominant trends confirm, once again, the conclusions of Ravenstein and others that, overwhelmingly, mid-nineteenth century migration was of a short-distance nature (PRYCE 1975).

This same large database of birthplace information has been analysed to explore, in detail, the major migration trends within the region itself. The findings reveal that the great majority of these local movements can be related to: (1) the size of the resident population in the sending areas; (2) the minimum distance over which migrants were obliged to travel to take advantage of new opportunities; and (3) there is evidence of selective migration in specific occupational groups (for example, Cardiganshire-born men were enumerated as miners in Flintshire's lead working districts), and amongst distinctive culture groups (migrants settled where their own language—Welsh or English—was already established).

From Fig 19-6 it is clear that market towns such as Rhuthun and St.Asaph in the rich agricultural lowlands of the Vale of Clwyd acted as major gathering points, together with industrial Holywell on Deeside. In the east, it was the developing townships on the inland coalfield—

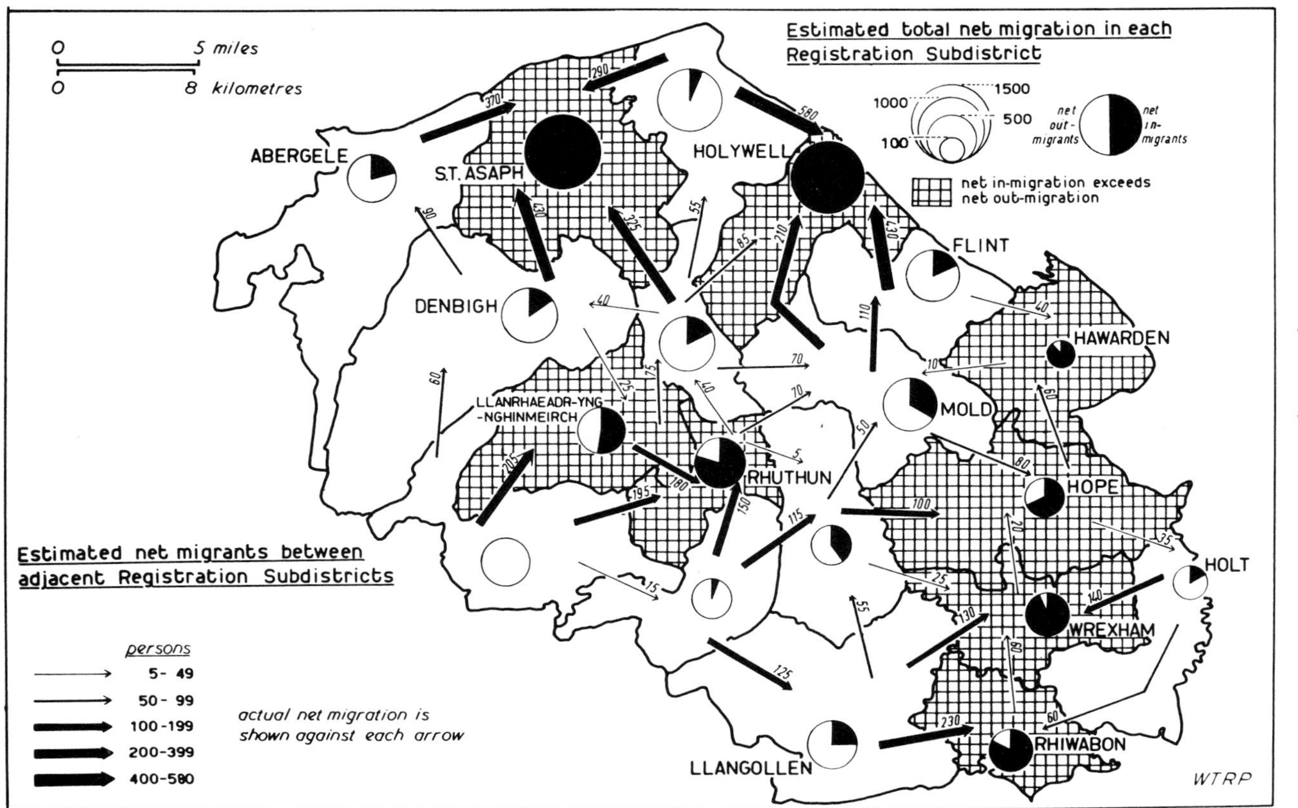


Fig 19-6 Life-time Migration Within North-East Wales, 1851 *Source:* based on W.T.R. Pryce (1975), 97.

Mold, Wrexham, Rhiwabon—that attracted migrants. But, as Ravenstein stated, every migration stream generated a flow of people in the opposite direction (Fig 10-5 again). Thus, we find that gross migration seems to have reached the most substantial flows between these colliery communities and there is substantial evidence of substantial two-way reciprocal movements between all the parishes on Deeside and westward along the coast as far as Abergele. Nevertheless, in all these centres inward migration was the dominant trend but—and this is of considerable importance in the context of research in family history—this was compensated by well-developed movements in the opposite direction.

In the rural west, as Fig 19-6 shows, migratory trends were of a very different nature. Here, long-term movements were, overwhelmingly, in one direction: from upland moorland and hill communities to the richer lowlands around Denbigh and Rhuthun—the land of rich agriculture, the land of milk and honey! Further analyses show that step-migration with replacement (Fig 19-4) was the underlying mechanism of movement. Parishes around smaller market centres such as Rhuthun functioned as collecting centres, or staging posts, in the migratory progress. People were 'collected' from surrounding parishes but subsequently their descendants moved away towards the coalfield, industrial Deeside or to the incipient resort centres along the northern coastline.

Further detailed analyses of the 1851 birthplace data from north-east Wales reveal that particular migration streams tended to focus on specific destinations within the coalfield communities. Migration flows from Welsh origins tended to focus on distinctively Welsh communities in terms of language and religious affiliation; and those from England flowed to villages and industrial enterprises where their fellow-countrymen were already established (for details, see PRYCE 1975). These phenomena are of the utmost interest to family historians and more information on the selective nature of migration will be presented further below.

## Migration and settlement in south Wales

This destination-specific nature of migration, which led eventually to the progressive building up of distinctive local communities, is indicative of chain migration. The first migrants, who had established themselves at a new destination, sent back news of new opportunities, personally, by letter or via third parties, to their home areas. In this way details of wages, living conditions, and offers of employment induced further migration to the same area, swelling the numbers of kinsmen and friends.

In recent years much new evidence for the operation of chain migration during the industrialisation process has come to light. The famous 'Blue Books' on education of 1847, which contain a vast amount of information for family historians on local conditions, observed that in Merthyr Tudful 'The workmen, who were perpetually immigrating [*sic*], live together very much in clans, e.g. the Pembrokeshire men in one quarter, the Carmarthenshire men in another and so on' (EDUCATION REPORT 1847, 304). This general statement has been confirmed from very detailed statistical analysis of the 1851 census enumerators' books covering Merthyr Tudful—the first distinctively Welsh industrial town of significance. These detailed findings reveal that it was west Wales (Cardiganshire, Carmarthenshire and Pembrokeshire) that supplied a large share of the in-migrant labourers to the iron-smelting townships of Dowlais, North Georgetown and Pentrebach; and, following the 'intervening opportunities' model (see Appendix), it is clear that these Welsh workers and their families later moved on into coal mining and other labour-intensive occupations (CARTER and WHEATLEY 1982, 27, 55-56).

The fact that migration streams seem to have been directed at specific destinations has also been examined closely by Dr P.N.Jones. Whereas in 1881 the migration of Welsh people to Glamorgan was directed primarily towards the developing coal mines in the valleys, migrants from England tended to seek out opportunities elsewhere in the agricultural Vale of Glamorgan and in the port towns of Cardiff and Swansea, away from collieries. This differentiation of Welsh and English migration streams was to begin to break down in later decades, certainly by 1911. From the closing decades of the nineteenth century, the market for coal and rocketing demands for labourers in the mines meant that in-migration led eventually to the anglicisation of what, hitherto had been Welsh communities (P.N.JONES 1969; 1988, 173-78). Similar trends have been identified in Gwent. Here, English-born labourers replaced Welsh migrants following a switch in the migration streams from rural Wales towards the Glamorgan coalfield (PRYCE 1990, 60-67).

Whilst much of the research on migration in nineteenth century Wales has focused on the returns for the 1851 census, the more recent studies have sought to explore the dominant trends a generation later in 1881. By this date the coal reserves in many more of the valleys of south Wales were in the process of development. The dates when a mine was sunk and began production varied from one part of the coalfield to another. Nineteenth century coal mining was a labour-intensive industry: invariably, the development of a new pit stimulated further movements of miners and labourers—initially from other parts of the coalfield but also, as labour demands escalated, by in-migration from the rural communities that lay beyond the colliery districts.

Recent studies by Dr P.N.Jones on migration and settlement up to 1881 in the Ogmore and Garw valleys reveal more clear evidence of chain migration. The patterns of migration, Jones concluded, comprised a complex migratory system. This involved:

> a series of locally-intensive clusters of origins derived in turn from tightly-drawn information fields. Heads [of households] and lodgers commonly originated from the same parish or hamlet, but the emphasis was different—the majority of heads originated from the shorter [migration] range, especially from within the south Wales coalfield, and the contribution of more peripheral [i.e. distant] places was lower . . . (P.N.JONES, 1987, 29).

Moreover, within these same mining villages the various migrant populations had settled in their own streets and house terraces:

> . . . clusters of people born in the same areas of origin forged links of neighbourliness, instigated further chains of migration, and acted as cornerstones for the establishment of community life (P.N.JONES 1987, 72).

Thus, the migration process was conceived by Dr Jones as a series of 'paths' and 'networks', succouring the milieu of communities that culturally, as well as in social terms, were already very distinctive. These migratory trends were to have an impact on many aspects of life. Although some 40 per cent of the English-born men in these communities had married Welsh girls, in general, marriages tended to reflect a strong ethnically Welsh or ethnically English basis (P.N.JONES 1987, 83).

Further detailed work by P.N.Jones on the 1881 Ogmore and Garw census returns was concerned specifically with the actual patterns of long-distance movements (defined as those over 30 miles). These aspects of the research involved a careful comparison (involving 648 individual migrations) of the birthplaces of fathers and their eldest co-residing child

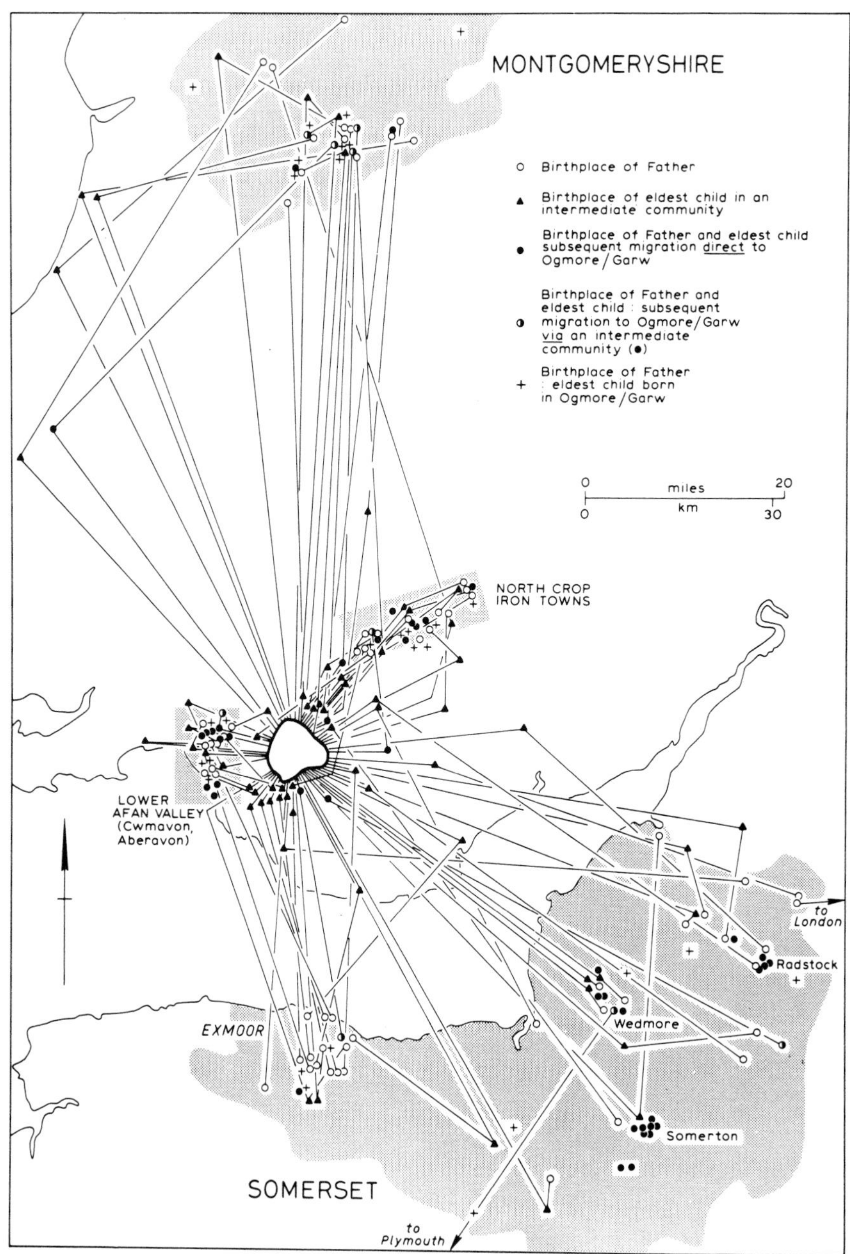


Fig 19-7 Migration Paths to the Ogmore and Garw Valleys, 1881
The map shows the routes followed by married men to Ogmore and Garw from selected source areas.
*Source:* P.N. Jones (1988), 195.

(Fig 19-7). For many, the first step in the migration process had been a long one that had brought the young men initially into the Glamorgan coalfield. This was soon followed by a much shorter move to another location within the coalmining area, presumably in response to better job prospects or wages.

Thus, from the census returns is revealed evidence that migrants had moved in response to a series of 'intervening opportunities', spending some time in other steam-coal valleys such as Rhondda, Cynon, or in the nearby Llynfi and Maesteg collieries before moving on to the Ogmore and Garw valleys. The English-born migrants were especially noticeable because they tended to settle in their own tight clusters—particularly the clusters of men who had originated either in the Exmoor villages of Cutcombe, Luxborough and Brompton Regis or in the Somerset coalfield (especially Radstock). The latter is a clear-cut example of the stepwise migration of specialists from another industrial area into Glamorgan (P.N.JONES, 1988, 195-97).

## Migration of the Welsh into England

Although in the nineteenth century it was industrialisation that was to provide many new opportunities for Welshmen in their own country, nevertheless, from time immemorial the Welsh have been moving into England. Estimates suggest that at least 6,000 Welsh-born persons had settled in London in the early seventeenth century, amounting to some seven per cent of the capital's resident population. By 1801, London's Welsh communities had been in existence for some four centuries—and it is clear that numbers had been fed and maintained by a small but continuous stream of migrants from Wales, temporary as well as permanent. During the nineteenth century the size of the London Welsh community increased still further, eventually reaching 35,421 in 1901. The Great Depression which, in particular, afflicted many mining districts, led to a very substantial flight of working people out of Wales, especially from the coalfields of Glamorgan and Monmouthshire. Many followed the traditional migration routes out of Wales, and, by 1931, the Welsh-born community in London had grown still more substantially to 59,751 (1.4 per cent of the resident population).

The whole fascinating story of the migration and settlement of the Welsh in London has been charted by Professor Emrys Jones (E.JONES 1981, 1985). The Welsh not only occupied high positions in law and the professions but, also, they cornered much of the dairy trade, especially in central districts such as Islington. Out of a total of 1,450 dairymen-farmers in 1895 in the city as a whole, over 500 had Welsh names: 103 of them were Joneses, 83 Davieses, 63 Evanses, 38 Williamses, 36 Morgans, 30 Jenkinses, 29 Edwardses and 22 Lewises (E.JONES, 1985, 150-53)! Moreover, the children of these migrants tended to intermarry, becoming, as Professor Emrys Jones puts it, 'people of substance'. This community developed to enjoy high standing as an achieving society and laid the foundations for what was to become that most influential body on developments back in Wales, namely the London-Welsh community.

Welsh communities existed in some 50 major towns in England, but, in 1851, only two of these, London and Liverpool, recorded more than 10,000 Welsh-born residents. A further five centres—Shrewsbury, Chester, Manchester, Bristol and Birmingham—each contained at least 1,000 persons from Wales. A generation later, in 1871, whilst London and Liverpool maintained their large numbers, the greatest increases of Welsh settlers were to be found in the smaller centres, suggesting that there was a progressive movement of Welsh people down the urban hierarchy into the smaller towns of England, including those centres that had involved considerable travel from Wales itself (POOLEY, 1983).

In general, Pooley's research findings confirm many aspects of Ravenstein's 'laws of migration'. In the decade leading up to 1871, Wales was still very much a rural country and out- migration conformed closely with general patterns of rural-urban movements. The great majority of migrants proceeded only a short distance into England: large numbers were enumerated by the census in all the border towns. Longer-distance movements were principally to the larger urban centres—London, the south coast, and to industrial north-east England (Fig 19-8A).

Ravenstein's interesting conclusions that migration was partly sex-selective in nature is confirmed in the ratios of Welsh-born men and women enumerated in each of these centres (Fig 19-8B). Women tended to be much more numerous where there existed a strong demand for personal and domestic services—the borderland towns close to Wales as well as in resort towns; and in stylish places further away, such as Bath and Brighton, where, during the later nineteenth century, it was fashionable for upper-class English families to have a Welsh maid. But Welsh-born women were numerous also where there existed a strong tradition of female labour—as in the textile mills and factories of Preston, Bolton and Huddersfield. In all these centres the women of

Wales outnumbered their countrymen. Conversely, there existed a 'surplus' of Welsh men in centres of heavy industry—in mining, metallurgy, in ship building and at the docks. Many of these towns—Tynemouth, South Shields, Sunderland, Middlesbrough, Barrow, Plymouth, Portsmouth—were a considerable distance from Wales and would have involved long-distance migration that was both sex- and skill-selective. As we shall see, in all likelihood movements to these destinations would have involved a series of temporary sojourns at intermediate locations elsewhere in England.

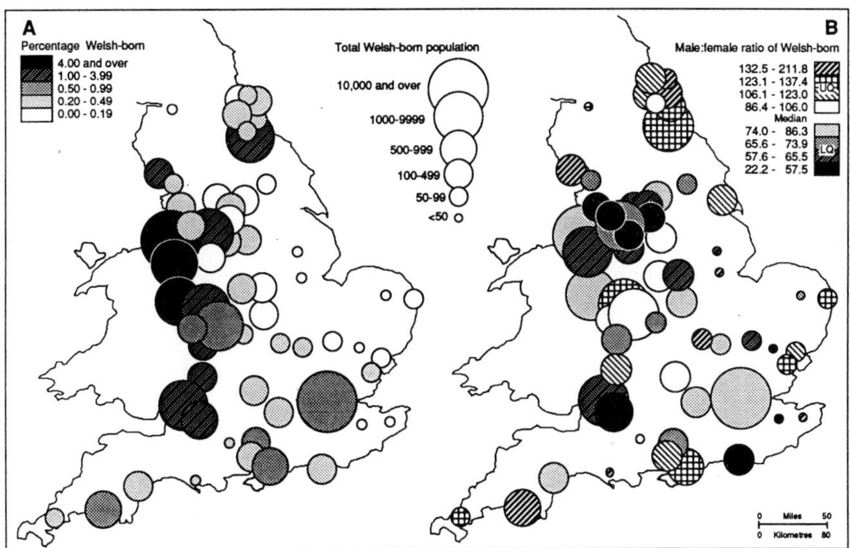


Fig 19-8 Welsh Migration to England, 1871
The circles are proportional to the numbers of Welsh-born migrants. Fig 8(A) shows Welsh-born persons as a percentage of the residential population in specific towns. Fig 8(B) shows men:women ratios amongst the Welsh. The darker shadings indicate centres where Welsh-born women (mainly domestic servants) outnumbered their countrymen.
*Source:* Pooley (1983), 291-92.

After London, north-west England, especially Liverpool and Merseyside, was a major destination for Welsh-born migrants—especially in the nineteenth century. Overwhelmingly, the great majority of these were drawn from the northern counties, especially

Anglesey, Caernarfonshire, Flintshire and Denbighshire (POOLEY 1983, 293-94). But, although much more numerous in districts such as Everton and Toxteth Park, the Welsh settled in every part of Liverpool: in contrast to the Irish, they did not congregate to form tight settlement clusters (POOLEY 1977). Nevertheless, as Dr Merfyn Jones has described, so ably (in R.M.JONES and D.B.REES, 1984), the Welsh did constitute a highly organised and very distinctive community within the city. The crucial agents in the formation of this community, as in London, were the Welsh nonconformist chapels.

By the 1890s, over 50 chapels, schoolrooms and missions, as well as two Anglican churches conducting services in Welsh, existed in Liverpool. Migrants arriving in the city found that a warm welcome awaited them in the chapels—and, moreover, a welcome that was articulated in their own native language. It is now clear that the chapel frequently acted as an agent in finding somewhere to live (lodgings for young migrants, houses for married couples), helped in the search for employment, and that general guidance was provided to newly arrived migrants on settlement in the English city. The chapel was the hub of a communications network that extended throughout Liverpool's Welsh communities as well as back into the sending areas in Wales itself. All migrants arriving in a large industrial city such as Liverpool shared an identity based, not, as at home, on kinship and proximity, but on the more universal and common linguistic and ethnic bonds of Welshness. Indeed, in the new cultural milieu of the city environment many became much more conscious of their Welshness in a way that was not possible in their home areas:

> To be Welsh in Wales was unremarkable, to be Welsh in Liverpool was to be visible and to be conscious of that position.

Marriage between in-migrants from different parts of Wales heightened this consciousness—and the chapel, ever aware of the needs of individuals, now provided a highly efficient dating system for this purpose much in the same ways as earlier it has provided labour exchange services. Thus, for the Welsh migrant the move to the city meant breaking with the isolation and relative parochialism of the previous rural life experience (R.M.JONES and D.B.REES, 1984, 23, 34).

As mentioned earlier, north-east England, and its industrial communities was another destination that attracted significant numbers of migrants from Wales in the last century. In 1851 the census recorded a Welsh community of some 1,500 persons in Middlesbrough, and, compared with earlier decades, increased numbers were recorded in neighbouring industrial centres (POOLEY 1983, 290-92). Here, in this English region that was so far away from Wales, as elsewhere, we are provided with a another splendid illustration of a well-developed migration stream that had been stimulated by news of major industrial developments of a kind that were attractive specifically to Welshmen, namely employment opportunities in metallurgy. Evidently it was Middlesbrough, a planned town laid out originally in 1830, that was the specific destination for many. In 1861, 216 of the town's householders (5 per cent of the total) had been born in Wales, primarily in the older metal-working districts of Glamorgan and Monmouthshire. The Welsh in this new urban setting kept in close contact with each other, settling down to live in neighbouring streets.

From the birthplaces of their children it is clear that many had arrived in north-east England by a series of migratory steps involving intermediate halts in the various iron- and steel-making districts of central and northern England. Moreover, as in the Ogmore and Garw valleys—and, no doubt, elsewhere—lodgers often recorded similar birthplaces to that of the man in whose house they were staying. This suggests that chain migration must have been of considerable importance in bringing the Welsh together in the relative remoteness from Wales of the lower Tees valley—a migration stream that embraced a specific occupational group that shared, in substantial measure, a common ethnic and national identity (GWYNNE and SILL 1976).

More recently, new research as to the nature of the migration process has involved the seeking out of Welsh-born individuals and families in the census enumerators' books of the major destinations in Liverpool, Shrewsbury and Middlesbrough in 1871; and then linking entries back to individuals in their home areas in Wales as recorded in the 1861 returns. By this means a whole series of longitudinal migration histories has been established in order to study underlying motives and the effects of the migration process on individuals. The linking of individuals in this way follows the same techniques as in conventional family history but it has to be admitted that these methods also suffer from similar problems of identification and the labour-intensive needs of the research.

The findings show that between 1861 and 1871, Welsh migrants to these particular towns did not, in general, record substantial changes of occupation. Nevertheless, there must have been some personal rewards in terms of economic enhancement. Evidently, large numbers of the migrants, especially long-distance movers from Dowlais (Glamorgan) to Middlesbrough, went as members of a family group. Thus, it seems that the main economic benefits were for those on the look-out for their first job, children and young adults. But the overall benefits were such that the larger labour market of the English town offered a better range of employment prospects for all members of the family than in Wales itself (POOLEY and DOHERTY, 1991).

All these local studies of Welsh migration to England are of considerable interest to family historians, particularly when such major centres as London or Merseyside or Middlesbrough figure in the story of a specific family. Further detailed studies are needed—particularly of major destinations like Sheffield, Manchester, Birmingham, Coventry and the west Midlands, and, of course, the city of Bristol, that long-standing outlet for a steady-stream of migrants. Before the railway age, and before the rise of the town ports of Cardiff and Newport, for many the city of Bristol was the nearest large urban centre that could provide, because of its world-wide connections, a good range of attractions and new opportunities. Unlike other places inland, in the pre-railway age this flourishing city could be reached easily in a matter of a few hours by sea—even from the remotest communities in the far west of Wales. Also, and in addition to further information on specific destinations, we need more studies of the movements that occurred within specific occupations such as the **merched y gerddi** (the country girls who worked in the market gardens), famous for their temporary seasonal migrations to work in London and the lower Thames valley (WILLIAMS-DAVIES 1977).

## Conclusions

The purpose of this chapter is to offer insights as to the nature and scope of migration research in the specific context of family history research in Wales. There is a marked tendency amongst family historians to concentrate all attention on factual matters, as revealed in documentary sources on the actual patterns of movements from place to place and from one generation to the next, without much consideration as to the processes of change that are inherent to migration.

But all our ancestors, every one of them, was a living person with feelings, opinions, preferences and an eager awareness to live his or her life to the full within the family setting, and in the context of their own time. Migration occurred within every family. The act of having to make a decision that would lead to a permanent shift of residence, often to a new unfamiliar milieu, wrought considerable changes to the way of life of all the individuals concerned—to the persons left behind as well as to the migrants themselves. Such an important decision was not taken without prior full and serious consideration.

**Acknowledgements**

The author is grateful to Dr P.N.Jones, University of Hull, for permission to reproduce Fig 19-7; to Dr Colin G.Pooley, University of Lancaster, for Fig 19-8 and new information on current research; to the Open University Press for Fig 19-4; and to Mr Richard Wall, Cambridge Group for the History of Population and Social Structure, for supplying information used in this chapter. Figs 19-3 and 19-8 have been revised and redrawn by John R. Hunt, Project Officer, Faculty of Social Sciences at the Open University.

**REFERENCES IN CHAPTER 19**

CARTER, H. (1986) 'Population movements into Wales: an historical review' in HARPER, P.S. and SUNDERLAND, E. (eds) (1986), 31-53.

CARTER, H. and WHEATLEY, S. (1982) *Merthyr Tydfil in 1851: a study of the spatial structure of a Welsh industrial town*. University of Wales Press, Cardiff.

EDUCATION REPORT 1847. *Reports, Commissioners of Inquiry into the State of Education in Wales*, Part 1: Carmarthen, Glamorgan, and Pembroke. London (for HMSO).

EMERY, F. (1967) 'The farming regions of Wales', in *The Agrarian History of England and Wales. Vol.IV 1500-1640.* Edited by H.P.R.Finberg. Cambridge University Press, 142- 47.

GWYNNE, T. and SILL, M. (1976) 'Census enumeration books: a study of mid-nineteenth century immigration [*sic.*]', *Local Historian*, 12, 74-79.

HARPER, P.S., and SUNDERLAND, E. (eds) (1986) *Genetic and Population Studies in Wales*. University of Wales Press, Cardiff.

JONES, E. (1981) 'The Welsh in London in the seventeenth and eighteenth centuries', *Welsh History Review*, 10, 461-79.

JONES, E. (1985) 'The Welsh in London in the nineteenth century', *Cambria*, 12, 149-69 (Part I in DAVIES, W.K.D. (ed) *Human Geography from Wales: Proceedings of the E.G.Bowen Memorial Conference*).

JONES, I.G. (1980) 'Language and community in nineteenth-century Wales' in *A people and a proletariat: essays in the history of Wales, 1780-1980*. Edited by David Smith. Pluto Press in association with Llafur, London, 47-71.

JONES, P.E. (1989) 'Migration and the slate belt of Caernarfonshire in the nineteenth century', *Welsh History Review*, 14, 610-29.

JONES, P.N. (1969) 'Some aspects of immigration [*sic*] to the Glamorgan coalfield between 1881 and 1911', *Transactions, Honourable Society of Cymmrodorion*, Session 1969, 82-98.

JONES, P.N. (1987) *Mines, migrants and residence in the south Wales steamcoal valleys: the Ogmore and Garw valleys in 1881*. Hull University Press.

JONES, P.N. (1988) 'Population migration into Glamorgan 1861-1911: a reassessment' in *Glamorgan County History: Vol.6, Glamorgan Society 1700-1980.* Edited by Prys Morgan. Glamorgan History Trust/University of Wales Press, Cardiff, 173-202.

JONES, R.M. (1981) *The North Wales Quarrymen*. University of Wales Press, Cardiff.

JONES, R.M. and REES, D.Ben (1984) *The Liverpool Welsh and their Religion*. Modern Welsh Publications, Liverpool and Llanddewi Brefi.

LAW, C.M. (1967) 'The growth of urban population in England and Wales, 1801-1911', *Transactions, Institute of British Geographers*, 41, 125-43.

LAWTON, R. (1968) 'Population changes in England and Wales in the later nineteenth century: an analysis of trends by registration districts', *Transactions, Institute of British Geographers*, 44, 55-74.

OWEN, L. (1959) 'The population of Wales in the sixteenth and seventeenth centuries', *Transactions, Honourable Society of Cymmrodorion*, Session 1959, 99-113.

POOLEY, C.G. (1977) 'The residential segregation of migrant communities in mid-Victorian Liverpool', *Transactions, Institute of British Geographers*, New Series, 2, 364-82.

POOLEY, C.G. (1983) 'Welsh migration to England in the mid-nineteenth century', *Journal of Historical Geography*, 9, 287-305.

POOLEY, C.G. and DOHERTY, J.C. (1991) 'The longitudinal study of migration: Welsh migration to English towns in the nineteenth century' in *Migrants, emigrants and immigrants: a social history of migration*. Edited by C.G.POOLEY and I.D.WHYTE. Routledge, London, 143-73.

PRYCE, W.T.R. (1975) 'Migration and the evolution of culture areas: cultural and linguistic frontiers in northeast Wales, 1750 and 1851', *Transactions, Institute of British Geographers*, 65, 79-107.

PRYCE, W.T.R. (1988) 'Language areas and changes, c.1750-1901' in *Glamorgan County History: Vol.6, Glamorgan Society 1780- 1980.* Edited by Prys Morgan. Glamorgan County History Trust/University of Wales Press, Cardiff, 265-313.

PRYCE, W.T.R. (1990) 'Language shift in Gwent', in *English in Wales: diversity, conflict and change*. Edited by N.Coupland. Multilingual Matters, Clevedon, 48-83.

RAVENSTEIN, E.G. (1885) 'The laws of migration', *Journal, Royal Statistical Society*, 48, 167-235.

REDFORD, A. (1926) *Labour migration in England, 1800-1850*. Manchester University Press. The second edition of this important book, revised by W.H.Chaloner, was published in 1964.

REES, D.Ben (1975) *Chapels in the Valley: a study in the sociology of Welsh nonconformity*. The Ffynnon Press, Upton, Wirral.

THOMAS, Brinley (1986) 'The Industrial Revolution and the Welsh language', in BABER, Colin, and WILLIAMS, L.J. (eds) *Modern South Wales: essays in economic history*. University of Wales Press, Cardiff, 6-21, 279-83.

THOMAS, Brinley (1987) 'A cauldron of rebirth: population and the Welsh language in the nineteenth century', *Welsh History Review*, 13, 418-37.

WILLIAMS, J. (1985) *Digest of Welsh Historical Statistics*. Vol.1. Government Statistical Office (Welsh Office), Cardiff.

WILLIAMS-DAVIES, J. (1977) ''Merched y Gerddi'': a seasonal migration of female labour from rural Wales', *Folk Life*, 15, 12-23.

## APPENDIX
## SOME KEY CONCEPTS IN MIGRATION STUDIES

**betterment migration**
migration primarily in search of improved status especially in pre-industrial times amongst those seeking craft apprenticeships and entry to the professions. Most movements are of a short-distance nature, from the countryside to the nearest town.

**gravity migration model**
explanations of migration based on the Newtonian idea of the gravity field. This model postulates that the volume/direction of migration is related to the relative sizes of population and the distances between the locations involved.

**host community**
the community that receives and accommodates in-migrants.

**intervening obstacles migration model**
explanations of migration that state that the volume and direction of movements is constrained by various negative features, perceived or existing, between places of origin and *potential* destinations.

**intervening opportunities migration model**
explanations of migration that state that potential migrants carefully evaluate and weigh the relatively moderate benefits to be derived from short-distance movements against the much more substantial rewards that could be derived from long-distance migration.

**life-cycle stage**
migration that occurs at specific stages in the life-cycle of individuals/families e.g. leaving the parental home in early adulthood, marriage, career development, or on retirement.

**macro scale**
studies involving large numbers of migrants/movements over large distances/areas.

**micro scale**
studies involving small numbers of migrants—individuals, a specific family, particular occupational, ethnic or cultural groups in a specific community/small area.

**migration barriers**
obstacles—physical, social, political, cultural, existing in reality or perceived—that prevent migration.

**migration field/hinterland**
the area/region from which migrants to a specific location (city or town) have been drawn.

**migration patterns**
specific directions/geographical patterns of movements amongst migrants

**migration processes**
(1) the underlying mechanisms by which the actual movements to a new destination are accomplished;
(2) the changes and effects that migration can have on population structures, and on the social, economic and cultural milieu of (a) the sending community, and (b) the receiving community, as well as on (c) the migrants themselves.

**migration triggers**
conditions/phenomena, existing or perceived, that give rise to migration.

**movers**
members of a family/community that become migrants (see 'stayers').

**pull factors**
factors—conditions/phenomena—that are attractive to out-migrants.

**push factors**
negative factors in the home area—existing or perceived—that persons/families try to avoid by becoming out-migrants.

**push-pull movements**
explanations of migratory behaviour that rely on negative and positive attractive factors. In practice, it is difficult to identify and quantify the roles played by 'push' and 'pull' factors in any migration movement.

**stayers**
members of a family/community that remain in a community after the out-migrants have departed.

**subsistence migration**
migration for reasons of economic necessity. In pre-industrial times, usually these movements involved the poorer, unskilled and lowly members of society, especially general labourers.

# 20. Emigration

David Peate

Once they set out on the ancestry trail, almost all overseas researchers with Welsh antecedents will alight on the interrogatives 'why?' and 'how?' Indeed all family historians are seeking the motivations for and methods of those inevitable migrations however localised which occur in families over generations. To some extent the impetus for and attraction of migration of the Welsh within the United Kingdom are similar to those which spurred them to leave their homeland for the other side of the Atlantic and, later, for the continents of Australasia, Africa and South America.

Even the most analytical of historical authorities will fail to reveal the reason for one person or family emigrating at any given moment. Because of the subjective nature and the scope of the topic, we are forced into generalisation and leave the ardent family historians the joy of particularisation with their own ancestors. Familiarisation with Montgomeryshire encourages us to view the scene in a confined way. Nevertheless, granting some idiosyncracies peculiar to a particular area, the content is relevant for Wales as a whole. It has been said that every Welsh family has a relative who emigrated in the nineteenth century and the validity of this saying has been proved repeatedly. Whilst the descendants of some emigrants have maintained contact with their Welsh kinfolk, others will still have that shared pleasure to come.

Although individuals from Wales had been involved in early British attempts at colonisation, it was William Vaughan of Llangyndeyrn, Carmarthenshire, who pioneered at his own expense the first Welsh settlement. This attempt was at Cambriol, Newfoundland, in 1617. This little community arose out of Vaughan's philosophy of a need to develop trade to strengthen England and Wales. Unfortunately, the experiment was unsuccessful and the colony was abandoned in the 1620s. For the next century and a half, the North American continent, incorporating the present United States, Canada and the West Indies, was the magnet for all emigrants from Wales.

During the period from 1618 when Britain had a mere toe-hold in New England, to the Restoration of Charles II in 1660, there was no particular Welsh flavour to the development of the transatlantic colonies which had been founded by individuals more or less experimentally. Many of those who made the crossing did so for land and trade and, to a large degree, were Anglican gentry; others were criminals and indentured servants. Some few people from Wales did emigrate during the Laudian persecution of the 1630s to gain religious and political freedom and were active in New England in the 1650s in evangelical reform; some of these emigrants returned to south Wales and were instrumental in the propagation of the Gospel consequent on the Cromwellian Act of 1650. One returning English emigrant captured the essential flavour of the refugees of the 1630s in a sermon to Parliament in 1645: 'I have lived in a country where in seven years I never saw beggar, nor heard an oath, nor looked upon a drunkard'.

The seventeenth century was a time of turmoil in English history with an ever-increasing allegiance to nonconformity, customarily generalised as puritanism. However, by 1642 at the outbreak of the first Civil War, Wales had scarcely been touched by the spirit of nonconformity and, despite the applied efforts of the Commonwealth to remedy this deficiency, the restoration of the Anglican church and the old order in 1660 was a cause for celebration in Wales. Nevertheless, proselytism had occurred on a minor scale. The religious repression of Restoration Parliaments hacked away at the outer skin of dissent and left a hard core of resistance which was to spearhead further emigration though with a definite Welshness. At random, we can point to pockets of dissenters in Carmarthen, Bridgend, Hay and Wrexham and in several parishes in Monmouthshire and Montgomeryshire. By the latter part of the seventeenth century, radical religious dissent in Wales, as in England, had segregated into sects with Baptists, Quakers, Presbyterians and Independents to the forefront.

The penal legislation of the Restoration under the Clarendon Code caused severe religious and social hardship for dissenters and for none more so than the Quakers, whose newly adopted passiveness after a period of radical militancy was mistrusted. At the same time, Wales was experiencing extreme economic problems. To a much greater extent than England, Wales consisted of a multitude of small tenant farmers whose plight was worsening with the concentration of land and power in the grasp of a prospering minority. Despite the Toleration Act of 1688 which allowed freedom of worship, religious dissenters were still excluded from many aspects of the political and social life of the nation. The American colonies offered the golden opportunity of relief; there was land available and the real prospect of total religious and political liberty. It is against this background that the first sizeable emigrations from Wales occur, though quality rather than quantity is the keystone.

In 1663, John Miles, the 'father' of the Welsh Baptists, led a party of mainly south Wales people to Massachusetts. Twenty years later, the Quakers, including Thomas Lloyd of Dolobran, Montgomeryshire, sought refuge in Pennsylvania in the Welsh Tract purchased from William Penn. These movements were quintessentially religious but with political and economic colouring. Between the Restoration and the turn of the century, probably some three thousand Welsh people crossed the Atlantic and, although there were movements of individuals, the overwhelming majority transferred in denominational groups and settled together.

**Case Study: to America 1683**

Thomas Lloyd, the third son of Charles and Elizabeth (Stanley) Lloyd, was born at Dolobran, Meifod, Montgomeryshire, on 17 February 1640. He was educated at Oxford and became a Quaker by convincement in 1662. He was briefly imprisoned for his belief in 1663 and was held again the following year until the Declaration of Indulgence in 1672. On his release, he moved to Maesmawr, Welshpool, and was subjected to arbitrary and illegal fines and confiscation of cattle. He married Mary Jones of Welshpool who bore him ten children. In 1683, he and his family made the eight weeks' voyage to Philadelphia on the *America* in company with fellow Quakers from Llanwddyn and Meifod. His wife died soon after their arrival and was the first to be interred in the Arch Street cemetery, Philadelphia. In 1684, Thomas married a widow, Patricia (Gardiner) Storey and was appointed president of the Provincial Council. William Penn appointed him a deputy-governor, a post which he held until the surrender of Penn's proprietary interest to the Crown in 1693 when he declined further service. He remained a leading Quaker and lived for some time in New York. He died on 10 July 1694 and was buried in Philadelphia.

Some individuals made their way to Barbados attracted by the success of the sugar plantations and moved on to the Carolinas whilst Jamaica offered similar, though later, commercial advantage. Whilst the eighteenth century witnessed further minor emigration to the colonies, the impetus of dissent and repression had disappeared though, from mid-century, the Methodist revival caused an unprecedented and lasting swing to moderate and low church religion with alienation from the Anglican church in 1811 and traditional Welsh nonconformity. Nevertheless, in America the Baptists in particular kept in contact with their Welsh brethren but, before we see any fresh Atlantic waves, an alternative channel was opened.

On 13 May 1787, the First Fleet of eleven ships sailed from Plymouth to Port Jackson (Sydney), Australia, with a consignment of convicts. This included two from north, one from central and one (female) from south Wales. Transportation to Australia lasted until 1868 and it is estimated that some 2,500 Welsh convicts experienced the hardships of the prolonged voyages. As with many statistics for Wales, these are certainly inadequate and represent only those people whose convictions resulted from crimes in Wales. There will be many others who will be classed as of English origin given the traditional subsumption of Wales in England. This inadequacy will be referred to again. We will pick up the thread of emigration to north America.

During the 1790s, Wales, in common with England, suffered a series of bad harvests with rising prices and economic and agricultural depression. The growing discontent of the populace was fired by the creed of revolutionary France and the flames were fanned by the Welsh intelligentsia in their demands for the natural rights of man. The eighteenth century was the age of enlightenment and an age of appreciation of antiquities and tradition in Wales. This fostered an aspiring intelligentsia which had been sympathetic to the aims of the American revolution with its freedom and equality. The political radicalism of this minority was intermingled with the radical theology of new religious dissent. In the whipped-up resurgent nationalism, whole tracts of central, west and south-west Wales were in a state of disorder and civil disobedience. There was a constant flow of correspondence between America and Wales which heralded a rage for emigration. The natural outlet for such economically and politically depressed dissidents was the Utopian vision of a free America and the prospect of available land. From 1794, with the departure of Morgan John Rhys and his followers from Bala and Wrexham, until the turn of the century, Welsh emigrants were numbered in their thousands. From all regions of the principality but especially the rural and upland areas they poured out of Liverpool, Bristol, Milford Haven, Caernarfon and other ports and were deposited in New York state, Pennsylvania and westwards in Ohio. They were not the dregs of Welsh society but consisted of farmer-weavers, artisans and men of some standing. The gregarious nature of these new Americans was determined by their religious and linguistic commonness and there is no reason to believe that there was a mass determination to establish a *Gwladfa*, a national homeland. In general, the Welsh were in the vanguard of applications for citizenship.

**Case Study: to America 1795**

George Roberts, whose brother was to become the minister of the Independent Hen Gapel, Llanbrynmair, was born on 11 February 1769 at Bron-y-llan farm, Mochdre, Montgomeryshire, the son of Evan Roberts by his first wife, Mary Green. Evan moved via Llanwnog to Llanbrynmair and his son joined him at the latter after some time in Carno. George married Jane Edwards of Llanerfyl on 20 May 1795. Llanbrynmair at that time was a hotbed of political unrest and the Roberts family had experienced those problems common to most tenant-farmers. In this climate, George Roberts, Ezekiel Hughes and others encouraged by the radical William Jones, Llangadfan, determined to emigrate. Hughes had already been prohibited from emigrating on an American ship at Liverpool to the north. They set out on the 11 July 1795 proceeding by foot via Machynlleth southwards to Carmarthen where they discovered that the *Maria* was too large to enter port. Because of feared trouble with a press-gang, the men walked on to Bristol leaving the women to follow in a sloop. The coaster was hindered by adverse weather and the women took to the road and, arriving at Swansea, they found passage for Bristol. Believing that the weather had changed favourably for the sloop, the master of the *Maria* set sail from port and encountered it in the Bristol Channel. After more intervening adventure, the men boarded the sloop back to Bristol where they were re-united with the women and they eventually embarked on the *Maria*. The vessel entered Delaware Bay on 16 October. A month later, the party walked to Cambria County. After a number of difficult years, George Roberts was appointed justice of the county in 1807 and, with a guaranteed income, was able to purchase lands. He was pastor at Ebensburg, Pennsylvania, where he died in November 1853.

The Napoleonic Wars compelled farmers to cultivate even waste areas with the need for home-produced food. This necessity relaxed after 1815 and Wales drifted into severe economic depression. The stress on the country was enhanced by a natural increase in population and Wales was crippled by a backward economy which was incapable of supporting its population. The cut-throat competition for farm tenancies inevitably led to excessive rack-renting by landlords. Yesterday's farmer became today's labourer. Whilst the infant industrial areas pulled out of the recession relatively quickly, the rural community fared badly until the hint of prosperity in the 1850s. From the middle of the nineteenth century other political, social and economic factors come into play. Though the Rebecca Riots of 1839 which plagued Carmarthenshire, Pembrokeshire and Radnorshire, and Chartist mutterings in Montgomeryshire in 1838, are significant indications of grievances, they did not amount to much on a national level.

Land was a luxury in Wales and the vast areas of America were a nostrum for the deprivation. Across the Atlantic, the frontiers were being pushed back daily opening the virgin tracts of Ohio, Wisconsin and Illinois. This was a period of desperate economic plight for Welsh tenant-farmers, agricultural labourers and weavers and they took full advantage of the glittering prize of good land and a stable economy. Industrial workers were also caught up by the craze for emigration though to a lesser extent. Although the United States and, less usually, Canada were the major sources for emigrants, the first half of the century witnessed competition from New South Wales and South Africa. The Australian colony was being populated by willing and unwilling emigrants alike.

### Case Study: Convict to Australia 1838

Born at Cwmbwch, Llanidloes, Montgomeryshire, Abraham Owen, the son of Aaron and Catherine Owen, was baptised in the parish church on 24 February 1792. It is possible that he served in the campaigns against the French as he was later referred to as 'an old soldier'. We pick up his threads as a widower with four children for whom he provided with his earnings as a weaver in the Llanidloes factories and with moderate parish assistance. He was quite literate and subscribed to 'subversive' literature. Abraham was active in the Chartist outbreak at Llanidloes in 1838 and was arrested on a charge of 'drilling and training'. He appeared before the Montgomeryshire County Assizes held discreetly at Welshpool where he was sentenced to seven years' transportation. With other Chartist transportees, he was taken by prison van to gaol at Shrewsbury and then by stage coach to Wolverhampton where they proceeded by rail to London.

Abraham was deposited in the hulks at Woolwich where he remained for over two months before being transferred to the convict ship *Woodbridge*. The vessel sailed on 16 October 1839 and, after a passage of 133 days, arrived at Sydney, New South Wales, on 26 February 1840. From Australian records, we learn that he was 5 ft 7 ¾ in, was ruddy and freckled with grey eyes and brown mixed with grey hair; he had various scars and had at some time fractured an arm. He received his certificate of freedom on 9 September 1846, which would have allowed him the options of returning home or remaining in Australia. He chose the latter and died in Australia on 10 June 1870 at the age of 80 when his birthplace is noted as Penzance, Wales!

As we have said, despite alternative destinations, the Welsh dream of America still held sway. There is a tendency to be complacent about the dream and it comes as a jolt to realise that some emigrants became very disillusioned and returned to their native land, to one of the larger English cities or moved on to other countries. Daniel Howell of Llanbrynmair was one who found that the promises of America were not realised and who returned to his origins having buried children abroad. The majority did, however, sleep on a bed of its own making.

**Case Study: to America 1839**

On 2 December 1797 at Cwmllydan farm, Llanllawddog, Carmarthenshire, John D.Jones was born. In 1824, he was accepted into membership of Pencader Independent chapel at Llanfihangel ar Arth, in which parish he resided for the remainder of his time in Wales. Shortly after he had married Jane Thomas, he and his wife decided to emigrate. John was a farmer and whether or not the unrest in the area which fostered the Rebecca Riots was the persuading factor is entirely speculative. Nevertheless, their departure took place in 1839. The couple with a child from one of Jane's two earlier marriages made the tedious journey to Liverpool where they embarked on the brig *Ark*. The vessel sailed on 21 April and berthed at Baltimore on 10 June. During the crossing, a son was born who was christened Owen Ark Jones, a lasting memory of the transatlantic passage. They summered in Baltimore with the infant and travelled via Wheeling and Cincinnati to the fledgling settlement at Gomer, Ohio; this was an arduous and dangerous journey. John D. purchased 120 acres of land for $710; the ground was cleared and a successful farm was established. He conducted family worship in his

> home each day and, in April 1851, took out American citizenship. John D.Jones died on 13 October 1875 at his farm and was buried in Pike Run cemetery in Gomer.

The pace of emigration gradually accelerated to reach its peak in the 1850s. Between 1815 and 1850, some three-quarters of Welsh emigrants originated in the south-west counties of Carmarthenshire and Cardiganshire and the central upland counties of Montgomeryshire and Merionethshire with concentrations in America in the states of New York, Pennsylvania, Ohio, Wisconsin, Illinois and, more specifically, in the counties of Oneida, N.Y., and Jackson, Allen and Gallia, Ohio. Besides the opportunities to own land and for higher wages and better conditions which were offered by America and the colonies, prospective emigrants received encouragement through press and mail. Emigration handbooks had been in existence since at least the 1790s and these were widely available in Wales giving increasingly current thoughts, views and advice. Newspapers played an important role through advertisements by emigration agents and shipping lines; in April 1859, the *Caernarvon & Denbigh Herald* ran an entry by White Star Line for 'Free grants of land of from 40 to 500 acres and upwards, in the fine province of Auckland, New Zealand' and, in the same edition, Black Ball Line, which was by then offering passage by auxiliary steam clippers, listed its north Wales agents—'Captain Tully, City of Dublin office, Holyhead; A.R. Martin, Bookseller, Bangor; M.T. Edwards, Conway; O.D. Aubrey, Festiniog; William Edwards, Druggist, Llangefni; A.S. Watts, Abergele; or to John Thomas, Ship Agent, Carnarvon'. Black Ball added that 'The Commanders are men of experience and noted for their kindness and attention to Passengers'. But the single most significant factor was the correspondence received in Wales from emigrant relatives. The letters home eulogised (though occasionally despaired of) the quality of life, the rewards through honest labour and the openings in receiving areas. These letters revealed spectacles which were in stark contrast with the deprivation and difficulties surrounding the readers and increased the waves of emigrants flowing across the oceans.

Although the mass exodus from Wales has been seen as a mostly rural phenomenon, industrial workers (for example, from the waning weaving factories of mid-Wales) did swell the numbers. The impetus for industrial emigrants surfaced in 1848 when we note, among others, miners from south, north and north-east Wales arriving in the Californian gold fields. Whereas the stream of Welsh flowed along the traditional course by road and by the new railways to Liverpool (in the main), London and Bristol and, occasionally, Aberystwyth, Bangor and Caernarfon bound for Baltimore, Philadelphia, New York, Quebec and New Orleans and the long arduous overland trek, many other Welsh 'forty-niners' made the voyage direct to San Francisco via Cape Horn or broke the journey at the Isthmus of Panama. The lack of success in the diggings led many Welsh prospectors to move on to British Columbia and Colorado in the 1850s to 1870s and even to transfer their attention to Australia.

The competition from the southern hemisphere was inhibited by the cost and the length of the sea-passage which could take four to five months to Australia. Assisted passages and the gradual reduction in sailing time made for less disadvantage. Australia had attracted the families of convicts and gradually more willing emigrants, especially with such inducements as free passages to surgeons in the 1850s and to artisans in the 1870s. New Zealand too was offering its broad sheep-pastures to the frustrated upland farmers of Wales. To a much greater degree than those destined for America, Australia had encouraged husbands and fathers to emigrate and to earn the passage monies for their wives and families to join them, often years later. The principal ports of embarkation were London and Bristol with Liverpool leading the way; Sydney, Melbourne, Perth, Auckland, Wellington and Canterbury were the major ports of disembarkation. From Melbourne 'passengers forwarded by steamers to all parts of Australia, Tasmania, &c'.

South Africa was also opening its arms to immigrants. Although the British had been in the Cape since before the turn of the eighteenth century, emigration did not get under way until the 1820s. It was in 1820 that the only two known organised movements of Welsh people occurred. Parties of some forty and thirty emigrants were led by Lieut. Valentine Griffiths, a half-pay officer of the Royal Marines from Newtown, and T. Phillips of Haverfordwest respectively. Griffiths eventually moved on to Australia. By 1824, settlers had filtered into Natal and this movement increased at the annexation in 1845 of Natal to the Cape. During the century many soldiers and some sailors were discharged and settled in South Africa; the South Wales Borderers were to the forefront in campaigns. The lure of South Africa was the open ranges, the chance to own and develop farms. Trade was beginning to broaden and the prospect of commercial success also beckoned. The discovery of gold in the 1850s produced an influx of diggers and many

Welsh moved on to the infant settlement at Johannesburg. There are still active Welsh societies in South Africa: the Witwatersrand Cambrian Society, Johannesburg, and Cape Cambrian Society, Cape Town. As with most other countries colonised by the British, there is little or no segregation of records to isolate the Welsh from the rest.

The real incentive of the southern hemisphere, however, was the gold rush between 1851 and 1857 in Victoria and New South Wales and the numbers of Welsh increased. As with their American kin, they were clannish and preserved the traditions of their homeland. In numbers, they settled mainly in Victoria, with concentrations near the gold-mining areas like Ballarat; in the 1860s, they nestled in Brisbane and, a decade later, they were battling with the Aborigines in Queensland. A little later, the process was repeated in New Zealand in the mining areas of Auckland and Dunedin. Emigrants from every corner of Wales were to be found in the southern dominions.

### Case Study: to New Zealand 1875

The head gardener of Powis Castle, Welshpool, had a number of children by his wife, Mary Jones. One of his sons was his namesake, affectionately called Teddie. Edward Jones junior had been trained by his father as a gardener at the castle and, later, took up employment in London. His experiences in the metropolis were unhappy and, in 1875, he decided together with his friend, Francis Bennet, to begin afresh in New Zealand. The pair left Westminster for Brunswick Wharf, Blackwall, where they passed the night with ninety other emigrants. Next day, they were sorted into messes of ten and then were obliged to wait for five days for the arrival of their ship. On 4 June, they embarked on the paddle-steamer *Sea Swallow* which ferried them to Gravesend where they boarded the *Rodney*. The vessel sailed on Sunday 6 June and, after experiencing severely adverse weather conditions, they arrived in Cook's Strait on 28 August 1875. Contrary winds and the lack of a pilot delayed her entry. On the evening of the following day, the steamer *Rangitira* towed the *Rodney* into Wellington. During the prolonged ocean voyage, there occurred eleven deaths and two births. Teddie Jones secured employment as a gardener in Auckland with 'the Major', a member of parliament. He was at Rotorangi in 1882 and is last heard of in 1886 as a gardener near Auckland. Whatever his fate was, he continued to send seeds home to his father for some years.

Whilst emigration to Australia and America reached its peak in the 1850s, there were still factors which maintained the exodus. The Tory and Liberal, Anglican and nonconformist conflict initiated political and quasi-religious evictions of tenant farmers in the 1850s and 1860s particularly in Merionethshire, Carmarthenshire and Cardiganshire. Agricultural depression in the last quarter of the century released more rural workers into the overseas market. The higher wages in the industrial areas of Pittsburg and Scranton, Pennsylvania, drew out many of the south and north-east Welsh. From the 1870s, steam replaced sail and passages were quicker; competition between shipowners encouraged cheaper and more comfortable passage; and the Acts of Parliament enforced greater care of ship and passengers. As the century wore on, the Welsh spread out from their comfortable congregations in America and had encompassed Iowa, Kansas and Missouri. In the third quarter of the century, a substantial volume of Welsh found a haven in Utah as converted Mormons. This religious migration owed much to Daniel Jones (1811-1861) of Abergele, who set up a publishing centre in Merthyr Tydfil after his conversion in America; in three voyages in 1849, 1852 and 1856, 'Captain Dan' escorted over a thousand Welsh converts across the Atlantic to the valley of the Salt Lake.

The most minor influx of the Welsh was into South America. In the middle of the nineteenth century they were found mining gold and coal in Brazil with their own colony at Nova Cambria, or copper-mining in Venezuela and cattle-ranching and working in the meat plants around the River Plate in Uruguay and Argentina. The settlement in the province of Rio Grande do Sul led by Evan Evans, Nantyglo, numbered some 200 in 1851 and included miners from the Rhymney Valley and from Anglesey and Denbighshire. Adverse climatic conditions led to the failure of the community and the scattering of its members throughout the east coast of South America. The active advertising by the Brazilian government in the 1870s influenced the arrival of more miners and farmers.

However, any thoughts of South America immediately conjure up visions of the Welsh in Patagonia. A party of 153 Welsh emigrants, who sailed from Liverpool, landed from the *Mimosa* on 28 July 1865 at Puerto Madryn which was a deserted area two hundred miles from the nearest settlement. After a few weeks, they tramped across the almost arid pampa to the valley of the river Chubut. Here they hoped to found a homeland, a true *Gwladfa*, in the four hundred square miles set aside for them to farm. The failure to farm successfully on the arid soil was overcome after a few years by diverting the river water and constructing irrigation canals. The little colony attracted further immigrants from Wales and the United States. The river valley was flooded in 1899 and this drove some of the colonists to head for Canada. There was an abortive attempt to remove the whole plantation to Australia and the few Patagonian Welsh who transferred to New South Wales, Western Australia and Victoria in the opening decades of the twentieth century were soon diluted and scattered; some even returned to Argentina. A further and final influx from Wales took place in 1911. Some four hundred miles west nestling at the foot of the Andes, the little settlement of Trevelin was established in 1888. Trelew, Gaiman and Dolavon between Madryn and Chubut were founded by the Welsh and the founding of the Chubut colony on 28 July is recognised by a traditional local holiday.

The inadequacy of statistics relating to Welsh emigration has already been noticed. The reports of the immigration authorities in the United States show that, between 1820 and 1950, some 90,000 Welsh had emigrated to the United States. This figure can be trimmed to account for the return of the disillusioned. In 1820, there were approximately one thousand parishes in Wales. In simplistic terms, this implies that, in a period of 130 years, an average of just ninety people from each parish emigrated to the United States. As early as 1857, writing during his unsuccessful attempt for a Welsh settlement in Tennessee, Samuel Roberts (S.R.) reported that 'of the people born in Llanbrynmair in the last fifty years there are more now living in America than Llanbrynmair'. That parish had a population of some 2,000. It is clear that emigration statistics have been seriously miscalculated and are unrealistic. On a rough and ready basis, it is considered that, during the years from 1820 to 1950, a conservative estimate of emigrants from Wales to the United States exceeds 250,000. Probably half of these passed through the port of Liverpool and many would have stayed in those lodging houses where strict temperance was a feature of the keepers' advertising.

To a limited degree, it is possible from an historical appreciation of the processes and causations of emigration to determine the general area from which emigrants originated. This is in itself an asset but it needs adequate support. If we discount the customary Welsh surnames of Jones, Evans and the like, it is surprising to discover how localised are the less common names. In isolated pockets, the lesser surnames are quite often as frequently occurring as such names as, say, Lewis, Hughes and Owen; this is reasonably valid up to about 1800 when the less usual surnames gradually broaden. Let us look at this in a little more detail. Take the following surnames: Bebb, Brees, Clayton, Jarman, Jehu, Peate, Rowbotham, Swancot, Tibbot, Tilsley, Wigley and Woosnam. This is quite a selection and representatives of all these families emigrated to America in the nineteenth century. Their common denominator is that they are old Montgomeryshire surnames many of which can be traced back to the sixteenth or seventeenth centuries in the county. Other localities have similar peculiarities in nomenclature.

The various records relating to emigration from Wales and England and to immigration into the receiving countries are legion. Because of the global nature of the subject it is impossible to identify all the sources and depositories. The material is voluminous and much transcription and consolidation has been and is being undertaken by individuals for their private purposes or as part of more wide-ranging programmes. Unless there is evidence accessible to the researching ancestor of a Welsh emigrant to enable him to be confident of the originating town or parish, it must be remembered that, as no complete official passenger lists are held by any national or local repository in the United Kingdom prior to 1890, the tracking down of an ancestor will be far more easily achieved in the country of destination. The census returns in the receiving areas are of paramount importance; in the United States, those from 1850 and each decade onwards will be of value.

A list of some of the sources which may be consulted when researching emigrants is given in the Notes to this chapter, together with some suggestions for further reading.

However, in the receiving countries, it is well worth contacting the local, county and state historical societies, many of which will have unpublished or out-of-print accounts of individuals. They may also have the various church histories with bio-sketches and the various commemorative and biographical records of local people. Diaries, letters and Bibles may have been deposited. These types of records are a particular feature of Welsh emigrants who are probably served better biographically than many other ethnic groups because of their gregarious settlements, their culture, language and religion. This leads on to Welsh language newspapers, particularly in North America and Australia, which include significant detail of immigrants and extensive obituaries. It is recommended that you should read anything concerning the Welsh in the area in which your ancestor settled as many items supposedly relating to named individuals incorporate many other names and details of relatives, friends and companions.

## NOTES TO CHAPTER 20

**General:**

Public Record Office, London. 'Emigrants & Documents in the Public Record Office'. Leaflet No.71.

T.V.H. FitzHugh, *The Dictionary of Genealogy* 3rd ed., (London: 1991).

*The Dictionary of Welsh Biography down to 1940*. (London: The Honourable Society of Cymmrodorion, 1959).

N.B. Numerous lists and indexes are available relating to British emigrants and many of these are noted in Terrick FitzHugh's book. Settlers in Natal are listed in publications by P.Phillips (1981) and S.O'B.Spencer (1981-7).

**Australia:**

Public Record Office, London. 'Australian Convicts: Sources in the Public Record Office'. Leaflet No.94.

Lewis Lloyd, *Australians from Wales*. (Caernarfon: 1988).

Deidre Beddoe, *Welsh Convict Women*. (Barry: S.Williams, 1979).

South Australian Family History Society (1989).

**Canada:**

Public Record Office, London. 'Records of the American and West Indian Colonies before 1782'. Leaflet No.23.

F.T. Rosser, *The Welsh Settlement in Upper Canada*. (London, Ontario: Univ. of Western Ontario, 1954).

National Archives of Canada, Ottowa. 'Tracing your ancestors in Canada' (revised 1987) Ministry of Supply and Services.

**New Zealand:**

Anne Bromell, *Family History Research in New Zealand* (revised 1989) The New Zealand Society of Genealogists Inc.

**South Africa:**

Kate Caffrey, *The British to Southern Africa*. (London: Gentry Books, 1973).

**South America:**

John E. Baurer, 'The Welsh in Patagonia', *Hispanic American Review* 34 (1954).

**United States of America:**

General Services Administration, National Archives, Washington, D.C. 'Genealogical Records in the National Archives'. Leaflet No.5.

Public Record Office, London. 'Records of the American and West Indian Colonies before 1782'. Leaflet No.23.

Public Record Office, London. 'Land Grants in America and American Loyalists' Claims'. Leaflet No.34.

Alan A. Conway (ed.), *The Welsh in America: Letters from the Immigrants* (Cardiff: UWP, 1961).

Gwyn A.Williams, *The Search for Beulah Land.* (London: Croom Helm, 1980).

T. Mardy Rees, *A History of the Quakers in Wales and their Emigration to North America.* (Carmarthen: Spurrell, 1925).

E.G. Hartmann, *Americans from Wales.* (Boston: Christopher, 1967). The bibliography is highly recommended.

**West Indies:**

Public Record Office, London. 'Records of the American and West Indian Colonies before 1782'. Leaflet No.23.

# 21. The Freeholders

Evan L. James

Family historians should be able to trace most branches of a Welsh family to ancestors born in the late eighteenth century by making use of the standard nineteenth century sources such as the census, civil registration and parish registers, which are dealt with elsewhere in this book. Further progress may be difficult for those localities for which parish registers and bishop's transcripts are not extant. In addition, even when registers are available, the lack of surnames, the use of a limited range of Christian names and the omission of the place of abode can make it difficult to identify a person unambiguously. However, in many parts of rural Wales where much of the population was tied to the land for many generations, their connection with the land can be used to particular advantage to help overcome these difficulties. That connection is likely to be recorded during the selling, mortgaging, leasing and renting of land, in disputes concerning ownership, as well as in family deeds such as wills and marriage settlements. Then again, the ownership or occupation of land resulted in a liability to pay taxes or for jury service, as well as (from land ownership) the right to vote.

The various classes of landowners include not only the aristocracy, esquires and gentry who owned considerable tracts of land (and whose estate records are discussed elsewhere), but also yeomen[1] who owned the land which they themselves farmed and the husbandmen or farmers who held land as leaseholders or yearly tenants.[2] In the fifteenth and sixteenth centuries a yeoman's land was assessed for taxation purposes as being worth either 20 shillings or 40 shillings a year, while an esquire's land might be between £20 and £40 a year, and a gentleman's land between £3 and £10 a year.[3,4]

But the class distinctions were neither static nor rigid, and could vary both with time and place. For instance, many a yeoman of England would have been far richer than many contemporary gentlemen of Wales. On the other hand, titles tended to become devalued with time, so that a yeoman of Wales owning his own farm in the seventeenth century might lay claim to descent from acknowledged gentry families. A person may be found to be described as a yeoman in one document and a gentleman in another, and the two descriptions may even be found within one and the same document. For example, a plea was filed at the Great Sessions of Cardiganshire in 1701 by Nathan Griffiths, esquire, against Griffith Rees, gentleman, of the parish of Llannarth, alias Griffith Rees, yeoman.[5] Thus there can be some difficulty in placing a person in a particular class, but, in general, the more land a person owned the higher his status, and it was his status which allowed him to become involved in the affairs of the community, whether as a churchwarden, juryman or magistrate. The names of churchwardens can be found in parochial documents; the records of the Quarter and Great Sessions provide the names of jurymen and magistrates.[6]

A considerable number of people owned land in Wales from the sixteenth century onwards, partly because the medieval Welsh law of gavelkind (the law of land tenure involving equal division of the intestate's property among his sons) had resulted in the fragmentation of estates into smallholdings. Even after the Act of Union (1536), which amongst other provisions abolished gavelkind, many of the minor gentry and yeomen continued to share their patrimony among their children and relatives. However, the higher gentry were more prone to practise primogeniture and to entail their estates by means of judiciously arranged marriages and by purchasing the land of small freeholders who found themselves in economic difficulties.[7] By the nineteenth century most of the land was in the hands of a few relatively large landowners, but there still remained a large number of freeholders who owned small estates, often of only a few acres.

A survey of landowners was conducted in 1873, and Fig 21-1 gives an analysis for Wales and the rural county of Cardiganshire,[8-11] one of the counties where the proportion of small proprietors was particularly

| | CARDIGANSHIRE | | WALES | |
|---|---|---|---|---|
| Class | No. of Owners | Acres | No. of Owners | Acres |
| Peers | 1 | 42,890 | 31 | 557,423 |
| Great landowners | 8 | 96,909 | 148 | 1,263,123 |
| Squires | 48 | 81,600 | 392 | 672,300 |
| Greater yeomen | 110 | 55,000 | 1,224 | 612,000 |
| Lesser yeomen | 304 | 51,680 | 2,932 | 498,440 |
| Small proprietors | 1,553 | 61,230 | 17,289 | 431,759 |
| Cottagers | 1,278 | 287 | 35,592 | 7,320 |

Fig. 21-1: Landownership—Wales and Cardiganshire, 1873

high. The categories are approximately as follows: 'great landowners' includes all estates held by commoners owning at least 3,000 acres with the rental of at least £3,000 per annum; 'squires' includes estates of between 1,000 and 3,000 acres, 'greater yeomen' 300 to 1,000 acres, 'lesser yeomen' 100 to 300 acres, 'small proprietors' one acre to 100 acres, and 'cottagers' includes all holdings of under one acre.

Thus in Wales nearly two and a half million acres were in the hands of 571 landowners, each owning an estate greater than 1,000 acres, while only one and a half million acres (approximately) were held by 21,445 landowners with estates of between one and one thousand acres. There were also 35,592 cottagers owning less than one acre each. Out of a total population of approximately 1,421,700 (in 1871) comprising 287,400 households, 57,608 persons owned land. Thus about one out of every five families owned land.

The pattern of land ownership varied within Wales. For instance, many parishes in north Wales were almost entirely in the hands of a single owner, whereas in south-west Wales some parishes were largely in the possession of small freeholders.

Another and more relevant picture of land ownership is given by an analysis of the schedules which were prepared for each parish in accordance with the Tithe Commutation Act of 1836. These schedules accompany what are generally known as 'tithe maps', three copies of which were made for each parish. One copy is kept at the National Library of Wales, another at the Public Record Office in London, and the third (which was originally left in the custody of the parish) may now be at the local county record office. The schedule records the names of landowners and occupiers, with the names and descriptions of their lands and premises.

A study by R.Moore-Colyer for the parish of Llanrhystud, Cardiganshire,[12] reveals that *circa* 1840 no more than 46% of the total area of land occupied was in the hands of 'significant' gentry, who owned 70 farms. There were, however, 52 small owners, 21 of them farming their own holdings.

It is the relatively numerous small owners that will be the concern of this chapter, as it is likely that most family historians will find a link with one of these freeholding families rather than with the gentry.

A landless man had little chance of acquiring land unless he was able to accumulate sufficient wealth from his profession or trade. An examination of wills of the period confirms that during the eighteenth century most land was either inherited or bought by members of the existing landholding families. Thus, later generations of the small freeholders very likely would have inherited at least some of their land. It is this fact that makes wills the single most important source of genealogical information for such families. Indeed it has been found possible to trace a freeholding family over many generations using wills alone, though usually other records are needed to bridge gaps and provide a fuller history of the family.

As an illustration, a freeholder family living in the parish of Llangrannog, Cardiganshire, will now be discussed. According to the Land Survey of 1873, David Jones of Trecregin owned 17 acres of land. In the 1871 census, when he was aged 45, his rank and occupation were given as landowner and farmer. He had inherited Trecregin from his father, another David Jones whose will was proved in 1862 at the Principal Probate Registry. This David Jones had a brother George Jones and they both described themselves in the 1851 census as freeholders and farmers of nine and 14 acres respectively. In the Tithe Schedule prepared in 1840 they were listed as owners of Trecregin West (12 acres) and Trecregin East (19 acres) respectively.

The schedule also shows that at this time the parish of Llangrannog, of total area 4,338 acres, was comprised of 75 holdings, 19 of which (782 acres) were owned by the local squire (Jordan, formerly Price, of Pigeonsford). There were two non-resident substantial owners (of Pentre and Gogerddan estates) who owned 1,073 acres between them in 13 holdings. The remainder was held by 23 small freeholders, of whom 19 were owner-occupiers like the brothers David and George Jones. The latter two were variously described in the church registers as freeholders, farmers and carpenters. They evidently found their holdings were too small for them to make a living solely by farming. Their father was James Jones, gentleman, of Trecregin, who referred to them in his will of 1808 as David *James* and George *James*. One of his daughters, named Bridgerd, received a life interest in a part of the real estate. This will, in the absence of a contemporary register of baptisms at the local parish church, is the sole evidence found for these family relationships. To extend the pedigree it becomes necessary to use not only wills but also other records.

From the 1798 land tax returns[13] for Llangrannog it is found that there were 19 owners of land, 12 of whom were owner-occupiers, a Bridget Jones of Trecregin being one of them. In the absence of a will made by Bridget Jones and the lack of relevant parish registers, no direct proof of a connection between Bridget Jones and James Jones has been found. Although it is known that she had several children, their names, other than that of a daughter Bridget, are not known. Ownership of the same tenement and the continued use of a rare name (Bridget) in succeeding generations of the family provide good reasons for believing that she was related to James Jones (possibly as his mother) and that he had inherited her land. Confirmation is provided by the remark made by Evelyn Hope,[14] a member of the family, that Trecregin was still in 1931 in the possession of descendants of Bridget.

Male freeholders owning land worth at least 40 shillings a year were entitled to vote in parliamentary elections and lists of such persons were prepared for a general election. A copy of the electoral roll for Cardiganshire in 1760 has survived,[15] which gives the name of the freeholder, his freehold property and of his abode. Among the 11 freeholders for Llangrannog was David John of Trecregin and George Price, esquire, of Rhydycolomennod (in English, Pigeonsford). George Price in his will proved in 1786 names David Jones as the husband of his 'sister Jones', and George's father William Price, gentleman, of Pigeonsford, in his will dated 1753 refers to him as David John Griffith (i.e., David son of John son of Griffith) of Trecregin, and the husband of his daughter Bridget. Family letters[16] indicate that Bridget had displeased her parents probably by marrying below her status as a gentleman's daughter, but that ultimately she was forgiven and a portion of Trecregin was settled on her and her heirs. Bridget's mother was Bridget Parry, the heiress of Pigeonsford, and a descendant of the Parry family of Cwmtydu, whose genealogy is included in the Golden Grove manuscript.[17] Bridget's father, William Price, had close relations living in Ireland, one of them being Arthur, Archbishop of Cashel, who died in 1752, leaving in his will £100 'to my poor relations in Cardiganshire, South Wales, to be divided among them as my cousin, David Price, Chancellor of Cashel, shall advise'. There were no fewer than 64 recipients of this bounty!

The genealogy delineated in Fig 21-2 provides a good example of a connection established between a family of small freeholders (the Joneses) and gentry families (the Prices and the Parrys). It is also interesting to contrast the history of the two families and their records.

The Price family of Pigeonsford grew in wealth and status mainly by making judicious marriages. George Price married Dorothy, daughter of James Bowen, esquire, of Llwyngwair, Pembrokeshire. His son, George Price, married Elizabeth, daughter of Barret Bowen Jordan, esquire, of Neeston, Pembrokeshire, and his grandson George Price

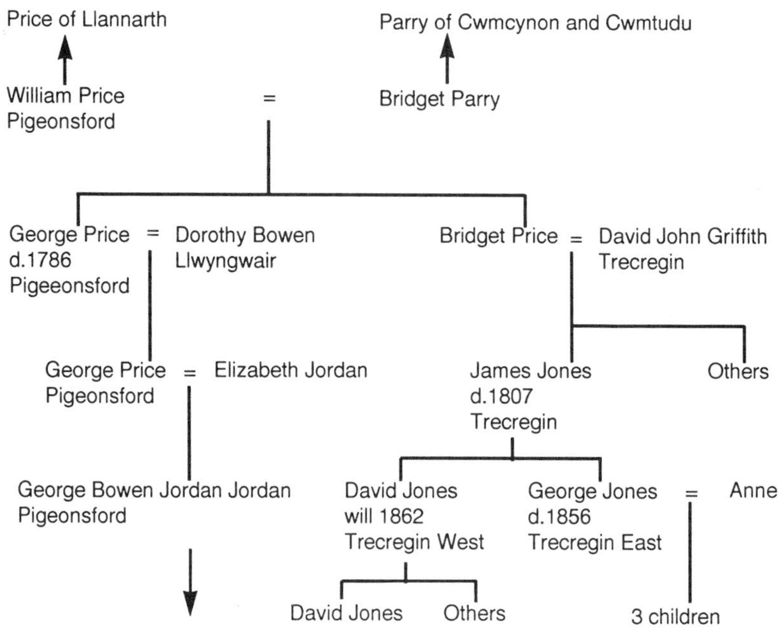


Fig. 21-2: Pedigree of Llangrannog families

(who adopted the surname Jordan) married Ellen, daughter of Sir John Owen, baronet, of Orielton, Pembrokeshire. Members of the Pigeonsford family became magistrates, high sheriffs and army officers. Pigeonsford is no longer the family home and the estate records (commencing mid-eighteenth century) are now in the National Library of Wales. The Jones family of Trecregin, on the other hand, though also descended from the Parrys of Cwmtydu, descended the social scale as a result of the successive division of their property, and they have no known collection of family records. In order to trace their history one has to turn to 'public' records which are generally available for the freeholder families, such as tax and electoral lists and wills.

Some of the descendants of the Jones family owned land at the end of the nineteenth century and are readily identified in contemporary records. These records may also enable other descendants of former landholding families who do not themselves own or hold land to be identified. The information on rank, profession or occupation which is entered on the census returns provides one means by which a connection with a landholding family may be established. It is obvious that esquire, magistrate, gentleman or freeholder would indicate such a connection. The description clergyman, army officer, lawyer, physician, surgeon or excise officer may indicate the person's former dependence on the financial resources of a landholding family during the course of his education or training. Such was the case of Daniel Owen Davies, a surgeon and farmer of the parish of Llangrannog (in 1851) and third son of David Davies of Moelon, Rhydlewis, who owned a small estate in Cardiganshire. His eldest brother, Griffith Davies, inherited the estate, while Daniel Owen Davies and his brother John both qualified as surgeons.

The descriptions 'independent', 'independent means', and 'annuitant' may also (particularly for women) be clues to connections with families of some wealth. The persons so described were frequently recipients of an annual income chargeable on the estate of a deceased relative or, occasionally, an employer.

Another indication of status in the community was the early adoption of a surname. Freeholding families were the first to adopt surnames and in some districts this occurred as late as the eighteenth century. A study of the 1760 list shows that most of the Llangrannog freeholders had surnames, though four still used either the patronymic system or were the first generation to use the father's name as a surname. There was no surname Jones, but there was a David John (of Trecregin) who was later known as David Jones.

Descent in the social scale often occurred, especially in large families: a freeholder's son might become a tenant farmer, and some of his children farm servants or agricultural labourers. If this happened earlier than the nineteenth century then in the absence of parish records it would be difficult to trace such a family. Tenant farmers are mentioned in land tax lists and tithe schedules, and in estate records such as rent rolls and tenancy agreements. Particularly useful are leases for lives (to be found among estate records) which give names and ages of more than one generation of a tenant family. But, in general, in contrast to a freeholder, a tenant farmer had a less permanent connection with a particular area and the continuity of a family's tenure of a farm is more uncertain.

Many tenant farmers also made wills, increasingly so in the nineteenth century, and particularly those who were related to families of freeholder status. The practice of making wills became ingrained not only in the landowners but also in other members of the family, even those who had become impoverished. It is not uncommon to find a series of wills enabling a family to be traced for many generations.

As an illustration, consider the ancestry of William Jones, who will be, by implication, William Jones (III), who died at the Aberaeron Union Workhouse in 1887, aged 93, and was buried in a pauper's grave. He had been successively a farmer, timber carrier and butcher. His father was William Jones (II) of Cefncoedisaf, Llanllwchaearn, Cardiganshire (a farm of about 100 acres), and a tenant farmer whose will was proved in 1843. His grandfather was William Jones (I), gentleman, who lived on his smallholding called Fforchgwm, Llanllwch-aearn, not far from New Quay, on the Cardiganshire coast. His estate amounted to about 20 acres and his cottage survived till about 1989 (see Fig 21-3, which illustrates the modest nature of some freeholders' homes).

In his will (proved in 1786) William Jones (I) bequeathed his fishing boat jointly to his wife and his son William, and shared Fforchgwm field by field among three of his children. His slate gravestone, with his name

Fig. 21-3: Fforchgwm, Llanllwchaearn, Cardiganshire

inscribed as William Jones, is the earliest that can be found in Llanllwchaearn churchyard. His name appears as William John in the list of 1760 Cardiganshire Freeholders, which indicates that William was the son of a person named John. Among the wills of the parish of Llanllwchaearn was found one made by his father John Richard, Fforchgwm, a yeoman who died in 1754. His will revealed that he, too, owned a fishing boat. A search for the will of a person named Richard yielded that of Richard David Jenkin, a leaseholder whose will was proved in 1721, in which his son John and other children were named. Richard David Jenkin farmed Cefngwyddil, adjoining Fforchgwm, and was the son of David ap Jenkin, yeoman, who, according to his will (1667), owned Penrhiwpistill and Troedrhiw near New Quay, an estate amounting to about 100 acres. His personal estate was valued at £41 16s.

A series of wills has thus enabled this family to be traced with certainty in the male line back to a yeoman who was born *circa* 1590 (see Fig 21-4). A search of the records available for the early seventeenth century (wills, lay subsidy lists and Great Sessions records), revealed that more than one David ap Jenkin lived in the area at that time. One was David Jenkin, the son of Dyddgu verch David, a widow of Llangrannog, whose will was proved in 1630. Her personal estate was valued at £187 11s and she was the mortgagee of properties in Llanllwchaearn. Her name appears in the lay subsidy lists and also in Great Sessions Records when she became involved in various land transactions and disputes. Two other sons, Evan Jenkin and Thomas Jenkin, had land in the parish of Llanllwchaearn, possibly inherited from their father Jenkin, and their names also appear in the lay subsidy lists. Unfortunately the absence of place-names in these particular records means that there is no definite proof that David ap Jenkin of Penrhiwpistill was the son of Dyddgu. However, his status as a yeoman in a small parish leads one to suppose that he might have been her son. As for Dyddgu, one can only say that she was probably descended from yeoman or gentry families.

Members of the yeoman class tended to marry wives from families of similar social and economic status, and some had to go farther than their own or neighbouring parishes to find them. For example, in the Llanllwchaearn family discussed above, John Richard married Catherine Jones, the daughter of John Rees, a freeholder of Nantypele, Llanllwchaearn (will, 1713), and Elizabeth Pugh. The parents of John Rees were Rees ap Evan Jenkin of Llangrannog (will, 1677) and Catherine James (will, 1704), the daughter of James ap Rees of Rhydarbennau, Llangeler, Carmarthenshire (will, 1662), an ancestor of Edmund Pryce,

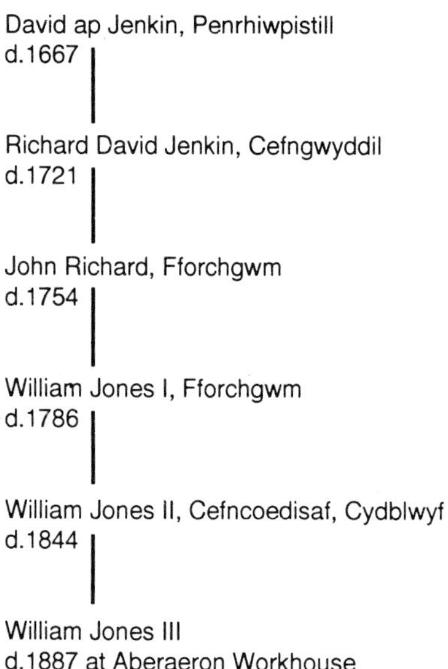


21-4: A family of Llanllwchaearn, Cardiganshire

a well-known genealogist. Likewise, William Jones (II) married Ann Jenkins, the daughter of Jenkin Griffith and Margaret Rees, both of yeoman families from Llandysul and Llangeler. Other marriages in this and other families confirm that the practice of marrying within the same class drawn from beyond the immediate neighbourhood was common among members of the yeoman class.

It is inevitable that research into yeomen (and gentry) families needs to be conducted over a wide area. A comprehensive study of the wills of a number of neighbouring parishes can be very revealing of previously unsuspected family connections. Other useful lists which should be systematically searched for a wide area are those of marriage bonds[18] and marriage settlements.[19]

It has been the purpose of this chapter to illustrate how a wide range of sources—the majority of which are dealt with in detail in other chapters—may be used in combination to trace families over many generations. In this way, a family historian who finds that one or more of his ancestors were freeholders will have increased substantially the chances that he can trace some branches of his family back to early periods. The technique is particularly valuable in the rural areas of west

Wales, from which the present examples have been drawn. The general principles may, however, be applied to research in most parts of Wales.

**NOTES TO CHAPTER 21**

[1]*Shorter Oxford English Dictionary*, 'yeoman: a man owning and cultivating a small estate; a freeholder under the rank of gentleman; loosely, a country man of respectable standing.' Cobbett is also quoted as follows: 'those only who rent are, properly speaking, farmers; those who till their own land are yeomen.'

[2]David W.Howell, *Patriarchs and Parasites* (Cardiff: UWP, 1986).

[3]W.Ogwen Williams (ed.), *Calendar of the Caernarvonshire Quarter Sessions Records*, vol.1: 1541-1558. (Caernarfon: Caernarfonshire Hist. Soc., 1956), p.lxix.

[4]PRO: Lay Subsidy Rolls for Cardiganshire, E 179/219/78.

[5]Wales 18/196, Plea Roll, Spring Will III, April 1701, at NLW.

[6]NLW Wales 4 and NLW Wales 13. Published lists can be seen in W.Ogwen Williams (op.cit.) and in K. Williams-Jones, (ed.), *A Calendar of the Merioneth Quarter Sessions Rolls, Vol.1: 1733-65* (Dolgellau: Merioneth County Council, 1965).

[7]H.J. Habakkuk, 'The Rise and Fall of English Landed Families, 1660-1800: i', *Transactions of the Royal Historical Society*, 5th ser., 29, (1979).

[8]*Return of Owners of Land 1873*, vol.ii. (HMSO, 1875).

[9]*Report of the Royal Commission on Land in Wales and Monmouthshire.* (HMSO, 1896), pp.244-5.

[10]J.Bateman, *The Great Landowners of Great Britain and Ireland*, 4th ed. (London, 1883).

[11]David W.Howell, *Land and People in Nineteenth-century Wales*, (London: Routledge and Kegan Paul, 1978).

[12]R.J.Moore-Colyer, 'Farmers and fields in nineteenth-century Wales: the case of Llanrhystud, Cardiganshire', *National Library of Wales Journal* xxvi (1989), p.32-57, gives a very detailed historical study of the ownership of land in one parish.

[13]PRO IR23/113.

[14]Evelyn Hope, *Llangranog and the Pigeonsford Family*. (Cardigan, 1931).

[15]J.H. Davies, 'Cardiganshire Freeholders in 1760', *Historical Society of West Wales Transactions* iii (1913), pp.73-116. The original manuscript is preserved in the Cwrt Mawr archives at the National Library of Wales.

[16]Evelyn Hope, op. cit. p.5.

[17]Golden Grove manuscript at the Carmarthen Record Office.

[18]'Marriage Bonds and Fiats of West Wales and Gower', *Historical Society of West Wales Transactions* iii-xii (1912-1927); NLW has a card index to marriage bonds in the Welsh dioceses.

[19]NLW Marriage Settlements Card Index.

# 22. Miscellaneous Sources

D. Emrys Williams and Others

This penultimate chapter is designed for two kinds of family historian: those who have successfully used most or all of the sources already described but who wish to explore the by-ways of the subject in the hope of tracing items of additional interest; and those who have had meagre success with normal sources, but who have not completely despaired of making some headway. Many of these less usual—and often unused—sources may be limited to particular areas, to certain occupations, professions or social classes, or to fairly well-defined periods of time. It must be borne in mind that the topics covered are, because of constraints of space, selective.

## Bidding Letters

An outstanding example of a source of genealogical information limited to one geographical area is the printed bidding letter. Broadly speaking this area is the greater part of the present county of Dyfed. More precisely it is the whole of Carmarthenshire, the most northerly part of Pembrokeshire, and Cardiganshire as far north as the vale of Aeron, together with the extreme western edges of the neighbouring counties of Brecknock and Glamorgan from Llanwrtyd in the north to Casllwchwr (Loughor) in the south. This distribution bears a striking resemblance to the area in which the Rebecca riots took place. The extant letters are largely limited to the nineteenth century, and although critics state that the custom was by the middle of the century 'confined to the lower classes', this claim is not entirely convincing.

The bidding letter was an invitation to a wedding celebration, usually held at the home of the parents of one of the contracting parties, together with a request for gifts. These could take the form either of repayment of donations previously made by the bride or groom or certain members of their families, or of donations by persons not hitherto associated in this way. In order to maximise the number of gifts the names and relationship of several members of both families were often appended, and it is these appendices which occasionally provide the family historian with invaluable nuggets of information. Occasionally information concerning the family of one of the parties is not given, and in a few instances even the name of the bride or groom is not specified. These peculiarities may be taken as evidence that the persons whose names were omitted had not participated in this practice, and were presumably strangers to the district in which the bidding was to be held.

An associated document was the bidding account book in which a record of the receipts, whether donations or repayments, was carefully kept. Around 500 bidding letters are known to have survived, but only about a dozen account books have been located. Nevertheless, their importance cannot be exaggerated as they usually contain the names of a few hundred people—relations, neighbours and friends. The sums donated and the order in which the guests parted with their gifts could be some guide to family or other relationships.

Around a quarter of the bidding letters were issued after the marriage had been solemnised, and would often be to events held at the home which had just been set up, while the substantial majority were invitations to a celebration to be conducted on the wedding day itself. The letter is usually dated three or four weeks before the proposed bidding and is, therefore, no proof that the marriage had actually taken place. In this way it corresponded to the calling of banns or the issuing of marriage licences, but although examples are known of marriages not being solemnised after these two statutory preliminaries had been set in motion, this is not the case with the bidding letters, and an extant bidding letter may be taken as fairly conclusive evidence of the solemnisation of a marriage.

Although a bidding could be held several months after the wedding, its location and date could well help to decide the time and place of the marriage itself. Bidding letters can also prove particularly useful when there are references to only one parent, to step-parents, or to grandparents. Most of these items are admittedly negative in character, but they may contain sufficient indications to open up new avenues of research, such as when a grandparent's surname differs from that of the bride or groom, suggesting that it was the mother's maiden name. The bidding letters of the children of David Evans ('Dewi Dawel', 1814-91) of Cwm-du in the parish of Talley (Carmarthenshire) illustrate some of these points:

1869, Aug 20. Son Dafydd to marry Jane Hancock Ellis: no reference to her family as she was a native of Devon.

1869, Dec 10. Son Daniel Goronwy to marry Mary Evans who had step-parents David and Martha Williams.

1882, Aug 30. Daughter Margaret had already married Daniel Davies: no reference to his family as he came from Llandysul, and so his family could not be expected to attend the bidding.[1]

The survival of the four groups of bidding letters in Fig 22-1 means that there is a preponderance of items from the areas and periods specified.

| No. | Period | Area | Compiler | Location |
|---|---|---|---|---|
| 73 | 1826-1851 | Lower Teifi Valley | Printer | NLW |
| 43 | 1862-1891 | Upper Cothi Valley | Innkeeper | NLW |
| 19 | 1852-1902 | Upper Cothi Valley | Landowner | NLW |
| 11 | 1827-1844 | Llanfihangel Aberbythych | Family | CRO |

Fig 22-1: The Survival of Bidding Letters

Future discoveries of substantial caches of bidding letters could modify this geographical and chronological distribution. It is also worth noting that there is a strong tendency in items belonging to the first of these groups to specify family relationships only and to omit personal names of family members.

Apart from being interested in his own kindred the family historian should take some note of demographic tendencies. Writers who have left us their impressions of the biddings consist of both advocates and detractors. The latter argue that they encouraged marriages at an early age before young people would normally consider setting up their homes unaided. Early marriage would also usually lead to larger families, while the repayment of bidding gifts would further drain the resources of such units, leading even to financial failure and probably to their departure to the industrial areas or emigration.

## Poetry

Welsh literary compositions, particularly poetry, contain much information of use to the family historian. These poems, which cover over six hundred years from the fall of Prince Llywelyn to the beginning of the present century, may be divided into two groups on grounds of both metre and content.

The earlier period lasts until the seventeenth century, and the main poetic form was the **cywydd** or rhyming couplet written in **cynghanedd** or strict metre with extensive use of alliteration. These rules often necessitated the intrusion of irrelevant phrases, and disentangling them is a prime task for the genealogical searcher. The works fall into two main categories: eulogies in praise of the noble person, sometimes on occasions such as marriage; and elegies composed after his or her death.

The following extract from an elegy by Siôn Tudur (died 1602), a landowning bard, on Ifan Llwyd ap Dafydd ap Maredudd of Hafod Unnos, Llangernyw, Denbighshire, shows some of these characteristics. The Welsh version is from a collection of Siôn Tudur's poetry edited by Enid Roberts,[2] while the English translation appears in the *History of Powys Fadog*:[3]

Bu'n ei oes ac yn byw'n ŵr,
Ddwy wragedd i oreugwr—
Un o Nannau yn union,
A'i ail ferch reiol o Fôn.
O'r rhain, fal llysiau'r henardd,
Y bu lwyn teg o blant hardd.
Ei fab hynaf, y pennaeth,
Yn ei fyw i nef aeth.

While he lived he lived a hero.
Two wives had this excellent man;
One from Nannau in direct descent,
And a royal maid of Mona for the second.
From these, like plants in an ancient garden,
There is sprung a fair grove of beautiful children;
The eldest son of my chief
In his life-time went to Heaven.

The poet proceeds to give information concerning Ifan's surviving children, the location of the homes of his six daughters being particularly valuable.

Much of the work of these strict metre bards has been collected in higher degree theses, mainly of the University of Wales, and much of the material which these contain has been published in books or articles. Comparatively little has, however, been translated. As most of this laudatory poetry was commissioned by members of the gentry, research undertaken on these patrons in various counties or districts may be of considerable interest to persons descended from such families.

The later period of these poetic works received a boost in the eighteenth century with the advent of the Methodist revival. Now the poems are in free metre, but despite this comparative freedom there is still much extraneous material, often in the form of Biblical allusions. Whereas the earlier poets commended their well-born patrons for their gallantry and nobility, their later counterparts praised the religious attributes of men and women who often hailed from quite humble beginnings.

Two elegies by the hymnologist William Williams, Pantycelyn, to fellow Methodists buried at Llansawel (Carmarthenshire) may be mentioned in this context. The earlier, to John Parry of the neighbouring parish of Talley who died towards the end of November 1770, must refer to the person buried at Llansawel on the 29th of that month—John Harry according to the burial register and John Harry Parry according to the bishop's transcripts. He also used to worship at the Methodist meeting-house at Llansawel, and these facts enable us to identify him as John, son of Harry David Harry or Harry Parry of Ffynnon-grech in the northern part of Talley parish and therefore fairly near to the village of Llansawel. He died at an early age, but had intended marrying 'Biddy', and one wonders whether she was the Bridget Morgan who married Morgan Rees of Llanfynydd, possibly another Methodist hymnologist, at Llangathen in 1773.

The other of these elegies is to William Jones of the large upland farm of Llywele-mawr who died on Sunday 10 April 1785. This information is useful, as the bishop's transcripts for that year do not give the dates of burial and this detail in the parish register is not at all clear.

A sub-section of these later elegies are the numerous ballads, composed particularly on the occasion of such calamities as murders and accidents. Mining fatalities are of particular interest as large numbers were often killed; for example, 41 miners lost their lives at Pentre pit in the Rhondda Fawr valley (Glamorgan) on 21 February 1871. A ballad gives particulars (names, ages, occupation—collier or labourer—and size of family) of the 20 bodies which were recovered, so just over half of those who died were not retrieved. Among the latter was Samuel Evans whose young widow and children returned to her native Carmarthenshire, where many of their descendants still reside, and it is significant that his name is absent from the index of deaths for the first quarter of that year.

Persons from the parish of Llanegwad in the Tywi valley (Carmarthenshire) are the subject of poetry in both periods. Lewis Glyn Cothi was an important fifteenth century bard whose name incorporates the river Cothi which flows into the Tywi in this parish. Although his compilations are by no means confined to this area and many of his poems praise the nobility of Radnorshire, he wrote an eulogy as well as an elegy on Hywel ap Dafydd ap Thomas ap Dafydd who had resided at Cefn-coed, or Cencoed, overlooking the confluence of these two rivers, but who had later taken up residence at Gwernant in the parish of Troed-yr-aur in south Cardiganshire.

William John of Glan Cothi, a Methodist exhorter, died in 1766 and was buried at Llanegwad. Although Thomas Dafydd who composed an elegy to his memory was a fellow-parishioner, he provides no genealogical information, only stating that the deceased was taken ill on his journey at Swansea and died a week later.

In the 1880s Llanegwad suffered the loss of two of its professional men, both in their thirties. The first was its vicar, Thomas Beynon Nicholl, who was buried there on 24 November 1881. Despite being only 38 years of age he had fathered a numerous family—ten according to a lengthy memorial poem by John Jones ('Emlynydd'), a schoolmaster at Abergorlech further up the Cothi valley. The following list of his surviving children has the advantage that it may be understood by someone with little or no knowledge of the Welsh language:

Yn ôl gwelwn y glwys Edward Beynon,
Charles Bowen mabaidd yn llawn cysuron,
David Whilmot a Theodore William,
Ethel Violet—Gwladys Maude ddi-nam—
John Newton yn ei arddull addawol,
Thomas Lloyd hygar gyda'i wên siriol,
A Lilly fach y plentyn ieuengaf.[4]

Many of these effusions were entered in competitions at local **eisteddfodau**, and distance was no object as the secretary or someone who had known the subject well could provide biographical details. John Jones used the same pro forma in published verses to Stephen Evans of Maes-pwll, near Lampeter, Cardiganshire, who died on his way to chapel on 2 November 1884. In a poem composed for the Maestir Eisteddfod of 21 September 1885 he again names the children of the deceased in order of age:

Jane fwyn, David, a Mary Anne dirion,
John, Samuel, ac Elizabeth ffyddlon,
Stephen Herbert, Evan James yr iengaf.[5]

The death occurred also in 1884 of Llanegwad's thirty-year-old doctor, William Lewis Jones of Glyn Cothi House. This, too, happened on the highway, on a visit to a patient, and the winning poem was again by a fellow-parishioner, Henry Davies, who styled himself 'Eryr Glyn Cothi' or the 'Eagle of the Cothi Valley'. The preface to the published verses is also important as it records the death in 1886 of the doctor's widow, leaving four orphaned children.

While staying in the same parish we now turn to a lower grade in the social order. Around the turn of the present century a competition was held for verses to the memory of Mary Rees of Tawelan. Again 'Eryr Glyn Cothi' was the winner, and he traces her movements from the uplands of the parish to the valley floor, and refers to the family illnesses and the deaths of her husband and their six children, all the burials being in the parish register. No date is given for the widow's death, and as she does not seem to have been buried with her family one wonders whether she was buried in a pauper's grave.

Certainly in the present century are printed bilingual verses in honour of Mrs Anne Lewis of Tŷ-coch, Llanegwad, who did not die until 21 July 1907, aged 74. The poetic quality is indicated by:

Mae ei phriod dan ei gur
A gyd-deithiodd hanner canrif . . .

Sorrow holds her husband tight,
He had sojourned fifty years . . .

She, too, had ten children, five of each sex, the sons being commended for their morals and the daughters for their good looks, but only the eldest son and his father's namesake, Thomas Lewis, is named, presumably as he had left for Sirhowy, Monmouthshire, while his siblings may have been still resident in their native locality.

Finally, we come to 1922 when John Walters of Clwte died. The verses to Anne Lewis record that she was buried in a nonconformist cemetery, while John Walters, a Calvinistic Methodist elder, was buried in Llanegwad churchyard with his wife.

## Monumental Inscriptions

Monumental inscriptions are well-known as a source of family history. A number of these were recorded before work of this kind became fashionable, such as the gravestones in the churchyard at Llanbadarn Fawr, Cardiganshire, towards the end of the nineteenth century,[6] while in recent years much work in the field has been undertaken by societies—family and local history and others—and individuals.[7] Many graveyards have been cleared and landscaped, and in the course plans and indexes have been compiled, although, unfortunately, some gravestones have been damaged in the process. It is worth enquiring if any such work has been undertaken, but in most cases there is no substitute for a visit to the cemeteries themselves.

No opportunity should be lost of speaking to other people in the vicinity—both local inhabitants and visitors. As members of the same family were buried near each other, gravestones other than those of immediate interest should be recorded. If the gravestones are not easily read, another visit at a different time of day or under different weather conditions could prove advantageous.

The information on these memorials varies considerably, being on the whole better in north Wales where slate was cheaper and more people adept at handling it. The Welsh language was commonly used, but as an example of a bilingual gravestone we may turn to John Jones, who used the bardic name 'Ioan Duad' and whose remains lie under a cracked table-top tomb in the churchyard of Cynwyl Elfed, Carmarthenshire, although there is no corresponding entry in the parish records. After providing the usual information (name, abode, date of death and age) in English, the sculptor turned to Welsh to allege that John Jones was descended on his father's side from the Joneses of Llanina in Cardiganshire and on his mother's side from the Howells of Cynwyl Elfed, who were descendants of the old princes of Caernarfon. This unusual information is followed by a verse or englyn by the bard being commemorated. Such verses are not uncommon, and various collections have been published.[8]

Many families have memorial cards or funeral leaflets in their possession, often recording the death of a person about whom very little is known. Although these were often only neighbours or friends, it is always worth searching for a family connection. Two collections of these cards in the National Library of Wales are of particular interest, one being collected in the Blaenau Ffestiniog area and commencing in 1862,[9] and the other those kept by a monumental mason from Llandinam in Montgomeryshire, covering the period 1852-1918.[10]

## Church Records

Until the middle of the nineteenth century the established church controlled many aspects of life which are now entirely outside its purview. Perhaps the most important of these was the proving of wills and associated acts (see Chapter 13). Disputes concerning grants of probate and the moral life of the people were also the concern of the church, and a large collection of papers concerning these activities have been preserved among the records of the church or consistory courts and have been meticulously scheduled. A series of articles by Walter T. Morgan on certain aspects of the consistory courts of St David's has appeared in the *Journal of the Historical Society of the Church in Wales*,[11] while John Addy's *Sin and Society in the Seventeenth Century* deals with these courts in the diocese of Chester, which included the detached part of Flintshire.[12]

## Ordination Papers

Church records, of course, deal largely with clergymen, and ordination papers are of particular importance. Before being accepted for ordination the candidate had to provide proof of his baptism, usually a copy of the entry in a parish register. If this was not available the candidate might have supplied an entry from a non-parochial register, an oath of a person who might have witnessed the christening, and perhaps a birth certificate. Before Evan Jones was ordained by the bishop of St David's in 1744, Clement Jones of the parish of Llanfihangel-y-Creuddyn, Cardiganshire, and Margaret his wife made oath before Lord Lisburne that their son Evan Jones was born in 1716, but that the parish register had been lost or mislaid for several years and a new one not procured till 1733. More than a century later, in 1857, Rachel Davies, aged 37, wife of Evan Davies of Silian in the same county and daughter of the late David Lewis of the same parish swore that she remembered the birth of her brother Titus Lewis, the ordinand, when she was around seven years of age (though she did not add that her father had been murdered and had been the subject of a ballad). A private family register is the authority quoted when Henry Jones, the son of a Carmarthenshire Congregational minister, sought ordination in the diocese of Bangor in 1861.

## The 'Notitiae'

Although diocesan records are more plentiful for the two bishoprics of the south than for the two sees of north Wales, one of the sources of the greatest use to the family historian relates to the diocese of St Asaph. These are the 'notitiae' from the 1680s. The publication of the documents for the parishes in the county was commenced in *The Montgomeryshire Collections* in 1965 and is still continuing in 1992. The information provided for persons surnamed Turnor in the parish of Aberhafesb may be regarded as typical.

| | No.in Family | Under 18 |
|---|---|---|
| Lewis Turnor | 11 | 14, 16 |
| Tho: Turnor | 6 | 16, 13, 6, 3 |

Lewis Turnor and his wife were under excommunication

It will thus be seen that this information combines some of the characteristics of the modern census with the concern of the consistory courts for the moral and spiritual welfare of the flock.

## Biographical Works

All researchers into Welsh family history should know of the existence of the biographical works published by the Honourable Society of Cymmrodorion in the 1950s: *Y Bywgraffiadur Cymreig* and its English-language counterpart, *The Dictionary of Welsh Biography*.[13] Although not many people will have members of their family noticed in these compilations, a perusal of their bibliographies could help them. Counties, towns, denominations, and even parishes, have books giving the histories of their famous inhabitants, often entitled *Enwogion* . . . ('Famous or eminent men of . . . '), such as three works bearing the same title, *Enwogion Môn* (Famous people of Anglesey) and *Eminent Men of Denbighshire* (Liverpool, 1946). Although two books on Cardiganshire people (*Enwogion Sir Aberteifi* and *Enwogion Ceredigion*) were published in 1868-69, the notebooks of John Evans ('John y Gwas') at the National Library giving brief biographies of persons from Cardiganshire and Carmarthenshire, and also of clergymen, may be mentioned. These compilations and the three editions of *Who's Who in Wales* (1921, 1933 and 1937) are particularly useful for the beginning of the twentieth century. Most local or parish histories also have a chapter giving biographies of noteworthy people connected in one way or another with the area.

The **cofiant** or life of ministers is a fairly common feature of Welsh nonconformity. The first chapter in such a book is the most important for the family historian as well as the most amusing as it often deals with the family background and the sins of the young man before his conversion to a religious life. A family tree may be included, as in *Cofiant y Parch T.Rees*[14] and *Cofiant y Tri Brawd*[15], which contain almost identical charts noting preachers descended from Harri William of the parish of Llanfynydd in Carmarthenshire. The 'three brothers' were surnamed

Stephens, and another biographical work bearing the same title gives accounts of the three Roberts brothers from Llanbrynmair in Montgomeryshire.[16]

## Newspapers and Periodicals

The first decade of the nineteenth century witnessed considerable advances in publishing in Wales. Until that time the only items of Welsh interest were those found in newspapers published in London or in a border city such as Chester or Gloucester, but two weekly newspapers in Wales commenced publication during those years—*The Cambrian* at Swansea in 1804, soon followed by *The Journal* at Carmarthen in 1810, although most of their contents at that time were far from local in character. A reader of a local newspaper should check whether more than one edition was published.[17]

Also important were the publications—usually monthlies—in the Welsh language. Although not all strictly allied to a particular denomination the following are usually regarded as such: *Yr Eurgrawn Wesleyaidd* (Wesleyan Methodist) 1809-; *Seren Gomer* (Baptist) 1818-; *Y Drysorfa* (Calvinistic Methodist) 1831-; *Yr Haul* (Church of England) 1835-; and *Diwygiwr* (Independent) 1835-. The latter is particularly important as it takes considerable pride in recording marriages in nonconformist chapels after the new act allowing such ceremonies came into force. These periodicals published particulars of births, marriages and deaths, but, of course, much depended on the local correspondent; for example, *Yr Haul*, although published in Llandovery, appears to have had a particularly good news gatherer in Llanidloes.

Welsh newspapers and periodicals were also published by Welshmen overseas, particularly in America, where the following were of considerable importance: *Y Cyfaill o'r Hen Wlad* (New York, 1838-); *Y Cenhadwr Americanaidd* (Utica, 1840-); and, in English, *The Cambrian* (Cincinnati, 1880-). In addition to news of Welshman in America, these often contain a foreign section—usually relating to Wales![18]

## Society Transactions

Wales has long been well-served by antiquarian, local history and record societies, who have been responsible for a considerable body of published material of interest and relevance to family historians. Such societies cover every part of Wales and extend to those based in London, such as the Honourable Society of Cymmrodorion. In a restricted space, it would be invidious to select a few illustrations of this wealth of articles, papers and reprints; rather, the reader should glance at the Notes attached to many chapters of this book to find a representative range of examples. Such items are of high quality and of greater length than can be accommodated in the journals of the relatively new family history societies.

Runs of these periodicals are to be found in local libraries within Wales and in larger libraries outside; the National Library of Wales has its extensive collection on open shelves. Libraries will also be able to provide contact addresses for the societies, whose officials are honorary and liable to change: back numbers and off-prints may be available.

The transactions themselves are frequently indexed (by volume or group of volumes)[19] and these indexes should be checked, both for personal names and for parishes. The various volumes of *The Subject Index to Welsh Periodicals*[20] form a general index. In addition, family historians should not ignore the genealogical guides referred to in standard textbooks: these form indexes to three-generation pedigrees in print and, therefore, are yet another key to genealogical material in Welsh county and area periodicals.[21] **(SR)**

## Taxation Records

As standard genealogical sources become scarcer for most families sooner or later, the importance of any list which indicates a name attached to a place and a date increases. For Wales, as elsewhere, there are many examples of such lists: among the most useful are records related to certain 'national' taxes. As with more local taxes—such as Church and Poor Rates which are dealt with in Chapter 15—the collection of money usually involved the keeping of careful and comprehensive records, often over long periods.

In the awkward period covering the late eighteenth and early nineteenth centuries, a study of land tax records may be particularly helpful in Wales, both in adding family information but also occasionally in providing clues to, for example, a date of death. Much has been written about these records in recent years and there is a useful guide to what has survived.[22] Because these records were used in the compilation of voting lists in the fifty year-plus period before electoral reform in 1832, they were relatively well-preserved in records of the Quarter Sessions and should be found in the County Record Office. There are gaps, inevitably, though a fairly recent discovery of 'missing'

Cardiganshire Land Tax Assessments, though incomplete, indicates that there is always hope of such gaps being filled.[23] For some Welsh counties, the only surviving records are those held at the Public Record Office in Kew for 1798, though there is a sad lack of even these for the county of Flint.

Where good records survive, as for much of Pembrokeshire 1786-1832, holdings of land may be traced throughout the period, and evidence of movement to other parishes is to be found.[24] The documents are stored in bundles, annually by hundred, and it can be a prolonged but satisfying task to search year after year to locate an ancestor who moved in pre-census times to a farm in another parish.

In the seventeenth century, the hearth tax is the primary example of useful lists which have survived on a large scale for Wales. The originals are held at the Public Record Office, Chancery Lane, and may be difficult to read. For some counties, transcripts exist, among the most useful being that of the 1670 Hearth Tax for Pembrokeshire.[25] This list is particularly useful in locating family members, since Pembrokeshire had varied and largely settled surnames at that time and identification of individuals is relatively easy. Normally, one must expect to combine a sighting in such records with, ideally, information from a will, and this becomes essential in a county such as Cardiganshire, where the listed names are largely patronymic. Fuller details of this tax and of similar lists are also in a Gibson Guide.[26] **(SR)**

## Soldier Ancestors

For centuries the poor quality of the land in Wales has limited the level of population which could be supported. As a result, pressures to move—merely to subsist—have made Wales a particularly fruitful place for recruiting parties, and Welshmen have always featured prominently in all the regiments of the British Army.

The main body of records relating to the British Army prior to 1913 are located at the Public Record Office at Kew. The use of those records for researching soldier ancestors has been well described in a wide range of publications. Two recent publications are, however, particularly worthy of note.[27]

For those with soldier ancestors who served in one of the regiments which (following successive amalgamations) have their headquarters in Wales, the museums at Cardiff[28], Brecon[29] and Caernarfon[30] could well have much to offer by way of letters, diaries, photographs, medals and a wide range of other military memorabilia. In addition, searchers may find something of value in two further museums at Monmouth[31] and Cardiff[32] which have rather more recent connections with Wales. However, few military museums are geared to serving the needs of family historians and they are only now beginning to catalogue their holdings in a systematic way. The help they may be able to give, therefore, is likely to be limited. A visit to the appropriate museum will, nevertheless, give an excellent insight into the military life experienced by a soldier ancestor. Opening periods and hours vary considerably and potential visitors should phone to check on these before visiting a particular museum. **(JBR)**

## Apprenticeship Records

The practice whereby a young person learned the 'craft or mystery' of a specific trade from an experienced practitioner is one of long-standing in Britain. It has the merit that it largely ensured the maintenance of adequate standards as, certainly for those trades covered by one of the guilds, it would not be possible to practise such a trade within a town or city without first having completed a suitable apprenticeship.

Basically there are two types of apprenticeship; trade apprenticeships and poor apprenticeships. In theory they offered a mechanism for individuals to better themselves and rise up the social classes. In practice the requirements for acceptance into trade (or guild) apprenticeships usually involved not only money but land or property qualifications as well. This inevitably put them out of the reach of many, and in particular out of the reach the labouring poor. This gulf between the two types of apprenticeship was accentuated by a sixteenth century statute which ensured that trade apprenticeships were not available to the children of those engaged in husbandry or as labourers.

### a. Trade Apprenticeships

These involved a voluntary agreement between a father (or widowed mother) and a master whereby a young person would be bound to that master for a period (typically seven or more years) to learn a specific trade. Although these apprenticeships were often the subject of a legal agreement, copies of those agreements were very much 'private' papers (kept by the parent and the master) and, inevitably, few have survived. However, the 1710 Stamp Act caused apprenticeships to be subject to tax and, as a result, a register of apprenticeships was kept for tax purposes up to 1811.

This register offers a great deal to the family historian, recording as it does (to 1750) the names, occupations and place of residence of all the parties. From 1750 the information is less full. The bulk of registers are to be found at the Public Record Office at Kew in the papers relating to the Inland Revenue (IR 1 and Indexes IR 17). Some original indentures are to be found at the Society of Genealogists which also has copies of the indexes to the registers at the PRO.

The significance of the survival of records for the period 1710-1811 will not be lost on the family historian with Welsh ancestry.

### b. Poor Apprenticeships

From the middle of the sixteenth century—but chiefly as a result of the Poor Law Act of 1601—parish officers were able to apprentice out poor children whose parents were unable to maintain them. Masters failing to carry out the conditions of the apprenticeship could be fined by the Justices.

Such apprenticeships were exempt from Stamp Duty so do not appear in the records of the Inland Revenue. However, they were very much the concern of the parish and reference to them may often be found in the Vestry Minutes (see Chapter 15).

In the case of a parish apprenticeship the agreement was between a public body and the master. As a result the likelihood of documents surviving which give details of the terms of the apprenticeship is much higher. An example of this is to be found in the parochial records for Bangor (Caernarfonshire) which are at the National Library of Wales. In that collection there is a draft indenture (dated 1811)[33] relating to Hugh Rowland—son of Margaret Rowland of 'Rallt, in the parish of Llandysilio (Anglesey)—and Rice Griffiths, Surgeon, Apothecary and Man Midwife of the City of Bangor. The proposed apprenticeship was for three years to enable Hugh Rowland to learn the 'Art, Mystery and Profession' of his proposed master. It was, perhaps, fortunate for the continued well-being of the people of that part of North Wales that the proposed term of three years had been struck out and the marginal note 'What can he learn in 3 years?' had been added.

In the above example, although the draft indenture had been drawn up by the parish, Margaret Rowland was also party to the agreement which indicates that she was being partly supported by the parish in securing this apprenticeship for her son. It also suggests that her husband had been a man of some substance (not 'engaged in husbandry or as a labourer') but that the family had fallen on leaner times following his death. If this is the case, there is every likelihood that without his death this might well have been a trade apprenticeship. **(JBR)**

## Welsh Gypsies

Welsh Gypsies have a long and colourful history and were first mentioned in Welsh literature in a **cywydd** by Morris Kyffin who died in 1598. The founder of Welsh Gypsies was Abram Wood and he is portrayed in literature by Twm o'r Nant (1739-1810) in his play *Pleser a Gofid*.

Abram Wood was buried at Llangelynnin (Merionethshire) on 12 November 1799 and the stone can be seen by the church door. Very little is known about him but the fortunes of his descendants have been thoroughly researched, the main source of information being Dr John Sampson, librarian at Liverpool University (1892-1928) who learned Romany and was warmly accepted by the Wood family.

Abram Wood had many descendants and his name is still in daily use in the idiom **teulu Abram Wood** which is used when referring to a large family.

The most noticeable characteristic of his descendants was their musical ability—mainly as fiddlers and harpists. One of the most famous of the musical descendants was Sir Henry Wood, founder of the London Promenade Concerts.

One of Abram's great-grandsons was John Roberts, *Telynor Cymru*, who won many Eisteddfod prizes for playing the harp. John Roberts and his nine sons played the harp for Queen Victoria when she stayed at Palé Hall near Bala in August 1889.

The definitive book on Welsh Gypsies has been written by Eldra Jarman, a descendant of Abram Wood, and her husband, Professor A.O.H.Jarman.[34] Abram Wood's family tree can be seen in the Journal of the Gypsy Lore Society for 1934. **(HCC)**

**NOTES TO CHAPTER 22**

[1]NLW: Department of Pictures and Maps: Posters and Broadsides, Folders 52-3 (including Bidding Letter Volume).

[2]Enid Roberts, *Siôn Tudur* (Caerdydd: 1980) (Cyf I, t. 250.

[3]J.Y.W.Lloyd, *History of Powys Fadog* (London: 1881-87), Vol IV, p397.

[4]NLW Misc Vol 365.

[5][Ed. John Jones, Abergorlech Board School] *Marwnadau i'r Diweddar Mr Stephen Evans, Maesypwll, ger Llanbedr* (Llanbedr: 1887).

[6]NLW MS 902A.

[7]As a contribution to the work of CAPEL: the Chapels Heritage Society, the Association of Family History Societies of Wales has compiled a list of those graveyards (both Nonconformist and Church in Wales) which have been transcribed. Copies of this list—which will be regularly updated—are made available to CAPEL, all the Family History Societies and the National Library of Wales.

[8]For example, by Gomer M. Roberts, *Mynwenta* (1980).

[9]NLW: J.W.Jones 1228a.

[10]NLW MS 22344F.

[11]*Journal of the Historical Society of the Church in Wales* (1957-1962)

[12]John Addy, *Sin and Society in the Seventeenth Century* (London: Routledge, 1989).

[13]*Y Bywgraffiadur Cymreig hyd 1940* (London: 1953) and *The Dictionary of Welsh Biography* (London: 1959).

[14]John Thomas, *Cofiant y Parch T.Rees, DD, Abertawy* (Dolgellau: 1888).

[15]John Thomas, *Cofiant y Tri Brawd, sef y Parch. J.Stephens, Brychgoed, D.Stephens, Glantaf, ac N.Stephens, Liverpool* (Liverpool: 1877).

[16]E.P.Jones, *Cofiant y Tri Brawd o Llanbrynmair a Conwy* (Bala [1892]).

[17]J.S.W. Gibson, *Local Newspapers 1750-1920* (FFHS, 1987) indicates locations of English language newspapers; an example of more detailed coverage (including title-changes) is found in *Local Newspapers in Dyfed* (Dyfed Archives).

[18]*Y Wasg Gyfnodol Gymreig/The Welsh Periodical Press* (NLW, 1987) provides an introduction to this subject.

[19]For example: Gareth Haulfryn Williams, *An Index to Y Cymmrodor and the Transactions of the Honourable Society of Cymmrodorion 1878-1982* (Hon. Society of Cymmrodorion).

[20]*Subject Index to Welsh Periodicals*, first published by the Wales and Monmouthshire Branch of the Library Association (Vol 1-7, 1934-1964) and latterly by the National Library of Wales (1978 to date).

[21]G.W.Marshall, *The Genealogist's Guide* (London: 1903; reprinted 1967) lists pedigrees in printed sources to 1903; J.B.Whitmore, *A Genealogical Guide* (London: Society of Genealogists, 1953) is a continuation of Marshall's work to 1953; G.B.Barrow, *The Genealogist's Guide* (Research Publishing Co., 1977) supplements the earlier works to 1975.

[22]Jeremy Gibson and Dennis Mills, *Land Tax Assessments* (FFHS).

[23]Now at NLW, temporary listing; most parishes have missing years in the late eighteenth/early nineteenth centuries.

[24]Those with Pembrokeshire ancestry should read Francis Jones, 'The Pembrokeshire Land Tax Assessments for 1786', *Journal of the Pembrokeshire Historical Society*, No. 2, 1986-87.

[25] *West Wales Historical Records,* vols. ix-xi, (1920-6).

[26] J.S.W.Gibson, *The Hearth Tax and other Stuart Tax Lists and the Association in Oath Rolls* (FFHS). Other transcripts, locally-held microfilm copies, etc, are also listed in this book. Other Gibson Guides, listed in Chapter 23, cover Wales for many possible listings (tax and others), and are revised periodically.

[27] Simon Fowler, *Army Records for Family Historians*, PRO Readers' Guide No.2 (London: PRO Publications, 1992) and Michael J. and Christopher T.Watts, *My Ancestor was in the British Army: How can I find out more about him?* (London: Society of Genealogists, 1992).

[28] Museum of the Welch Regiment, Cardiff Castle (0222 229367).

[29] The South Wales Borderers and Monmouthshire Regimental Museum, Royal Regiment of Wales, The Barracks, Brecon (0874 623111).

[30] 23rd Royal Welsh Fusiliers Museum, Caernarfon Castle (0286 673362).

[31] Museum of the Royal Monmouthshire RE Militia (TA), Monmouth (0600 712935).

[32] Museum of the 1st The Queen's Dragoon Guards, Cardiff Castle (0222 222253).

[33] Parochial Records (NLW, Bangor Diocese, Bangor Item 14).

[34] Eldra Jarman and A.O.H.Jarman, *The Welsh Gypsies, Children of Abram Wood* (Cardiff: UWP, 1991).

# 23. Select Bibliography

This final chapter contains suggestions for further reading made by many of the authors of the preceding chapters, together with works recommended by the editors. Inevitably, the authors' lists had many suggestions in common and, since space did not permit the repetition involved in chapter by chapter bibliographies, broader headings are used here. There have had to be some arbitrary decisions about the category in which a widely useful book is placed as a result of this; but readers are, in any case, advised to consult the endnotes to individual chapters for specific recommendations of books and, in particular, for references to articles in journals or chapters within books, which could not be duplicated here.

The editors have chosen many of the additional titles for their value and relevance to the *family* historian, and have paid particular attention to the merits of their bibliographies. To help the general reader in the limited space available, emphasis has had to be given to works written in English, but a few valuable Welsh titles are included. Readers should consult the latest edition, on microfiche, of *A Bibliography of the History of Wales,* Cardiff: University of Wales Press, 1989) for wider information on the topics discussed here.

The place of publication is London, unless otherwise specified.

### Abbreviations

FFHS—Federation of Family History Societies
NLW—National Library of Wales
*NLWJ—National Library of Wales Journal*
PRO—Public Record Office
SoG—Society of Genealogists, London
*THSC—Transactions of the Honourable Society of Cymmrodorion*

### The Anglican Church: Its Organisation and Records


Burn, J.S., *The History of Parish Registers in England*, 2nd edn (1862; repr. 1976)

Cox, J.C., *The Parish Registers of England* (repr. Wakefield: 1974)

Gibson, J.S.W., *Bishops' Transcripts and Marriage Licences, Bonds and Allegations: A Guide to their Location and Indexes* (FFHS, 1985)

Guy, J.R., *The Diocese of Llandaff in 1763* (Cardiff: 1991)

Humphrey-Smith, C. (ed.), *The Phillimore Atlas and Index of Parish Registers* (Chichester: 1984).

*Parish Register Copies in the Society of Genealogists* (SoG, 1992)

Richards, T., *The Religious Census of 1676* (1927)

Steel, D.J., *National Index of Parish Registers, I: General Sources of Births, Marriages, and Deaths before 1837*, 3rd edn (repr. 1968)

Veysey, A.G., *Guide to the Parish Records of Clwyd* (Clwyd Record Office, 1984)
Walker, D., (ed.), *History of the Church in Wales* (Penarth: 1976; repr. 1990)
Williams, C.J. & Watts-Williams, J., *Cofrestri Plwyf Cymru/Parish Registers of Wales*, Vol.13: National Index of Parish Registers (NLW and others, 1986)
Williams, G., *The Welsh Church from Conquest to Reformation* (Cardiff: 1962)

**Biographical Works**

Jenkins, R.T.(ed.) *The Dictionary of Welsh Biography down to 1940* (Honourable Society of Cymmrodorion, 1959)
Jenkins, R.T., and Jones, E.D., (ed.) *Y Bywgraffiadur Cymreig 1941-50* (1950)
Jones, E., *Enwogion Cymreig* (Caerdydd: 1908)
Mee, A., (ed.), *Who's Who in Wales* (Cardiff: 1921)
*Who's Who in Wales,* 2nd, 3rd edns (1933, 1937)
Pike, W.T., (ed.), *Edwardian Biography: South Wales and Monmouthshire* (1907; repr. Edinburgh: 1986)
Rees, T.M., *Notable Welshmen 1700-1900* (Caernarfon: 1908)
Roberts, T.R., *A Dictionary of Eminent Welshmen* (Cardiff & Merthyr Tydfil: 1908)
Williams, R., *Enwogion Cymru: A Biographical Dictionary of Eminent Welshmen* (Llandovery: 1852)

**Civil Registration and the Census**

*District Register Offices in England & Wales*, 8th edn (East Yorkshire FHS, 1991)
Dunn, F.I., *Registration in Cheshire, 1538-1987: a brief history to mark 150 years of civil registration, 1837-1987* (Chester: Cheshire County Council, 1987).
Gibson, J.S.W., *Census Returns 1841-1881 on Microfilm: A Directory to local holdings* (FFHS, 1990)
Gibson, J.S.W., *General Register Office and International Genealogical Indexes: Where to find them* (FFHS, 1988)
Gibson, J.S.W., *Marriage, Census and other Indexes for Family Historians* (FFHS, 1992)
Higgs, E., *Making Sense of the Census: the Manuscript Returns for England and Wales, 1801-1901* (HMSO, 1989)
Lumas, S., *Making Use of the Census*, Public Record Office Readers' Guide No.1 (PRO, 1992)
Lumas, S., *An Introduction to the Census Returns of England and Wales* (FFHS, 1992)
McLaughlin, E., *St. Catherine's House: the General Register Office* (The author).
Nissel, M. *People Count, a History of the General Register Office* (1987)
PRO Information Leaflets:
—Records of Births, Marriages and Deaths
—Censuses of Population 1801-1891
Rosier, M.E.B., *Index to Census Registration Districts* (1992)

**Education**

Davies, M., *Glynogwr and Gilfach Goch: A History* (Cowbridge: 1981)
Evans, L.W., *Education in Industrial Wales 1700-1900* (Cardiff: 1971)
Evans, W.G., *A History of Llandovery College* (Llandovery: 1981)
Foster, J., *Alumni Oxonienses 1500-1714* (Oxford & London: 1891-2)
——— *Alumni Oxonienses 1715-1886* (Oxford & London: 1887-8)
Gruffydd, W.J., *Cofiant O.M.Edwards* (Aberystwyth: 1937)
Jenkins, R.T., *Edrych Yn Ôl* (Llundain: 1968)
Kissack, K., *Monmouth: the Making of a Town* (1975)
Owen, G.D., *Elizabethan Wales* (Cardiff: 1964)
*Report of the Commissioners of Inquiry into the State of Education in Wales* (HMSO, 1847)
Richards, T., *History of the Puritan Movement in Wales* (1920)
Seaborne, M., *Schools in Wales 1500-1900: A Social and Architectural History* (Denbigh: 1992)
Venn, J., and J.A., *Alumni Cantabrigienses, from the Earliest Times to 1900*, (Cambridge: 1922-54)

**Emigration**

Beddoe, D., *Welsh Convict Women*. (Barry: 1979)
Blackwell, H., *A Bibliography of Welsh Americana*, 2nd edn (Aberystwyth: 1977)
Bromell, A., *Tracing Family History in New Zealand* (Wellington: 1991)
——— *Family History Research in New Zealand* (Auckland: NZGS, 1989).
Brownfield, L.T., (ed.) *History of Welsh Settlements in Jackson and Gallia Counties of Ohio* (1896; transl. Columbus: 1988)
Bull, E., *Aided Immigration from Britain to South Africa 1857-1867* (Pretoria: 1991)
Caffrey, K., *The British to Southern Africa* (1973)
Conway, A.A., (ed.), *The Welsh in America: Letters from the Immigrants* (Cardiff: 1961)
Evans, W., *The Diary of a Welsh Swagman 1869-1894* (Melbourne: 1975)
Glenn, T.A., *Welsh Founders of Pennsylvania*, 2 vols (Oxford: 1911, 1915)
——— *Merion in the Welsh Tract* (Norristown: 1896)
Hartmann, E.G., *Americans from Wales* (Boston: 1967)
Jenkins, H.M., *Historical Collections relating to Gwynedd, a Township of Montgomery County, Pennsylvania* (Philadelphia: 1897)
Lloyd, L., *Australians from Wales* (Caernarfon: Gwynedd County Council, 1988)
Matthews, A., *Hanes Wladfa Cymreig yn Patagonia* (1894; repr. Gaiman: 1977)
O'Byrne Spenser, S., *British Settlers in Natal 1824-1857* (1981-87)
Phillips, P., *British Settlers in Natal 1795-1819* (1981)
Rees, T. Mardy, *A History of the Quakers in Wales and their Emigration to North America* (Carmarthen: 1925)

Rosser, F.T., *The Welsh Settlement in Upper Canada* (London, Ontario: 1954)
Williams, D., *Cymru ac America/Wales and America* (Cardiff: 1946)
Williams, D.J., *One Hundred Years of Welsh Calvinistic Methodism in America* (Philadelphia: 1937)
Williams, G., *The Welsh in Patagonia, the State and the Ethnic Community* (Cardiff: 1991)
Williams, G.A., *The Search for Beulah Land* (1980)
Williams, R.B., *Cymry Patagonia* (Aberystwyth: 1942)

**Genealogical Guides**

Barrow, G.B., *The Genealogist's Guide: An index to printed British pedigrees and family histories, 1950-1975* (1977)
Marshall, G.W., *The Genealogists's Guide*, 4th edn (repr. Baltimore: 1967)
Whitmore, J.B., *A Genealogical Guide: An index to British pedigrees* (1953)

**Genealogical Method and Sources**

*Genealogical Sources at the National Library of Wales* (NLW, 1986)
Bevan, A., and Duncan, A., *Tracing Your Ancestors in the Public Record Office*, 4th edn (HMSO, 1990)
Colwell, S., *Family Roots: Discovering the Past in the Public Record Office* (1991)
——— *Dictionary of Genealogical Sources in the Public Record Office* (1992)
FitzHugh, T.V.H. [revised by B. Christmas] *The Dictionary of Genealogy* (1991)
Pelling, G.,*Beginning Your Family History* (FFHS, 1990)
Riden, P., *Record Sources for Local History* (1987)
Saul, P. & Markwell, F.C, *The Family Historian's Enquire Within* (FFHS, 1991)
Todd, A., *Basic Sources for Family History—1: Back to the Early 1800s* (Ramsbottom: 1987)

**Heraldry**

Siddons, M.P., *The Development of Welsh Heraldry* (Aberystwyth: NLW, vol. I, 1991; vols. II and III to be published early in 1993)
Woodcock, T., and Robinson, J.M., *The Oxford Guide to Heraldry* (Oxford: 1988)

**History (Background)**

Davies, R.R., *Conquest, Coexistence and Change 1063-1415* (Oxford and Cardiff: 1987)
Evans, D.G., *A History of Wales 1815-1906* (Cardiff: 1989)
Jenkins, G.H., *The Foundations of Modern Wales 1642-1780* (Oxford and Cardiff: 1987)
Jenkins, J.G., *Life and Tradition in Rural Wales* (1976; Alan Sutton, 1991)

Jones, D.J.V., *Before Rebecca: Popular Protest in Wales 1793-1835* (1973)
——— *Rebecca's Children: Study of Rural Society, Crime and Protest* (Oxford: 1989).
Jones, I.G., *Explorations & Explanations: Essays in the History of Victorian Wales* (Llandysul: 1981)
——— *Communities: Essays in the Social History of Victorian Wales* (Llandysul: 1987)
Jones, J.G., *A Pocket Guide: The History of Wales* (Cardiff: 1990)
Morgan, K.O., *Rebirth of a Nation: Wales 1880-1980* (Oxford and Cardiff: 1981)
Morgan, P.J. and Thomas, D., *Wales: the Shaping of a Nation* (David & Charles, 1984)
Owen, T.M., *A Pocket Guide: The Customs and Traditions of Wales* (Cardiff: 1991)
Williams, D. *The Rebecca Riots: A Study in Agrarian Discontent* (Cardiff: 1955, paperback 1986)
Williams, G., *Recovery, Reorientation and Reformation c.1415-1642* (Oxford and Cardiff: 1987)
Williams, J., *Digest of Welsh Historical Statistics,* 2 vols (Welsh Office, 1985)

**The Land and its People**

Carr, A.D., *Medieval Anglesey* (Llangefni: 1982)
Chapman, J., *A Guide to Parliamentary Enclosures in Wales* (Cardiff: 1992)
Colyer, R.J., *The Welsh Cattle Drovers* (Cardiff: 1976)
Gibson, J., *Agriculture in Wales* (Aberystwyth: 1879)
Gresham, C.A., *Eifionydd: A Study in Land Ownership from the Medieval Period to the Present Day* (Cardiff: 1973)
Howell, D.W., *Patriarchs and Parasites: the Gentry of South-West Wales in the Eighteenth Century* (Cardiff: 1986)
——— *Land and People in Nineteenth Century Wales* (1978)
Howells, B. (ed.), *Early Modern Pembrokeshire* (Pembrokeshire County History, Vol. III) (Haverfordwest: 1987)
Hume, I. and Pryce, W.T.R. (eds), *The Welsh and their Country* (Llandysul: 1986)
Humphreys, T.M., 'Rural Society in Montgomeryshire in the Eighteenth Century', (unpublished PhD thesis, University of Wales, 1978)
Jenkins, D., *The Agricultural Community in South-West Wales at the turn of the Twentieth Century* (Cardiff: 1971)
Jenkins, P., *The Making of a Ruling Class: The Glamorgan Gentry, 1640-1790* (Cambridge: 1983)
Jones, F., *Historic Carmarthenshire Homes* (Carmarthen: 1987)
Lloyd, T., *The Lost Houses of Wales: a survey of country houses in Wales demolished since c.1900* (1987)
Moore, D. (ed.), *Wales in the Eighteenth Century* (Swansea: 1976)
Owen, D.H. (ed.), *Settlement and Society in Wales* (Cardiff: 1989)

Parry, J.G., 'Stability and Change in Mid-Eighteenth Century Caernarvonshire', (unpublished PhD thesis, University of Wales, 1978)
Pryce, W.T.R., *The Photographer in Rural Wales* (Llanfair Caereinion: 1991)
Smith, P., *Houses of the Welsh Countryside* (HMSO, 1988)
Thomas, D.L., *A Digest of the Welsh Land Commission* (1896)
Thomas, H.M., *A Catalogue of Glamorgan Estate Maps* (Glamorgan Archives, 1992)
Vincent, J.E., *The Land Question in North Wales* (1896)
——— *The Land Question in South Wales* (1897)

**The Legal System**

Abbott, C., *Jurisdiction and Practice of the Court of Great Sessions of Wales upon the Chester Circuit* (1795)
Coke, Sir E., *Institutes of the Laws of England* (1628) [The Great Sessions are considered in the third part of this work]
Davies, J.W., *Montgomeryshire Pleadings in the Court of Chancery 1558-1714* (Aberystwyth: 1991)
Foley, R., *The Practice of the Court of Great Sessions for Carmarthen, Pembroke and Cardigan* (1792)
Fox, K.O., 'An edited calendar of the first Brecknockshire Plea Roll of the Courts of the King's Great Sessions in Wales July 1542', *NLWJ* (1965-6)
——— 'The Records of the Courts of Great Sessions'. *Journal of the Society of Archivists* (1966)
Gibson, J.S.W., *Quarter Sessions Records for Family Historians* (FFHS, 1992)
Gibson, J.S.W, and Rogers, C.D., *Coroners' Records in England and Wales* (FFHS, 1989)
Hawkings, D.T., *Criminal Ancestors: A Guide to Historical Criminal Records in England and Wales* (Stroud: 1992)
Oldnall, W.R., *The Practice of the Court of Great Sessions* (1814)
Phillips, J.R.S., *The Justices of the Peace in Wales and Monmouthshire 1541 to 1689* (Cardiff: 1975)
*Rules and orders of the Court of Chancery of the Great Sessions for Brecknock, Glamorgan and Radnor—A Book of Practice (1818)* [Preserved in the PRO, London]
Sherrington, E.J., 'The Plea-rolls of the Courts of Great Sessions 1545-1575', *NLWJ* (1963-4)/5
Simpson, A.W.B., *An Introduction to the History of the Land Law* (Oxford: 1961)
Vaughan, R., *Practica Walliae or Proceedings of the Great Sessions of Wales* (1672)
Williams, W.O., *Calendar of the Caernarvonshire Quarter Sessions Records 1541-58* (Caernarfonshire County Council, 1956)
Williams, W.R., *The History of the Great Sessions in Wales 1542-1830* (Brecknock: 1899)
Williams-Jones, K., *A Calendar of the Merioneth Quarter Sessions Rolls 1733-65* (Merioneth County Council, 1965)

**Local Administration and the Poor**

Grant, R.J.K., *On the Parish* (Glamorgan Archives, 1988)
Oxley, G.W., *Poor Law Relief in England and Wales 1601-1834* (Newton Abbot: 1974)
Tate, W.E., *The Parish Chest*, 3rd edn, (repr. Chichester: 1983)
West, J., *Village Records* (Chichester: 1982)
West, J., *Town Records* (Chichester: 1983)

**Locations: Maps and Place-Names**

*Place Names on Maps of Scotland and Wales* (Southampton: Ordnance Survey)
Booth, J. *Antique Maps of Wales* (1978)
Charles, B.G., *Non-Celtic Place-Names in Wales* (1938)
——— *The Place-Names of Pembrokeshire* (Aberystwyth: 1992)
Davies, E, *A Gazetteer of Welsh Place-Names* (Cardiff: 1975)
Harley, J.B, *Maps for the Local Historian: A guide to the British sources* (National Council of Social Service, 1972)
Harley, J.B, & Phillips, C.W., *The Historians' Guide to Ordnance Survey Maps* (National Council of Social Service, 1984)
Lewis, S., *Topographical Dictionary of Wales* (1833, etc)
Richards, M., *Welsh Administrative and Territorial Units* (Cardiff: 1969)

**Maritime**

Chappell, E.L., *The History of the Port of Cardiff* (1939)
Coppack, T., *A Lifetime with Ships* (Prescot: 1973)
*Cymry a'r Mor/Maritime Wales* (Caernarfon: Gwynedd Archives & Museum Service, No.1, 1976—No.15, 1992)
Davies, J.I., *Growing Up Among Sailors* (Caernarfon: 1983)
Eames, A., *Ships & Seamen of Anglesey* (Cardiff: 1981)
——— *Meistri'r Moroedd* (Dinbych: 1978)
——— *Ship Master* (Caernarfon: 1980)
——— *Gwraig y Capten* (Caernarfon: 1984)
——— *Machlud Hwyliau Cymry/The Twilight of Welsh Sail* (Cardiff: 1984)
——— *Ventures in Sail* (Greenwich: 1987)
Elis-Williams, M., *Bangor, Port of Beaumaris* (Caernarfon: 1988)
George, B., *Pembrokeshire Sea-trading before 1900* (Field Studies Council, 1964)
Hughes, E., and Eames, A., *Portmadog Ships* (Caernarfon: 1975)
Jenkins, D., *The Jenkins Brothers of Cardiff* (1985)
Jenkins, J.G., *The Maritime Heritage of Dyfed* (Cardiff: 1982)
——— *Maritime Heritage, The Ships & Seamen of Southern Ceredigion* (Llandysul: 1982)
——— *Evan Thomas Radcliffe, Cardiff Shipowning Company* (Cardiff: 1982
Jenkins, J.G. and Jenkins, D., *Cardiff Shipowners* (Cardiff: 1986)

Lloyd, C., *The British Seaman 1200-1860* (1970)
Lloyd, L.W., *The Unity of Barmouth* (1977)
——— *The Amity of Aberdovey* (Aberystwyth: 1983)
——— *The Brig Susannah of Aberdyfi* (Harlech: 1985)
——— *The Port of Caernarfon 1793-1900* (Harlech: 1989)
——— *Pwllheli, the Port & Mart of Llŷn* (Harlech: 1991)
Stickings, T.G., *The Story of Saundersfoot* (1970)
Rees, J.F., *The Story of Milford* (1954)
Rodger, N.A.M., *Naval Records for Genealogists* (HMSO, 1988)
Swansea Maritime & Industrial Museum, *Swansea Cape Horners Remember* (1990)
Thomas, N.L., *The Story of Swansea* (1969)
Watts, C.T., and M.J., *My Ancestor was a Merchant Seaman—How can I find out more about him?* (SoG, 1992)

**Migration**

Camp, A.J., *My Ancestor was a Migrant (in England or Wales): how can I trace where he came from?* (SoG, 1987)
Carter, H., and Wheatley, S., *Merthyr Tydfil in 1851: a study of the spatial structure of a Welsh industrial town.* (Cardiff: 1982)
Harper, P.S., and Sunderland, E., (eds) *Genetic and Population Studies in Wales.* (Cardiff: 1986)
Jones, P.N., *Mines, migrants and residence in the south Wales steamcoal valleys: the Ogmore and Garw valleys in 1881* (Hull: 1987)
——— 'Population migration into Glamorgan 1861-1911: a reassessment', *Glamorgan County History*: Vol.6, Glamorgan Society 1700-1980, ed. P. Morgan (Cardiff: 1988)
Jones, R.M., *The North Wales Quarrymen* (Cardiff: 1981)
Jones, R.M., and Rees, D.B., *The Liverpool Welsh and their Religion* (Liverpool and Llanddewi Brefi: 1984)
Redford, A., *Labour migration in England, 1800-1850* 2nd ed. (Manchester: 1964)

**Monumental Inscriptions: Some Published Collections**

Evans, M. & C., *Awelon, Dewch i Wylo* (Llanrwst: 1982)
Hughes, J.E., *Englynion Beddau Dyffryn Ogwen* (Llandysul: 1979)
James, M.E., *Englynion Beddau Ceredigion* (Llandysul: 1983)
Jones, E., *Dagrau Gwerin* (Caernarfon: 1982)
Jones, G.G., *Meini sy'n Llefaru* (Y Bala: 1980)
Jones, G.L., *Lloffion o'r Llan* (Penygroes: 1982)
Jones, J., *Gleanings from God's Acre within the Hundred of Lleyn and Commot of Eifionydd* (Pwllheli: 1903)

Roberts, G.M., *Mynwenta* (Abertawe: 1980)
Roberts, G.T., *Llais y Meini* (Caernarfon: 1979)

**Nonconformity: Its Organisation and Records**

Bassett, T.M., *The Welsh Baptists* (Swansea: 1977)
Breed, G.R., *My Ancestors were Baptists* (SoG, 1988)
Clifford, D.J.H., *My Ancestors were Congregationalists in England & Wales: with a list of registers* (SoG, 1992)
Davies, D.E., *They Thought for Themselves* (Llandysul: 1982)
Gandy, M., *My Ancestor was Jewish* (SoG, 1982)
Griffith, S., *A History of Quakers in Pembrokeshire* (Llandysul: 1990)
Jones, I.G., and Williams, D., *The Religious Census of 1851: A Calendar of the Returns relating to Wales: Vol. 1, South Wales* (Cardiff: 1976) and Jones, I.G., *Vol. 2, North Wales* (Cardiff: 1981)
Leary, W., *My Ancestors were Methodists* (SoG, 1990)
Martin, A.J., *Hanes Llwynrhydowen* (Llandysul: 1977)
Milligan, E.H., and Thomas, M.J., *My Ancestors were Quakers* (SoG, 1983)
Palgrave-Moore, P., *Understanding the History and Records of Nonconformity* (Norwich: 1988)
Rawlins, B.J., *The Parish Churches and Nonconformist Chapels of Wales, Their Records and Where to Find Them—Vol. 1: Cardigan—Carmarthen—Pembroke* (Utah: 1987)
Rees, D.B., *Chapels in the Valley: a study in the sociology of Welsh nonconformity* (Wirral: 1975)
Richards, T., *Wales under the Penal Code* (1925)
Roberts, G.M., *Hanes Methodistiaeth Galfinaidd Cymru,* 2 vols. (Caernarfon: 1973, 1978)
Steel, D.J., *Sources for Nonconformist Genealogy and Family History* (SoG, 1973)
Steel, D.J., and Samuel, E., *Sources for Roman Catholic and Jewish Genealogy and Family History* (SoG, 1974)
Williams, A.H., *Welsh Wesleyan Methodism 1800-1858: Its origins, growth and secessions* (Bangor: 1935)

**Pedigrees—Manuscript**

Bartrum, P.C., *Early Welsh Genealogical Tracts* (1966)
——— 'Notes on the Welsh Genealogical Manuscripts', *THSC* (1968)
——— 'Further Notes on the Welsh Genealogical Manuscripts', *THSC* (1976)
——— 'Notes on the Welsh Genealogical Manuscripts (Part III)', *THSC* (1988)
Evans, J.G. (ed.), *Reports on the Manuscripts in the Welsh Language* (1898-1910)
Jones, F., 'An Approach to Welsh Genealogy', *THSC* (1948)
——— *A Catalogue of Welsh Manuscripts in the College of Arms* (Harleian Society Publications, 1988)

Owen, E., *A Catalogue of the Manuscripts Relating to Wales in the British Museum* (1900-22)

## Pedigrees—Printed Collections, including County Histories

Bartrum, P.C., *Welsh Genealogies, AD 300-1400* (Cardiff:1974; microfiche, 1980)
——— *Welsh Genealogies, AD 1400-1500* (Aberystwyth: 1983)
Bradney, J.A., *A History of Monmouthshire* (1907-32)
Clark, G.T., *Limbus Patrum Morganiae et Glamorganiae* (1886)
Dwnn, L., (ed. Meyrick, S.R.) *Heraldic Visitations of Wales* (Llandovery: 1846)
Green, F., (ed.) *West Wales Historical Records*, 14 vols Carmarthen: 1912-29)
Griffith, J.E., *Pedigrees of Anglesey and Carnarvonshire Families* (Horncastle: 1914; repr. Wrexham: 1985)
Griffith, T.C., *Achau ac Ewyllysiau Teuluoedd De Sir Gaernarfon* (Chwilog: 1989)
Lloyd, J.Y.W., *History of Powys Fadog* (1881-7)
Meyrick, S.R., *The History and Antiquities of the County of Cardigan* (repr. Brecon: 1907)
Nicholas, T., *The Annals and Antiquities of the Counties and County Families of Wales* (1872; repr. Baltimore: 1991)

## Probate Records

Camp, A.J. (ed.), *An Index to Wills Proved in the Prerogative Court of Canterbury, 1750-1800*, 6 vols (SoG, 1976-1993)
Cox, J., *Wills, Inventories and Death Duties: A provisional guide* (PRO: 1988)
Gibson, J.S.W., *Probate Jurisdictions: Where to look for Wills* (FFHS, 1989)
Milward, R., *A Glossary of Household, Farming and Trade Terms from Probate Inventories* (Chesterfield: 1982)
NLW Leaflet, *Probate Records in the National Library of Wales*

## Reading Documents

Buck, W.S.B., *Examples of Handwriting 1550-1650* (Chichester: 1973)
Cheney, C.R., *Handbook of Dates* (Royal Historical Society, 1978)
Dawson, G.E., and Kennedy-Skipton, L., *Elizabethan Handwriting 1500-1650: a Guide to the Reading of Documents and Manuscripts* (1968)
Emmison, F.G., *How to read Local Archives, 1550-1700* (1967)
Grieve, H.E.P., *Examples of English Handwriting, 1150-1750* (Chelmsford: 1974)
Ison, A., *A Secretary Hand ABC Book* (Reading: 1982)
Morris, J., *A Latin Glossary for Family and Local Historians* (FFHS, 1990)
Munby, L., *Reading Tudor and Stuart Handwriting* (Chichester: 1988)
Webb, C., *Dates and Calendars for the Genealogist* (SoG, 1989)

**Surnames**

Cottle, B., *The Penguin Dictionary of Surnames* (Harmsworth: 1978)
Ekwall, E., *Concise Oxford Dictionary of English Place-Names* (Oxford: 1960).
Guppy, H.B., *The Homes of Family Names* (1890)
Hanks, P., and Hodges, F., *A Dictionary of Surnames* (Oxford: 1988)
McKinley, R.A., *A History of British Surnames* (1990)
Morgan, P., *Background to Wales* (Llandybïe: 1968)
Morgan T.J. and P., *Welsh Surnames* (Cardiff: 1985, 1986)
Reaney, P.H., *The Origin of English Surnames* (1967, 1980)
——— *Dictionary of British Surnames* (1961)

**Taxation Records and other Nominal Lists**

Gibson, J.S.W., *Unpublished Personal Name Indexes in Record Offices and Libraries* (FFHS, 1987)
——— *The Hearth Tax, other later Stuart Tax Lists and the Association Oath Rolls* (FFHS, 1985)
Gibson, J.S.W., and Dell, A., *Tudor and Stuart Muster Rolls* (FFHS, 1989)
Gibson, J.S.W., and Medlycott, M., *Local Census Listings 1522-1930: Holdings in the British Isles* (FFHS, 1992)
——— *Militia Lists and Musters 1757-1876* (FFHS, 1990)
Gibson, J.S.W. and Mills, D., *Land Tax Assessments c.1690-c.1950* (FFHS, 1986)
Gibson, J.S.W., and Rogers, C., *Poll Books c.1696-1872: a directory to holdings in Great Britain* (FFHS, 1989)
——— *Electoral Registers since 1832; and Burgess Rolls* (FFHS, 1990)

**Urban Development and Industrialisation**

Baber, C., and Williams, L.J. (eds) *Modern South Wales: essays in economic history* (Cardiff: 1986)
Dodd, A.H., *The Industrial Revolution in North Wales* (Wrexham: 1990)
Edwards, G., *The Coal Industry in Pembrokeshire* (Field Studies Council, 1963)
Jenkins, J.G., *The Welsh Woollen Industry* (Cardiff: 1969)
John, A.H., *The Industrial Development of South Wales 1700-1950* (Cardiff: 1950)
Jones, G.E., *Modern Wales: A Concise History, 1485-1979* (Cambridge: 1984)
Lewis, E.D., *The Rhondda Valleys* (Cardiff: 1984)
Lewis, W.J., *Lead Mining in Wales* (Cardiff: 1967)
Lindsay, J., *A History of the North Wales Slate Industry* (Newton Abbott: 1974)
Minchinton, W.E. (ed.), *Industrial South Wales 1750-1914* (1969)

**The Welsh Language**

Evans, H.M., and Thomas, W.O., *Y Geiriadur Newydd: The New Welsh Dictionary* (Llandybïe: 1953)

Evans, H.M., and Thomas, W.O., *Y Geiriadur Mawr: The Complete Welsh-English, English-Welsh Dictionary* (Llandybïe: 1968)
Evans, H.M., and Thomas, W.O., *Y Geiriadur Bach: The Welsh Pocket Dictionary* (Llandybïe: 1969)
Jenkins, M., *A Welsh Tutor* (Cardiff: 1959)
Jones, T.J.R., *Living Welsh* (Teach Yourself Books, 1977)
Morris-Jones, J., *An Elementary Welsh Grammar* (1921; 1938); also under the title *Learn Welsh for English Speakers* (USA: Saphograph Corp., 1975)
Williams, A.E., *Termau Archifau: Archive Terms* (Gwynedd County Council, 1986)

Audio-cassette, *Say that Again: a guide to the pronunciation of Welsh place names.* (Theatr Felin-fach/Dyfed County Council)

**Useful Addresses**

The Welsh National Language Centre, Nant Gwrtheyrn, Llithfaen, Pwllheli, Gwynedd LL56 6PA
Welsh National Language Unit, The University of Glamorgan, Brook Street, Treforest, Pontypridd, Mid Glamorgan
The University of Wales Centre for Teaching Welsh to Adults, 22 Park Place, Cathays Park, Cardiff CF1 3DQ

# Index


account books (seafarers), 128-9
Act for the better preventing of clandestine marriages, 14
admission registers (schools), 161
Alban, 11
*Alumni Cantabrigienses,* 154-5
*Alumni Oxonienses*, 154-5
Angle
  vestry minutes, 1819, 168
Anglican Church: organisation and records
  bibliography, 298-9
  *see also* parish registers
    parochial records
apprentices
  indentures (seamen), 131-2
  paupers, 176-7, 294-5
  trade, 293-4
*Archaeologia Cambrensis,* 219
archive repositories, 3-7
  addresses, 6-7
Arminianism, 41
Association of Family History Societies of Wales, 11
attendance registers (schools), 161
bailiffs, 200
Ballard, William, March King of Arms, 214
Bangor Diocese
  bishop's transcripts, 23
  parish registers, 17
Baptists, 21, 37, 39, 40, 41, 42, 46
Bennet, William
  manuscript collection, 221
Bernau index, 183, 184
bibliographies, 298-309
bidding letters, 280-2
biographical works, 162, 289-90
biography
  bibliography, 299
Births and Deaths Registration Act, 1858, 46
bishop's transcripts, 23-4
Blethin family, Shirenewtown, 223
Bodleian Library, Oxford, 221
bonds of indemnity, 177
borough courts, 185
Bowen, Thomas, Cae Howell, 198
Brigstock, Elizabeth, 96
British and Foreign Schools Society, 159, 162
British Library, 220
calendars of probate, 145
Calvinistic Methodists, 21, 37, 41, 42
  baptisms in Anglesey, 49-51
  records, 4, 45
*Cambrian, The,* (Cincinnati), 290
*Cambrian, The,* (Swansea), 47, 290
Capel—the Chapels Heritage Society, 43-4
Capel-y-Graig, Trelech a'r Betws
  distribution of local christenings, 49, 50
Cardiff Central Library
  genealogical manuscripts, 221
Carew
  churchwardens' accounts, 1738/1770, 170-1
*Cenhadwr Americanaidd, Y,* 290
census, 1, 2, 6, 32-4
  bibliography, 299
  transcripts, 34
Chaloner, Jacob, 217, 221
Chaloner, Thomas, 215, 220
chapels
  computerised gazetteer, 45
  records, 43
  *see also* nonconformist records
    nonconformity
charity school movement, 155
chief constables, 200
chief stewards of the lordships and manors, 200
churchwardens, 270
  accounts, 170-1
circulating schools, 156-7
civil registration, 2, 29-35
  bibliography, 299
clandestine marriages, 18, 20
Clwyd FHS, 8, 9
  centre at Ruthin, 9-10
coal miners, 3
*Cofiant y Parch T. Rees,* 289
*Cofiant y Tri Brawd,* 289
*Cofrestri Plwyf Cymru/Parish Registers of Wales,* 14, 74, 76, 168
College of Arms, 220-1
colleges, 164
Congregationalists, 37
consistory courts, 144, 288, 289
coroners, 200
cottagers, 270, 271
county record offices, 4-5, 165
  addresses, 6-7
  electoral registers, 5
  enclosure awards, 5

land tax assessments, 5
nonconformist records, 5
parish registers, 5
poll books, 5
quarter sessions, 5
county militia, 175-6
Court of Augmentations, 184
Court of Chancery, 183
Court of Common Pleas, 184-5
Court of Exchequer, 184
Court of Great Sessions, 4, 182-3, 188-207
articles of misdemeanour, 205
attorneys, 192
Bill books, 196
calendar of prisoners, 199-200
challenge pedigrees, 194, 195, 209-10
chancery proceedings, 195-6
civil proceedings, 191-2
coroners' inquests, 205-06
criminal proceedings, 198-9
Decree and Order books, 196
docket rolls, 192
examinations, 200-01
fines, 192, 193
gaol files, 191, 198-9, 208
indictments, 203-04
jurisdiction, 189-91
jurors, list of, 193, 202-03
location, 191
miscellaneous correspondence and papers, 206
Nomina Ministrorum, 200
origins, 188-9
petitioners, 204-05
plea rolls, 192-3, 208
pleadings, 197-8, 208
presentments, 204
prisoners, schedules of, 203
process writs, 205
prothonotary papers, 195
quarter sessions records, 200
recognizances, 202
writs, 195
voting lists, 291
Court of King's Bench, 184-5
Court of Requests, 183
Court of Star Chamber, 183
Court of the Duchy of Lancaster, 184
courts,
English, 183-5
local, 185
Welsh, 181-3
crew lists and agreements, 131, 133-7
*Cyfaill o'r Hen Wlad, Y,* 290
Cynwal, Wiliam, 215, 216, 217, 220, 221
cywyddau (Welsh poems), 82, 282
Dafydd Benwyn
pedigree book, 216, 221
Davies, David, Moelon, Rhydlewis, 275
deeds of settlement, 149
*Dictionary of Welsh Biography down to 1940,* 82, 289
*Directory of Members' Interests,* 9
disbursement books (seafarers), 128-9
*Diwygiwr,* 290
Dr Williams' Library, 46
*Drysorfa, Y,* 53, 290
Dwnn, Lewys, 215, 216, 218, 220
Dyfed FHS, 8
*Early Welsh Genealogical Tracts,* 218
education
bibliography, 300
records, 152-65
Education Reports 1847, 159-60, 240
Edwardes, David, Rhyd-y-gors, 215, 217, 220, 221
eisteddfodau, 43, 285-6
electoral registers, 5, 6
elementary schools, 158-9
Ellis, Peter, 217
emigration, 254-68
America, 256-9, 260-3, 265
Australia, 257, 259-60, 262, 263
bibliography, 300-01
Canada, 259
New Zealand, 262, 263-4
Patagonia, 264-5
South Africa, 262, 263
South America, 264-5
Welsh language newspapers, 266
*Eminent Men of Denbighshire,* 289
englynion (Welsh verse), 82, 287
*Enwogion Ceredigion,* 289
*Enwogion Môn,* 289
*Enwogion Sir Aberteifi,* 289
escheators, 200
estate records, 5, 104-21
abstract of title, 119
adminstration, 112-17
labourers, 119
leases, 117
manorial records, 118-19
marriage settlements, 118
rentals, 114-17

servants, 119
surveys, 118
tenant farmers, 112-17
wills, 118
estates
decline of large, 111-12
inheritance, 108
marriages, 105-08
purchases, 108-11
*Eurgrawn Wesleyaidd, Yr,* 290
Evans, Alcwyn
manuscripts, 220
Evans, David (Dewi Dawel, 1814-91), Cwm-du
bidding letters, 281-2
Evans, Evan, Nantyglo, 264
Evans, Evan, New Quay, 130
Evans, Gwenogfryn
manuscript report, 219
Evans, Stephen, Maes-pwll, 285
extra-mural departments, 11
Family History Societies of Wales, 8-12
farming records, 6
Federation of Family History Societies, 12
Fellow, William, Lancaster Herald, 214
folklore, 6
foresters, 200
freeholders, 269-79
Fulk ap Hywel, Lancaster Herald, 214
gavelkind, 270
*Gazetteer of Welsh Place-names,* 74, 77
Genealogical and Heraldic Society of Wales, 8
genealogical guides
bibliography, 301
Genealogical Society, Utah
bishop's transcripts, 24
General Register Office, 14, 29-32
Geneu'r Glyn Hundred
surnames, 62, 63
Gibbs, Philip, 97
Glamorgan FHS, 8
Golden Grove Book, 217, 220, 221
grammar schools, 153-4
Green, Francis, 220
Griffith, George William, 220
Griffith, T. Ceiri, 219
Griffiths, Lieut. Valentine, 262
Gruffudd Hiraethog, 215, 216, 220, 222, 224
Guild of One-Name Studies, 11
Gutun Owain, 220, 221
Gwent FHS, 8
Gwynedd FHS, 8
gypsies, 295
Hamon, Isaac, 220
Harleian manuscript collection, 220
*Haul, Yr,* 290
hearth tax, 292
Hen Gapel, Yr, Tre'rddol
museum, 45
heraldry, 212-15
bibliography, 301
history
bibliography, 301-02
*History of Breckonshire,* 219
*History of Monmouthshire,* 219
*History of Powys Fadog,* 219
Hitchings, Griffith, St Nicholas, Pembroke, 98
Holmes, Randle, 215, 217, 220
Hopkin ab Einon, 217
Hopkins, Walter, 217
Hughes, Griffith, 217
collection of Flintshire pedigrees, 221
husbandmen, 269
Hywel ap Dafydd ap Thomas ap Dafydd, Cefn-coed, 285
Ifan Llwyd ap Dafydd ap Maredudd, Hafod Unnos, Llangernyw, 283
IGI
*see* International Genealogical Index
Independents, 21, 37, 39-40, 41, 42
industrialisation
bibliography, 308
International Genealogical Index, 9, 24, 93-103
arrangement, 94-8
compact disc version, 93, 101-03
contents, 93-4
editions, 101
microfiche version, 99-101
wills, 98-9
*Jane Brown,* slate trader, Barmouth, 128-9
Jews, 21
John, William, Glan Cothi, 285
Jones, Daniel, Abergele (1811-1861), 264
Jones, David, Trecregin, 272
Jones, Evan, Llanfihangel-y-Creuddyn
ordained in 1744, 288
Jones, Major Francis, 219, 220
Jones, Henry
ordained in 1861, 288
Jones, John (Ioan Duad)
bilingual gravestone, 287
Jones, John D. (1797-1875) Llanllawddog, 260-1
Jones, Teddie, head gardener, Powis Castle, 263
Jones, Thomas, Tregaron (Twm Siôn Cati), 217

Jones, William, Fforchgwm, Llanllwchaearn, 276, 277, 278
Jones, William, Llywele-mawr, 284
Jones, William Lewis, Glyn Cothi House, Llanegwad, 285-6
*Journal, The,* 290
jurymen, 193, 202-03, 270
justices of the peace, 185, 200
Kyffin, William
  challenge pedigrees, 193, 194
labourers, 119
land
  bibliography, 302-03
land tax records, 291
landed estates
  *see* estate records
landowners, 269-79
law, 181-7
  bibliography, 303
Lewes, William, Llwynderw, 217, 220
Lewis, Anne, Llanegwad, 286
Lewis, Griffith Thomas, headmaster of Tregaron, 155
Lewis, Titus, Silian, ordinand, 288
*Limbus Patrum Morganiae et Glamorganiae,* 219
Llanbadarn Fawr
  graveyard inscriptions, 286
Llandaf Diocese
  bishop's transcripts, 23
  parish registers, 17, 18, 19
Llanfihangel ar Arth
  bonds of indemnity, 177
Llangrannog
  freeholders, 272-5
Llanllwchaearn
  freeholders, 276-8
Llanrhystud
  landowners, 271
  poor rate assessments for a group of farms, 169-70
  surnames, 62
Llanstephan manuscripts, 219
*Lloyd's List,* 124, 130
*Lloyd's Registers of Shipping,* 124, 130
Lloyd, Thomas, Dolobran (1640-94), 256
Llyfr Baglan, 218-19
Llyfr Cedwyn, 218
Llyfr Silin, 218
London-based Welsh FHS, 11
magistrates, 270
maps, 2, 4, 271
  bibliography, 304
  Ordnance Survey, 77-8
maritime records, 5, 123-39
maritime Wales
  bibliography, 304-05
  history, 123-6
*Maritime Wales/Cymru a'r Môr,* 129
marriage bonds, 278
Meredith, 11
Methodist Archives and Research Centre, 46
migration, 227-53
  bibliography, 305
  historical trends, 228-30
  into England, 235, 243-8
  into North Wales, 235-9
  into South Wales, 239-43
  key concepts, 252-3
  key terms, 228
  Ravenstein's laws of, 1885, 231-4
  within Great Britain, 231-5
Miles, John, 256
military ancestors, 175-6, 292-3
mining records, 5-6
*Montgomeryshire Collections,* 219
monumental inscriptions, 286-7
  bibliography, 305-06
Mormons, 264
  Family History Centres, 30, 33
  International Genealogical Index
  *see also* International Genealogical Index
Mostyn manuscripts, 219
*My Ancestor was a Merchant Seaman,* 128, 132
National Library of Wales, 3-4, 5
  address, 6
  Baptist archives, 46
  bishop's transcripts, 4, 24
  calendars of probate, 145
  Calvinistic Methodist records, 4, 45
  census holdings, 33
  chapels
    computerised gazetteer, 45
  civil registration, indexes of, 30
  Court of Great Sessions holdings, 191
  department of manuscripts and records, 3, 4
  department of pictures and maps, 3
  department of printed books, 3
  diocesan records, 4
  marriage allegations and bonds, 4
  nonconformist records, 4
  parish registers, 4, 15
  pedigree collections, 4, 219-20
  Peniarth collection, 217, 219-20
  probate records, 4, 147-8
  research service, 25
  street indexes, 34

tithe maps, 4, 271
Wesleyan records, 45
National School Society, 158-9, 162
newspapers, 2, 6, 163, 266, 290
Nicholl, Thomas Beynon, 285
Non-Parochial Registers, 46
nonconformist records, 40
at National Library of Wales, 4
at PRO, 46
content, 47-54
location 44-7
nonconformity, 36-56
bibliography, 306
history, 37-43
periodicals, 47
*North Wales Scholarship Association Reports, 1879-1894,* 163
notitiae, 288-9
Oakley, John, Winnington, 201
one name studies, 11, 101
ordination papers, 288
overseers' accounts, 170-1
Owen, Abraham, Cwmbwch (1792-1870), 259-60
Owen, Edward
catologue of manuscripts, 219
Owen, George, Henllys, 216, 220
parish registers, 4, 5, 13-28
content, 19-20, 22-3
copies, 24
indexes, 24
location, 14-15
nonconformity, 20-2
photocopying, 25
researching of, 25
survival, 15-19
transcripts, 24
parochial records, 166-80
location, 167-8
origins, 166-7
Parry, Cwmtudu, 274
Parry, John, Talley, 284
Parry, Richard, Cwrt Gilbert, 220
pedigrees, 4, 209-26
bibliography, 306-07
*Pedigrees of Anglesey and Carnarvonshire Families,* 219
Peniarth collection, 217, 219-20
periodicals, 47, 82-3, 290
Phillips, T., Haverfordwest, 262
Pigeonsford, Llangrannog, 272, 273, 274
place-names, 73-80, 223
bibliography, 304
surnames derived from, 64-5
Plomer, Thomas, 97
poetry, 282-6
political records, 6
Pontypridd Historical and Cultural Centre, 45
poor
apprenticeships, 176-7, 294-5
bibliography, 304
settlement and removal, 171-5
Powys FHS, 8
Presbyterians
*see* Calvinistic Methodists
Price, Pigeonsford, 273-4
private academies, 155
private schools, 163
*Probate Jurisdictions: where to look for wills,* 150
probate records, 4, 307
Prothero, 11
Protheroe Collection, 221
Public Record Office
apprenticeship records, 293-4
census returns, 33
courts records, 182
land tax records, 292
maritime records, 131, 134
military records, 292
nonconformist records, 46
probate records, 147
street indexes, 34
public schools, 154
Quakers, 21, 37, 39, 45-6, 52
quarter sessions, 5, 39, 185, 200
rate assessments, 169-70
reading documents
bibliography, 307
*Record of Caernarvon,* 210
Rees, Mary, Tawelan, 286
Register of Masters, 130
Register of Masters, Mates and Engineers, 133
Register of Merchant Seamen, 132-3
Registration Act, 1695, 51
residential courses, 12
Rhys Cain, 216, 217
Rice, Mary, Llanrhystud, 175
Roberts, George, Mochdre (1769-1853), 258
Roberts, S. R., Llanbrynmair, 265
Rowland, Hugh, Llandysilio
draft indenture, 294
Royal Institution of South Wales, 6
St Asaph diocese
bishop's transcripts, 23
notitiae, 288-9
parish registers, 17

St David's diocese
  bishop's transcripts, 23
  parish registers, 17, 18-19, 20
sale catalogues, 118
Salesbury, John, Erbistock, 217, 220
Salesbury, Owen, Rug, 217, 220
schools
  biographies, 162
  histories, 162, 164
  log books, 161
  *see also different types of schools*
seafarers
  census returns, 127
  gravestones, 127
  parish registers, 127
  probate records, 127-8
secondary schools, 163
*Seren Gomer,* 47, 290
settlement and removal, 171-5
shipping registers, 124, 130-1
Simwnt Fychan, 215, 216, 221
Siôn Cain, 217, 220
Society of Friends (Quakers) records, 5, 45
Society transactions, 290-1
soldiers' records, 292-3
South Wales FHS, 8
steel workers, 3
*Subject Index to Welsh Periodicals,* 291
Sunday schools, 43, 157-8
Supreme court, 185
surnames, 57-72, 94, 222-3, 275
  bibliography, 308
  distribution, 67-9
  IGI indexes, 93-103
  modern names, 69-70
  non-Welsh, 65-7
  occupational, 64
  patronymic, 1, 57-60, 142
  permanent, 60-1
  personal characteristics, 63-4
  place-names, derived from 64-5
  time-scale of formation, 61-3
*Susannah,* brig, Aberdyfi, 128-9, 132
Swansea City Archives, 6
Taicroesion Book of pedigrees, 220, 221
taxation records, 291-2
  bibliography, 308
Test and Corporation Acts, 40
Thomas, Hugh, 215, 217, 220
Thomas, John, Burton, 96
Thomas, John, St Ishmaels, 96
Thomas, Rees, Llansamlet (1840-1914), 52-4
Thomas, Thomas, Shrewsbury
  settlement at Pembroke, 173-4
Thomas, William, Llanelly (bapt., 1817), 95-6
tithe maps, 4, 271
Toleration Act 1689, 39
trade apprenticeships, 293-4
trade directories, 2, 6, 163
trade union records, 6
*Transactions of the Honourable Society of Cymmrodorion,* 219
Trelech a'r Betws
  distribution of local christenings, 49-50
Trinity House Petitions, 129-30
Turnor, Aberhafesb, 289
Tŷ Meirion, Dolgellau
  Quaker museum, 46
Unitarians, 37, 41
*Unity,* sloop, Barmouth, 128-9
University College, Swansea, 6
University College of North Wales, Bangor, 4, 5-6, 221
Vaughan, Charles
  challenge pedigrees, 193, 194
Vaughan, Robert, Hengwrt, 216, 217, 220
vermin control, 178-9
vestry minutes, 168
Vincent, Augustine, 221
Walters, John, Clwte, 286
*Welch Piety,* 157
*Welsh Administrative and Territorial Units,* 74, 76
Welsh Church Commission, 1910, 44
Welsh Folk Museum, 6
*Welsh Genealogies 300-1400,* 9, 11, 218
*Welsh Genealogies 1400-1500,* 9, 11, 218
Welsh language, 81-92, 160
  bibliography, 308-09
  glossary, 88-92
  grammar, 83-5
  mutations, 84
  pronunciation, 85-7
Welsh manuscripts, 87
*Welsh Surnames,* 58
Wesley Historical Society Library, 47
Wesleyan Methodist Metropolitan Registry, 46
Wesleyan Methodists
  records, 45
*West Wales Historical Records,* 219
*Who's Who in Wales* (1921, 1933 and 1937), 289
Wiliam Llŷn, 215, 216, 217, 220
Williams, Richard, Llywel, Breconshire, 221
wills, 140-51, 271-2, 275-8
  Church of Latter-day Saints, index to, 148

distribution of, 150
indexes, 9, 147
location, 147
strays, 148
*Wills and their Whereabouts,* 150
Wood, Abram, 295
Wood, H. J. T., 220
Workers' Educational Association, 11-12
works school, 158
Wynnstay estate
formation of, 105-07, 109
rentals, 115, 117
yeomen, 269, 270, 271